DRUGS IN THE CLASSROOM
A CONCEPTUAL MODEL FOR SCHOOL PROGRAMS

Remember when HIPPIE meant big in the hips,
    and a TRIP involved travel in cars, planes or ships?
When POT was a vessel for cooking things in,
    and HOOKED was what grandmother's rug may have been?
When FIXED was a verb that meant mend or repair,
    and NEAT meant well organized, tidy and clean,
    and GRASS was a ground cover, normally green?
When lights and not people were SWITCHED ON and off,
    and THE PILL might have been what you took for a cough?

When GROOVY meant furrowed with channels and hollows,
    and BIRDS were winged creatures like robins and swallows?
When FUZZ was a substance, fluffy like lint,
    and BREAD came from bakeries and not from the mint?
When ROLL meant a bun and ROCK was a stone,
    and HANGUP was something you did with the 'phone?
When CHICKEN was poultry, and BAG meant a sack,
    and JUNK trashy cast-offs and old bric-a-brac?

When CAT was a feline, a kitten grown up,
    and TEA was a liquid you drank from a cup?
When a SWINGER was someone who swings in a swing,
    and a PAD was a sort of cushiony thing?
When WAY OUT meant distant, and far, far away,
    and a man wouldn't sue you for calling him GAY?

Words once so sensible, sober and serious
    are making the freak-scene like psycho-delirious.

It's groovy, man, groovy, but English it's not.
Methinks that the language has gone straight to pot.

                              TSR
                      (Source unknown)

DRUGS IN THE CLASSROOM

A CONCEPTUAL MODEL FOR SCHOOL PROGRAMS

HAROLD J. CORNACCHIA, Ed.D.

Professor of Health Education, California State University, San Francisco,
San Francisco, California

DAVID J. BENTEL, M.A., D.Crim.

Consultant in Drug Abuse, National Clearinghouse for Drug Abuse Information, National
Institute for Mental Health, Washington, D. C.

DAVID E. SMITH, M.D.

Assistant Clinical Professor of Toxicology, Department of Pharmacology,
University of California Medical Center; Founder and Medical Director, Haight-Ashbury
Free Medical Clinic, San Francisco, California

SAINT LOUIS   1973

THE C. V. MOSBY COMPANY

Copyright © 1973 by The C. V. Mosby Company

All rights reserved. No part of this book may
be reproduced in any manner without written
permission of the publisher.

Printed in the United States of America

International Standard Book Number
0-8016-1053-2
Library of Congress Catalog Card Number
72-88507

Distributed in Great Britain by Henry Kimpton,
London

CB/CB/B   9   8   7   6   5   4   3   2

PREFACE

Schools have been expected to help resolve the youth drug problem that exists in the United States today. Approximately 60% to 90% of the young people are using alcohol, 40% to 60% tobacco (with a million new teen-age smokers yearly), 6% to 40% marijuana, 5% to 15% LSD, and 1% to 3% heroin. In addition, 750 aspirin pills are used by every man, woman, and child yearly, and about $161 is spent each year on legal drugs for every person in this country. Expectations of school participation in solving the problem run high, but the formidable task confronting these institutions has not been adequately evaluated. Despite recent noble efforts, schools have been the subject of adverse criticisms because of their ineffective results.

Schools have been faced with the dilemma of trying to provide viable programs with limited funds, with no guidelines, and with no models for use to determine appropriateness or adequacy of such programs. We have recognized this need as a result of our many school experiences and numerous contacts with national, state, and local education leaders. We have worked closely with specialists at one of the four National Training Centers in Drug Education conducted at California State University, San Francisco, by the United States Office of Education and in on-site visitations and consultations that followed in 1970 to 1971 in twelve western states and two territories. Emerging from this exposure was the discovery of numerous difficulties that led to the writing of this book, the purpose of which is to introduce a conceptual model of a multidimensional, differential school drug program designed to meet the needs of the variety of student drug users and abusers as well as the nonusers. It is a new approach to the attack on the drug problems of youth that should prove useful to all school personnel.

The focus herein will be on the preventive aspects of the drug problem for grades kindergarten through twelve, with emphasis on the behavorial approach in drug education. The proposal includes education, identification, and assistance for drug abusers as well as suggested ways to modify the school atmosphere to make it more conducive to learning. This volume will help schools resolve the dilemma they are now facing by providing directions so desperately needed. It will render practical assistance for a variety of school and community individuals.

This text could not have been written five years ago. Much of the information and support did not exist to provide the impetus necessary to move forward in schools on preventive drug programs of the magnitude now being attempted in the United States. There have been many dramatic activities and changes in drug education in recent years at the national, state, and local levels. Much political and community interest for action has developed, with funds becoming available for programs from a variety of sources. This volume, therefore, has synthesized and organized the most promising demonstrations, activities, and information available from an array of sources in order to provide functional solutions to the problems facing schools. It has organized data and material into practical approaches and usable forms for pre-service and in-service teachers, administrators, counselors, nurses, and other school personnel at all levels. Every effort has been made to provide the best directions for school drug programs. These guidelines have evolved from a comprehensive review of the latest data available in the literature, the array of school programs in operation, the vast experiences of federal, state, and local leaders, and our own extensive experiences and involvement in the drug scene.

In addition to school use, this book should be valuable for community organizations including parents. It will help them understand the school drug program and encourage them to initiate action for the development of such programs. School programs should not be developed in isolation from community programs, since drugs affect and are used by all people in varying ways and degrees. The greatest impact on students will undoubtedly be achieved through coordinated efforts of the school and the community.

Teachers, nurses, or other school personnel will find this text a valuable resource to have available for use in the instructional program and in other ways. Counselors will find it helpful in dealing with drug abusers. Administrators will find it useful in handling numerous administrative problems in conjunction with drug problems of youth. Curriculum directors will find guidelines for the development of curriculums and teaching units. Some additional features of the text include the following:

1. Utilization of current curriculum ideology, including the concept approach
2. Identification of behavioral goals at the primary, intermediate, junior high, and senior high school levels as categorized in the cognitive, attitude, and action domains
3. Over 400 teaching techniques gathered from the review of 60 curriculum guides and other sources and grouped under these four headings: alcohol, drugs, tobacco, and psychic-social-spiritual techniques
4. More than 160 sources of education materials
5. Films and filmstrips recommended for use by the National Coordinating Council on Drug Education
6. A variety of illustrative evaluative instruments that may be used, or adapted, for local situations, including a quantitative-qualitative device to assess the total school drug program
7. Physical and behavioral signs and symptoms of drug abusers and suggested procedures for aiding them
8. Guidelines for development, with illustrative policies and procedures in terms of sale, use, and possession of drugs in schools

Although the main emphasis in the volume is on the conceptual model of a school drug program and its implementation, the early chapters provide fundamental information about the school dilemma and the drug scene. Such background is necessary to better understand the program that has been introduced. It is also useful for the classroom teacher.

Part I of the text covers the dilemma faced by the schools. Part II discusses the drug scene: a current synthesis of pharmacological, psychological, and sociological aspects of drugs; rehabilitation and treatment resources; and the law and law enforcement procedures. In Part III is found a conceptual model of the school drug program, which includes (1) drug education with specific suggestions for curriculum development and practical ideas for use by classroom teachers, (2) drug services to identify drug abusers and procedures for helping these students, (3) school atmosphere needed to understand student unrest, what to do about the physical and emotional needs of students, and provision for humanism in the school, and (4) coordination of the school drug program necessary for an administrative structure to develop policies and procedures, to conduct in-service programs, and for other purposes. Part IV, a summary, provides evaluation guidelines and suggestions for use by teachers, administrators, and others, with illustrative procedures.

The reader must be aware that drugs are a problem of people and not of substances. Therefore, understanding of the individual as an organismic and integrated whole—his physical, psychological, social, and spiritual aspects—must receive consideration in any proposed attempt to resolve the problem. This book focuses on these factors, providing a unique approach that offers unusual potential for use in school drug and drug education programs.

Harold J. Cornacchia
David J. Bentel
David E. Smith

CONTENTS

PART 1·INTRODUCTION

CHAPTER 1
THE DILEMMA

Fifty state drug co-ordinators, educators, psychologists, and other people . . . met here to discuss the do's and dont's of drug education . . . the delegates agreed that most schools and most other groups are doing a bad job of teaching about drugs . . . they disagreed . . . about what works and what doesn't work in drug education, and even about the purpose of drug education.

MARK R. ARNOLD[1a]

The nation's schools have not yet launched a concerted attack on the growing problem of drug abuse among the young. Although more and more schools are working to combat the problem, many others are still ignoring the issues, assuming that 'it can't happen here' . . . of 500 schools surveyed, 35% said drugs were of no particular concern to them; 32% had no drug abuse program; 44% said they had no inservice teacher-training program in drug education.

Schools have touched on the drug problem in the past, but the effort was generally inept and ineffective.

EDUCATION USA[15]

Parents, legislators, and the community have expected schools to help in the resolution of the drug problem among young persons in the United States. Laws have been passed, funds have been authorized, and pressures have been applied for appropriate action. Schools and school districts have made sincere efforts to comply by developing programs in recent years without guidelines, without the models needed for direction, and without qualified leadership. Bland best describes the action of schools when she says, "In the rush to teach about drug abuse, we resemble Stephen Leacock's mythical character who 'flung himself from the room, flung himself on his horse, and rode off in all directions!' "[4] The result has been that numerous fragmented, piecemeal, "crash," poorly planned, misguided, and frequently uncoordinated programs have been developed. Is it any wonder that schools have been ineffective? Is it any wonder that schools have not had much impact on the young? When you realize the complexity of the drug problem, which by itself does not have simple answers, the community expectations for action have created a dilemma for the schools. Therefore the variety of criticisms that have been advanced regarding the ineffectiveness of programs needs further examination despite well-meaning efforts by schools and their dedicated personnel.

Numerous authorities have said they believe that educational programs have had little if any impact on students. Mounting evidence reveals this to be true. It has been stated that, although such programs may provide an increase in drug information, they may encourage student experimentation and use of mind-altering chemicals. Recent studies in Pennsylvania and California indicate that drug use rather than diminishing tended to increase after students were exposed to limited information-centered drug education programs. Some schools, parents, and communities have proceeded cautiously or have failed to take any action along educational lines because of this possible hazard. Other individuals point to the laws concerning teaching about narcotics and dangerous drugs that have been operative in most states for many years. They claim that these laws have had practically no effect on pupils. Still others ask the question: how many pupils have schools turned off drugs?

Whether the criticisms of school programs are justified, and whether education is causing students to turn on or to turn off drugs has not been ascertained to date. Perhaps it is a little early to evaluate programs except in terms of predictive indications. Nevertheless the comments appear to have validity.

The school problem is the result of a variety of factors. One important matter is the failure to define adequately the precise objectives of the educational program. Dr. Warner from Pennsylvania State University recently conducted a study of eighth grade, eleventh grade, and college student programs and discovered that: "You're not going to stop kids from taking drugs. If that's our goal we'd better re-examine it. . . . All education can do is maybe make them examine their motivations, steer them away from bad drugs, let them know what the risks are, unless you have a real alternative for them in terms of something to really absorb their energies."[51] Thus the question must be asked as to what educational goals have been established by the schools. At present little has been done to clearly identify criteria except by adults who wish to indoctrinate the young against the use of illegal drugs or to see how many they can turn off drugs unpopular with adults. Should not youths also be encouraged to avoid legal drugs?

However important the establishment of educational objectives is, other questions must be raised. What are the frames of reference from which the critics are making judgments? What should be the nature and type of drug program to be conducted? There are no model programs,

although some constructive patterns are developing. There are no clear standards, although guidelines are being prepared. Add these difficulties to the lack of generally acceptable, identifiable, educational goals and much confusion exists over the following: (1) the nature of the school drug program: is it more than, or solely, educational? (2) the differentiation and the interrelationships between school and community drug educational programs, (3) the distinction between formal and informal education and the place of each in the school program, (4) the definition of prevention and its application within the school, (5) the types of student users and abusers of drugs and the application of this information to the school program, and (6) whether provisions for multiple programs to meet the needs of differing students should be made in schools.

In summary, the problem is one of defining the role of the school in helping to resolve the drug problem among youth. Therefore, however appropriate and necessary they may be, the criticisms now appearing must be given consideration only in the light of the factors just presented. They may be premature at this time.

RECENT DEVELOPMENTS IN SCHOOL DRUG PROGRAMS

Further understanding of the school dilemma can be obtained by a review of some recent developments and problems related to drug programs.

Prior to 1970 many school drug programs, including drug education, were being conducted in various parts of the United States, with minimal financial support provided by the federal government, by state legislatures, by local school districts, and by other sources. In 1969 the federal funds available for drug education amounted to approximately $2.5 million. In addition to these funds, schools received limited personnel, cooperation, and materials from a variety of community sources. School programs, although relatively numerous in some states, were sporadic, limited, or nonexistent in many other states. The nature and support of the programs differed greatly. Overall they were not extensive and occurred with inconsistent frequency.

In March 1970 a massive, nationwide effort to reach all schools was made when President Nixon released $3.5 million for the development and implementation of educational programs. This money was distributed to all states in the form of grants-in-aid in proportion to the number of youths in each state's schools, with the amounts ranging from $40,000 to $200,000 per state. For many states this was the only money available. However, numerous state legislatures, local districts, and communities provided additional funds; in other states the previous level of financial aid was maintained. Each state was permitted to develop its own proposal for the use of the federally allocated funds under broadly defined guidelines established by the Office of Education, but the financial support was primarily earmarked for the stimulation of drug education programs in all schools throughout the United States.

A portion of the federal funds authorized by President Nixon in 1970 was set aside to establish four national training centers in New York, Wisconsin, Texas, and California. We directed the California center at San Francisco State College. In the summer of 1970, administrators, teachers, students, parents, and community leaders representing a variety of racial and ethnic minorities from each state were sent to the centers for training. These individuals were to be prepared to assume leadership roles in drug education and were expected to train other leaders within their states, who, in turn, would prepare still other drug educators. This action would hopefully multiply, in geometric proportions, the number of school personnel capable of conducting drug education programs. The goal was to reach every school and every teacher in the nation by June 30, 1971. It became abun-

dantly clear before the prescribed date that such an accomplishment was impossible within the designated time period. It was also clear that it was impossible to develop quality programs within a 1-year period. More time would be needed to organize, to qualify people, and to test ideas and proposals.

Although the guidelines for the conduct of the training centers had been established, they were not precisely defined and were subject to varying interpretations, as evidenced by the difference in programs that were developed at each of the centers. However, the efforts did provide the desired stimulus, and drug education programs in schools became quite numerous in all states. It is estimated that every state department of education is now involved in drug education and that a majority of the 17,000 school districts have made efforts in this direction.

The need for the extended development of educational programs in the United States undoubtedly aided in the passage of the Comprehensive Drug Abuse Prevention and Control Act of 1970, which provided more grant-in-aid funds for the states. In 1971 and 1972, $6 million was appropriated, with approximately one half given to states for their school educational programs and the remaining one half distributed to agencies and organizations for community education programs. Thirteen million dollars is expected to be available for 1972 and 1973.

Numerous governmental agencies that have been and continue to be involved in drug education programs in recent years include the following: the Office of Education, the National Institute of Mental Health, the Justice Department's Bureau of Narcotics and Dangerous Drugs, the Office of Economic Opportunity, many state and local governmental agencies, and a variety of voluntary and professional organizations and commercial companies at national, state, and local levels. It is estimated that more than $14 million has been spent to date by several federal agencies for a variety of drug education programs and activities. (This amount will undoubtedly be somewhat greater by the time this book is published.) The efforts of these groups have resulted in the production and distribution of pamphlets, books, films, and curriculum guides. In addition, provision has been made for speakers, workshops, advisory committees, information and other services for students and parents, funds, and help in many other ways.

It should be obvious that school drug and other drug education activities and programs have been growing and developing in recent years. Despite the need for greatly improved coordination between agencies and organizations, numerous creative and innovative methods, ideas, and materials have been developed and prepared, many of which are being piloted, or are now in use in schools throughout the country. These new approaches include "drop-in" centers, "hot-lines," use of peer groups in teaching, use of ex-addicts, improved school and community relationships, greater involvement of parents and students in planning and conducting programs, crisis intervention procedures, policies for handling drug users and abusers, "rap" sessions, and publication of numerous books, pamphlets, curricula, and visual materials.

SCHOOL PROBLEMS

Despite the variety of efforts now taking place to cope with the tremendous drug problem in schools, there is still much to be done. We have discovered the following problems are in need of attention:

1. Lack of understanding of the nature of the total school drug program in which education is but one important phase
2. Numerous educational programs with goals that primarily emphasize the acquisition of pharmacological or physiological information without consideration of the psychological, sociological, and spiritual aspects associated with drug use
3. Unclear understanding of the independent roles of the school and the community as well as the importance of cooperation and coordination of these programs at federal, state, and local levels with police departments and other community agencies and organizations
4. Lack of communication procedures for alerting the community regarding the drug problem and for gaining support for school drug programs
5. Failure in designing programs to meet the special needs of students in ghetto areas
6. Inadequate consideration of the involvement of students, parents, and community representatives, including minorities, in drug programs together with insufficient understanding of effective ways of utilizing such persons; that is, the use of ex-addicts and of students in planning and implementing the curriculum
7. Fragmented, piecemeal, uncoordinated, and frequently ineffective programs in schools and school systems
8. Lack of adequate, continuous, and dedicated leadership in some areas of the nation (There was a change in the state drug leadership personnel in approximately one half of 12 western states during 1970 and 1971; in some schools and school districts no administrative leadership has been provided to date.)
9. Unfamiliarity with the distinction between formal and informal education, especially on the part of community people
10. Failure to recognize the need for differring types of school drug programs and drug education to meet the variety of types of student users and abusers found in schools
11. Inadequate consideration and emphasis in school drug programs of the behavioral and humanistic relationships
12. Lack of understanding and development of more effective communica-

tion with students, especially drug users

13. Use of "scare" tactics, sensationalism, assembly programs, and speakers as the main, or sole, approach to educational programs

14. Need to clarify the roles of administrators, teachers, nurses, counselors, and other school personnel

15. Apathetic attitude toward change and toward attempts to develop creative and innovative approaches to the drug problem by administrators, teachers, community leaders, and others

16. Insufficient recognition of and inadequate attention to important administrative concerns related to the drug program such as the curriculum, the place of education in the curriculum, the objectives to be achieved, teacher qualifications, inservice preparation of personnel, methodology, the financial support and cost of programs, and the establishment of policies and procedures for handling drug users and abusers

17. Lack of procedures to assess the effectiveness of programs quantitatively and qualitatively

CONTRIBUTING FACTORS IN THE SCHOOL DILEMMA

How to best attack the drug problem in society has not been determined. It is a difficult problem to resolve because drugs are not the cause but rather the effect. That is to say that the legal and illegal use and abuse of drugs is more symptomatic of a people's problem than of a drug problem. As one pharmacist has noted, "Drugs have been on my shelves for years and never caused anybody any problem. It's the people that cause the problems." It is certain that a variety of approaches must be made, including involvement of the schools. There is an acute need for a coordinated and cooperative effort on the part of every American community to face the current epidemic of youthful drug abuse and to

deal with it compassionately and maturely, involving the home, the school, and the community organizations and agencies.

Presently much confusion exists regarding the proper role of the school in handling the increasing drug problem. Very little of the massive amount of literature addressed to this matter deals either with this problem or with the alternatives open to schools in preventing or dealing with drug abuse. It is not surprising that many schools have in desperation initiated fragmentary, superficial, incomplete, and uncoordinated programs that have done little to resolve the problem.

Although schools and teachers cannot solve all humanity's ills, they have a special role to play in drug misuse and abuse.* They can be instrumental in helping to reduce the drug problem through preventive action.

The difficulty of role identification is compounded by a number of contributing factors that add to the school dilemma. Confusion exists about the nature of drug use in society, especially among youth, the meaning of prevention or preventive action, the types and numbers of drug users and abusers in schools, and the conflicting views about drug education.

There are, of course, no simple answers or simple solutions. That is why the problem has not been resolved. But there are useful alternatives that may need modification to fit the particular needs of every community. The situation is far from hopeless. Perhaps this book will provide some of the needed guidelines for schools.

Nature of drug use in society

Man uses drugs to awaken in the morning, to keep awake or to sustain himself throughout the day, to lose weight, to flush out his bowels, to enhance social and religious experiences, for pleasure and relaxa-

---

*Drug use = consumption of a drug; drug misuse = periodic or occasional improper or inappropriate use; and drug abuse = interference with the individual's health or his economic or social adjustment (Chapter 2).

tion, to escape from reality, to go to sleep, to treat disease and medical conditions, before and after dinner, and for a variety of other purposes. Man has used a variety of drugs for centuries and probably will continue to use them for thousands of years in the future. Lipscomb says:

The United States is a drug-using culture. On any given day an American adult is likely to ingest 4-5 identifiable chemical compounds that are pharmaceutical in nature. Consider the individual who arises in the morning, brushes his teeth with toothpaste containing fluoride, downs a Bromo-Seltzer, has two cups of coffee containing caffeine, takes a dexedrine to help him with his weight problem, lights his post-coffee cigarette containing nicotine and heads for a round of events in the business or professional world which may include cocktails and wine with meals followed by brandy and a good cigar—this individual is more likely to be typical than unusual. While for the most part individual adults do not get into trouble through their use of drugs, some unfortunates do experience complications—social and medical.*

Pharmacologically, drugs are generally grouped into a variety of categories, among which are stimulants, depressants, psychedelics, and narcotics (Chapter 4). Drugs may also be classified as legal and illegal. Legal drugs refer to those that may be purchased in two ways—over the counter or by prescription. A person may buy such drugs as alcohol, tobacco, aspirin, laxatives, and cough syrups whenever desired in any drug store, supermarket, or liquor store by paying the requested over-the-counter price. A person may also acquire legal drugs such as pep, sleeping, and relaxing pills when they are prescribed by a physician for some personal ailment that is in need of treatment or cure. Illegal drugs such as marijuana, heroin, and cocaine, however, are considered narcotics by law and may not be purchased through the usual legal channels. Some legal drugs such as pep and sleeping pills may be considered illegal because they are obtainable and sold through unlawful channels.

We live in a drug-oriented society. Many persons throughout the United States are using, misusing, and abusing numerous legal and illegal drugs. The drug problem is not one involving only youth and the military. It is one that may affect the life of every individual to a greater or lesser degree. There are many individuals at all social and economic levels, in homes and in business, who are using drugs and who are creating problems. Why is the focus only on illegal drugs? The drug problem is one in which not only illegal drugs but also the readily available legal drugs are involved. The prevalence of drug misuse and abuse continues to grow at alarming rates in all of society, with the legal drug problem being far greater than the illegal one.

Numerous persons are engaged in the self-diagnosis of physical, mental, and emotional ailments; they attempt to treat or cure these conditions with readily available legal drugs and possibly through the use of illegal drugs. Nowlis identifies this problem when she says, "Relying more on medication than on the physician, the person medicates himself excessively and indiscriminately. He uses medication as a kind of magical protector and depends on medication rather than people to handle certain emotional drives and needs."[38] The magnitude of the drug problem is identified by Lennard, who reports:

Although most of the current voluminous writing about the misuse of drugs concerns the misuse of psychoactive agents by young people, and especially the use of drugs obtained illegally, it seems no use to decry the use and misuse of drugs by young people while paying so little attention to the growing use and misuse of psychoactive agents in general, both those prescribed by physicians and those obtained over the counter without prescription, is highly misleading and unproductive.*

The steady and marked increase of the legal psychoactive drugs has gone unnoticed. Louria states, ". . . it is reasonable

---

*Lipscomb, W. R.: An epidemiology of drug use-abuse, J. Public Health **61:**1794-1800, 1971.

*Lennard, H. L., et al.: Mystification and drug misuse, San Francisco, 1971, Jossey-Bass, Inc., Publishers.

to estimate that half of the sedatives and tranquillizers prescribed by physicians are given unnecessarily."[29]

Alcohol, cigarettes, cough syrups, laxatives, sleeping aids, vitamins, aspirin, and other nonprescription items are readily obtainable. Billions of dollars are spent yearly on prescription drugs alone. In 1970, 202 million legal prescriptions for psychoactive drugs—stimulants, sedatives, tranquilizers, and antidepressants—were filled in pharmacies for patients of physicians.

Alcohol is perhaps the most popular social drug used in the United States. About two thirds of the population over 15 years of age, or over 70 million people, drink alcoholic beverages.[35] About 90% drink in moderation and are not adversely affected by their drinking practices. Thus approximately 7 million do have problems. About 15 billion aspirin tablets (27.2 million pounds) are consumed yearly by Americans.[5] This amounts to about 750 pills for every person per year (approximately two daily). Some 8 billion amphetamine tablets are produced yearly and 50% of these get into illegal traffic—35 doses of 5 milligrams each for every man, woman, and child in the United States.[47] It is estimated that there are 70 million smokers in this country, with 1 million new teen-age smokers each year.[25]

Food and Drug Administration Commissioner Dr. Edwards[16] as well as Halleck[23] indicates that the so-called legal drugs are at least as great a societal problem as the abuse of illegal drugs.

The public is constantly being encouraged to purchase and use drugs through the mass communication media; television has contributed extensively to bringing the medicine man into every household. Thus individuals may be more prone to self-diagnosis of bodily ailments and self-medication of their problems as a result of the media influence.

An indication of the possible extent of legal drug use may be obtained from these data, which represent approximations of the funds expended for the purchase of selected legal drugs and drug products in the United States in 1970[13]:

Alcoholic beverages	$15,760,000,000
Tobacco accessories	9,225,000,000
Prescriptions	5,220,000,000
Cough and cold items (cough syrups, nose drops, etc.)	580,000,000
Internal analgesics including aspirin	559,000,000
Dentifrices	361,000,000
Vitamin concentrates (30% by prescription)	322,000,000
Laxatives and other elimination aids	201,000,000
Diet aids	138,000,000
Antacids	104,000,000
Diarrhea remedies	70,000,000
Sleeping aids	28,000,000
Motion sickness preparations	21,000,000
	$32,589,000,000

It may be generalized from this information that approximately $161 for each man, woman, and child was spent for selected legal drugs in 1970.

A variety of drugs such as sleeping and pep pills, marijuana, heroin, and LSD are readily available on the illegal market despite police surveillance and control. The Federal Food and Drug Administration estimates that 10 billion barbiturate and amphetamine pills are produced yearly, and that one half of these are bootlegged through illegal channels. In recent years the increase in the use of amphetamines, barbiturates, hallucinogens (including LSD) and sedative-hypnotics (including marijuana), has been extensive. Yolles[52] estimates there are 7 million experimenters, 5 million moderate users, and 3 million chronic users of illegal drugs. President Nixon's Commission on Marijuana[9] claims 24 million Americans (over 11 years of age) have tried marijuana at least once and 8.3 million are current users. The incidence of use is greatest in young people: 6% among 12 to 13 year olds, 27% among 16 to 17 year olds, and 40% among 18 to 21 year olds.[36]

A recent survey of drug use conducted by the New York State Narcotic Addiction

Commission revealed the information found in Table 1-1. Rayburn F. Hesse, chairman of the National Association of State Drug Abuse Program Coordinators, included this information in his testimony before the U. S. Senate Appropriations Committee on May 31, 1972.

The extensive use of legal and illegal drugs provides documentation that society is faced with an extensive, difficult, and complex problem if it hopes to curtail or reduce the use, misuse, and abuse of drugs. Drugs have become deeply ingrained in people's life-styles despite the adverse effects they may have on the life, health, and welfare of many people, both young and old. The drug problem has grown in recent years because of the involvement of a large percentage of young people, the experimentation with drugs by the so-called middle class, the advent of television, and more recently, the participation of military personnel. Drugs may now be found in the classroom and on school campuses. They are creating a tremendous dilemma for parents, teachers, administrators, and other school personnel. A recent Gallup poll[20] showed that two thirds of the adults in the United States and 40% of the students believe the schools have a significant problem with which to contend. This same poll identified the use of drugs by students as the sixth leading problem facing schools today.

Preventive approach

Prevention has many meanings for many people. Although a precise definition is not readily available and may be difficult to clearly identify, it is necessary to provide a frame of reference for a better understanding of the purpose of this book. Literally, to prevent is to keep from happening or occurring. More specifically, in medicine it refers to a prophylactic or procedure that arrests the threatened onset of a disease or condition. Application of these statements to the drug problem leads to the conclusion that education, laws, and law enforcement as well as rehabilitation and treatment are preventive procedures. All of these elements have features with which schools must be concerned and involved. However, the role of the school is primarily

Table 1-1. New York State survey of drug use*

DRUGS	USERS TRIED†	USERS REGULAR‡	POPULATION REGULAR§	FROM LEGAL SOURCES	USE AT SOCIAL AFFAIRS	REGULAR USERS EMPLOYED	USE ON JOB
Antidepressants		39,000	0.3%				
Barbiturates		361,000	2.7%	10%	31,000		
Cocaine	101,000	6,000	0.05%				
Diet pills		222,000	1.5%	20%	16,000		
Heroin		125,000-250,000	1%-1.7%			34,000	11,900
LSD	203,000	45,000	0.3%			25,000	5,000
Marijuana	1,043,000	487,000	3.5%			293,000	67,938
Methadrine	111,000	35,000	0.3%				
Narcotics—controlled		17,000	0.1%				
Pep pills		110,000	0.8%	50%	45,000	10,000	6,000
Sedative-hypnotics		187,000	1.5%	15%	18,000		
Tranquilizers (major)		71,000	0.5%	5%	4,000		
Tranquilizers (minor)		525,000	4.0%	5%	36,000		

*Data from the New York State Narcotic Addiction Commission.
†Tried = in last 6 months.
‡Regular user = at least six times per month.
§Percentages based on 13.7 million people age 14 years and older in the state of New York.

an instructional one and it is in this context that prevention will be defined.

Prevention involves primary, secondary, and tertiary aspects. Their application to the drug scene will be interpreted in the descriptions that follow.

PRIMARY PREVENTION

Primary prevention refers to action taken to prevent something from happening or measures to stop something before it starts. It is the attempt to encourage and help students, or other people, primarily through education, either (1) to refrain from or reduce the misuse and abuse of drugs or (2) to make more intelligent use of drugs. This type of prevention may take place inside the school or in the community. Within the school, the education may be formal or informal and may be provided for students, parents, school personnel, and members of the community.

SECONDARY PREVENTION

Procedures taken after something has occurred to forestall the condition from growing worse or from becoming more advanced constitute secondary prevention. It is the steps or actions taken to provide help or service to individuals who are using, misusing, or abusing drugs and who are present in schools. These pupils may attend school under the influence of drugs or the use of drugs outside the school may affect their ability to learn effectively. The services rendered may include crisis intervention, information on alternatives to drug use, understandings toward more intelligent use of drugs, guidance to a community agency, or therapy. This aid may come in the form of counseling, education, or treatment.

Since schools are not expected to provide treatment services that are preventive, this assistance must take place outside the school; it is similar to that provided in medical clinics with outpatient services by physicians, psychiatrists, and others. In the school the nontreatment assistance may be analogous to the health services phase of the school health program, whereby student health deviants are identified and follow-up procedures are initiated to provide the help needed to enable the student to learn better. Such services may include informal education, guidance and counseling, diagnostic examinations or procedures, observations of symptomatic behavior, first aid, referral to community agencies, adjustment of programs, and improvement of teacher-pupil relationships. The assistance may be rendered by counselors, nurses, physicians, psychologists, and others, and may include rap sessions, drop-in centers, and hot-lines. Such services may be located inside, outside, or adjacent to the school. They may or may not be conducted by school personnel.

Secondary prevention is generally of short-term duration and may occur within the school or elsewhere in the community.

TERTIARY PREVENTION

Tertiary prevention is an extension of secondary prevention wherein action is taken to ward off the development of more serious conditions resulting from drug misuse and abuse. It refers to long-term, extensive, technical health, rehabilitation, and educational services rendered by such persons as physicians and psychiatrists to save lives, prevent serious personality damage, provide crisis intervention, and aid in the adjustment of individuals to society. Such services usually are of an inpatient type and generally take place in a hospital, rehabilitation center, or other appropriate therapeutic communities such as Synanon, "The Family" at Mendocino State Hospital, California, Daytop Village in New York, and the Haight-Ashbury Free Clinic Social Rehabilitation Project in San Francisco. Extended care may also be given in some clinics such as those established in the methadone maintenance programs. Tertiary prevention takes place outside the school.

• • •

The school setting can provide primary and secondary prevention to the extent previously defined. This will be discussed more fully later in the text. Justification for the services identified as secondary prevention is based on the premise that, although parents are primarily responsible for the medical and health care of their children and youth, they (1) often do not recognize problems, (2) frequently do not know what to do when a health deviation occurs and may look to the school for guidance, and (3) often ignore their responsibilities and continue to send pupils with drug problems to school to be educated. Children and youth who are physically, mentally, or socially ill will have trouble learning under the best environmental conditions. Thus schools must have available educational services that will inform, guide, encourage, and direct parents and students to action, thereby enabling pupils to attain the highest levels of wellness.

SCHOOL-COMMUNITY COORDINATION IN PREVENTION

The school and community must coordinate their efforts in drug prevention to render the best possible service to students. Children and youth with drug problems who are attending school may need to be referred to resources outside the school for assistance. Such help may be available from a physician, psychiatrist, guidance clinic, drop-in center, or other agency or organization. However, if such services are in short supply, the school may need to become active in trying to promote their development. By the same token, if schools are not attending to students with drug problems, the community organizations may find it necessary to encourage schools to take action. In addition, community educational programs may be transmitting information that is in conflict with that presented in the school. For example, the school may be teaching that marijuana use is always injurious to health. Community representatives may be indicating that marijuana use may cause little or no danger to humans physiologically. These differing views may create un-

necessary difficulty between students and parents as well as between students, teachers, and the school. Such differences, if they exist, must be recognized by the teachers and the school; measures must be taken to resolve them.

These illustrations should make it apparent that schools and communities, each with their independent programs, cannot act in isolation but must function cooperatively to satisfactorily attack the drug problem. The need for clear identification of the roles of the school and of the community, including their relationships, should be evident. Such clarity and cooperation does not often exist with any degree of regularity in the United States, although there is growing evidence of improvement in these relationships.

Classification and numbers of drug users and abusers

Most if not all adolescents use drugs in some form at some time in their lives. However, not all young persons who use drugs are problems, nor do many who use drugs develop problems. This is especially true when consideration is given to such legal drugs as alcohol and tobacco, but it is also applicable to the illegal drugs. Marin and Cohen state, "Hard narcotics are always destructive and their spread is frightening, but the soft drugs—marijuana, the psychedelics—are more variable. Some of them give some trouble to some adolescents at some time; but not always, not even most of the time."[30] Marin and Cohen also indicate that illegal drug use generally starts at the high school level but that in some places it may occur as early as the fifth or sixth grade, at ages 10 and 11. They claim that most young persons merely try drugs out by tasting or testing them. They believe that if adolescents are tuned into the world, are energetic, and are minimally adjusted, the use of drugs should not create serious problems. However, knowledge of the types of student users and of the extent to which they are using, misusing, and abusing drugs is necessary not only to further understand the nature of prevention but, more importantly, to design school programs.

CLASSIFICATION OF USERS AND ABUSERS

David E. Smith, director of the Haight-Ashbury Free Medical Clinic, has categorized student drug users as nonusers, experimenters, periodic users, compulsive users, and relapse users.

Nonusers use no drugs. Frequently this categorization of students refers only to those not using the illegal drugs, but occasionally it includes alcohol and tobacco. Actually if all legal drugs were included, it is conceivable that there are no nonusers of drugs.

Experimenters try drugs for short periods of time and then abandon their use. This is the largest group of users. Their numbers as well as the extent of their experimentation will vary with the drug used.

Periodic users use drugs regularly at social-recreational and religious-ritual affairs, but not necessarily every weekend. They may use prescription or over-the-counter drugs for medical reasons. They may use drugs in a group setting. The usage tends not to be habitual, although regular, and may fit only one segment of their life-style. This is the largest group of users of drugs who do so regularly, for example, at periodic cocktail parties or occasional marijuana parties. In numbers they may not be large, except possibly for the prescription and over-the-counter drug users. These individuals generally can stop using drugs if they so desire.

Compulsive users are habituated or addicted to the use of one or more drugs. They may be called "potheads," "acidheads," "speed freaks," or alcoholics, depending on the drug used. They use and seek drugs regularly. They are heavy users and drugs are part of their life-style. They constitute a very small percentage of the population.

Relapse users have ceased to be compulsive users and are fighting the craving for drugs. They also form a small but increasing percentage of the population, including alcoholics in Alcoholics Anonymous and ex-addicts in rehabilitation centers.

NUMBERS OF DRUG USERS AND ABUSERS

Data clearly identifying the numbers and percentages of junior and senior high school students using various kinds of drugs are not available. However, there have been a number of scattered studies that have been carefully researched and provide helpful information. Generalizations made from these studies provide substantive indicative data. The best estimates, however, are probably "guestimates," for so many variables are involved in the collection of such data. Social, economic, racial, ethnic, and religious factors differ so widely in communities, as do the types of drugs used, that conclusions made in the discussion that follows should be reviewed in the light of these variables.

One of the more extensive and complete surveys on drug usage was compiled for grades 7 to 12 over a 3-year period in San Mateo County, California.[19] A more recent preliminary report of the fourth year of this study will be found in Tables 1-2 to 1-4. In addition, Table 1-5 provides interesting summary material from several studies. These data together with information from other studies[3] in Massachusetts, Maryland, Utah, Idaho, and New York serve as the basis for the following generalizations regarding the extent of drug use among junior and senior high school students:

1. The percentage of compulsive and relapse users is relatively small and the numbers and percentages of these users are probably the lowest of all categories. In some ghetto areas the use of heroin may be as high as 6% or higher, while in other communities it may 0.5% or less. The percentages of use of LSD, amphetamines, and barbiturates may be a little higher, with marijuana possibly being used by as much as 15% or more of the population in some communities.

2. The numbers and percentages of peri-

Table 1-2. Percentage of drug use reported by San Mateo County, California, in male high school students*

| | ANY USE DURING PAST YEAR | | | | TEN TIMES + DURING PAST YEAR | | | | 50+ USE | |
| | Date of survey | | | | Date of survey | | | | Date of survey | |
	1968	1969	1970	1971	1968	1969	1970	1971	1970	1971
Alcoholic beverages										
Freshmen	61.0	66.3	66.1	74.0	21.4	26.8	26.4	36.2	11.3	17.6
Sophomore	64.5	75.2	76.8	76.5	24.7	36.8	38.9	45.0	18.0	24.4
Junior	70.7	78.9	79.2	82.4	35.6	43.5	45.9	54.7	23.4	32.3
Senior	76.5	81.7	80.6	83.6	41.6	52.6	49.9	59.3	26.9	36.9
Tobacco										
Freshmen	57.1	51.2	49.9	54.4	34.0	31.2	29.4	32.5	22.8	24.6
Sophomore	54.3	50.1	51.4	51.1	34.6	33.7	33.5	33.0	27.2	26.8
Junior	56.7	55.0	50.5	54.6	39.4	38.7	34.9	38.3	28.9	31.6
Senior	58.3	58.1	52.1	53.5	41.5	42.1	36.7	37.7	30.7	31.3
Marijuana										
Freshmen	26.8	34.9	34.1	44.4	14.3	20.2	19.6	26.1	11.5	17.2
Sophomore	32.3	41.7	45.5	49.7	18.1	25.7	29.3	33.3	19.6	23.2
Junior	36.9	45.5	48.9	57.9	22.5	30.3	34.1	42.3	23.5	30.2
Senior	44.6	50.1	50.9	59.1	25.6	33.9	34.2	43.7	22.0	32.3
LSD										
Freshmen	8.1	11.0	10.9	12.5	2.6	4.5	4.3	4.4	2.0	2.0
Sophomore	11.1	16.9	16.4	16.1	4.2	7.2	6.1	5.9	2.0	2.7
Junior	14.6	19.2	18.5	21.2	5.7	8.5	7.3	8.6	2.6	3.9
Senior	16.6	23.0	17.4	21.1	6.6	10.5	6.9	7.3	2.6	3.4
Amphetamines										
Freshmen	12.0	14.9	13.8	17.9	4.0	5.0	4.2	6.3	1.9	2.9
Sophomore	15.8	19.1	18.5	19.5	5.6	7.2	6.0	7.0	2.6	3.0
Junior	17.9	22.1	20.7	24.6	7.0	9.5	8.2	10.7	3.9	4.9
Senior	20.5	25.7	18.8	27.0	8.5	11.5	7.2	10.9	3.3	5.6
Barbiturates										
Freshmen			12.5	16.8			3.9	5.4	1.8	2.6
Sophomore			16.6	16.8			4.8	5.7	2.3	2.2
Junior			17.3	19.8			6.5	7.7	3.6	3.8
Senior			14.3	18.6			5.1	7.3	2.4	3.7
Heroin										
Freshmen				3.7				1.8		1.4
Sophomore				3.9				1.8		1.4
Junior				4.9				2.4		1.8
Senior				5.9				3.0		2.0

	1968	1969	1970	1971
Number of responses				
Freshmen	2,349	3,129	3,161	3,084
Sophomore	2,332	2,826	3,183	2,804
Junior	2,064	2,579	3,019	3,037
Senior	1,799	2,034	2,352	2,467

*From a Preliminary release report prepared by the Department of Public Health and Welfare, San Mateo, Calif., Nov. 8, 1971.

Table 1-3. Percentage of drug use reported by San Mateo County, California, in female high school students*

	ANY USE DURING PAST YEAR				TEN TIMES + DURING PAST YEAR				50+ USE	
	Date of survey				Date of survey				Date of survey	
	1968	1969	1970	1971	1968	1969	1970	1971	1970	1971
Alcoholic beverages										
Freshmen	52.0	63.2	62.6	68.3	13.4	20.9	20.9	30.8	6.5	12.8
Sophomore	60.1	67.4	73.3	74.1	15.1	25.0	31.2	38.9	12.3	17.4
Junior	67.4	71.4	76.0	78.4	24.0	30.4	35.0	41.5	12.9	19.3
Senior	71.1	75.7	76.7	79.1	27.0	34.3	36.6	42.5	13.1	18.5
Tobacco										
Freshmen	52.0	56.1	52.1	56.2	27.3	31.3	29.5	33.7	20.2	23.6
Sophomore	55.4	55.5	57.0	56.3	34.0	32.7	36.9	37.7	28.1	30.1
Junior	57.4	54.8	54.8	55.6	35.4	37.5	35.4	38.7	27.6	31.8
Senior	55.1	57.5	52.7	53.7	36.7	39.7	37.3	36.4	30.6	30.4
Marijuana										
Freshmen	22.9	31.8	31.9	40.5	10.6	18.0	16.2	23.3	7.2	11.6
Sophomore	28.1	35.5	42.1	48.1	14.9	21.2	26.6	31.1	14.1	17.0
Junior	31.7	38.3	42.6	49.6	16.7	23.3	26.2	32.6	14.4	19.3
Senior	31.9	38.0	40.3	48.3	17.4	22.3	24.1	30.6	15.0	18.5
LSD										
Freshmen	6.9	11.2	9.2	11.7	1.9	3.5	2.2	3.0	.7	1.0
Sophomore	8.3	12.8	15.0	13.6	2.5	4.4	4.8	4.1	1.4	1.4
Junior	9.2	13.0	12.4	15.0	3.6	4.6	3.3	3.9	.8	.4
Senior	9.4	10.8	11.7	12.1	3.3	3.7	3.2	3.0	.7	1.0
Amphetamines										
Freshmen	12.9	19.5	17.3	22.5	3.7	6.3	5.4	7.6	1.6	2.5
Sophomore	16.1	20.1	24.4	26.8	6.1	8.3	9.4	11.0	3.6	4.0
Junior	17.1	21.5	22.3	25.5	6.4	8.1	8.3	11.2	2.9	4.6
Senior	16.1	19.8	19.9	22.8	6.7	8.2	7.5	10.4	2.4	4.3
Barbiturates										
Freshmen			14.5	18.0			4.6	5.3	1.5	1.5
Sophomore			20.3	19.2			7.7	6.2	3.0	2.3
Junior			15.0	17.9			4.5	6.8	1.7	2.7
Senior			13.7	15.0			4.4	5.3	1.3	2.2
Heroin										
Freshmen				1.9				.6		.5
Sophomore				2.0				.8		.5
Junior				3.3				1.1		.7
Senior				2.6				1.1		.6

	1968	1969	1970	1971
Number of responses				
Freshmen	2,526	3,156	3,378	3,220
Sophomore	2,473	2,920	3,053	2,821
Junior	2,205	2,850	3,004	2,982
Senior	1,892	2,287	2,632	2,363

*From a Preliminary release report prepared by the Department of Public Health and Welfare, San Mateo, Calif., Nov. 8, 1971.

Table 1-4. Percentage of drug use of students in grades 7 and 8, San Mateo County, California*

	BOYS						GIRLS					
	Any use			Used 10+ times			Any use			Used 10+ times		
	1969	1970	1971	1969	1970	1971	1969	1970	1971	1969	1970	1971
Alcoholic beverages												
Grade 7	52.3	49.0	55.1	10.9	11.7	16.4	38.4	42.0	43.0	8.2	6.7	10.7
Grade 8	60.2	61.4	68.0	18.3	22.6	30.6	50.6	53.8	63.4	16.2	15.0	22.7
Tobacco												
Grade 7	43.6	38.2	41.6	17.4	12.3	15.8	39.8	34.0	36.0	14.0	11.9	14.3
Grade 8	51.0	51.0	50.1	25.5	23.6	25.7	50.1	44.9	49.0	25.3	21.4	26.3
Marijuana												
Grade 7	10.9	9.9	17.6	4.1	2.7	5.3	10.7	7.2	12.6	1.7	1.4	4.1
Grade 8	23.9	22.5	29.1	11.6	10.3	14.6	21.8	16.6	25.8	7.4	6.9	12.4
Amphetamines												
Grade 7	5.1	3.7	5.3	1.7	0.6	1.3	5.9	2.8	5.9	1.1	0.4	1.3
Grade 8	11.8	9.5	10.9	3.4	2.8	3.5	10.4	8.2	13.2	1.5	2.1	3.0
LSD												
Grade 7	2.8	1.3	2.7	0.2	0.2	0.9	2.1	0.9	2.3	0.4	0.1	0.3
Grade 8	8.7	4.9	6.2	2.4	0.9	2.0	6.0	4.0	6.3	1.3	0.8	1.3
Barbiturates												
Grade 7		3.4	5.9		0.5	1.2		3.1	5.4		0.4	1.0
Grade 8		9.6	11.0		2.3	3.7		7.7	12.3		2.1	3.6

	1969	1970	1971	1969	1970	1971
Number of responses						
Grade 7	530	2,268	2,619	523	2,356	2,777
Grade 8	553	2,215	2,638	597	2,166	2,762

*From a Preliminary release report prepared by the Department of Public Health and Welfare, San Mateo, Calif., Nov. 8, 1971.

odic users is probably somewhat higher than that of the compulsive and relapse users, but there are little if any data indicating how much higher.

3. The experimenters form probably the largest group of users. The percentages according to the drug used are as follows: alcohol, 60% to 80%; tobacco, 40% to 60%; marijuana, 5% to 30%; LSD, 1% to 25%; amphetamines and barbiturates, 2% to 20%; and heroin, probably 1%. Nyswander and Millman[39] claim that it has been reported that 60% of students enrolled at several New York City high schools have used heroin. Moderate drinking is the norm for male adolescents.[8] Daily drinking, frequent episodes of ex-cessive use, and personal complications with alcohol are rare among youth.

4. The percentage of nonusers differs with the types of drugs used. Overall, the San Mateo County study shows that among high school students only 20% reported using no drugs whatsoever, 3% used only tobacco, 13% used only alcohol and tobacco, or a total of 46% used no drugs if alcohol and tobacco are excluded.[19] The same study noted that the percentage of nonusers of all drugs, including tobacco and alcohol, was highest in the seventh grade (44%) and decreased each year in school thereafter to 16% in the senior year of high school. In the state of Idaho[49] the percentages of nonusers of drugs were

Table 1-5. Compiled data of high school student drug use

PERCENTAGES*

	Never used						Ever used					
DRUGS	Dallas, Texas[45]	Idaho[49]	Portland-Multnomah, Ore.[24]	San Mateo, Calif.[19]	Utah[1]	Five other studies[3]	Dallas, Texas[45]	Idaho[49]	Portland-Multnomah, Ore.[24]	San Mateo, Calif.[19]	Utah[1]	Five other studies[3]
Alcohol	29	37	14	21	—	20- 40	71	63	86	79	—	60-80
Tobacco	56	44	41	42	—	40- 60	44	56	59	58	—	40-60
Marijuana	86	88	87	53	88	70- 94	14	12	13	47	12	6-30
Amphetamines	92	94	87	75	90	85- 95	8	6	13	25	10	5-15
LSD	—	92	94	87	95	—	—	8	6	13	5	—
Barbiturates	—	94	91	82	—	—	—	6	9	18	—	—
Solvents	92	92	89	—	93	89- 97	8	8	11	—	7	3-11
Heroin	97	97	—	95	—	97-100	3	3	—	5	—	0- 3

*Data for each location derived from sources cited in references.

as follows: alcohol, 37%; tobacco, 44%; marijuana, 88%; inhalants, 92%; hallucinogens, 92%; barbiturates, 94%; amphetamines, 94%; and heroin, 97%.

5. The San Mateo County study also revealed the percentage of users of drugs other than alcohol and tobacco to be lowest in the seventh grade (approximately 10%) increasing yearly to approximately 49% in the senior year of high school. It is interesting to note that the use of alcohol ranged from 46% in the seventh grade to 78% in the twelfth grade, and tobacco ranged from 36% in the seventh grade to 53% in the twelfth grade.

DATA CONCERNING HIGH SCHOOL DRUG USE. The data in Table 1-5 were extrapolated and compiled from five major studies and a variety of other reports. The analysis of data in each research effort was treated differently; hence this information should only be considered indicative of the reported findings. In addition, a number of the reports of the studies were incomplete and fragmentary. It was difficult therefore to precisely organize the material. In reviewing the evidence, it may be generalized that the use of drugs was less frequent in grades 7 and 8, and be-

came increasingly greater as students progressed through high school. Also, boys tended to use drugs more often than girls, although the differences were not always very dramatic.

• • •

Knowledge of the extensiveness of drug use and abuse as well as of the types of drug users among youth identifies the need for the development of varieties of preventive procedures and of differing educational programs. However, the meaning of drug education is widely misunderstood and is in need of clarification. Responsible individuals attempting to develop programs have been confused. This has caused difficulties in determining the differing roles of the school and of the community and has led to problems in communication and coordination of school and community efforts.

The meaning of drug education

Drug education is often identified synonymously as drug information or drug knowledge. Frequently phrases such as "give them the facts" and "scare the hell out of them" are used. President Nixon identifies drug education in this manner, "There is no priority higher in this administration than to see that children and the public learn the facts about drugs in the right way and for the right purposes."[37] Others believe drug education to be learning that goes on in a classroom in which there are 30 to 40 students and a teacher who didactically warns them of the evils and hazards of using drugs. Some people think drug education is a talk by a noted speaker, physician, pharmacologist, psychiatrist, or other authority describing the effects of drugs on the human body to an assembly with 500 to 1000 students in attendance. The showing of a film and the distribution of a pamphlet are other references that some individuals believe to be education. There are many other points of view regarding the meaning of drug education, but perhaps these illustrate the varieties of understandings that exist.

Actually all of the activities described have educational possibilities. However, what learning takes place under these circumstances may be solely factual, or informational. It may be accurate as well as inaccurate in its content. It may be a series of biased, prejudiced, and false exhortations. The evidence is overwhelmingly supportive of the fact that without the concern for the personal attitudes, without individuals being actively engaged in the learning process, factual information by itself is meaningless, is useless, and will have little effect on the way persons behave toward drugs. In fact, data indicate that such "facts" may create "pro" attitudes toward drugs by removing the uncertainty of the hazards and thereby increasing the experimental use of drugs.

Unfortunately much of the so-called drug education that has occurred in the schools has been of the informational kind. This may be one of the main reasons for the ineffectiveness of many of the drug education programs.

Learning about drugs can be considered an overly simplified definition of drug education. Such learning may take place inside or outside the school. It may occur in a formal or an informal manner for children, youth, parents, teachers, counselors, administrators, and the general public. It may be provided for nonusers, experimenters, periodic users, compulsive users, and relapse users of drugs as part of primary, secondary, and tertiary prevention programs.

FORMAL EDUCATION

Formal drug education generally refers to organized or planned learning that usually takes place in a classroom and may involve a teacher, a curriculum, a textbook, and such audiovisual aids as films, filmstrips, and tape recordings. Drug education as such usually is not considered to be a separate subject area in the curriculum for grades kindergarten through 12, but probably is taught as part of another subject such as health education, science, social studies, or as a separate unit of work in these same courses. It may be a specific course or series of presentations for teachers, counselors, nurses, parents, or community representatives in a college or in a university. It involves the use of a variety of teaching techniques, including speakers. Such education may also occur outside the school without the involvement of school personnel: a city health department may hold a series of meetings concerning drugs for parents, industrial leaders, and educators; a medical center may conduct formal sessions for the community at large or for physicians and paramedical personnel.

Formal drug education is more easily presented in schools or in the community when its purpose is to provide only pharmacological information. It becomes more complex and more difficult to conduct when the objectives include social, psychological, and possibly spiritual emphases—when the focus is on changing behavior or attitude. Thus expediency and the need for a simple, direct attack may be reasons for the factual emphasis in many formal drug education programs.

INFORMAL EDUCATION

Informal education refers to the learning that takes place without structure and, without much, if any, planning. It may occur in the classroom, in the school, outside the school, in the home watching television, reading a newspaper or magazine, talking to a parent, or in the community talking to a friend, neighbor, or anyone else. It may take place in discussion on a one-to-one basis or in small groups. It is an activity in which a person usually participates voluntarily.

BEHAVIORAL APPROACH

Drug education today must be centered on behavioral changes that include not only a knowledge or understanding of drugs but also attitudes toward drugs and drug practices. In the current vernacular of educators the appropriate goals must be stated in terms of their cognitive, affective, and action emphases. Education must cover more than merely the pharmacological and physiological effects of drugs on body systems. It must give consideration to student feelings, values, interests, and actions about and with drugs. It must include the why of drug use and abuse as well as the social effects of drugs on individuals and the community. It must provide students with alternatives to drug use. It should permit students to make their own decisions about the use of drugs after all the favorable and unfavorable aspects of such usage are presented. It should encourage the development of values. This approach is referred to as the behavioral approach in drug education.

One of the objections to the previously mentioned statement by President Nixon concerns his emphasis on factual information in drug education. The available evidence clearly indicates that facts by themselves, information by itself, and knowledge alone. are not sufficient to change or affect human behavior. Facts are singularly ineffective in changing the opinions of persons who are emotionally committed to their own way of looking at an issue.

This is especially true of those users and abusers of drugs who may feel they are more sophisticated about drugs than the teacher or the speaker who may be presenting drug information. However, factual data are prerequisite to intelligent action if such information is accurate, if it is acquired within a context that provides proper motivation, and if the student understands the facts to be meaningful, applicable, and useful in the environment in which he lives. Thus in drug education a teaching approach of much wider scope than merely the presentation of facts becomes mandatory.

Schools have encountered difficulties with, have not been aware of, or have not frequently used the behavioral approach. The result has been that drug education programs have been primarily information oriented and ineffectual in their impact on the drug problem. This may be the most significant justification for the criticism that has been made about the ineffectiveness of drug education programs. One of the purposes of this book is to help schools develop behaviorally centered curricula with behaviorally stated objectives so that the desired impact on students can be achieved.

Both formal and informal drug education must take place in the schools as part of programs of primary and secondary prevention in order to provide differential learnings for the different types of student drug users found in schools (Chapter 7).

Generally it may be concluded that formal education should be the main educational focus for nonusers and for experimental drug users, provided there are numerous opportunities for informal education as well. Informal education, which should also be a part of the services phase (Chapter 8) of the drug program, should be used to try to reach the periodic, compulsive, and relapse drug users.

The dilemma of the schools can be resolved by giving attention to the total school drug program introduced in this book. Such a program must provide differential phases to accommodate the variety of drug users and abusers as well as the non-users in the local school community. It should focus on the primary and secondary prevention aspects of the problem. It must include both formal and informal education, services to identify and assist drug users and abusers, consideration for improvement of the school atmosphere, and coordination of the total drug program within the school and with the community.

References

1. Advisory Committee report on drug abuse: summations and recommendations, Salt Lake City, 1969, Utah Governor's Citizen Advisory Committee on Drugs.

1a. Arnold, M.: The trouble in drug education, Natl. Observer 10:16, 1971.

2. Barrins, P. C.: Drug abuse: the newest most dangerous challenge to school boards, Am. Sch. Board J. 157:15-18, 1969.

3. Berg, D. F.: Illicit use of dangerous drugs in the United States: a compilation of studies, surveys, and polls, Washington, D. C., 1970, Drug Services Division of the Bureau of Narcotics and Dangerous Drugs, U. S. Department of Justice.

4. Bland, H. B.: In Hafen, B. Q., editor: Readings on drug use and abuse, Provo, Utah, 1970, Brigham Young University Press.

5. Bureau of Narcotics and Dangerous Drugs, U. S. Department of Justice: Guidelines for drug abuse prevention education, Washington, D. C., 1970, Government Printing Office.

6. California State Department of Education: Drug abuse: a sourcebook and guide for teachers, Sacramento, 1969, State Printing Office.

7. Cornacchia, H. J.: Teaching in difficult areas of health, J. Sch. Health 41:193-196, 1970.

8. Demone, H. W.: Implications from research on adolescent drinking. In Alcohol Education Conference proceedings, Washington, D. C., 1966, U. S. Department of Health, Education and Welfare.

9. Drive to curb hard drugs gets no. 1 priority, U. S. News World Rep. 72:37, April 3, 1972.

10. Drug abuse: a reference for teachers, rev., Trenton, N. J., 1968, Division of Curriculum and Instruction, New Jersey State Department of Education.

11. Drug education handbook, Denver, 1970, Alcohol and Drug Dependence Division, Colorado State Department of Public Health.

12. Drug education in Maine, Augusta, 1970, Maine State Department of Education.

13. Drug trade news, Oradell, N. J., Oct. 7, 1971, Topics Publishing Co.

14. Drugs and the educational antidote, Nat. Sch. 85:49-52, 1970.

15. Education USA, Washington, D. C., Sept. 27, 1971, National School Public Relations Association.

16. Edwards, C. C.: Drug Educ. Rep. 1:4, 1971.

17. Eisner, V.: Adolescent drug abuse, Calif. Sch. Health 4:1-9, 1969.

18. Finlator, J.: The drug scene: the scope and the problem faced by schools. In Teaching about drugs: a curriculum guide, Kent, Ohio, 1970, American School Health Association.

19. Five mind altering drugs (plus one), San Mateo, Calif., 1970, Department of Public Health and Welfare.

20. Gallup, G.: Public's attitude toward the public schools, Phi Delta Kappan 52:99-112, 1970.

21. Globetti, G.: The use of beverage alcohol by youth in an abstinence setting, J. Sch. Health 39:179-183, 1969.

22. Greenberg, J. S.: Drug abuse and the schools, J. Drug Educ. 1:171-175, 1971.

23. Halleck, S.: The great drug education hoax, The Progressive 34:30, 1970.

24. Johnson, K. G., et al.: Survey of adolescent drug use, Am. J. Public Health 61:2418-2432, 1971.

25. Laun, W. L.: Priority topics for inclusion in health instruction programs, Ill. J. Educ. 60:12-18, 1969.

26. Lawler, J. T.: Peer group approach to drug education, J. Drug Educ. 1:63-76, 1971.

27. Lennard, H. L., et al.: Mystification and drug misuse, San Francisco, 1971, Jossey-Bass, Inc., Publishers.

28. Lipscomb, W. R.: An epidemiology of drug use-abuse, J. Public Health 61:1794-1800, 1971.

29. Louria, D.: Nightmare drugs, New York, 1966, Pocket Books.

30. Marin, P., and Cohen, A. Y.: Understanding drug use: an adult's guide to drugs and the young, New York, 1971, Harper & Row, Publishers.

31. Matchett, W. F.: Who uses drugs? a study in a suburban public high school, J. Sch. Health 41:90-93, 1971.

32. McGrath, J. H., and Scarpitti, F. R.: Youth and drugs: perspective on a social problem, Glenview, Ill., 1970, Scott, Foresman & Co.

33. Meeds, L.: Education: key to the drug problem, Soc. Educ. 33:664-666, 1969.

34. Miller, T. J.: Drug abuse: schools find some answers, Sch. Manage. 14:22-28, 1970.

35. Mullin, L.: Alcohol education: the school's responsibility, J. Sch. Health **38**:518-522, 1968.

36. National Commission on Marijuana and Drug Abuse: Marijuana: a signal of misunderstanding, first report of the Commission, Washington, D. C., 1972, Government Printing Office.

37. Nixon, R. M.: Quoted in Tune in: drug abuse news, Washington, D. C., 1971, National Institute for Mental Health, National Clearinghouse for Drug Abuse Information.

38. Nowlis, H.: The student and his culture. In McGrath, J. H., and Scarpitti, F., editors: Youth and drugs: perspective on a social problem, Glenview, Ill., 1970, Scott, Foresman, & Co.

39. Nyswander, M. E., and Millman, R. B.: Slow detoxification of adolescent heroin addicts in New York City. In Proceedings of the Third National Conference on Methadone Treatment, Washington, D. C., 1970, National Institute of Mental Health.

40. Peterson, R. C.: Suggestions for educators, In Resource book for drug abuse education, Washington, D. C., 1969, National Institute of Mental Health, National Clearinghouse for Mental Health Information.

41. Petrillo, R. F.: Comprehensive action model to combat drug abuse in high school, J. Sch. Psychol. **8**:226-231, 1970.

42. Plesent, E.: A community and its school's efforts to understand and deal with drug abuse, J. Drug Educ. **1**:85-91, 1971.

43. Prettyman, R. L., et al.: Drug abuse and the school scene, Sci. Teacher **37**:45-47, 1970.

44. Randall, H.: Patterns of drug use in school-age children, J. Sch. Health **40**:296-301, 1970.

45. Report of the Ad Hoc Committee on Drug Abuse, Dallas, 1970, Superintendent of Schools, Dallas Independent School District.

46. Resource book for drug abuse information, Washington, D. C., 1969, National Institute of Mental Health, National Clearinghouse for Drug Abuse Information.

47. Sandusk, J. F.: Size and extent of the problem, J.A.M.A. **196**:707-709, 1966.

48. Selected drug education curricula, drugs and hazardous substances, grades K-12, San Francisco, 1969, San Francisco Unified School District.

49. Survey of drug use among junior and senior high school students in the state of Idaho, May, 1970, Idaho State Department of Public Instruction.

50. A teacher resource guide for drug use and abuse for Michigan schools, Lansing, 1970, Michigan State Department of Education.

51. Warner, R., Jr. Reported in Arnold, M. R.: The trouble in drug education, Natl. Observer **10**:16, 1971.

52. Yolles, S. F.: Prevention of drug abuse. In Resource book for drug abuse education, Washington, D. C., 1969, National Institute of Mental Health, National Clearinghouse for Mental Health Information.

53. Yolles, S. F.: Prescription for drug abuse education, J. Drug Educ. **1**:101-103, 1971.

54. Yolles, S. F.: Statement on control of drug abuse before the Subcommittee to Investigate Juvenile Delinquency of the Committee on the Judiciary, United States Senate, Sept. 17, 1969.

PART II · THE DRUG SCENE

CHAPTER 2

SOCIETY AND DRUGS

The exploding problem of drug abuse in the United States is of paramount public concern. Drug experimentation and drug dependency have spread with frightening speed among all age, social, racial, and economic groups; drug use and abuse by our young people threatens the physical and mental fiber of the next generation of citizenry. President Richard Nixon has warned, "Any nation that moves down the road to addiction . . . that nation has had something taken out of its character."[14] Pointing out that, although the United States produces no heroin, it uses more heroin than any other country in the world, the President in March of 1972 declared the control of narcotics traffic to be "the number one priority" for law enforcement in his administration.

Drug abuse is currently so extensive that all youths are exposed to it (especially if one includes the experimentation with alcohol by those who are underage) even though they are not actually involved. Almost all young persons have tried one illegal drug at some time or other, and no one today is exempt from the possibility of becoming a drug abuser.

Here is an enormous challenge to education. To ignore this challenge or to pretend that it does not exist, or that it is not so widespread and serious, is irresponsible. To fail to deal adequately with this problem is to fail one of the most pressing educational needs of our time. Our schools —administrators and teachers as well as students—must provide viable programs that will positively direct the young away from drug abuse. One of the keys to productive educational programs is the involvement of youth. Many programs have failed because the young were left out of the planning or given only token responsibility. School personnel must try to understand the values, life-style, and world of the drug user and want to help find realistic answers to his problems, answers that offer *alternatives* to drug abuse However, they must realize that not all drug use is destructive or a sign of deviance or personality disturbance. Schools must help students, both as individuals and as a group, to become involved in making wise choices about drugs. Efforts must extend beyond the school grounds to the fostering of better communication between young people and adults. The school must become a catalyst in changing and modifying community attitudes. Adults need information and education about drugs as much as if not more than youths.

Drug use and abuse patterns have shifted so significantly that much of the information once used as a basis for education and prevention programs has lost credibility and now must be supplemented and reinterpreted in the light of more sophisticated thinking.

WHAT IS THE DRUG PROBLEM?

The problem of drug abuse is the complex interaction of pharmacological, psychological, and sociological variables and affects all strata of society, not just youth. Ours is a drug culture but, unfortunately, many of our reactions to the problem are based on emotional responses rather than on factual information placed in perspective. The lack of information and perspective has acutely compromised the effectiveness of many, if not most, of our educational and training efforts. Historically, the moralistic attack on drug-abusing addicts and youth seems to have lacked insight or logic, and has even added more confusion to an already complex medical, social, and legal problem. As drug abuse educator Helen Nowlis[15] has pointed out, most people believe that drugs are good or bad, safe or dangerous, legal or illegal, and that individuals are either drug users or nonusers and either good citizens or criminals.

Most persons in our society have fallen into the simple dichotomy of either-or and have been largely unwilling or unable to make the subtle distinctions necessary for understanding and intelligent action. Any useful or meaningful action or program relating to what we carelessly label "drug abuse," for want of a better title, must be based on careful discrimination not only among drugs and types of drug use and overuse but also among the different types of people who use drugs, including how and why they use them. We must be concerned with what specific drug is being abused and more concerned with what it is that the person thinks the drug is doing for him.

CONFLICTS OF REALITY: DIFFERENT WAYS WE THINK ABOUT DRUGS

What do we really mean by drug use, drug abuse, and drug misuse? It should be fairly obvious that the words are used in so many different contexts that many of the great debates about the drug issue are largely semantic. The terms have lost their meaning, if they ever had much, and have caused endless confusion, misunderstanding, and hysteria.

The issue, as stated somewhat more academically by sociologists, is whether or not those drugs that are defined as addicting, habituating, or indicative of psychological dependence and criminality have been so defined *not* because of the drug's inherent chemical nature but because of the *cultural framework* within which these drugs presently exist. Sociologists suggest that many of the so-called dangers of drugs are in large part defined by the social circumstances of their use.[3] It is certainly true that we approve of some drug use and that we do not approve of others regardless of health factors.

We feel that to fully understand the problems and complex issues of drug abuse education one must first become aware of hidden determinants in our cultural patterns that are crucial in forming our attitudes about just what the drug problem is and what should be done about it. Each of us has a mental set, a belief system, that affects the way we see social issues and the way we formulate solutions to problems. One of the false positions that each of us adopts in this age of technical and scientific expertise is assuming that our "expertness" is more than simply our opinion when it is nothing more than that. So let us look at some common opinions about drugs and drug abuse and consider their validity.

Conceptual views of drug abuse

We have divided popularly held opinions about drugs into three general models or belief systems. They are as follows: (1) legal-morality model, (2) medical-psychiatric model, and (3) sociological-psychological model. The basic ideology of these models can be found in the "conventional" wisdom about drug abuse of the uninformed, average person and in the technical and popular literature.

LEGAL-MORALITY MODEL

The legal-morality model is a rigid perspective through which some people perceive, identify, and label the behavior and life-style of others. Such perceptions have actually fostered much of the present crisis surrounding certain drug use in this country. According to this view, which is held by many of the "solid citizens" of our society, anyone who overuses drugs or indulges in drugs that are presently in disfavor with the dominant majority of society is a sinner and a criminal who should be punished and sent to jail. This community stereotype of the drug user, which has evolved within the last 50 years, represents a fusion of several strands within the American experience, including an essentially biblical interpretation of "man's weakness and fall from Grace." The drug user is viewed as essentially a sinner[6] or a disciple of the devil.

The foremost aim of the legal-moralists is to provide more severe criminal penalties in order to deal with the increasing use and sales of illegal drugs such as marijuana. This group maintains, in the face of scientific evidence to the contrary, that marijuana is a serious threat to our society and strongly resists the findings of the President's Commission on Marijuana. If such a position seems overly dramatic, remember that just a few decades ago we had newspaper headlines about "mad dog drug fiends" who, "crazed" on marijuana, rampaged about town in an orgy of raping, looting, and killing. Harry Anslinger, the former director of the then Federal Bureau of Narcotics, called the "dope fiend" America's "Public Enemy Number One."[11]

Increasingly, however, thoughtful persons were able to see through the shallow, vindictive stereotypes that falsely label without really explaining. An excellent analysis of the formative period in our nation's "drug history," including the creation of the drug fiend stereotype, is provided by Lindesmith in his book *The Addict and the Law.*[11] We shall not take time here to explore historical developments, but we will consider the implications of the legal-morality view for the many communities that discover "our kids take drugs!" One of the results of these implications is that youthful drug abusers have been segregated into a community of deviants and punished.

The emphasis of the official legal-morality view has been primarily functional and expedient: how can the user or trafficker in illicit drugs be identified, apprehended, and punished? The most preferred form of punishment is that which permanently removes this social pariah from the larger community. He, like Adam and Eve, is literally to be cast out of concerned humanity because of his transgression. An extreme example of this was the sentencing of a young man in the state of Texas to a thousand years in prison for the possession of a small amount of marijuana.

Spokesmen for the legal-morality model have never appreciated the term "clinic," nor do they feel that any medical definition should be applied to what they see as essentially a problem for criminal justice. Indeed, some critics have gone so far as to suggest that the development of free clinics for drug-involved youth in this country raises a grave moral issue and that such clinics aid and abet persons who should receive whatever help, if any, in a government penal institution such as the original Federal Narcotic Rehabilitation Program at Lexington, Kentucky. The legal-moralists believe that local medical assistance provides drug addiction and illegal drug use with a convenient source of "official respectability" and acts as an excuse to maintain individuals in a perpetual state of disease.

Much of the present controversy over the effectiveness of treatment with the drug methadone (Chapter 4) is confused by the issue of whether a person with drug problems ought to be *treated* at all or if he ought to be simply *forced* to conform to the law. Methadone, it has been stated over and over again, maintains individuals in a perpetual state of disease and hence is immoral.[19]

The legal-morality view is best observed in the speeches and writings of those who feel it is their duty to enforce the community's prohibitions against particular types of drug misuse. In fact, the view of legal-moralists has been incorporated into much of the legal code surrounding the use and sale of drugs in this country. The legal-morality assumptions, explicitly stated or not, underlie almost all of our present national and state legislation, except that expressly concerned with providing treatment. Maximum sentences of 40 years and life imprisonment are found in many state laws, and in some states there are provisions for the death penalty on conviction for the sale of narcotics or of any of a number of specified dangerous drugs to a minor. Only recently has there been a thrust in legislation to reduce the penalties for first-time possession of marijuana for personal use.

Meanwhile, the pharmaceutical drug industry in America makes compulsive users and abusers out of millions of us. Physicians admit they overprescribe. Massive advertising and miseducation have convinced people that pills can improve almost every aspect of life—curing a cold, getting rid of a headache, putting one to sleep or waking one up, and making us all feel happy even if we are not. But to persons who adhere strictly to the legal-morality belief system, a certain special type of person, a "drug user," invariably falls into the classification of a deviant and a law breaker. Even though many persons who at one time subscribed to this punitive, rigid attitude have recently become more tolerant, the view of the drug user as a criminal still pervades most of our attitudes in teaching about drugs. We should be aware of this and rationally decide whether this is a reasonable state of affairs.

Most of the drugs used by the young have been outlawed for them by their elders, a fact that not only polarizes the existing ideological conflict between generations, but that technically makes criminals of the young. Smith sees this fact alone as creating a pivotal issue for adolescent rebellion. This is one of the sorry results of our national policy. Yet in no other form of deviance is the distinction between what constitutes criminal behavior and what is not criminal behavior so blurred as it is with drug use.

Too often the community's response to adolescent drug activity (Chapter 5) is not guided by an informed articulation of its causes. Instead a vaguely conceived panacea of "education" is proposed without any real understanding of what education is supposed to do, or even what it means. Too often "educating the community about youth and drugs" involves the assumption that drug use or nonuse is a matter of personal decision making and principally of individual wrong doing. Such an attitude obscures rather than grapples with the complex social and group dimensions of drug use. Focus on the individual drug abuser alone denies that his drug use has important causal links with peers and with the peer-group social system. Drug use is largely a group experience. Yet the orientation of the legal-moralists is to support what has been called the "rotten apple" view of mankind. The sociologist Skolnick says, "Under this doctrine, crime and disorder are attributable mainly to the intentions of evil individuals; human behavior transcends past experience, culture, society, and other external forces and should be understood in terms of wrong choices, deliberately made."[18] Educators must become more aware of the social surroundings in which drug taking occurs and of the social as well as the personal meaning of its use. Education must be *about* drug taking as well as *against* drug taking.

MEDICAL-PSYCHIATRIC MODEL

We shall return to some of the issues passed by, dealing with them in more detail in later chapters, but let us look at a second model, the medical-psychiatric. Although more benign and humanitarian than the legal-morality view, which stresses detection, isolation, and punishment, the medical-psychiatric view nevertheless still defines the problem in essentially individual and personal terms. The pathology still resides in the individual. Use of and addiction to heroin can be viewed as a disease in the following analogy: Almost nobody "catches" the disease (starts using dope) except from someone else who has it (uses). Therefore it is presumed that if somehow addicts or users can be kept separated from nonusers, the chances of the disease spreading are minimized.

When drug abuse is viewed as a disease, within the medical-psychiatric framework, it becomes an affliction that requires hospitalization and treatment. Doctors, psychiatrists, and other health professionals strongly urge a transfer of social control from the justice department to the medical profession. We are in basic accord with this view but maintain certain reservations that will be described later.

Today there is a crying need for inexpensive (to the patient), nonjudgmental, and humanitarian medical care for drug-dependent persons, particularly addicts.[21] But most physicians do not understand drug abuse treatment and do not want to get involved. Also the medical establishment in this country has long been disenfranchised by criminal justice in the drug abuse area. Passage of the Harrison Narcotic Act and the activities of the then Federal Bureau of Narcotics forced the medical profession, through dire threats, to abdicate completely its role and responsibilities in establishing and maintaining standards by which physicians could treat drug addiction and adverse drug reactions. Even today, over a half a century after the passage of the Harrison Act, physicians are being threatened with the most extreme sanctions and brought to trial for attempting to treat drug abusers in normal medical settings.*

There has been in the last 15 years a slow shift from emphasizing the criminal nature of addiction toward the "new humanism"—a concern for the well-being of the individual and not just of the state. The increasing acceptance of this approach may in part be due to the fact that it offers advantages to law enforcement and to the bureacracy as well as to the health care professions. Behind the new rhetoric are many old, punitive practices. Even so, more institutions are demonstrating genuine care and concern for the plight of the addict. The way has opened for massive assistance programs from the federal health institutes, and financial support has been

---

*The Koning and Frazier trial is an example discussed in Smith, D. E., and Bentel, D. J.: Drug Abuse Information Project, the fifth annual report to the legislature, San Francisco, 1972, University of California, San Francisco Medical Center.

developed for many communities previously unable to undertake remedial projects.

A second half of the medical approach, the psychiatric, still views the problem as residing within the disturbed psyche and flawed personality of the user, particularly in the case of the narcotic addict. A focus on unstable personality as a critical factor in drug usage has resulted in a whole range of treatment strategies devised originally for those identified as mentally ill. Again we must point out that trying to tinker with the body or the mind of the user bears little relevance to the underlying social causes. Nevertheless the medical perspective on drug use is a major advance when the user is classified as sick rather than as criminal.

SOCIOLOGICAL-PSYCHOLOGICAL MODEL

Our third major concept is the sociological-psychological model. This is essentially a behavioral approach that views drug use as a social activity arising out of group and individual needs. Although such use can lead to a serious pathological condition on the part of the user, perhaps warranting medical and psychiatric intervention, the usage itself is seen as a normal response to the environment and to peer pressure. Whereas the legal-moralistic view stresses free will, free choice, and individual volition, the sociological-psychological model considers the taking or not taking of various drugs to be largely the consequence of environmental circumstances in which the individual plays a limited role. The normal, healthy, curious child will naturally experiment with drugs in our contemporary permissive atmosphere. He will take drugs because of "peer-group pressure" and the aura of mystery and forbiddenness surrounding drugs. At a time when drug use is epidemic, the possibility is strong that he will become a statistic in the total epidemiology of disease. Rather than focusing on the user himself, the sociological-psychological approach examines the individual and social characteristics of the user population. Drug abuse or illegal drug use is often a central ritual in the lives of those attempting to develop a unique or counter-culture style of life.

Factors affecting drug use and abuse

Here we shall attempt to briefly examine and assess the role of different drugs in American life among adults as well as among the young.

ABUSE OF MEDICINES AND DRUGS

Many legitimate medicines and drugs are widely abused by adults and youth (Chapter 1). Among these drugs are stimulants such as amphetamines, diet pills, and "stay-awake pills" and depressants such as barbiturates, sleeping pills, and tranquilizers. These preparations are often used for reasons other than to alleviate specific diseases and can be dangerous. The number of drug-induced injuries runs into the thousands each year, and there are an estimated 1 million cases of drug poisoning annually. Half of these cases involve small children who get their hands on poisonous drugs, but the remainder is largely the result of adults attempting to treat or overtreat themselves.

The increasing, almost universal use of chemicals to alter the physical and emotional state has become accepted practice in the United States. The American people are subjected to massive amounts of advertising propounding the self-prescribing of drugs and medicines for various conditions ranging from the common cold and arthritis to tension headaches, irritability, depression, and even to "staying regular." Innumerable types of drugs, both prescription and nonprescription, are readily available.

The home medicine cabinet contains an average of 22 different drugs. For many Americans the medicine chest has become the one place to find comfort, energy, and sleep. One out of six Americans reaches for the pill bottle at the first sign of nervousness or anxiety. By taking more than the amount prescribed by a doctor, frequently refilling prescriptions, and repeatedly turning to the medicine cabinet when they are upset, millions of people flagrantly misuse drugs yet would never consider themselves in the same category as a "junkie" or other deviant.

Children become accustomed to seeing their parents freely use or misuse these different substances, and for many different reasons. Most parents give medicines to children, including a variety of vitamins, pain killers, sedatives, and "children's aspirin" for mild childhood upsets. These medicines are selected for children from a variety of pleasant forms—candies, gums, and syrups—and condition children to seek drugs as a "first line" solution to many physical and mental problems. The home medicine cabinet nearly always contains one or more analgesics (aspirin) and sedatives, which can be dangerous and even fatal if not adequately guarded from children.

ILLEGAL USE OF DRUGS

The legality of drug use is a factor that cuts through this complex issue of drugs without clarifying any crucial points or distinguishing between drugs on the basis of abuse potential. It is simply a fact of legislation that some drugs are outlawed and some are not. Legally, some nonnarcotic drugs are classified with narcotics and carry the same harsh penalties for possession or use. But making the use of a drug a crime solves neither the problem of use nor that of control.

As early as 1957, for example, government officials recommended that marijuana not be classified as an opiate, additionally suggesting pointed inquiry into the wisdom of punishment for the mere possession of marijuana. The findings of the recent President's Commission on Marijuana, 15 years later, support these earlier recommendations.[18] Meanwhile, millions of Americans have smoked marijuana, many regularly, with apparently minimal harm. Yet sale, use, or possession of marijuana is still a felony and may result in a prison term on conviction.

The "legal pushing" of socially acceptable and widely distributed drugs is big business and involves the liquor and pharmaceutical industries. Alcohol use has resulted in chronic alcoholism for 6 to 9 million persons and has contributed to 15,000 deaths and 200,000 traffic injuries yearly. Ten billion barbiturate and amphetamine tablets are produced annually to be prescribed by doctors for health care; yet these, too, are frequently misused. Thus millions of people legally use and abuse purchased or prescribed drugs (alcohol and pharmaceuticals) and millions more illegally use and abuse them.

Clearly, when so many people live in violation of the law, and when abusable substances can be found in almost every home, the law is either not enforced—which is mostly the case—or is enforced selectively. Faced with an impossible task, law enforcement can only exercise token control, taking action only in areas where criminal activity is visible, where drug distribution and use patterns lie outside legitimate big business, or where persons with little influence, prominence, or prestige can be apprehended.

In general we believe that it is futile to seek regulation solely through police efforts. Law enforcement, although given great fiscal support, has been temporary and limited. Perhaps through better education we can seek more effective alternatives for social change.

Basic definitions of drugs and drug abuse
DRUGS AND MEDICINE

A *drug* may be defined as any chemical agent other than foodstuffs that significantly affects the structure or function of a living organism. All drugs are chemicals or contain chemicals that interact with the complex biochemical system of the human body. Such compounds are also referred to as medicine. *Medicine* is any substance or preparation used in treating disease, whereas a drug is usually defined as any chemical substance that alters bodily functions or structures. In current terminology, medicine usually refers to chemicals used to treat specific ailments, whereas the term *"psychoactive"* drug generally refers to chemicals used to relieve pain or that affect the mind or are mood modifiers. Many thousands of psychoactive drugs are now available and thousands of new ones are on the horizon.

A medicine (drug) then is any substance used to treat illness, protect against disease, or promote better health, whereas a psychotropic or psychoactive drug mainly affects mental processes. The term "psychotropic," like "psychoactive," refers to drugs with predominant effects on the mind rather than on the body.[5] Such effects are produced by stimulants, depressants, psychotomimetics, and so on. Although we will use psychoactive in this text, use of the term "psychotropic" might be preferred because it has the advantage of being widely employed, has a carefully defined scientific definition, and there is more general agreement as to its meaning.[5]

Functionally, drugs may be grouped into two major overlapping categories: (1) those drugs used for medical purposes (prescribed by a physician for a specific therapeutic effect, such as Seconal or secobarbital for sleep induction) and (2) those that are used for purely social purposes (no specific therapeutic use, such as caffeine in coffee, nicotine in cigarettes, and ethyl alcohol in beer, wine, and hard liquor). The social uses of drugs may be further divided into the categories legal and illegal, since it is clear that people also use drugs for social or nonmedical purposes that are prohibited by the law.

Drugs are chemicals that effect changes in the perceptions, feelings, and behavior of the organism. The kind and extent of these changes depend on the nature of the ingested substance, the amount present in the body at any one time, the route and speed of administration, the physiological characteristics and current physiological state of the individual, the physical and social setting when the substance is ingested, the reason(s) it is taken, and what changes the substance is expected to make in the feelings of the individual (Chapter 4).

Drugs, then, may be viewed as powerful catalysts that induce changes of an exceedingly complex social, psychological, and biochemical nature. Before we describe the role that drugs play in these complex events, all drug-related terms that are in everyday usage must be defined. Either through ignorance or intent, official and unofficial information about psychoactive drugs is often inaccurate, slanted, or hysterical rather than factual. Even the scientific terms used to describe drugs have been given such highly emotional connotations that they are used essentially as accusations. A straightforward, culture-free definition of the words "drug use," "drug misuse," and "drug abuse" is needed.

DRUG USE, DRUG MISUSE, AND DRUG ABUSE

The term "drug use" means no more than the consumption of a drug. A "drug user" then is just about everybody.

The term "drug misuse" refers to the periodic or occasional improper or inappropriate use of either a social or a prescription drug. Misuse means the *improper* use. For example, society might condone the behavior of a star player of a football team who gets "smashed" (drunk) after losing a game. Yet from a medical point of view, this would still be inappropriate behavior and would be drug (alcohol) misuse, even if society might define such behavior as appropriate under the circumstances. In addition, if this person were underage, his use of alcohol would be illegal drug-taking.

The term "drug abuse" is an epithet as well as a social concept. The user of the term typically writes in whatever meaning it has for him. For many, it simply means the use of some drugs (illegal or illicit) that are more favored by a minority (typically youth) and disfavored by the majority (the older "establishment"). Drug

abuse refers to the use of drugs that society has outlawed, in contrast to the use of other abusable drugs that are socially acceptable. For some, drug abuse means the ill effects or unacceptable behavior accompanying certain drug use, as reported by the popular press. For still others, it has strong political overtones and becomes a partisan rallying cry, a call for action to prevent the destruction of the conventional American value system and way of life. Thus the concept of drug abuse has consisted of part myth and part hysteria, obscuring any real understanding of a serious social and medical problem.

Although the term "drug abuse" is used to describe just about any relationship between man and chemical of which someone disapproves, we must take a position that distinguishes certain man-drug relationships as abuse from others that are not abuse. Smith's definition of drug abuse will be used in this book to mean the *use of any drug to the point where it interferes with an individual's health or with his economic or social adjustment.*[20] Notice that this term does not touch on whether or not the use of the drug is legal. By our health-oriented definition, marijuana smoking is not *necessarily* drug abuse, for although an outlawed drug such as heroin does possess a high degree of inherent abuse potential, so do cigarettes and alcohol, which are legal. Our concern is whether drugs are harmful, not whether they are socially acceptable. First we ask, does a substance harm the body? If so, in what ways and to what degree? Does the substance have the capacity to cause either physical or psychological dependency?

DRUG ADDICTION, DRUG DEPENDENCE, AND HABITUATION

Before defining drug dependency, let us first consider the word "addiction." The term has acquired many shades and degrees of meaning; we even speak of being addicted to golf. Clearly the flexibility of modern usage has influenced the preciseness and utility of the word. Dr. Harris Isbell[9] of the Addiction Research Center in Lexington, Kentucky, says that national laws and international treaties imposing special controls on drugs have lumped together substances of such diverse natures that it becomes difficult and confusing to try to discuss these varying forms of drug abuse under a single term. For these reasons, the Expert Committee on Addiction-Producing Drugs of the World Health Organization has recommended that the terms "addiction" and "habituation" be dropped and replaced by the term *"drug dependence."*

Drug dependence, Dr. Isbell adds, "is defined as a state of psychic and physical dependence, or both, which arises in a person following chronic administration of that drug either periodically or continuously."[9] Since the characteristics of drug dependence will vary with the particular agent involved, and since the damage to the individual and to society will also vary with particular drugs, it is always necessary to specify the particular type of drug dependence in each case. For example, one must speak of drug dependence of the "morphine type" or of the "barbiturate type."

At this point we should distinguish *physical dependence* from *psychological dependence*. In physical dependence, the user experiences acute physical symptoms such as nausea, vomiting, anxiety, watery eyes and nose, withdrawal and abstinence syndrome, and an overwhelming compulsive desire to seek the drug if deprived of it for any period of time. To maintain normal body functioning without discomfort, the drug is needed at regular intervals.

In psychological dependence, or what we still like to term "habituation" (despite the WHO definition), the individual demonstrates a strong emotional motivation to continue the use of a drug either because of the pleasure that it gives, or because it relieves real or imagined discomfort. If the drug is withheld, the user may experience anxiety, but will suffer no acute

or otherwise serious physical discomfort. Escape from tension, the dulling of unpleasant reality, and euphoria (being "high") are some of the other reasons drugs come to be used habitually. (To this end they may even prove to exert significant therapeutic properties.)

Unfortunately such drugs often contribute their own dependence, the inner need for repeated use. Nicotine in cigarettes, alcohol, caffeine, marijuana, and amphetamines, each of which possesses no inherent addictive properties, are all often involved in psychological drug dependence and often result in injury to body tissue as well.

Psychological dependence on a drug is not necessarily abuse, although it might become so. Psychological dependence is what we are referring to when we say that a person has a bad "habit." Nail biting and cigarette smoking (particularly chain smoking) are compulsive habits suggesting psychological dependence. That regular, first cup of coffee to start the morning is a type of dependence. Yet there is nothing inherently addicting in the drugs in coffee. The body and the mind, however, may be habituated to the ritual of drinking as well as to the lift that caffeine produces. Navy chiefs and Scandinavians have in common a reputation for the use of coffee bordering on the excess. Coffee drinking becomes a compelling social ritual. But the drinking of coffee is also associated with allergies and kidney malfunction, making its habitual use a health problem for some people, and thus, drug abuse.

When cigarette smoking is associated with spells of coughing, poor health, emphysema, and even cancer, then its sustained use also constitutes drug abuse. Millions of Americans, in increasing numbers, are abusing cigarettes despite substantial medical evidence documenting their danger (Chapter 4). Since such a wide variety of substances consumed by humans on a daily basis are capable of inducing this same psychological dependence, we feel that, as a conceptual aid, the term "habituation" is useful, since it strongly suggests a habit!

In closing our discussion of drug dependence, we hope it is understood that there is not simply one unified phenomenon that can be labeled drug dependence. A variety of different types of drug dependence exists, each having its own typical syndrome of use or abuse. Each of the drugs that we will discuss has specific characteristics, particular problems associated with it, and often a particular style of use and social setting, or life-style. Therefore the common or general term "drug abuse" has extremely limited relevance or utility.

SUMMARY OF DRUG TERMS

The World Health Organization Expert Committee on Addiction-Producing Drugs created the following definitions that are used worldwide*:

addiction A state of periodic or chronic intoxication produced by the repeated consumption of a drug and involving tolerance, psychological dependence, usually physical dependence, an overwhelming compulsion to continue using the drug, and detrimental effects on both the individual and society. Its characteristics include (1) an overpowering desire or need (compulsion to continue taking the drug and to obtain it by any means); (2) a tendency to increase the dose; (3) a psychic (psychological) and generally a physical dependence on the effects of the drug; and (4) detrimental effects on the individual and society.

dangerous drugs A legal term that applies specifically to barbiturates, amphetamines, and other drugs (except narcotics) which are officially determined to have a potential for abuse because of their depressant, stimulant, or hallucinogenic effect on man.

desire (for drugs) A persistent but not overpowering wish for a drug to an undeniable compulsion to take the drug and to obtain it by any means.

drug A medicine or a substance used in the making of medicine and, when used within the context of the illegal use of drugs, has been interchanged freely with the term "narcotics."

drug abuse The illegal self-administration of drugs, narcotics, chemicals, and other substances to the possible detriment of the individual, of society, or of both.

drug dependence A state arising from repeated administration of a drug on a periodic or continuous basis.

habituation A condition, resulting from the repeated consumption of a drug, which involves little or no evidence of tolerance, some psychological dependence, no physical dependence, and a desire (but not a compulsion) to continue taking the drug for the feeling of well-being that it engenders. Its characteristics include (1) a desire (but not a compulsion) to continue taking the drug for the sense of improved well-being which it engenders; (2) little or no tendency to increase the dose; (3) some degree of psychic dependency on the effect of the drug, but absence of physical dependence and hence of an abstinence syndrome; and (4) detrimental effects, if any, primarily in the individual.

physical dependence A condition in which the body has adjusted to the presence of a drug and, when forced to function without the drug, reacts with a characteristic illness, called "abstinence syndrome," or "withdrawal illness."

psychic dependence The individual who receives satisfaction from his first use of a drug tends to make repeated use of the drug. Through continued repetition he may find it necessary to utilize the drug as an instrument in his adjustment to life, relying upon it for fulfillment which others achieve without the help of drugs.

tolerance A condition in which body cells protect themselves against toxic substances by developing resistance to them. Tolerance is manifested when repeated doses of the same amount of a drug become diminishingly effective and progressively larger doses are required to secure the desired effect.

COMMONLY ABUSED DRUGS

Although we will be dealing at much greater length in Chapter 5 with various categories of drugs and individual drug syndromes, the following will briefly introduce five important categories of widely abused drugs. They are the central nervous system stimulant group; the central nervous system (sedative-hypnotic) depressant group with its subgroup of inhalants, the volatile hydrocarbons; the psychedelic or hallucinogenic group; the narcotic drugs; and finally, the common over-the-counter or nonprescription drugs.

---

*Drug dependence, its significance and characteristics, W.H.O. Bull. 32:721-723, 1965.

Central nervous system stimulant drugs

A serious drug abuse problem among middle-class youth is the use and abuse of the central nervous system stimulant drugs, our first category of abusable drugs. This group consists largely of the amphetamines, of which methamphetamine is the most commonly used. Methamphetamine (Methedrine, Desoxyn), or "speed" and "crystal" as it is called on the street, stimulates all parts of the central nervous system. "Meth" excites the individual, suppresses his appetite, and prevents him from sleeping, particularly when injected rather than taken orally (oral use of amphetamines is much more common than intravenous use). Because of the massive stimulation of the nervous system by the amphetamines and perhaps indirectly because appetite and sleep patterns are disturbed, prolonged use of these compounds may cause a state of acute toxic psychosis.

Toxic psychosis, a major break with reality, may be characterized by hallucinations, tremendous panic or fear reactions, and paranoia to a point where the individual feels that various individuals are trying to harm him. One does not become physically dependent on the central nervous system stimulants in the classic sense of the word. However, when prolonged dosage is discontinued, the individual falls into a state of exhaustion, then eats ravenously, and then often lapses into a prolonged depressive reaction.[20]

MINOR STIMULANTS. The nicotine contained in cigarette tobacco places cigarettes in the category of minor stimulants. Although it is the nicotine that gives the physiological lift to the smoker, it is the high temperature of the gases inhaled by the smoker and the tar and particulates that cause most of the serious health problems.

Central nervous system depressant (sedative-hypnotic) drugs

The second major category is central nervous system depressants, or sedative-hypnotics. The most commonly abused sedative, which may lead to chronic physical dependence, is ethyl alcohol. Alcohol still represents the biggest drug problem in the United States. It, and not the psychedelics, is the major problem drug with school-age youngsters.

ALCOHOL. In the United States, ethyl alcohol is the most widely used social drug; it is legal and accepted by our culture. Used in large amounts, alcohol leads to a state of acute intoxication, in which the depression of various elements of the central nervous system seriously interferes with the individual's motor and mental functioning. As now recognized, the disease of alcoholism is one in which chronic, repeated intoxication with alcohol has seriously compromised the individual's ability to function normally or to be casual about his drinking. It is important to note that one can become physically dependent upon alcohol. Physical dependence is present if the use of a drug reaches the point where the body's metabolism is dependent upon that agent in order to function. If that particular chemical agent is withdrawn, a physical abstinence syndrome is seen, characterized by extreme anxiety, hyperactivity, and often hallucinations. The most severe withdrawal state seen in medicine today is that of withdrawal from alcohol, not heroin. Delirium tremens, a physical condition caused by abrupt withdrawal during physical dependence on alcohol, is responsible for a high death rate. Persons in the final stages of alcoholism often die of delirium tremens.

Millions of Americans are addicted to alcohol. In the United States it is the foremost addictive drug; yet because of public demand an age limit is the only restriction placed on its use.

BARBITURATES. Other commonly abused sedatives are the barbiturates. Prescribed by physicians for sleep or relaxation, these agents are commonly abused by adults. The use of the barbiturates can produce a state of disinhibition similar to that caused by excessive dosages of alcohol. The user may also consume the drug repeatedly, taking progressively larger doses to the point where he also becomes physically dependent. Withdrawal from barbiturates presents a severe medical situation and can result in convulsions and death. In fact, withdrawal from sedatives generally is more dangerous than withdrawal from heroin. Withdrawal from barbiturates, as from alcohol, may be a life-or-death matter.

INHALANTS—THE VOLATILE HYDROCARBONS. Other types of sedatives include the volatile hydrocarbons, which are inhalants. For example, certain young people sniff glue and a variety of other substances such as gasoline, kerosene, and paint thinner. This is actually inhalation of an anesthetic-like chemical, toluene, which in higher vapor concentrations depresses the central nervous system and causes many of the same abuse problems as alcohol. Such sedative abuse is a problem in certain school areas and in lower socioeconomic groups, although youth involved in the hippie subculture use few sedatives and, in general, reject alcohol as a primary intoxicant, along with the inhalants. Inhalants are typically abused by younger brothers and sisters who cannot obtain more sophisticated drugs.[10]

Psychedelic (hallucinogenic) drugs

LSD (lysergic acid diethylamide) is the prototype of the psychedelic or hallucinogenic drugs, a new group of selective central nervous system stimulants. The use of this relatively new drug has spread widely among middle-class youth throughout the nation, and there are potentially hundreds of LSD-like chemicals that can be assembled from a variety of laboratory, plant, and animal sources. For example, LSD is made in the chemical laboratory and is a semisynthetic derivative of ergot, a mold of rye grain. Mescaline, which produces LSD-like mental effects, is derived from the peyote cactus. Bufotenine, another psychedelic substance, is derived from an animal source—the skin of a toad.

A dose of LSD as small as 250 micrograms (this amounts to only a speck that could rest on the head of a pin) generates startling perceptual alterations, synesthesia (the translation of one sensory phenomenon into another, such as feeling color or sound, or hearing light), and other major psychological changes that can last for up to 8 hours. For example, an individual under the influence of LSD may see colored vibrations coming from music produced by a record player. He may experience disorientation in time and place. Cognitive changes produce striking alterations in value judgments and severely disorient the user. Such disorientations may or may not be perceived as pleasurable.

Because of the action of LSD on the central nervous system, the individual, in fact, sees and perceives his environment in a way that he has never seen it before. Many individuals describe this as a valuable experience, but many others have what they consider a "bad trip." That is, the perceptual alterations produce panic to the point where the individual, under the influence of LSD, loses control of his mental processes and reacts in a manner often destructive to himself. Subjectively he might be described as "crazy." To predict which individuals will react positively to LSD and which individuals will react negatively is difficult because such an equation involves not only the drug itself, but also the personality of the individual as well as the setting in which he takes the drug. The drug trip may change from minute to minute. The use of LSD in unsupervised circumstances increases the likelihood of an adverse reaction.

Two patients illustrate the different types of reactions one sees with unsupervised LSD use. A 19-year-old girl from a middle-class background in her second year of college had used alcohol, occasionally smoked marijuana, but never used any other drug. She was vaguely unhappy with school, but described no other mental problems and had no history of psychiatric care. One day she was given some LSD by a friend. Although she knew nothing about the chemical, she took the drug and described the experience as beneficial, or a good trip. No long-term residual effects followed this drug experience.

In the second example a 19-year-old boy of a similar background was persuaded by a friend to take LSD in an equally casual fashion. After taking the drug, he became frightened. The perceptual alterations and distortions he observed in his environment (everyone looked like a meaningless body) made this reaction a bad trip. After recovery, he continued to feel that life was meaningless and developed a severe depression, resulting in an attempt at suicide. Ten months after his experience with LSD, the boy was still significantly depressed and under psychiatric care.

MARIJUANA. Where does marijuana belong in this discussion of sedatives and narcotics? Marijuana is pharmacologically *not* a narcotic and *does not* produce physical dependence. Whether or not it is a psychedelic drug is a subject of argument even among experts. Among middle-class youth the drug is used primarily because in limited doses it produces a mild euphoria and is a pleasant relaxant. Occasionally, as with alcohol, an individual may take large doses and achieve a classic state of intoxication with central nervous system depression.

Marijuana and its various preparations are known by different names all over the world. The weed marijuana *(Cannabis sativa)* grows just about everywhere. Known and used for its special properties over the centuries, marijuana is grown as a commercial crop (although it is classed as a weed) in Mexico, India, Nepal, Ceylon, and Afghanistan. It grows wild and is illegally cultivated in the United States as well. There is evidence of Chinese hemp cultivation as early as 3000 B.C., but whether or not it was raised for its psychoactive properties is unknown. Historically, its commercial uses have been as the fiber for hemp ropes and for the oil from its seeds.[4]

Until a decade or so ago, the use of the drug marijuana in the United States was limited to nonwhite minorities, primarily Mexican-Americans who brought the habit with them from Mexico, and to a few avant-gardes and jazz musicians. Smoking marijuana was not prestigious and was considered the vice of the criminal and the degenerate. Violence and sadism were attributed to its use as with heroin. Marijuana users were classified with the worst dope fiends, and legal penalties, until the present, have been severe.[2, 17]

Pharmacology. From a health viewpoint, the abuse potential of marijuana is approximately that of alcohol or less. The use of marijuana among both middle-class youth and adults of today is similar to that of alcohol by the older generation. It is a social drug that is taken in group settings for its mild high, or intoxication. Prolonged or heavy dosage of marijuana can produce impairment of physical or mental functioning, although most of the marijuana available is of too low a concentration to cause such reactions. In contrast to alcohol, marijuana does not suppress appetite nor does one become physically dependent on the drug. From a health viewpoint, it is ironic that in many states the possession of one drug, marijuana, is a crime, and indeed a felony upon conviction of a second offense, yet possession of another drug, alcohol, which has many similar properties and even greater demonstrated abuse potential, is socially accepted. This suggests, perhaps, a need for more rational criteria in making judgments about drugs.

Narcotic drugs

The fourth major category of drug abuse includes drugs of the narcotic type, the most common of which is heroin. Narcotics include the opium derivatives such as morphine, semisynthetic opiates such as heroin, and the purely synthetic opioids such as Demerol, the chemical name of which is meperidine. Heroin, as with other morphinelike analgesics, is a narcotic derived from the sap of the opium poppy.

OPIUM. Long known to man, perhaps as long as 6000 or 7000 years, opium has probably been the most singularly important herbal medicine in history. It is almost a magic drug in the way in which it relieves pain, replacing suffering with a feeling of euphoric well-being. The juice of the opium poppy *(Papaver somniferum)* not only has solved many medical problems but also has served to maintain the credibility of early and rather unreliable medicine. Besides its other euphoric properties, opium induces sleep and corrects dysentery.[16]

Pharmacology. Prolonged or regular use of the opium drugs alters body chemistry so that the organism's metabolism becomes dependent on its continued use. If use of the addicting chemical is discontinued, a disruptive general physiological reaction called the abstinence syndrome occurs. The body hunger for the addicting drug may produce great mental and physical discomfort. In the case of heroin addiction, acute discomfort may occur over a period of several days unless relieved by the administration of the addictive drug or various other psychoactive drugs that help alleviate the withdrawal symptoms. These symptoms do pass after several days, but the psychological craving for this drug of choice and for the life-style surrounding it may persist for months or even years.

Heroin addiction used to be associated primarily with the youth of the economically and socially deprived areas, that is, the ghettos of the Negro and Mexican-American communities. It appears that young persons who become addicted to heroin utilize the drug as an escape from their poverty-stricken surroundings. Today heroin use is found increasingly in many of our schools and is one of the most significant and serious drug problems among the middle-class youth of school age. One of the major problems of addiction, or of dependency, is that the user must have the drug on a regular basis

or experience a physical and mental crisis. In some types of drug dependence, such as with some sedative-hypnotics, rapid withdrawal of the drug may precipitate a life-threatening emergency for the user. One addicted to barbiturates, or "downers," as they are called by youth (Seconal or Nembutal, the generic drugs secobarbital and pentobarbital, respectively), may lapse into coma and convulsions and, in extreme cases, may die.

With narcotics such as heroin, withdrawal (that is, deprivation of the drug) will cause moderate to severe discomfort, depending on how much pure drug the user is accustomed to ingesting. Moderate withdrawal typically causes aching muscles, nausea, cramps, and vomiting. This may be accompanied by the symptoms of flu—runny nose, runny eyes, muscle cramps, and general malaise. Rarely is such withdrawal of narcotics life threatening, but the process fosters a strong emotional and physical resistance to "getting off dope." Death may also result from an overdose of heroin, a situation causing respiratory depression and heart stoppage, but death is not usually precipitated by withdrawal.

Because of increased physical tolerance, the narcotic user may continue to maintain his drug habit long past the point where he no longer gets a thrill, or euphoric effect. He keeps using drugs, in large part, because such use helps him avoid the discomfort of withdrawal and because it has become a habit and a way of life. Narcotics use becomes a complete life-style.

Over-the-counter or nonprescription drugs

Our last major category is the over-the-counter drugs. When considering categories of drugs that are the source of considerable abuse, this category is almost always overlooked, or at best, given little consideration. Few books on drug abuse, in fact, even mention the over-the-counter drugs.

Chemical comforters, as Nowlis[15] states, change the way a person feels about himself and the world, which says as much about the world in which the user lives as it does about the drug he chooses. The largest number of these chemical comforters, or mood-altering drugs, are the over-the-counter pain relievers, tranquilizers, antidepressants, antianxiety drugs, stimulants, and sedatives found in almost every medicine cabinet in the nation. An enormous variety of these nonprescription preparations is used by millions of Americans on a daily basis. The essential difference between prescription drugs and proprietary (over-the-counter or nonprescription) drugs is the provision in the latter case for self-diagnosis.

Providing drugs for self-diagnosis is currently at least a $2.5 billion a year industry.[7] Over-the-counter (which we shall refer to from here on as OTC) preparations are chemicals considered to be safe for general unsupervised use by the public. These are drugs of a relatively mild nature used to treat minor "everyday" (the ads say) ailments. The directions for use provided in the package or on the label of each product are considered sufficient to protect the consumer and to direct proper usage.

One assumption now being challenged is that OTC drugs are weak enough that abuse potential in all cases is extremely limited. Recent investigations, however, disclose that these drugs, when used in high dosage, may be abused, are being abused, can be toxic, and can even be lethal. All OTC drugs have multiple effects, depending on the dose and the physical as well as the psychological and social setting of the user. All of these drugs have side effects that may be serious. At higher and higher dosage levels, all may be dangerous. Many of them should be taken rarely or not at all. Few healthy persons, for example, should have to regularly use laxatives or sleep inducers.[12]

ASPIRIN. One of the most widely used medicines in the world is aspirin. Americans consume nearly 30 million pounds annually—almost 7 pounds per person per year. More than 1000 medical products sold in the United States contain aspirin. Also, some 200 deaths annually in this country result from overdoses of aspirin, with children the most frequent victims. This drug, invaluable as it is, often is misused. Pathologically, aspirin causes minute hemorrhages in the viscera and affects the central nervous system. Excessive use has been linked to kidney damage, ulcers, and anemia. The symptoms of aspirin poisoning are headache, dizziness, ringing in the ears and loss of hearing, nausea, vomiting, gastric hemorrhage, mental confusion, and, in some instances, convulsions, delirium, and coma. Severe cases are difficult to treat and require highly specialized medical care and laboratory examinations.

ANTIHISTAMINES. There are few cough syrups that do not contain antihistamines. Antihistamines dry the mucus of the respiratory tract and may be helpful in the early congestive stages of the common cold. They are mild sleep inducers and often act as minor tranquilizers (that is, they counteract tension without acting on the central nervous system). Antihistamines also relieve symptoms of hay fever and other allergies, motion sickness (Dramamine is an antihistamine), insomnia, and Parkinson's disease.

Habitual or excessive use of antihistamines may result in drowsiness, dizziness, ringing in the ears, lack of coordination, fatigue, blurred or double vision, euphoria, nervousness, insomnia, and tremors. There may also be a loss of appetite, nausea, vomiting, abdominal pain, constipation or diarrhea, dryness of the mouth, urinary frequency and burning, headache, tightness of the chest, heaviness, and weakness of the hands.

COUGH MEDICINE. Cough remedies are among the most common nonprescription drugs available. All are mixtures containing from two to five or more drugs, including antitussives, antihistamines, expectorants, and decongestants. Cough elixirs (not syrups) are sometimes used as "kick-inducers." Some mixtures may contain as much as 50% ethyl alcohol (the equivalent of 100-proof whiskey). Since many states still have no limitation on the purchase of these cough mixtures, many medical authorities believe they should be made prescription items because of their abuse potential.

DIET PILLS. Dieting has become an American way of life. In their compulsion to lose weight, people are often indiscriminate in their use of the many popular OTC diet pills. The major ingredients of these nonprescription preparations are stimulants that act on the body in various ways. For example, sugar substitutes such as saccharin are widely used, although they have been known to have a harmful effect on children, pregnant women, and persons with kidney failure.

Diuretics, used in diet preparations, purge the body of excess water, but they have a wide range of possible side effects, including rash, headache, constipation, dizziness, restlessness, fatigue, sweating, and a tingling feeling in the arms and legs. On rare occasions convulsions and blood and kidney diseases have developed. Diuretics can also frequently cause the user to lose too much natural salt. Although an individual may lose weight using a diuretic, this effect is temporary. The body will usually begin to retain water once again when its use is discontinued.

CAFFEINE. Long-haul truck drivers and students are the most flagrant, although hardly the sole, abusers of the popular OTC pep pill preparations such as No-Doz, Vivarin, and Comeback. These nonprescription drugs are concentrated caffeine preparations, although they contain less caffeine than the average cup of coffee.

Commercial or industrial caffeine is a white powder obtained from tea leaves. If taken orally, it stimulates the cortex of the brain, temporarily increasing alertness. The user thinks faster and performs mental functions more easily. In short, he is more awake. The sense of touch is intensified and drowsiness and fatigue disappear for a while. Caffeine, however,

is habit forming. Moreover, large doses may cause rapid and irregular heart action, muscle twitching, agitation, and possibly even convulsions. Caffeine also stimulates the flow of gastric juices and should not be used by persons with peptic ulcers. Caffeine certainly is no substitute for rest.

SLEEPING PILLS. There are countless sleep-inducing prescription drugs such as barbiturates, but numerous sleeping aids such as Sominex can be purchased over the counter. Such preparations usually contain an antihistamine (methapyrilene hydrochloride) to induce drowsiness and scopolamine, an anticholinergic drug that has a number of sedative properties. Sleeping pills, after prolonged use, generally disrupt healthy, normal sleeping habits. Possible side effects of sleeping pills include blurred vision, rapid pulse, dizziness, and drying of the mouth. Excessive doses of scopolamine and methapyrilene in the form of these nonprescription relaxants can produce delirium. Medical researchers have studied recent cases in which patients who took popular brand-name sleeping pills suffered toxic reactions that appeared to be the early stages of acute schizophrenia. There is no conclusive evidence to indicate that their disorders resulted from the drug, although it may have helped precipitate the psychotic reaction.

INFLUENCE OF MASS MEDIA

We have mentioned just a few of the OTC drugs, one category of abusable substances, and the dangers inherent in their use. The researchers Mannheim and Mellinger,[12] studying patterns of legal family drug use, found American medicine cabinets and bathroom shelves practically pharmaceutical houses, stocking every imaginable drug. From diet pills to headache powders, the average American home is a drugstore. Industry promotes such use. The mass media expend large sums of money selling drug products to the public. They create a belief structure in which the normal, accepted way to achieve pleasure, health, happiness, relief from life's pains and anxieties, as well as to achieve sexual prowess is to smoke, drink, eat, or swallow a drug. Do the media have impact? Particularly, do the media have impact on youth?

During 1969, Dr. Donald Kanter, then professor of consumer psychology at the University of Southern California, served as a research consultant to the Coronado Unified School District in a study to clarify for educators the processes that occur when drug advertising (direct or indirect) impinges on students.[8] The results of this initial research with hundreds of students clearly indicated, "There is no doubt . . . that there is a relationship between drug use and certain kinds of advertising. . . . The nature of the relationship is complex."

1. Drug and cigarette advertising affects the very young (subteens) and encourages them to experiment with certain palliatives.
2. Experimenting takes the form of increasing dosage, to see what kind of a kick can be obtained.
3. Pleasure and relief are depicted in many advertisements, particularly drug and cigarette commercials. These depictions of relief and personal satisfaction act as reinforcing agents to general teen-age usage.
4. Teen-age initial experimenting and drug advertising do not seem directly related; but early excessive usage of Bufferin, Midol, etc., widely advertised products, could be the seedbed for later experimentation. "To ignore advertising's reinforcing function in the general world of the teen-ager as well as the subteen seems also incorrect."

SUMMARY

It should now be apparent that drug abuse is a much broader issue than it is popularly understood to be. Most persons wish to see drug abuse as only the misbehaving of the young despite the fact that our entire society indulges in temperate drug use and also in drug abuse. Most people support the myth that they themselves would never succumb to what are assumed to be the temptations that drugs hold only for the evil or the degenerate. The doper, the junkie, and even the chronic alcoholic are seen as almost an untouchable caste, a population of deviants with some inherent character flaw that makes them deserve what they get because they are immoral, weak willed, or have criminal leanings.

Yet anyone, given the right set of circumstances, might become a junkie or a chronic drug user and many people have who do not even recognize the extent of their own involvement. Much of our current understanding about drugs and the young is hypocritical. One need only examine the statistics on the number of conventional housewives who are abusing amphetamines and barbiturates as well as alcohol. Society, for unexplained reasons, still seems reluctant to accept the responsibility for creating and sustaining conditions that both encourage addictive behavior and work aggressively against attempts at therapeutic modification. Addiction and dependence and habituation are primarily social and health issues, not criminal ones.

References

1. Bauer, W. W.: Today's health guide: a manual of health information and guidance for the American family, Chicago, 1965, The American Medical Association.
2. Blum, R. H.: Society and drugs, San Francisco, 1969, Jossey-Bass, Inc., Publishers.
3. Carey, J. T.: The college drug scene, Englewood Cliffs, N. J., 1968, Prentice-Hall, Inc.
4. Chein, I., et al.: The road to H; narcotics, delinquency, and social policy, New York, 1964, Basic Books, Inc., Publishers.
5. DiPalma, J. R., editor: Drill's pharmacology in medicine, New York, 1971, McGraw-Hill Book Co., Inc.
6. Goldfarb, J.: The medieval legacy of crime and delinquency, Speech delivered at the School of Criminology, University of California at Berkeley, 1967.
7. Handbook of non-prescription drugs, Washington, D. C., 1971, American Pharmaceutical Association.

8. Kanter, D.: Innovative solution to teen- and subteen-age drug abuse, 1968-70, from material prepared under the Elementary and Secondary Education Act, Title III Project by Coronado Unified School District.

9. Isbell, H.: Paper presented at the International Physicians' Conference on Drug Abuse, University of Michigan, Ann Arbor, Nov., 1970.

10. Kitzinger, A.: Narcotics and dangerous drugs: a manual of basic information for teachers, Sacramento, 1964, California State Department of Education.

11. Lindesmith, A. R.: The addict and the law, Bloomington, 1965, Indiana University Press.

12. Mellinger, G. D.: Society's dilemma: pills, pills, pills, Unpublished paper presented to the Contra Costs Mental Health Association, Diablo Valley College, May 25, 1967.

13. National Commission on Marijuana and Drug Abuse: Marijuana: a signal of misunderstanding, first report of the Commission, Washington, D. C., 1972, Government Printing Office.

14. Nixon, R. M.: Quoted in San Jose Mercury News, San Jose, Calif., Mar. 21, 1972.

15. Nowlis, H.: Perspectives on drug use, J. Soc. Issues 27:7, 1971.

16. Over the counter drugs—easy does it. In Attack, Spring, 1971.

17. Ray, O. S.: Drugs, society, and human behavior, St. Louis, 1972, The C. V. Mosby Co.

18. Skolnick, J. H.: The politics of protest, 1969, New York, Ballantine Books.

19. Smith, D. E., and Bentel, D. J.: Drug Abuse Information Project, the third and fourth annual reports to the legislature, San Francisco, 1969-1970, University of California San Francisco Medical Center.

20. Smith, D. E., and Luce, J.: Love needs care, Boston, 1971, Little, Brown & Co.

21. Smith, D. E., et al.: The free clinic: a community approach to health care and drug abuse, Beloit, Mich., 1972, Stash Press.

CHAPTER 3

PSYCHOSOCIAL FACTORS AND THE ADOLESCENT

The misuse and abuse of drugs by young people involve a variety of psychological and sociological factors that need understanding in order to be familiar with the drug problem. No attempt herein will be made to completely segregate the psychological from the sociological aspects because both are frequently interrelated and such a separation would be impossible. Instead those essentials will be identified that should be known and utilized by school and community personnel in their drug programs.

PATTERNS OF DRUG ABUSE

The patterns of drug abuse, particularly among adolescents and disaffiliated youth, have changed dramatically in the last 10 years. Prior to the 1960s, whatever constituted drug abuse was relatively constant and predictable, with illegal drug use largely confined to racial, ethnic, and philosophical minorities submerged in urban ghettos. The white middle-class representative of the dominant culture usually restricted his use to alcohol, tobacco, and a few prescription psychoactive drugs.[4]

Contemporary drug-use patterns have become much more widespread and varied. The available evidence suggests that drug use has become a *majority* phenomenon among both youth and adults.[2] Cohen states dramatically, "Even excluding alcohol, coffee and cigarettes, it is now safe to estimate that more than 50% of the total American population over 13 years of age has at least tried some powerful mind-altering drug via prescription or on the illicit market."[5]

In May 1970 the National Institute of Mental Health estimated that there were 125,000 "active narcotic abusers" in the nation. The number of persons directly involved with other dangerous drugs was placed somewhere between one-quarter and one-half million. The number having experimented with marijuana was estimated to be 20 million persons. In addition the Pentagon reports that about 50% of the American troops in Vietnam smoke marijuana. The soldiers themselves say that the percentage is even higher.

Large universities report marijuana use by more than 50% of their undergraduate student bodies. High school, junior high, and even elementary school students are using a variety of drugs and intoxicants at an increasing rate.

John Finlator, former deputy director, Bureau of Narcotics and Dangerous Drugs, estimated the number of "pot" smokers to be probably close to 8 million, although the figures of 12 million and the prediction of increases to 20 million or more are common.[8] But according to Finlator, in the last few years we have seen a strong movement of heroin into the affluent suburbs, into the high schools, and even into the junior high schools. Our addict population is increasing, he added, especially among those under 18, and the Bureau now estimates that there are 315,000 addicts (opiate) in the United States. More recent data indicate this number may be as high as 500,000. The Bureau of Narcotics and Dangerous Drugs also estimates that 2.7 billion amphetamine and 700 billion methamphetamine dosage units are produced per year at present, with about 20% diverted to the illegal market.

In addition to the usual drugs of abuse, young persons are continually experimenting with other preparations. Some have smoked catnip, nutmeg, or oregano or have injected deodorant, milk, or mayonnaise in their reckless search for a high. Not infrequently such experiments result in death.

The *New York Times* reported on January 17, 1971, that marijuana and wine are now becoming the preferred drugs at universities on the East and West coasts. However, experimentation with other mind-altering drugs is still spreading among high school and university students in other geographical locations. Some influences against the use of drugs may include natural living, communalism, religious groups, and the objectionable increasing commercialization of youth culture and of drug abuse. A less encouraging trend reported in the article is a growing incidence of heroin abuse despite student campaigns against it.

√ On the school grounds today there is a readiness to use a wide variety of drugs. Although alcohol, especially wine, is the favored and most consumed intoxicant, almost anything, including heroin, is likely to be used; sniffing of glue, gasoline, and lighter fluid is fairly common. The use of barbiturates and amphetamines begins to develop. The smoking of marijuana enters into the repertoire. If no drugs are available, youngsters—at least some of them—seek out substitutes. We obtained reports of youths using nutmeg or crushed aspirin in cokes, sniffing the vapors of burned plastic combs, consuming the cotton inserts from Vicks and Valo inhalers, smoking tea, injecting wine intravenously, "dropping" amphetamines, barbiturates, and hypnotic compounds, and sniffing paint thinner and a variety of unclassified materials.

Grown-ups are serious offenders, too. Tens of thousands of adults are being given prescriptions for amphetamines or barbiturates in situations where accepted medical practice would indicate that the prescription should not have been issued. Many persons with prescriptions for such drugs take them more frequently and in greater doses than their doctors intended. The result is a substantial amount of harm to the individual involved, in many cases leading to irreversible personality damage or near addictive patterns or both, involving extreme dangers to the user and others.

One survey found that 25% of all American women over 30 years of age currently had prescriptions for amphetamines, barbiturates, or tranquilizers; the percentage was found to be as great as 40% to 50% for those of higher income families. Thus we reiterate a point made in other chapters—drug use of some sort has become a *social norm* in our drug-oriented culture. Before there can be real understanding of the drug problem, the concept of drug usage as a minority phenomenon must be discarded. Given the right conditions, almost anyone is susceptible. The popular notions that drug abusers are a distinct breed of people or a separate social group and that they are to be identified as deviants and as willful, aggressive troublemakers must be buried.

Society's view of drug abuse must change as profoundly as the nature and extent of the drug problem has changed. No longer is it acceptable to label the psychoactive chemicals nicotine and alcohol as nondrugs, thus perpetuating their enormously harmful influences under the comfortable disguise of respectability, and at the same time to point with alarm and indignation at drug abuse in the youth culture and to demand that offenders and malefactors be rooted out and punished.

This ill-informed, sometimes hypocritical attitude has not worked and will not work in remedying the causes of the current and ominous drug epidemic. Until there is a more realistic understanding of the drug problem there will be no solution.

THE WORLD OF THE ADOLESCENT

To understand the youthful drug abuser one must understand the world of the adolescent with its cultural group life so distinctly different from the adult. Most adults at least vaguely realize that a separate and different adolescent culture exists but the extent of their awareness creates more puzzles than solutions. They may not recognize the world of the adolescent for what it is—a compelling social force often more influential in the life of the youngster than parent, home, or the mores, rules, and practices of adult society.

This is not a condition that youth has deliberately sought. He has been pushed or, perhaps more accurately, sucked into this position to fill a vacuum in his life created by our twentieth century society. Society does not incorporate youth into full membership. Therefore if a young person is to have the group affiliation and status that he needs for his psychological security, he must create his own group with its own rules, standards, and conduct. As Henry has noted:

> In many primitive cultures and in the great cultures of Asia, a person is born into a personal community, a group of intimates to which he is linked for life by tradition; but in America everyone must create his own personal community. Where one is born into an inalienable personal community, social appeal is relatively unimportant, but in American culture, where no traditional arrangement can guarantee an indissoluble personal community, every child must be a social engineer, able to use his appeal and his skill at social maneuvering to construct a personal community for himself.*

It is necessary, then, to see the adolescent social system as an ad hoc arrangement by the young for dealing with their own problems or with their peer group.

Two views of adolescence

Two major competing views attempt to define the relationship of the adolescent social system to adult institutions, the transitional or functional and the segregationist. One group holds that adolescence is merely a transitional period whereby youth are gradually socialized into the adult world. This "functional" view sees youth passing through a series of socializ-

*From Henry, J.: Culture against man, New York, 1963, Random House, Inc.

ing institutions that prepare him for adult life. The other, or "segregationist," view sees the adolescent as segregated from the social institutions of adult life and subordinated to second-class citizenship.

As Smith has put it, "The primary function of youth culture is that of bringing the normal movement of youth from the parental family to the marital family."[18] According to this functional view, adolescence is a transitional period wherein young persons are weaned from the dependent situation of a child to the independent status of an adult. Adolescent deviance, including the abuse of outlawed drugs, is understood in terms of blocked access to adult status and adult commodities. In fact, Bloch and Niederhoffer[1] have interpreted adolescent cliques in school and adolescent gang behavior as the functional equivalents of puberty rites in primitive societies. Whereas puberty rites function to prepare youth for adult responsibilities, the gang provides adolescents with the symbolic equivalent of adult behavior denied them in bars, cars, and travel. Because American society has not made adequate preparation for the induction of adolescents into adult status, juvenile delinquency is an attempt, symbolically, to become adult by imitating certain superficial symbols of adulthood. The functionalists, rather than seeing this deprived status as inimical and destructive, see in segregation and powerlessness the necessary preparation and training of young adulthood. Parsons illustrates this point in noting: "At the same time [youth] is frustrated by being deprived of power and influence in the current situation, though it recognizes that such a deprivation is in certain respects essential, if its segregation for purposes of training is to be effective."[14] This is the Protestant ethic of delayed gratification: sacrifice now for future rewards.

The other view of the adolescent is the segregationist one in which the young person is separated from the social institutions of adult life and subordinated to second-class status. One of the functions of the high school, Reuter[16] observed, is to exclude adolescents from meaningful participation (and also competition for the labor market) in society. The trade union movement has been particularly effective in limiting the job market. This segregationist view contends that the proliferation of extracurricular activities (athletics, band, etc.) has operated to contain and entertain adolescents who have no function in the modern economy. Friedenberg[9] draws an analogy with colonial exploitation.

Extensive literature on the historical development of the adolescent social system in our industrial society is available. Under preindustrial conditions, each person was a useful member of society from an early age. This is no longer true as a consequence of two significant developments: (1) The shocking exploitation of children in eighteenth century industrial England created social pressures for reform, resulting in our contemporary child labor laws. Children are no longer allowed to work as they did in the past. (2) The transition from an agricultural to an industrial economy, with its accompanying shift from rural to urban life, also helped create a marginal, noncontributing adolescent group.

Youth has lost its economic importance as a producer, with an accompanying loss of social position, pride, and self-esteem. The adolescent is a total dependent, with all the internal and external implications inherent in total dependency.

The growth of technology is also significant because it has changed the character of the occupational structure. The need for technical training, requiring years of education, means that occupational knowledge and skills are no longer transmitted from father to son. Most youngsters do not even understand the work their parents do. So the vocational preparation of youth has also passed from the family to the school system.

The inevitable consequences of these various changes have been the removal of an enormous and growing group of young persons from the mainstream of life and the denial to them of meaningful participation in the general community. Youth's self-created alternative is the adolescent society, with its own set of standards and values. In the last decade some of the older youth have become so segregated from the adult world that, as Messer has noted, "The generation gap seems to have widened to the extent that it is now a cultural gap."[13] This cultural gap is most apparent in the proliferation of hippie communes, "long hair" communities such as Haight-Ashbury, and the rapid diffusion of these life-styles to younger adolescents. The parent who puzzles over the generation gap and decries adolescent rejection of his value system fails to grasp the reasons why the dichotomy he so resents has become established. Invariably he will assign the wrong reasons for the emergence of practices unacceptable to his world—including that of drug abuse.

A meeting ground for both functionalist and segregationist positions is found in a concensus among students of adolescence that youngsters are subjected to an overly long and prolonged period of dependency. On that, at least, everyone agrees.

Rationales for drug abuse

Young people may use drugs for one or more of the following general purposes: (1) to achieve detachment from personal problems and troubles and to produce a state of well-being, (2) to establish an involvement with the subculture that offers an identity and an identification in society, and (3) to express hostility toward respectable society and as a protest against the injustices and restrictions imposed by the establishment. These reasons may be and are affected by a variety of psychological and environmental or social influences, including (1) personal conflicts, (2) television, and (3) commercial exploitation.

PERSONAL CONFLICTS

Personal factors involved in drug abuse may center around overwhelming intrapsychic conflict, present especially during adolescence and centered around adult sexuality, hostility, dependency-independency issues, and identity diffusion. These conflicts are the results of demands for conformity placed on the individual by society.

Secondary factors, arising largely from the first group, may include the following:

1. Fear of competition and failure
2. Fear of homosexuality
3. Fear of threatening mental illness or mental disintegration
4. The need to rebel
5. The need to be caught and punished
6. The need to explore the limits of one's body and psyche and to challenge one's resources
7. The need for a hedonistic or orgiastic experience
8. The need to belong to a group or subculture
9. The need for instant relief or instant answers (Chemicals produce the most instant change.)

TELEVISION

A constant emphasis on drugs as the solution to every physical and mental problem has created an atmosphere leading to a normality of drug overconsumption that borders on the unreal. This atmosphere is an influencing factor in the drug abuse problem. Television has probably had a profound influence on our habits as drug consumers and has especially impressed the young. As a result of this influence, there is a total diffusion of the drug culture through every social and economic level.

Television is no longer just a machine but has become the national babysitter, the substitute parent, the teacher, the preacher, the indoctrinator, and almost an extension of our bodies. Children spend an enormous amount of time in front of television before they are old enough to select and judge. They are stuck in front of the television set, which then acts as a tranquilizer so that mother can get on with her housework or so that parents may entertain their friends without interruption.

On Saturday mornings channels on television are directed at children. By the time a child has reached 6 years of age, he may have seen on television over 20,000 acts of violence. He learns that violence is all right and that death is reversible because, "if the guy gets killed today, he still comes back next Saturday."

The child's fantasies about his own omnipotence are maintained by the fact that he can, at will, change the channel or switch off the program he does not like. Children deprived of communication with their parents or with other children lack the ability to express themselves verbally; their own initiative, inquisitiveness, and exploratory behavior is stifled. They begin to speak in monosyllables and, by identifying with the television set, talk in terms of "turning on," "tuning out," "tuning in," "turning off," and "dropping out." This, of course, has also become the language of the new psychedelic generation.

Society is in endless search of escape; one of the quickest temporary means of escape is drugs. Television offers drugs as the solution to all disaffections of body and mind. Seductive pharmaceutical advertisements promise to make one feel more tranquil, happier, younger, sexier, and more attractive. The advertising industry has for many years employed some of the best psychologists. They know that one good way to persuade people to buy is to promise relief from suffering and from feelings of inadequacy. Sex, strength, youth, and virility are implied; we are gulled into a delusion that chemicals are safe, when many are not.[11]

COMMERCIAL EXPLOITATION

The continuing intensification of group consciousness among adolescents during the last 25 years has led to their economic exploitation and is another factor related to the drug problem. Business and industry have effectively used the teen-age group pressure for conformity to create a multimillion dollar market. The word "teen-ager" itself seems to have had a commercial origin, recognizing an identifiable subgroup within society that might be exploited.[11]

In 1946 Eugene Gilbert invented a business that involved the sale of information concerning the tastes and behavior of teen-agers to commercial organizations. In 1958 MacDonald reported that Gilbert was making between $500,000 and $1 million a year for his services. His clients included Borden's milk, *Seventeen,* Hollywood V-ette, Vassarette brassieres, Van Heusen shirts, and the U. S. Army. In 1944 the magazine for adolescents, *Seventeen,* bulging with advertisements directed at teen-agers, published its first issue. In 1958, 17 million teen-agers purchased $9.5 billion worth of commodities with their own funds.[12] It was estimated this figure would rise to $14 billion by 1964.

Advertisers exploit peer-group status and personal insecurities expertly in the promotion of their products. In most instances the appeal is made not to the individual, but to the group; the youngster is reminded again and again that a particular product will enable him to stand in good stead with his peers. He can prevent isolation and minimize that left-out feeling by buying or accepting the commodity being offered.

Advertising offers to solve many adolescent problems—loneliness, sex, intimacy, personal community, instability—through the purchase of commodities such as face creams, perfumes, pimple preparations, hair oils, after-shave lotions, deodorants, soaps, mouthwashes, and shampoos. These products are fetishized solutions to real adolescent problems.

The inevitable consequence of the commerical exploitation of adolescent group psychology has been to intensify the conformity urge. Group drug abuse and the teen-age drug epidemic reflect the same kind of motivation that causes the typical teen-age girl to own an average of seven bras, the first of which she bought at the age of 13 years.

Psychological motivations

Young people, in their efforts to achieve detachment from personal problems and troubles, identify a number of specific reasons for the use, misuse, and abuse of drugs, including curiosity, peer-group pressure, insecurity, escape, boredom, rebelliousness, and "kicks."

CURIOSITY. Curiosity about drugs is engendered by our adult drug culture, which includes the use of tobacco, alcohol, tranquilizers, sleeping pills, diet pills, and pep pills, all advertised openly and widely by the media. What other teen- and subteen-agers say about the fun they have turning on also creates curiosity.

PEER-GROUP PRESSURE. It is almost becoming a puberty rite to have experimented with drugs by the time one is 13 years old. The real change in recent months has been the large numbers of elementary school children turned on by others in elementary school or by older brothers, sisters, and friends. The "I dare you to" has become simply "why don't you have fun like we do and you can belong to our 'in' group."

INSECURITY. A timeless condition among teen-agers has been a sense of insecurity and the desire for affection and identity (recognition). Failing to find security at home, feeling a lack of affection and concern for who and what they are and to whom, teen-agers have throughout history resorted to various types of behavior designed to satisfy these needs. In numbers increasing for almost a decade, thousands of insecure young persons have resorted to drugs to find a sense of security, to attain affection (from others in the drug culture), and to identify with peers who are also involved.

ESCAPE. Drugs of all kinds, including marijuana, LSD, hashish, and other psychedelics, have the ability to provide an escape from reality; they can reduce and, for the moment at least, can wipe out the internal conflicts and the normal insecurities of young people (thus preventing these persons from coming to grips with their problems at the time, place, and age where they normally need to "face up" if they are to mature). These persons can escape in this way without losing consciousness, and, for the duration of their high, they can live in a new and marvelous world—one recreated again and again by getting "stoned."

BOREDOM. Boredom with school or routine living lacking the interst and stimulation to engage the youngster in meaningful experience drives some young persons to drug experimention.

REBELLIOUSNESS. Youth sees drugs as a way to get parents or teachers "up tight," frightened, or anxious, resulting in over-reaction by parents, society, school officials, and civic and law enforcement personnel. Instead of curing the situation, this leads to further "bugging" of the adult world by the youngsters, which results in new levels of overreaction (for example, demands for new and more stringent laws and sentences when the present ones are ineffectual and unenforceable).

KICKS. Last and probably most important, both for the experimenting young group and for those who become dependent, is using drugs for kicks, substituting synthetic fun for the development of meaningful relationships with other people. Some youth lose their shyness in this way; some lose their drabness or plainness and become, for a time, beautiful and handsome.

STUDENT NEEDS JUSTIFY BEHAVIOR

According to some students, drugs aid in the formation of friendships and the development of a better understanding of people. Rap sessions and interpersonal communications are "easier when zonked out on pot." The drugs create an atmosphere of relaxation and pleasure (hedonism). The question is whether the pleasure-to-risk ratio always favors the user.

The enrichment of life that students claim they gain through the use of drugs includes an enhancement of creativity and an increased appreciation of beauty and nature. Drugs are said to have inspired some persons to write, paint, compose music, and perform. It is possible that sensitivity in these areas may be heightened, although this is not the norm.

The contemporary quest for a deeper in-sight into the self and the universe incorporates the use of drugs. Some students use drugs as a panacea for emotional troubles, as a method for improving one's personality, or to cure hangups. Although chemicals produce the instant results desired, any enlightenment gained is always artificial and does not last. The use of drugs in do-it-yourself psychology has been a two-way street with sometimes traumatic results.

Search for identity

Time and again one hears teen-agers asking the questions, phrased according to their age and verbal skills, "Who am I?" and "What am I doing here?" Some social scientists have called this the search for identity or for meaning. More and more young people, freed from considerations of economic survival, find it hard to accept the basic value system that modern civilization has emphasized—materialism and the quest for affluence and material achievement. Less and less are young persons satisfied with a system that seems to push them toward a greater amount of education designed to help them attain more prestigious jobs, leading to higher income and social status. To many teen-agers, it makes no sense, especially because it has not led to widespread personal satisfaction and happiness in the adults most visible to them. This rejection of the values associated with material acquisition has led to confusion, to a vacuum in meaningful goals, and to a search for something "inside." A further discussion is included in Chapter 9.

VALUES

Offspring of the middle class are particularly sensitive in perceiving that the "old myths" are unrewarding and meaningless. Members of the psychedelic revolution have been conspicuously concerned with values, with, as they put it, "where we're at." This preoccupation reflects their search for new personal identities and new ideologies to guide their lives.

Since the establishment possesses virtues as well as shortcomings, and those virtues and shortcomings are relative, not absolute, perhaps a different kind of teaching about our national ideals, achievements, and failures would help to counteract the youthful disillusionment that leads to disaffiliation. An honest and forthright examination of our national qualities in social science textbooks and classrooms, in a constructive rather than either a flag-waving or a negative perspective, certainly would provide less basis for a counter-society of hostile, contemptuous youth. Meanwhile a close link exists between the social-cultural attitudes of young persons and their abuse of drugs. This is discussed further in Chapter 7.

Rejection of the culture

Among the young there is widespread disillusionment with American ideals and American values, which appear phony to them in the light of reality. They perceive that the basic American ideologies often clash conspicuously with ongoing practices, and, in the adolescent manner of making absolute judgments from limited or two-dimensional evidence, they cross off entirely the establishment's claims to righteousness.[16] When as conspicuous an example as the Vietnam war involves them personally and acutely, threatening their very existence and trampling on their ideals, rejection of the establishment and everything it stands for results. From this disaffirmation it is an easy, even natural, step to challenge the sanctions aginst drugs and then to create a rationale of complete justification for their use. In 1967 Blumer touched on this point when he described the collective beliefs of young drug users he had studied:

. . . they viewed with contempt the use of opiates and rejected with evidence the claim that use of harmful drugs led naturally to opiate use. They pointed out that the break-up of home life, with which many of them were very familiar, was due to other factors than the use of drugs; they were able to show that the limitations of their career opportunities came from other conditions than the use of drugs as such. They

met the fear of arrest by developing greater skill and precautions against detection in the use of drugs. Added to these stances was a set of collective beliefs that justified their use of drugs, so that such use resulted in harmless pleasure, increased conviviality, did not lead to violence, could be regulated, did not lead to addiction, and was much less harmful than the use of alcohol, which is socially and openly sanctioned in our society.[*]

An example of how teen-age rejection of the American culture has lead to drug abuse is in the identification of white students with the "Negro revolt" and their sharing of the Negro and lower class culture. As the civil rights movement developed and the American culture crisis grew in scope, marijuana smoking acquired increasingly political and ideological significance for college students affiliated with the New Left. The transfer of drug habits to the recruit was an inevitable consequence of joining up with causes. The contagiousness of drug abuse amply justifies the term "epidemic" in referring to the lightning spread of its use among youth groups.

The alternate drug scene has an undeniable attraction for youngsters hard pressed to cope with our enormously complex environment. It appears to offer the same kind of escape from the onerous demands of growing up that the circus offered to youth of a generation or so ago. So many young persons roll up their blankets and take off. On a Friday afternoon they spot the highways from San Francisco to Big Sur, dressed in costumes carefully chosen for their picturesqueness from Salvation Army and Goodwill Industries used clothing racks, thumbing rides to "where the action is." The action includes the use of drugs, and those who join such alternate cultures have been effective intermediaries in transmitting drug usage to the larger youth population.

The use of drugs is an apparent alternative. After all, our culture and communica-

[*]From Blumer, H.: The "Ad" Center Project report on drug abuse, Berkeley, 1968, University of California Press.

tions media teach children that one solves almost all problems by turning on—drugs for headaches, constipation, sleeplessness, "nerves," and for whatever other maladies beset us. Taking drugs is the *common* palliative in our society, not a deviant one. Thus it is difficult to fashion public health approaches without realizing the cultural logic and appeal of mind-altering drugs, although their unlawfulness and uniqueness would seem to set them apart from the mainstream of drug use.

AFFLUENCE AND PERMISSIVENESS

Bored teen-agers with a car, money, no responsibilities to a family or to the community, and with no meaningful or rewarding work easily succumb to the thrill of drug experimentation. These youngsters have little directed play after school or on weekends, no chores, no music lessons, and no scouting tests to pass to strengthen the ego and to gain rewards; they turn to challenging, aberrant behavior, including a whole range of marginal or unacceptable behavior, part of which is the use of drugs. This behavior begins as early as the third grade. The absence of standards of behavior, dress, and speech go along with a lack of zest, challenge, and satisfaction to promote drug abuse. Open and unchallenged violation of laws, morals, and manners, as seen among many adults, cause a child to question the whole set of social rules and to wonder whether crime does not pay very well indeed.

Since the Civil War there has been a continuing trend toward the elimination of corporal punishment in the rearing of children and an increasing rejection of the stern exercise of parental authority. The earlier puritanical conception of evil saw the child as "damned with all mankind in Adam's fall." This creature of original sin was full of disobedience and rebellion against God's laws. Corporal punishment was necessary to break his congenital will to do evil.

Even at the beginning of this century the baby was a dangerous bundle of impulses

that had to be curbed. By the 1940s his aberrant manifestations were viewed more complacently as exploratory gestures by which he learned about the world. The trend since then has been consistently toward less authoritarian discipline and parental domination of children's lives. Increasingly children have been given independence and self-determination within the sphere of the family. "The child should learn to live his own life; his parents cannot live it for him."

Parents have had a traditional role in determining educational policies in the public schools; this has enabled parents to extend into the classroom an insistence on freedom of action for the child without meaningful punishment for transgressions. Whether as a consequence or merely concurrently, the fifties saw sudden public concern over juvenile deliquency. It has been pointed out that the decline in parental authority could not be blamed for any sudden increase in deliquency because permissiveness had been a long-term, gradual development. Instead, it was suggested, the extension of public education to absorb all economic and racial classes might be the explanation. In 1900 only 11% of the nation's high school age population was in high school; in 1930, 51%; in 1960, over 90%. The majority of these children came from working-class and farm families; these adolescents were found by Coleman[7] to dominate the high school social system. Increasing exposure of middle-class children to this group, it was proposed, was resulting in the adoption of patterns of behavior unacceptable by prevailing white middle-class majority standards. Such behavior was alien, subversive, and consequently threatening. The negative reaction of adults to "rock 'n roll" in the fifties was based on the alien quality of its sound and delivery, which was of Negro and southern backcountry origin.

Whether or not permissiveness was a contributing factor to the youth drug epidemic, the youngster of the 1960s and 1970s who chose or was pressured into the drug scene by his peers had a high degree of autonomy in taking that route. A conspicuous absence of parental influence appears in the case studies of drug abusers.

Summary of motives for drug use

There is no need to dwell on the motives leading to drug abuse. Curiosity, social pressure, rebellion against authority, and escape from social and emotional problems, the desire for kicks—all these are relevant in many cases but add little to our capacity to understand the recency and magnitude of contemporary drug abuse. Beyond these obvious aspects are cultural and psychological factors that come to the attention again and again, glibly articulated by college students and teen-agers and subconsciously manifested by those in their pre-teens.

The theme of these factors is disenchantment and alienation, particularly in the area of values. Increasing numbers of young persons have been struck with a sense of futility regarding the basic institutions of society. They charge social and political hypocrisy and reject governmental and social policies that seem headed toward more war, hate, and injustice. Youth has begun to challenge the goals of the educational system that trains them for jobs incapable of guaranteeing personal satisfaction. They criticize parents, citing a basic lack of understanding and discrimination of what is really important. They are put off by organized religion—symbolized by rite and dogma—because it seems to deny inherent human worth and to exist for hypocritical adults who attend church without seeming to be touched with love for God or for their fellow men.

The psychedelic scene is a middle and upper-middle socioeconomic class phenomenon that reflects youth's disillusionment. It operates from material oversufficiency, not economic deprivation. Pot and acid are not functional to the ghetto individual and the poverty-stricken minority member. Their drugs of choice are alcohol, barbiturates, heroin, and other depressants or "consciousness-contractors." The use of psychedelics has not flourished among the economically underprivileged, perhaps because they need to forget what already is. Children from affluent families can suffer a different kind of pain—a need to find that which they do not have.

THE "COP-OUT" FROM SOCIETY

By now it should have become obvious that illegal drug use, drug-using subcultures, social protest movements, politically inspired violence, destructive encounters between generations, and increasing rejection of our society by the young are merely symptomatic of a profound upheaval in contemporary life. Today's youth is attempting to resolve an identity crisis perhaps unparalleled in history. His abuse of drugs is directly associated with a sense of despair and rejection, with a failure to achieve self-realization and self-fulfillment, to discover a meaningful place in our contemporary world. Certainly our society is falling far short of providing him with such an environment.

It must be recognized, then, that the drug crisis is in large measure the product of complex, interacting social and psychological variables. But whatever their setting, most are aspects of the struggle and failure of youngsters to relate to what is for them a disrelated, disoriented, dehumanized, but enormously complicated culture. Their use of illicit drugs is frequently both a social protest and an escape mechanism. It is a self-defeating problem-solving procedure—but an attractive one. In the initial stages, at least, drug usage is exciting and pleasurable. Many drugs are relatively cheap and easily available; the rationale for their use is seductive. Carey's study[3] of the college drug user identifies the frequently recreational use as one of the unique features of the contemporary drug scene. But the significant fact here is that such use has developed within the context of a life-style that offers an alternative to an unacceptable social world epitomized by the organization man.

One of the fallacies that appears in discussions of drug education is that drug use and abuse are somehow different from the conventional problems of youth and education. Drug use seems to bear little relationship to the larger context of adolescent peer-group relationships and the school environment. As a consequence, proposals emerging from such discussions may not penetrate the realities. They do not come to term with the social causations. Drug education must be made to relate to the actual, specific causes of drug abuse before it can achieve any significant influence.

Unfortunately, few persons either in teaching or in administration have the training and experience to equip them to deal effectively with youthful drug abuse. Moreover, much uncertainty exists regarding the proper role of the school. This is particularly true in dealing with the increasing drug traffic on the school grounds. Unfortunately the specifics of these difficult individual situations are likely to obscure the need for dealing with the problem in its larger social dimensions.

THE SCHOOL ENVIRONMENT

The school is the staging ground for the adolescent social system. In the usually small neighborhood elementary school the youngster continues the association with his young friends from down the street or around the block. His social relationships are extended to the school grounds; parental and neighborhood influences still strongly affect his environment, which tends to be familiar and secure.

When the individual leaves the neighborhood school to enter the large, impersonal, and heterogeneous junior or senior high school, he is without a well-defined and continuous identity for the first time in his life. In this new and confusing setting he must both meet academic requirements and strive to establish identity and status with his peers. Here the adolescent may be chosen or rejected, he may not know whether he has been chosen or rejected, and those he numbers in his personal community one day may not be there the next. This situation makes for great uncertainty in interpersonal relations. It also makes for great sensitivity to group standards and practices and reinforces the compulsion to conform. The fact that the adolescent social system creates a world of superficial social contacts rather than a climate of loyalty and intimacy explains the tremendous pressure for comformity. It helps to explain the epidemic appeal of drugs once they are accepted or used by the prestige members of the peer group. The compulsion to "go along" is very strong.

The school can no longer effectively intervene in the affairs of students because (1) the power of the administration has been diffused by the size of the school and the fragmentation of classes and (2) because the authority of the teacher over student conduct has been restricted. Consequently when the youngster enters this new and expanded student community where he must scramble for membership, the strongest influence in his life is apt to be the peer group that takes him in. If it is a drug-using group, then there is a strong possibility that he will soon be a drug user.

Rejection of the school culture

The diffusion of drug use among high school populations has grown apace with student rejection of traditional school culture. The old symbols of participation associated with that culture—athletics, the block letter, membership on committees, student government offices, rallies, and the "rah rah" emphasis long identified as "school spirit"—have been drained of meaning for youngsters sharply aware of the racial crisis, the deteriorating environment, war, violence, and poverty. These issues have been imposed upon their consciousness by the mass media and by first-hand personal observation. For these youngsters the traditional school culture is empty. Its failure is not that it does not provide the opportunity to grow, achieve, and find emotional outlets, but that it provides the *wrong kind* of opportunity. This is also discussed in Chapter 9.

Results of the irrelevance of school to the lives of students have ranged from the undramatic withdrawal of students from school activities and even from school itself at one extreme, to the highly dramatic hippie movement and student political radicalism at the other. A thorough reexamination of the assumptions underlying the traditional high school culture has long been needed. The research for such analysis is not adequate, but nevertheless some information is available. One thing appears clear—the extracurricular activities to which the school attaches the greatest rewards (athletics, student government, etc.) are those that serve the school, not the student. Athletes perform a role that enhances the prestige of the school and establishes solidarity with the local community. To the extent that their energies are channeled into such service rather than into their own growth, social prestige is gained at the expense of personal development.[10]

In contrast, activities that bear little relationship to enhancing the school's public image—art and science, for example—foster only individual growth; hence they carry little prestige. The system increasingly turns off students, so that now the star halfback passes among them unnoticed, and the student body president's denunciation of the lack of school spirit goes unheard. Instead the students seek identification with alienated groups: hippies, radicals, black militants, Chicanos, antiwar groups, youth for Jesus, and so on. And, of course, they also choose alternative groups (including some of the aforementioned and others not so easily identified by label) that embrace drug use.

The traditional school culture has fostered a climate of adolescent irresponsibility because most of the areas of student initiative have been usurped by the school.[17] Such a climate facilitates an adolescent ethos of kicks, fun, and impulse release with little regard for consequences.

Under circumstances where adolescents are not expected to be responsible agents, it is unlikely that they will be.

The schools have been largely concerned with the "technology game"—teaching young persons the skills necessary to enter the commercial enterprise system. But fewer and fewer young people want to learn what the schools are teaching. The concepts of grades and pure achievement are no longer incentives for students, but lead to the rejection of the school culture.

Schools could get students so totally involved that grading would become largely irrelevant. In fact, Paula Gordon has stated:

In general then I see a change in grading as being a means to vastly increasing a young person's mobility out of a failure syndrome as well as a means of removing one of the underlying causes that may have landed him there in the first place. It is also important because a young person's desire to achieve would then no longer be based on a fear of failure as it may be seen to be at present. . . .

Such a change in grading systems would not do away with the notion of failure altogether. It would simply make a sense of failure dependent upon internally established criteria rather than externally imposed ones. In this way also, self-development and growth would be nurtured, rather than thwarted as they often are under present systems.*

Soskin,[19] a psychologist who developed an innovative drop-in center for school-age children states:

Schools—like shopping plazas, these educational super markets for the young—could only have been conceived by efficiency-minded adults who think in terms of persons as units to be processed through a system rather than children to be guided humanely and wisely to the full ripening to the human potential. Hundreds of thousands of tired and troubled teachers, as their classes grow more restless and querulous and as daily absence rates mount despite their most conscientious efforts, must be asking themselves about the adequacy and relevance of the educational experiences we provide our young. For,

---

*From Gordon, P., editor: Guide to ideas on drug abuse programs and policies, ed. 2, Berkeley, Calif., 1970, Committee for Psychedelic Drug Information.

despite the architectural innovations and the electronics innovations and the "system" innovations, the stark fact is that our schools are in grievous trouble, and our young people are trying to tell us this, if we could only comprehend the meaning of their anger or alienation.*

Development of a school program responsive to human needs

Soskin,[19] among others, believes that schools, as their primary purpose, ought to teach young persons to understand themselves better. Experience in living and the complexities and subtleties of interpersonal relationships ought to be explored to help young persons develop more quality in their lives. Schools should begin to deal with essential human traits and values (Chapter 7). These include openness, honesty, dependence, and trust instead of fear, anger, and loneliness. Alternatives to the "speeding" of modern life as well as to the compulsion for achievement could be provided. Schools should do more than merely program young minds to unquestioningly absorb the dominant cultural values. Getting grades—pure achievement—should be secondary to fostering self-acceptance, enjoyment of life, self-expression, and creativity.

The most important thing that needs to be done to improve education is to make it more responsive to basic human needs. The educational experience must be both relevant and stimulating. When it fails to be meaningful, stimulating, and relevant to the problems and life experiences of the child, he becomes bored, dissatisfied, and may be seriously handicapped emotionally and spiritually. Charles Silberman's *Crisis in the Classroom* (1970) is only the latest in a series of studies documenting the nonproductive and psychologically destructive nature of much of our educational system today.

Contemporary emphasis in education has tended to be on information and on a limited form of critical analysis. What has been missing is an emphasis on assimilating and using such information in daily living and on developing goals, values, and ideals that would give a basis for the enjoyment of a meaningful and happy life.

Young persons need direction and guidance. Answers to basic questions are being sought by them, but are not being found. These questions concern the meaning of life, the significance of actions, the reasons for being discriminating in what one does, the relevance of a moral life, the ways of finding inner peace and self-understanding, and the place of happiness, humor, and love. School should be a place where the student can deal with such realities.

There seems to be a tendency today for educators, parents, and adults in general to shy away from taking personal stands, from stating personal opinions, from arguing against what they know is wrong and false, and from defending what they have learned from their own experience to be true. Such evasive tendencies may be seen as related to an inner uncertainty as to what is right or true. The trend seems to be toward a "hands off" policy of giving youth the facts they presumably need, presenting them with a neutral view of alternatives, and turning them loose to make their own choices and mistakes, but punishing them, of course, if they do not follow the majority and conform.

Persons, whether teachers, parents, or other adults, do not develop expertise overnight in giving moral guidance, especially when they may be uncertain as to what their own convictions are. Educational programs that do not have an ethical basis do youth a definite disservice. It would seem that education must renew its focus upon the understanding, inculcation, and awakening of ideals and goals. It is essential that the lives of exemplary individuals and exemplary societies and civilizations, both Eastern and Western,

---

*From Soskin, W. F.: Project community and the children of the good life, Unpublished monograph, Berkeley, Calif., 1970.

Table 3-1. Alternatives to drugs*

LEVEL OF EXPERIENCE	CORRESPONDING MOTIVES (EXAMPLES)	POSSIBLE ALTERNATIVES (EXAMPLES)
Physical	Desire for physical satisfaction; physical relaxation; relief from sickness; desire for more energy; maintenance of physical dependency	Athletics; dance; exercise; hiking; diet; health training; carpentry or outdoor work
Sensory	Desire to stimulate sight, sound, touch, taste; need for sensual-sexual stimulation; desire to magnify sensorium	Sensory awareness training; sky diving; experiencing sensory beauty of nature
Emotional	Relief from psychological pain; attempt to solve personal perplexities; relief from bad mood; escape from anxiety; desire for emotional insight; liberation of feeling; emotional relaxation	Competent individual counseling; well-run group therapy; instruction in psychology of personal development
Interpersonal	To gain peer acceptance; to break through interpersonal barriers; to "communicate," especially nonverbally; defiance of authority figures; cement two-person relationships; relaxation of interpersonal inhibition; solve interpersonal hangups	Expertly managed sensitivity and encounter groups; well-run group therapy; instruction in social customs; confidence training; social-interpersonal counseling; emphasis on assisting others in distress via education; marriage
Social (including sociocultural and environmental)	To promote social change; to find identifiable subculture; to tune out intolerable environmental conditions, e.g., poverty; changing awareness of the "masses"	Social service; community action in positive social change; helping the poor, aged infirm, young, tutoring handicapped; ecology action
Political	To promote political change; to identify with antiestablishment subgroup; to change drug legislation; out of desperation with the social-political order; to gain wealth or affluence or power	Political service; political action; nonpartisan projects such as ecological lobbying; field work with politicians and public officials
Intellectual	To escape mental boredom; out of intellectual curiosity; to solve cognitive problems; to gain new understanding in the world of ideas; to study better; to research one's own awareness; for science	Intellectual excitement through reading, through discussion; creative games and puzzles; self-hypnosis; training in concentration; synectics—training in intellectual breakthroughs; memory training
Creative-aesthetic	To improve creativity in the arts; to enhance enjoyment of art already produced, e.g., music; to enjoy imaginative mental productions	Nongraded instruction in producing and/or appreciating art, music, drama, crafts, handiwork, cooking, sewing, gardening, writing, singing, etc.
Philosophical	To discover meaningful values; to grasp the nature of the universe; to find meaning in life; to help establish personal identity; to organize a belief structure	Discussions, seminars, courses in the meaning of life; study of ethics, morality, the nature of reality; relevant philosophical literature; guided exploration of value systems

*From Cohen, A. Y.: J. Psychedelic Drugs **3:**16-21, 1971.

Table 3-1. Alternatives to drugs—cont'd

LEVEL OF EXPERIENCE	CORRESPONDING MOTIVES (EXAMPLES)	POSSIBLE ALTERNATIVES (EXAMPLES)
Spiritual-mystical	To transcend orthodox religion; to develop spiritual insights; to reach higher levels of consciousness; to have divine visions; to communicate with God; to augment yogic practices; to get a spiritual short-cut; to attain enlightenment; to attain spiritual powers	Exposure to nonchemical methods of spiritual development; study of world religions; introduction to applied mysticism, meditation; yogic techniques
Miscellaneous	Adventure, risk drama, "kicks," unexpressed motives; pro-drug general attitudes, etc.	"Outward Bound" survival training; combinations of alternatives above; pro-naturalness attitudes; brain-wave training; meaningful employment, etc.

be studied with such objectives in mind. Young people are looking for direction and purpose, and the prescripts that they receive today appear to be having little or no positive impact upon their lives.

The techniques of critical analysis have made students more inclined to take apart and find fault rather than to approach problems and situations in constructive and creative ways. The educational process has failed if the young person leaves secondary school unable to cope constructively with the day-to-day problems he is certain to face. The educational process has failed if the young person is left without a sense of direction and some basic personal values by which he can guide his life.

Ideally, the educational process should play a key role in the child's spiritual, emotional, and characterological development. Ideally, the educational experience should help to inculcate a young person with an attitude of caring about what happens to himself and to others. At present the educational experience, as well as the home experience, too often fails to stir these natural feelings. Human needs and aspirations seem to be bypassed. If children are to be rendered "drug abuse proof," higher goals and values must be internalized for them.

Educators can play a key role in helping young persons to develop goals and values, a sense of direction, a capacity for meeting problems, solving them, and finding a sense of inner satisfaction in life. The more humor, love, care, and simple respect for their students that teachers bring to their classrooms, the more human the educational process will become. Real interest is contagious; so are happiness, hopefulness, trust, humor, love, and an attitude of caring. If these attributes become a manifest part of the teacher's life, the child will begin to naturally acquire some of the same attitudes and attributes.

The drug problem is but one symptom of a deeply rooted discontentment. When life itself is not valued, then health itself will very likely also be disregarded. Health education can stress the merits of *not hurting;* it can help to inculcate persons with deeper regard for health. It can also help by instructing them to exercise safeguards and to discriminate as far as what they do to their minds and bodies. But it would seem most unlikely that health education alone can provide the motive force needed for the young to find themselves and to begin to build values and to discover meaning in living.[17]

ALTERNATIVES TO DRUGS

"Youngsters use drugs because they want to, and they would stop doing it if there were something better." This hypothesis may appear weak in that it ignores the complex psychosocial aspects that we have discussed at length, but if we say the same thing in a little different way it will sound more credible. Let us say that if there were satisfying alternatives for youth, such alternatives would serve to interrupt a drug-using life-style. Alternatives could be used to help develop legitimate personal aspirations, which are more effective than drugs. (Cohen[6] has provided a table of alternatives that matches motives with relevant concerns.) Opposite from each level-motive category in Table 3-1 are examples of types of alternatives that might replace, ameliorate, or prevent drug abuse. Dohner[7a] includes other alternatives such as self-reliance development, vocational skill training, and meditation through the achievement of a state of heightened consciousness by focusing attention, daydreaming, and "mind-tripping."

There is, however, as Cohen points out, another major alternative not specified here, and that is stopping drug use. Even junkies stop using drugs when the use itself or the life-style of using becomes simply unbearable. They are faced with too many "rip offs" (exploitation), too many hassles (interpersonal confrontations), and often too many "bummers" (unpleasant drug experiences). Exposing this side of drug use could act as a deterrent to new users.

Our emphasis here is not to demonstrate the supposed evils of drug abuse but to show the benefits of nonuse. The concept of viable alternatives may be effectively applied in the field of drug education. The idea that making children afraid of drugs will stop them from using drugs has completely lost credibility. The real possibilities lie in educational alternatives, what people can do with and about their own lives. That is what drug abuse prevention should stress.

The present national policy that singles out particular drugs and makes their unauthorized possession or use a crime should be changed. We believe that the individual and social harm accomplished by imposing criminal sanctions on drug users far outstrips the benefits of this approach. Handling drug users as criminals has created widespread disrespect for the drug laws, has resulted in selective enforcement, has possibly done more to encourage than to discourage illegal drug use, has undercut bona fide educational efforts to explain the important differences between the physical and mental damage caused by the different types of drugs, and has deterred drug abusers from seeking necessary help. There is a strong need for the decriminalization of the drug laws.

Most of those who advocate a public health approach disapprove strongly of the unsupervised use of dangerous drugs, especially by young persons. Our conclusion is based rather upon a recognition that the present penal methods of handling the drug abuser are at best ineffective, and at worst counterproductive, and that other approaches must be tried.

We feel that, as a first step in bringing the problem back into perspective, criminal penalties for the possession of illegal drugs for personal use only should be abandoned, just as criminal penalties for public intoxication are now being abandoned in many jurisdictions. This is in conformity with the recent recommendations of President Nixon's Commission on Marijuana.

If the confrontation over the role of criminal law in enforcing private moral judgments or choices of drugs were eliminated, the country might then be able to unite behind an intensified approach to research, prevention, treatment, and law enforcement; this latter should be directed against the upper echelons of the illegal drug traffic: the importer, the pusher, and the dealer. Restrictions on scientific research inquiries into particular drugs might then be lifted and substantial public and private funds more easily directed toward the understanding of how drugs work on the mind and body and what effects, both short- and long-term, they produce. The education of young people against the reckless use of powerful substances that affect the mind could proceed in a free and open climate more calculated to affect behavior.

In the meantime, however, the present realities make it necessary to deal with the facts of illegal usage and with the stipulated penalties. The law makes the unauthorized consumption of a large number of drugs criminal. Those who use them are thus defined as criminals, irrespective of how leniently specific laws are enforced. Teachers should know the law, legal and government policy, and how the laws apply. This is discussed further in Chapter 5.

References

1. Bloch, H., and Niederhoffer, A.: The gang: a study in adolescent behavior, New York, 1958, Philosophical Library, Inc.
2. Blum, R. H., et al.: Students and drugs, San Francisco, 1969, Jossey-Bass, Inc., Publishers.
3. Carey, J. T.: The college drug scene, Englewood Cliffs, N. J., 1968, Prentice-Hall, Inc.
4. Chein, I., et al.: The road to H; narcotics, delinquency, and social policy, New York, 1964, Basic Books, Inc., Publishers.
5. Cohen, A. Y.: Inside what's happening: sociological, psychological, and spiritual perspectives on the contemporary drug scene, Am. J. Public Health 59:2092, 1969.
6. Cohen, A. Y.: The journey beyond trips: alternatives to drugs, J. Psychedelic Drugs 3:16-21, 1971.
7. Coleman, J. S.: The adolescent society, Glencoe, N. Y., 1961, The Free Press.
7a. Dohner, V. A.: Alternatives to drugs: a new approach to drug education, J. Drug Educ. 2:3-22, 1972.
8. Finlator, J.: Speech at the National Training Center in Drug Education, San Francisco State College, July, 1970.
9. Friedenberg, E.: Coming of age in America, New York, 1963, Random House, Inc.
10. Gordon, W. C.: The social system of high school, Glencoe, N. Y., 1957, The Free Press.
11. Gottlieb, D., and Ramsey, C.: The American adolescent, Homewood, Ill., 1964, Dorsey Press.
12. MacDonald, D.: Profiles: a caste, a culture, a market, The New Yorker 34:57-94, 1958.
13. Messer, M.: Epilogues: running out of era; some non-pharmacological notes on the psychedelic revolution, J. Psychedelic Drugs 2:157-165, 1968.
14. Parsons, T.: Youth in the context of American society, Daedalus 91:97-123, 1962.
15. Poveda, A. G.: Drug use among the major social types in high school, Unpublished doctoral dissertation, University of California, 1970.
16. Reuter, E.: The education of the adolescent, J. Educ. Sociol. 14:67-68, 1940.
17. Smith, D. E., and Bentel, D. J.: Drug Abuse Information Project, The third, fourth and fifth annual reports to the legislature, San Francisco, 1969-1972, University of California San Francisco Medical Center.
18. Smith, E. A.: American youth culture, Glenco, N. Y., 1962, The Free Press.
19. Soskin, W. F.: Project community and the children of the good life, Unpublished monograph, Berkeley, Calif., 1970.
20. Turner, R.: The social context of ambition, San Francisco, 1964, Chandler Publishing Co.

CHAPTER 4

PHARMACO-LOGICAL ASPECTS OF DRUG ABUSE

Drugs possess the potential for unlocking a variety of mental and physical experiences. They are also catalysts that energize complex body processes. Although we shall discuss the actions of just a few dozen psychoactive (mood-altering) drugs, the number of psychoactive (psychotropic) substances available runs in the thousands, and their effects are many. Under certain conditions, which vary with the individual, psychotogenic drugs can precipitate a pleasant, even a euphoric, experience. Under other conditions, those same drugs may conjure up a veritable nightmare of horror and misery. The obscure passages leading to an understanding of these effects are only partly explored. What is known, however, demands public awareness if our society is to deal effectively with the problems of drug abuse.

PHYSIOLOGICAL ACTION OF DRUGS
The nervous system[5, 16]

To maintain a physiological and biochemical balance in the body, man is equipped with a complex, self-adjusting, and self-regulating biological system. All functions are thus kept within certain tolerance limits. For example, when physical exertion generates excessive heat, the body signals peripheral blood vessels (those close to the surface of the skin) through the nervous system to dilate and allow more blood to circulate and cool the body. When exposed to cold the body conserves heat in the central cavity by restricting peripheral blood flow through constriction of blood vessels.

These self-adjusting characteristics are called homeostasis. The mechanisms that exercise this complex control include the brain, the nervous system, and the endocrine system. Messages about the condition of the body must be transmitted to the brain, processed, and fed back to body centers through the nervous system to adjust conditions that are in imbalance. Such electrical messages are sped along the complex network of the nervous system. Chemical messages are communicated through the bloodstream by the endocrine system; the time of travel and duration of effect may vary from a few seconds to several weeks.

The nervous system may be conceptualized as a fine network of electrical wires (neurons) running throughout the body, along which millions of signals, or messages, pass each second. But where a wire is continuous, nerves are not. Nerve fibers consist of billions of cells, end to end, that almost but do not quite touch each other. There is a gap called the synapse. Nerve cells are long and thin —many hundreds of times longer than their own width. A message, or signal, travels from one end of a nerve cell to the other as an electrical pulse. To move that pulse across the gap to the next nerve, chemicals must be produced to fill the gap and to generate a corresponding electrical pulse in the adjacent nerve. It is these billions of signals across and along nerves that not only regulate our body chemistry but also create for us our whole world of perception and feeling. All of our experiences, thoughts, and emotions are nothing more than electrical activity that occurs in some part of the brain.

Normal nerve functioning depends on the regular manufacture by the body of the nerve chemicals, called nerve transmitters, their release to create an electrical impulse, and their breakdown after achieving the desired effect. The internerve cell gaps where the chemistry of nervous transmission occurs is also the point of chemical action for many psychoactive drugs. Some psychotomimetic drugs have characteristics similar to the nerve transmitters so they can occupy the spaces between the nerves and activate the nerves. Others block the transmitter effect because they occupy but do not activate the receptor site.

The messages that are transmitted through the nervous system must be sorted out and carried to the body organs for action. This is accomplished by the two divisions of the entire nerve structure— the central nervous system (CNS) and the autonomic nervous system (ANS). The CNS is voluntary and comprises the brain, which includes the forebrain, midbrain, hindbrain, and the spinal cord, which is an extension of the brain. The ANS is involuntary and comprises the sympathetic and parasympathetic segments that control visceral functions—heart, blood vessels, glands, abdominal organs, and others.

Encapsulated in the skull and continuing down the back as the spinal chord is the central nervous system. The CNS gathers the myriad items of information coming from stimuli inside and outside the body (all that is heard, seen, and felt), integrates it with information from internal sources, and then sends out messages to all the muscles and glands for action. The CNS "computerizes" what is happening to us and how we react.

A second integrating system is the ANS, which forms a network of nerves along each side of the vertebral column, the spine. The CNS and the ANS work together to perform certain chores; the ANS operates mostly to regulate organ functions and to maintain a stable internal environment. This might be called the "unconscious" nervous system, which maintains our body functions. When we run, without conscious thought, our heart beats faster. When we are cold, we get "goose-bumps" where the hair shafts have been raised to preserve heat. These reactions are controlled by the ANS.

The ANS may be divided into two units —the sympathetic and parasympathetic systems. The first functions principally to mobilize the body for action; the second generally operates to maintain ongoing production of necessary materials via the digestive system.

Mobilizing the body for action is part of a process of stimulation. Forces or pressures both outside and inside the body activate the organs and parts through the nervous and endocrine systems. Body machinery is speeded up and mental alertness is increased. We breathe faster, our heart rate speeds up, and blood flow increases. We may grow flushed, as when angry or excited. Our blood pressure rises and our pupils dilate. Our appetite and other food and waste processing functions are suppressed for the moment. Some of the drugs that we call stimulants, such as cocaine and the amphetamines, produce just these effects on the CNS.

Sometimes, however, we say we are depressed. This is both a state of mind and a physical condition. Drugs called sedative-hypnotics, which are known as central nervous system depressants, act in just this way. Barbiturates and alcohol slow us down. Depressants may lower our body temperature, slow breathing, and decrease blood flow so that we look pale and anemic.

Additional drugs cause a variety of other body reactions through the nervous and endocrine systems. These drugs will be identified later.

Drug effects

The effects of drugs on people are dependent on four factors: individual dose response, biological variability, potency of the drug, and tolerance.

DOSE RESPONSE. A fundamental concept in understanding drug actions is the "dose response curve." This term refers to the fact that, as the amount of a drug in use is changed, there may be a change in the reaction of an individual, which may be shown as a curve on a graph. Generally speaking, the greater the dose, the greater the response. Ranging from a dose that is too weak to achieve any effect on an organism to a lethal dosage, the dose response may be plotted along two axes of a graph, or chart; one axis illustrates the low to high dosage and the other shows the small to great effect. The resulting figure is called the dose response curve. Different dose response curves are influenced by biological variability of individuals, the type and dosage of drug used, and other factors.

Since drug effects result from the collective action of many molecular interactions, the more molecules at the site of a drug's action, the more interactions will take place and the greater will be the effect of the drug. For each type of drug, however, there must be a minimum number of molecules to produce the smallest response; this amount is referred to as the threshold dose. Some drugs may necessitate a large amount of the substance for reaction. Threshold dose refers to the minimum amount of a drug needed to stimulate a bodily reaction. The threshold dose of LSD is 10 to 50 micrograms.

Other dose responses include therapeutic, toxic, or lethal: therapeutic refers to the amount of a drug that will aid in the solution of a medical problem; toxic means that the prescribed dose will have adverse effects on the body; and a lethal dose will result in death.

In contrast, at a certain point the organism may become drug saturated and increasing the dosage or the amount of the drug does not increase the response. The affected system shows maximal response, and additions of the drug have no further effect on it. But as the dosage level is increased beyond saturation for one particular response, new response systems may suddenly be affected. Some biological systems have higher thresholds than do others or are less accessible to the drug. Therefore

to fix an exact dosage for a set response may prove to be both complex and uncertain.

BIOLOGICAL VARIABILITY. In all living organisms there is substantial variability in biochemical response. This is particularly true with ingested drugs. Dose response curves vary widely between persons. Some individuals are generally more sensitive to drugs than others. Some persons will show the desired effect at lower dosage levels and others, equally drug sensitive, will have more bad side effects at the set levels.

Some persons have a much higher drug threshold, which additionally may mean that there is a longer delay before drugs become effective and start to work. Thus a person may continue to increase the dose for a time without feeling any effects, then —rather suddenly—succumb to overdose. Street people call this "OD-ing." Other individuals may "get off" on much smaller dosages and be able to maintain a high with no additional dose reinforcement.

With some drugs, like alcohol, the range between a subthreshold dose (not causing any result) and a lethal dose is very large. With cocaine, an example of the opposite extreme, the dosage range is small. It takes little to cause an effect and very little more to kill.

The *effective dose* is the amount of drug needed to cause a particular reaction or desired response in a certain percentage of persons. The lethal dosage is measured by the percentage of animals that die within a specified period of time. The safety margin is the dose range between an acceptable level of effectiveness and a dose that results in a 1% lethality level among animals.

The wide variability of response in these dosage ranges is not completely understood, but some of the most apparent considerations are the rate of absorption of the drug from the digestive tract and the activity of the drug-metabolizing enzymes in the liver. Dose-response is a complex relationship.

POTENCY. The potency of a drug is determined by the amount that must be given to obtain a particular response; the smaller the amount needed to achieve that result, the more potent the drug. Intrinsic chemical strength, efficiency, and maximum effect are not measures of potency. If the dosage of a drug is increased past the point of maximum therapeutic effect, the drug effect may be prolonged, but the primary result is an added number and degree of undesirable side effects. It may become toxic to the individual. An excessive dose of aspirin, for example, does not stop a headache more efficiently, but rather produces gastric irritation and bleeding if usage is prolonged.

Cumulative effects result from the addition of a second dose before the body has assimilated the first dose. An example of this is alcohol. With this drug, the effects continue to increase as the dosage is increased.

Additive effects of drugs are similar to cumulative effects in that they represent an increase in response corresponding to an increase in dosage. But additive effects result from a combination of drugs acting on the same system. Although small doses of each of several drugs may be taken without adverse effects, together the effect may be the same as a larger dose of a single drug. Alcohol and the barbiturates are drugs that show additive effects; they may be lethal. The depressant effects of both together are more than the latent effect of either drug alone. Unfortunately the result of this little understood phenomenon is that many people unwittingly kill themselves.

TOLERANCE. Tolerance refers to a condition in which repeated administration of a drug results in a gradually diminishing effect. That is, the second dose does not produce as much effect as the first; the third dose is less effective than the second, and so on. To achieve the same result as previously, the dose must be increased. But increasing the dose also increases the unwanted side effects. With some drugs, like LSD, tolerance builds

very rapidly; with others, such as morphine and barbiturates, it builds more slowly; with alcohol, tolerance is minimal. We learn how to handle higher and higher alcohol dosage levels, but we still get just as drunk. Marijuana, in quite the opposite way, seems to lead to sensitization rather than to tolerance. The more one smokes, the less one needs in order to get high.

Tolerance can occur with both stimulants and depressants, but physical dependence occurs only with depressants.

CATEGORIZING DRUGS

A drug is any substance other than food that, by its chemical or physical nature, alters structure or function in the living organism. Drugs can be classified in many ways, ranging from their chemical structure to their effects on biochemical, physiological, or behavioral systems, as well as according to their social uses. Physicians, pharmacologists, chemists, lawyers, psychologists, and users all have drug classification schemes that serve their special purposes. As Ray has explained:

A compound such as an amphetamine might be categorized as an anti-appetite agent by many physicians since it reduces food intake for a period of time. It might be classed as a phenylethylamine by a pharmacologist since its basic structure is a phenyl ring with an ethyl group and an amine attached. The chemist wastes no time and says flat-out that amphetamine is 2-amino-1-phenyl propane. To the lawyer amphetamine may only be a drug of abuse falling in Schedule II of the 1970 federal drug law, while the psychologist may simply say that it is a stimulant.*

Drugs may be called by (1) their trade name—the manufacturer's own brand name, (2) their generic name—the pharmaceutical name of the compound, (3) their chemical name, (4) their pharmacological category, and (5) their common or street name. Thus we have Benzedrine (made by Smith, Kline & French Laboratories), generically *dl*-amphetamine, chem-

---

*From Ray, O.: Drugs, society, and human behavior, St. Louis, 1972, The C. V. Mosby Co.

ically 1-phenyl-2-aminopropane, which is catalogued as a CNS stimulant and is called a stimulant or an "upper."

The molecular structure of a compound is described by its chemical name. This description is based on the rules of organic chemistry for naming compounds. Because of the complexity of chemical names, their use is usually confined to the laboratory.

The American Medical Association, the American Pharmaceutical Association, the U. S. Pharmacopeial Convention, Inc., and the Food and Drug Administration have standardized the legal names of drugs. These are official generic (or nonproprietary) names and, because of their simplicity, are much more commonly used than chemical names. A generic name is assigned to a specific chemical structure and may be freely used by anyone (is in the public domain) and is not protected by a trademark.

The brand name is the registered title of a drug and identifies a particular manufacturer and formulation of a generic product. Companies try to make brand names as simple and meaningful in terms of use as possible. These names are protected by trademarks.

Drugs that are available only on prescription are called legend drugs. Each prescribed drug must be marked with the legend "CAUTION: Federal law prohibits dispensing without prescription."

We have developed a classification that we hope will be useful to educators and still maintain pharmacological accuracy. Drugs are grouped into socially meaningful clusters of compounds. (See p. 94.)

The first category is the central nervous system *stimulants*; they increase functional activity. These stimulants include the amphetamines (Table 4-1), amphetamine-like drugs, or equivalents, as well as the so-called minor stimulants, the social drugs nicotine (Table 4-3) and caffeine (Table 4-4). Cocaine (Table 4-2), used as a local anesthetic, is included in this group. Although cocaine is also an analgesic (pain killer), its primary activity is one of stimulation.

Caffeine in coffee, tea, and cola drinks, and nicotine in tobacco are natural or "organic" stimulants; the amphetamines are synthetic stimulants. Stimulants are identified by their primary effect of excitation of the central nervous system, resulting in behavioral arousal and activation.

The second category is the nervous system *depressants* (Tables 4-5 and 4-6), sometimes known as *sedatives* or sedative-hypnotics. These hypnotic anesthetics induce the opposite physical effects of those produced by stimulants; they have a calming effect. Alcohol, popularly considered a stimulant, is a depressant, as are barbiturates.

There is confusion regarding the classification of marijuana. It is considered by law to be a narcotic; at high doses it has psychedelic properties and therefore people use it for this reason; but pharmacologically it has properties that enable it to be called a sedative-hypnotic. Therefore marijuana has been included at this point but is descriptively discussed later in the chapter. Table 4-7 has been prepared to identify some of its unique characteristics. The main physiological effects of marijuana are disinhibition, euphoria, which is interpreted by the user as a "high," and mild sedation, much the same as alcohol. The case of marijuana illustrates how so often drugs are classified on moral, ethical, political, or legal grounds.

Also included among the depressants are a variety of substances that emit intoxicating vapors—the *inhalants*. Most of these products contain volatile (evaporate into the air) hydrocarbons. Model airplane cement is the most common inhalant.

We have called the third category *psychedelics* (Table 4-8) instead of the more frequent term "hallucinogens." Many of the so-called hallucinogens do not technically cause hallucinations. An hallucination, according to *Dorland's Illustrated Medical Dictionary*, is "a sense perception not founded upon objective reality," such as the hearing of unreal sounds and the seeing of things that are not there. This would be true for some LSD trips, but most experiences with the mind-altering drugs are *distortions* of reality rather than *illusions.*

In the fourth category we place the better known *narcotics* (morphine, heroin) (Table 4-9), all produced from the juice of the opium poppy. The *opiates* are noted for their remarkable properties of sedating, suppressing pain, and unfortunately addicting the repeated user.

The fifth category, *tranquilizers* (Table 4-10), antidepressants, and diverse psychoactive agents, represents a more diverse and mixed collection of substances. They are lumped together rather than distributed through other categories because they possess certain common characteristics, although they are only cousins rather than brothers or sisters.

The tranquilizers and their cousins are all psychotherapeutic agents used in psychiatric medicine. One of the revolutions in pharmacology was the introduction in the early 1950s of the antipsychotic phenothiazine tranquilizers for treatment of the mentally ill. These drugs affected the mind but not the body. They virtually revolutionized the treatment of schizophrenia and made thousands of totally institutionalized mental patients ambulatory and minimally functional in society.

Although it will not be discussed here, our sixth and final major category deals with OTC (over-the-counter) drugs, some of which have already been listed in other categories (Chapter 2). The sixth category includes the mild analgesics, or pain relievers, the sleep aids and sedatives, the mild stimulants (caffeine and nicotine, also mentioned earlier), and the cough suppressants and cold remedies, such as antihistamines. These drugs will be discussed with the categories in which they fall pharmacologically.

CENTRAL NERVOUS SYSTEM STIMULANT DRUGS
Amphetamines[2]

The amphetamines are known to most people as diet or pep pills. Like all psychoactive agents, they exert certain effects on both the peripheral and the central

nervous systems. The peripheral actions of the compounds include an increase in blood pressure, dilation of the pupils, constriction of the blood vessels on such mucosal surfaces as the lips and the lining of the nose, relaxation and dilation of the bronchial muscles of the respiratory tract, relaxation or a spasmodic contraction of the gastrointestinal tract, and a secretion of sparse, thick saliva. The drugs' dilating action on the bronchial passages explains their former use in treating hay fever and asthma.

Although these peripheral actions are both marked and potentially therapeutic, amphetamines are generally employed today only for their more profound stimulative effects on the CNS. Of these, the three most pronounced actions are the suppression of appetite, the elevation of mood, and the forestallment of fatigue. The first property is used medically in the control of weight; the second is employed in the treatment of some forms of psychological depression.

Although amphetamines are now classified as dangerous drugs under state and federal law, over 153,000 pounds of the compounds were obtained through doctors' prescriptions alone during 1968 in the United States. The American pharmaceutical industry advertises the drugs as panaceas for fatigue, boredom, depression, and many other human emotional problems. Some physicians indiscriminately dispense them to their patients. As a result, and despite their high abuse potential, millions of people today ingest amphetamines to induce euphoria. Even low-dosage amphetamine consumption can cause tremulousness, anxiety, drying of the mouth, alteration of sleep habits, and other unpleasant effects.

No fatalities have been recorded as a direct result of high-dose consumption, but these drugs commonly produce restlessness, hypertension, extreme anxiety, impaired judgment, hyperventilation (a state of excessively rapid breathing), hallucinations, and possibly psychosis. Sedatives may be profitably employed in treating acute toxicity, but patients may require isolation

Table 4-1. Amphetamines

BRAND NAME	GENERIC NAME	SLANG NAME	USUAL SINGLE ADULT DOSE	DURA-TION OF ACTION
Benzedrine	Amphetamine sulfate	Bennies, beans, whites, cross tops, truck drivers, cart wheels	2.5-5.0 mg up to 15 mg	4-6 hr
Dexedrine	Dextroamphetamine sulfate	Dex, dexies, oranges, hearts	2.5-5.0 mg up to 15 mg	4-6 hr
Dexamyl	Dexedrine, amobarbital	Christmas trees (spansule form)	2.5-5.0 mg	4-6 hr
Biphetamine-T	d- and dl-Amphetamine	Black beauties	2.5-5.0 mg	4-6 hr
Methedrine, also Desoxyn	Methamphetamine hydrochloride	Meth, crystal, crank, speed	2.5-5.0 mg	4-6 hr
Preludin	Phenmetrazine	Diet pills	2.5-5.0 mg	4-6 hr
Didrex	Benzphetamine		2.5-5.0 mg	4-6 hr
Tenuate	Diethylpropion		2.5-5.0 mg	4-6 hr

Method of administration—Swallowing pills or capsules and intramuscular (I.M.) or intravenous (I.V.) injection

Legitimate medical uses (present and projected)—Treatment of obesity, narcolepsy, fatigue, and depression

Potential for psychological dependence—High

Potential for tolerance leading to increased dosage—Yes

Potential physical dependence—???

Overall potential for abuse—High

Usual short-term effects—CNS stimulants; increased alertness; reduction of fatigue; insomnia; often euphoria

Usual long-term effects—Restlessness; irritability; weight loss; toxic psychosis (mainly paranoid); diversion of energy and money; habituation

Form of legal regulation and control—Available in large amounts by ordinary medical prescription that can be repeatedly refilled or obtained from more than one physician; widely advertised and "detailed" to doctors and pharmacists; other manufacture, sale, or possession prohibited under federal drug abuse and similar state dangerous drug laws; moderate penalties; widespread illicit traffic

and reassurance that they are not suffering heart attacks or losing their sanity.

More serious and increasingly common in this country is *chronic amphetamine toxicity*. The chemicals are not addictive in small doses, but persons who take larger amounts do experience extreme psychological dependence and may even suffer mild physical withdrawal symptoms when deprived of the drugs. Such dependence is complicated by the fact that, as the body develops a tolerance to amphetamines, increasingly larger doses are required to maintain the drug effect. Prolonged high-dose amphetamine consumption often results in physical deterioration and in a toxic psychosis characterized by perceptual alterations, visual and auditory hallucinations, severe depression, and a state that resembles paranoid schizophrenia. It may also lead to organic brain damage and personality change, as studies of amphetamine abusers in Japan seem to reveal.[10]

STREET USE OF AMPHETAMINES. *Speed* is a street name for amphetamines and any number of substances that provide the same CNS stimulation. Although the words "speed" and "Methedrine" were once used synonymously in the San Francisco Bay Area underground, young persons in Haight-Ashbury and elsewhere apply the term "speed" to any stimulant that will bring them up, just as they use the word "downer" to describe alcohol, opiates, barbiturates, and all other depressants. Speed is also referred to on Haight Street as "splash," "uppers," "rhythm," "crank," "meth," and "crystal"; the latter three terms apply particularly to a powdered form of methamphetamine.

The "speed binge" can be divided into an action phase and a reaction phase. During the action phase the user may inject methamphetamine intravenously from one to ten times a day. With each injection he experiences a "flash," which he describes as a "full body orgasm." Between injections the user is euphoric, hyperactive, and hyperexcitable. This action phase may last for several days, during which time the individual does not sleep and rarely eats. It is terminated for a number of reasons. The user may stop voluntarily because of fatigue; he may become confused, paranoid, or panic stricken and stop "shooting"; or he may simply run out of drugs.

Whatever the reason for termination, the action phase is followed by the reaction phase in which the user goes rapidly from a hyperexcitable state to one of extreme exhaustion. The "speed freak" may sleep for 24 to 48 hours and upon awakening eat ravenously. When his food and sleep needs are satisfied, he often enters a prolonged phase of extreme psychological depression. This depression is often so intolerable that he starts another speed binge. The cycle is repeated, leading to even deeper

depression as well as the paranoid-schizophrenic psychoses characteristic of chronic amphetamine toxicity. He may suffer terrifying hallucinations, mistake friends for police officers, and lash out with murderous rage at any real or imagined intrusion. Some users start new runs at this point to escape their depressions; some people inject barbiturates to induce sleep. Other speed freaks should be hospitalized and restrained before they can do physical harm, especially if they were "going up" or "coming down" in crowded places. Reactions, of course, differ with the individual.

Cocaine: new uses of an old drug[22]

Cocaine, called the "champagne" of drugs because of its scarcity, cost, and great euphoric properties, traditionally was abused only in the inner-city ghetto. Recently its widespread usage has developed among both minority groups and middle-class white youth.

Most of the cocaine that comes into the United States is derived from the leaves of the *Erythroxylon coca* tree, which grows mostly in Colombia and the Peruvian Andes. The drug moves northward, through Mexico, is smuggled over the border, and —increasing in value all the time—finally ends up in major cities all around the country.

Although used in medicine as a local anesthetic, cocaine has been described by "coke heads" (users) as having euphoric effects almost indistinguishable from amphetamines. In the Controlled Substances Act it is classified as a Schedule II substance—a drug having a high abuse potential with severe psychic or physical dependence liability. Although the subjective effects of cocaine are generally considered to be more intense and the abuse potential more significant than with the amphetamines,[5] there has been no definite evidence to support this position. An equivalency with amphetamines in terms of effect may be assumed. Stereotyped, repetitious, and compulsive behavior is common with both speed (amphetamines and methamphetamines) and coke (cocaine). Both cocaine and amphetamine users attempt to cope with the tense, "wired" effect of these CNS stimulants by using sedatives and narcotics, including heroin. The mixture of opiates and either cocaine or an amphetamine is known as a "speedball."

Cocaine produces a strong state of psychological excitation involving feelings of euphoria more pronounced than those seen with practically any other psychoactive agent, including heroin. Psychological depression, however, follows this state in a rather short time (30 minutes). This depression is in such marked contrast to the previous pleasurable sensations induced by sniffing and intravenous use of cocaine that users may be motivated to repeat the dose immediately in order to recapture the original state. A cycle may then develop, with the user injecting the drug at short intervals (as little as 10 minutes) in an attempt to maintain a constant euphoric state.

The repeated administration of cocaine tends to increase the severity of excitatory symptoms. Users may become so psychologically excited and agitated that they develop an intense anxiety state with gross paranoid features. In this state, hallucinations are not uncommon, and abnormal sensations induced by cocaine in the peripheral nerves may convince the hyperex-cited user that animals are burrowing under his skin.

BEHAVIORAL ASPECTS OF COCAINE USE. The technique for using cocaine consists of raising the powder to one nostril, closing the other, and sniffing deeply. What follows are 15 to 20 minutes of very pleasurable exhilaration and then several hours of nervousness and depression similar to the aftereffects of amphetamine abuse. Other aftereffects of high-dose cocaine use can include extreme irritability, loss of the sense of heat and cold, tightening of muscles, jerking or convulsions, and finally respiratory arrest and cardiovascular collapse. The last two symptoms, of course, are those of a fatal overdose. Although this has been relatively rare up to now, it becomes increasingly likely because of the various adulterants contained in most of the cocaine presently available.

Cocaine addicts have been reported to use up to 10 grams in a single day, a potentially lethal dose. Yet after a long period of abstinence (which is not accompanied by notable severe symptoms) the user may be able to tolerate the same dosage levels that have been reached gradually during an earlier period of chronic use.

Pharmacological investigations have failed to uncover any characteristic withdrawal syndrome after the cessation of chronic cocaine use. In a strict sense, then,

Table 4-2. Cocaine

GENERIC NAME	SLANG NAME	USUAL SINGLE ADULT DOSE	METHOD OF ADMINISTRATION	DURATION OF ACTION
Cocaine	"C," candy, coke, flake, snow, dust, Bernice, Charlie	Variable	Swallowing pills, I.M. or I.V. injection, sniffing	4 hr

Legitimate medical uses (present and projected)—Anesthesia of the eyes and throat
Potential for psychological dependence—High
Potential for tolerance leading to increased dosage—Yes
Potential for physical dependence—No
Usual short-term effects—CNS stimulant; increased alertness; reduction of fatigue; loss of appetite; insomnia; often euphoria
Usual long-term effects—Extreme irritability; toxic psychosis
Form of legal regulation and control—Same as narcotics

the drug cannot be termed addictive. However, a pattern of psychological dependence on cocaine can develop with a number of adverse consequences for the user.

Cigarettes and tobacco[24, 26]

Until the twentieth century cigarettes were neither a major article of consumption nor an important threat to public health. Individuals used tobacco mainly in the form of cigars, chewing tobacco, pipe tobacco, and snuff. In 1900 only about 4 billion cigarettes were manufactured; more than 580 billion are now being manufactured annually.

As a major article of consumption, then, cigarettes are relatively new. Their sudden enormous increase in popularity came about because they provide the user with many gratifications that other forms of tobacco do not. They are convenient, relatively clean, can be smoked quickly, and are mild enough so that they can be inhaled. Smoking cigarettes, however, can rather quickly become addictive for many persons—addictive in the sense of building up a psychological dependence and perhaps, for some individuals, a physiological dependence as well.

CHARACTERIZATION OF THE TOBACCO HABIT (NICOTINE). Of the known chemical substances present in tobacco and tobacco smoke, only nicotine has been given serious pharmacological consideration in relationship to the tobacco habit. Lewin stated, "The decisive factor in the effects of tobacco, desired or undesired, is nicotine . . . and it matters little whether it passes directly into the organism or is smoked."[11]

Nicotine is present in tobacco in significant amounts, is absorbed readily using all routes of administration, and exerts detectable pharmacological effects on many organs and structures, including the nervous system. The physical and psychological effects of smoking vary. Wilder summarized the literature by noting ". . . observations that cigarette smoking obviously serves a dual purpose: it will mostly pick us up when we are tired or depressed and will relax and sedate us when we are tense and excited."[27]

Smokers and users of tobacco in other forms usually develop some degree of dependence on the practice. At the extreme point significant emotional disturbances occur if the smoker is deprived of its use. The evidence indicates this dependence to be psychogenic in origin. In medical and scientific terminology the practice should be labeled habituation to distinguish it clearly from addiction, since the biological effects of tobacco, coffee and other caffeine-containing beverages, betel nut chewing, and such, are not comparable to those produced by morphine, alcohol, barbiturates, and many other potent, addicting drugs.

Psychogenic dependence is the common denominator of all drug habits and the primary drive that leads to initiation of and relapse to chronic drug use or abuse. Although a pharmacological drive is necessary, it does not need to be a strong one or to produce profound subjective effects for habituation to the use of the crude material to become a pattern of life. Besides tobacco, the use of caffeine in coffee, tea, and cocoa is the best example of psychogenic dependence in the American culture.

Scientists became suspicious of cigarettes as a cause of illness and death as early as the 1930s. One of the reasons they were concerned was an increase in the incidence of lung cancer. In 1930 fewer than 3,000 Americans were listed as dying from this disease; by the 1950s, this number had grown to 18,000 annually. In 1965 the number was approximately 50,000. In 1962 a damning indictment of smoking was issued by Great Britain's Royal College of Physicians of London and in 1964 this was followed by the report of the U. S. Surgeon General's Advisory Committee on Smoking and Health. Its conclusions were summed up in the sentence: "Cigarette smoking is a health hazard of sufficient importance in the United States to warrant appropriate remedial action."[25]

In the years since publication of that report an unprecedented amount of pertinent research has been completed, continued, or initiated in this country and abroad under the sponsorship of governments, universities, industrial groups, and other agencies. No evidence has been revealed that questions the conclusions of the 1964 report. The health consequences of smoking can, in the judgment of the Public Health Service, be summarized as follows[26]:

1. Cigarette smokers have substantially higher rates of death and disability than their nonsmoking counterparts in the population. This means that cigarette smokers tend to die at earlier ages and experience more days of disability than comparable nonsmokers.

2. A substantial portion of earlier deaths and excess disability would not have occurred if those affected had never smoked.

3. If it were not for cigarette smoking, practically none of the earlier deaths from lung cancer would have occurred; this is also true for a substantial portion of the earlier deaths from chronic bronchopulmonary diseases (commonly diagnosed as chronic bronchitis, or pulmonary emphysema, or both) and a portion of the earlier deaths of cardiovascular origin. Excess disability from chronic pulmonary and cardiovascular diseases would also be decreased.

4. The cessation or appreciable reduction of cigarette smoking could delay or avert a substantial portion of the deaths that occur from lung cancer, a substantial portion of the earlier deaths, and a substantial portion of the excess disability of cardiovascular origin.

Smoking-related diseases have been defined by the Public Health Service as cancer of the lung, larynx, lip, oral cavity, esophagus, bladder, and other urinary organs; chronic bronchitis and emphysema; arteriosclerotic heart disease, including coronary artery disease; specified noncoronary cardiovascular disease; cirrhosis of the liver; and ulcer of the stomach. These are the diseases, for whatever cause or reason, that occur significantly more often among cigarette smokers than among nonsmokers.

Figs. 1 to 5 are adapted from studies by the American Cancer Society, based on 3,764,571 person-years of experience and 43,221 deaths occurring in 1,003,229 persons.[17]

As may be seen, death rates within each age group and for every cause of death listed are greater for smokers than for those who never smoked regularly. The differences are striking for the 65 to 79 year age group, and for those diseases most clearly associated with cigarettes, such as lung cancer and coronary heart disease. A study reported at the 1967 World Conference on Smoking and Health by E. C. Hammond[7] of the American Cancer Society shows that important differences exist between the life expectancies of smokers and nonsmokers, and also between the life expectancies of heavy smokers and light smokers.

The 25-year-old man who never smoked regularly can expect to live 48.6 more years, which is 4.6 years longer than the man who smokes 1 to 9 cigarettes a day; 5.5 years longer than the 10 to 19 cigarette-a-day smoker; 6.2 years longer than the 20 to 39 cigarette-a-day smoker; and 8.3 years longer than the heavy smoker who uses two packs a day or more. Similar differences exist at other ages.

A high correlation exists between death rates and exposure to cigarettes, whether the exposure is expressed as the number smoked, the degree of inhalation, or the time elapsed since smoking began. Increased consumption of cigarettes is accompanied by higher death rates for both men and women. Among men 45 to 54 years of age, the death rate for those smoking 10 to 19 cigarettes per day is more than double that of nonsmokers. In all age groups from 45 to 74, a greater number of cigarettes smoked per day is consistently associated with a higher death rate.

A pronounced increase in both male and female mortality from lung cancer and

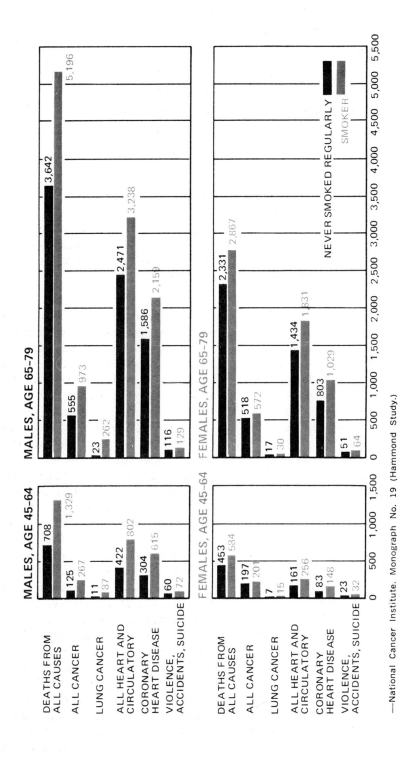

—National Cancer Institute. Monograph No. 19 (Hammond Study.)

FIG. 1

Death rates of smokers versus those of nonsmokers. (From U. S. Department of Health, Education and Welfare: Chart book on smoking, tobacco, and health, Washington, D. C., 1969, Government Printing Office.)

Age	Never Smoked Regularly	Cigarette Smokers By Daily Amount			
		1-9	10-19	20-39	40+
25	48.6	44.0	43.1	42.4	40.3
30	43.9	39.3	38.4	37.8	35.8
35	39.2	34.7	33.8	33.2	31.3
40	34.5	30.2	29.3	28.7	26.9
45	30.0	25.9	25.0	24.4	23.0
50	25.6	21.8	21.0	20.5	19.3
55	21.4	17.9	17.4	17.0	16.0
60	17.6	14.5	14.1	13.7	13.2
65	14.1	11.3	11.2	11.0	10.7

FIG. 2
Estimated life expectancy of males age 25 to age 65 years in the United States. (Data from the American Cancer Society's epidemiology study of over 1 million men and women; reprinted from Proceedings, world conference on smoking and health, New York, 1967, National Interagency Council on Smoking and Health.)

coronary heart disease corresponds with an increase in the number of cigarettes smoked. The death rates associated with cigarettes smoked per day provide one of the most striking examples of the dangers of smoking for women. Although those who smoke 1 to 9 cigarettes per day have death rates comparable to those who do not smoke at all, those who smoke more than this show consistently higher death rates. In the case of women in the 45 to 54 age group, the death rate for two-pack-plus smokers is almost double that of those who do not smoke.

There is also a consistent upward trend in the death rate in relation to the depth of inhalation. Those who inhale deeply have death rates more than double the rates of those who do not smoke.

The longer a person smokes, the greater the risk of early death. Men who began smoking before they were 15 years old have death rates about double those of men who started in their 30s.

In 1967 the Public Health Service issued a report based on interviews with members of 42,000 households.[15] The findings show that a man who smokes more than two packs of cigarettes a day is away from work half again as many days as the non-smoker, spends more than half again as many days ill in bed, and suffers nearly twice as many days of restricted activity. Comparisons between women smokers and nonsmokers yield similar, or worse, statistics.

Chronic conditions are those illnesses that last for a long time—months, even years. In the Health Interview Survey, any illness that began more than 2 months before the time of the interview was considered a chronic condition. Both men and women cigarette smokers reported more cases of chronic illness than those who never smoked. More chronic illness existed among the heavy smokers than among those who smoked fewer cigarettes or had never smoked at all. Smokers also reported more chronic conditions per person.

When data from the Public Health Service's report are interpreted to reflect the entire population, some indication may be gained of the magnitude of the total economic burden associated with cigarette smoking. For the nation as a whole, in the year the survey was made, there were 399 million workdays lost because of illness. A total of 77 million of these days, or 19%,

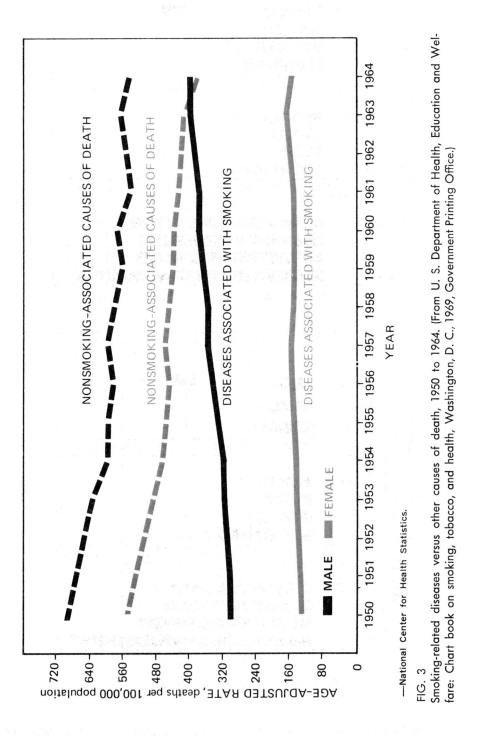

—National Center for Health Statistics.

FIG. 3

Smoking-related diseases versus other causes of death, 1950 to 1964. (From U. S. Department of Health, Education and Welfare: Chart book on smoking, tobacco, and health, Washington, D. C., 1969, Government Printing Office.)

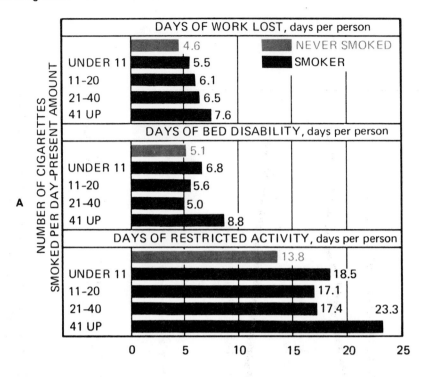

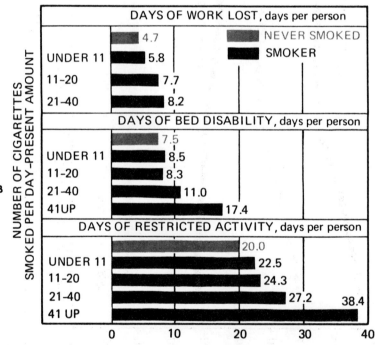

—National Center for Health Statistics.
Chart shows age-adjusted number of days per person per year,
1965.

FIG. 4
Smoking and disability. **A,** Males. **B,** Females. (From U. S. Department of Health, Education and Welfare: Chart book on smoking, tobacco, and health, Washington, D. C., 1969, Government Printing Office.)

Table 4-3. Nicotine

SOURCE	SLANG NAME	USUAL SINGLE ADULT DOSE	METHOD OF ADMINISTRATION	DURATION OF ACTION
Cigarettes	Fags, smokes, coffin nails	1-2	Smoking and/or inhalation	1-2 hr
Cigars		1		
Pipe tobacco		1 pipe		
Chewing tobacco		1 "chaw"	Chewing plug or loose tobacco	1-2 hr
Snuff		1 pinch	Sniffing or chewing	1-2 hr

Legitimate medical uses (present and projected)—None (used as insecticide)
Potential for psychological dependence—High
Potential for tolerance leading to increased dosage—Yes
Potential for physical dependence—No
Overall potential for abuse—Moderate; potential for compulsive use high
Usual short-term effects—CNS stimulant; relaxation or distraction in the process of smoking
Usual long-term effects—Lung and other cancer; heart and blood vessel disease; cough; habituation; diversion of energy and money; air pollution; fire
Form of legal regulation and control—Available but advertising banned on TV; minimal regulation by age, content, and labeling of packages

Table 4-4. Caffeine

SOURCE	SLANG NAME	USUAL SINGLE ADULT DOSE	METHOD OF ADMINISTRATION	DURATION OF ACTION
Coffee	Java	1-2 cups	Swallowing liquid	2-4 hr
Tea		1-2 cups		
Colas		16 oz		
No-Doz and similar products		5 mg	Swallowing pill	2-4 hr

Legitimate medical uses (present and projected)—Mild stimulant; treatment of some forms of coma
Potential for psychological dependence—Moderate
Potential for tolerance leading to increased dosage—Yes
Potential for physical dependence—No
Overall potential for abuse—None
Usual short-term effects—CNS stimulant; increased alertness; reduction of fatigue
Usual long-term effects—Sometimes insomnia or restlessness; habituation
Forms of legal regulation and control—Available and advertised without limit; no regulation for children or adults

were excess in the sense that they would not have been lost if persons who smoked cigarettes had the same rate of illness as those who have never smoked. Using this same method of analysis, there were 88 million excess sick days related to smoking, or 10% of the national total, and 306 million excess days of restricted activity, or 13% of the national total.

The loss of human life, of productive time, and of wages, and the costs of hospitalization and medical care that are a consequence of smoking are appalling. It seems indeed ironic that the current great popular concern over drug abuse should be focused to such a small extent on the use of tobacco and its almost incalculable injury to our society.

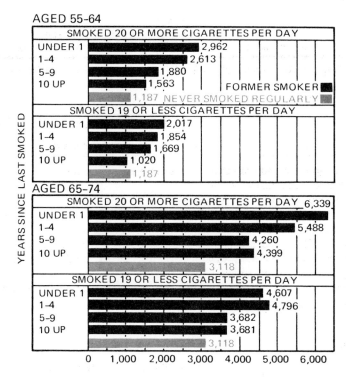

—National Cancer Institute. (Hammond Study.) Rates per 100,000 person-years.

FIG. 5
Death rates of males who were formerly smokers. (From U. S. Department of Health, Education and Welfare: Chart book on smoking, tobacco, and health, Washington, D. C., 1969, Government Printing Office.)

CAFFEINE. Caffeine (Table 4-4) is a substance found in popular beverages, including coffee, tea, chocolate, and cola drinks. It is also an ingredient used in several over-the-counter drug products. It is commonly used and readily available for purchase.

CENTRAL NERVOUS SYSTEM DEPRESSANT (SEDATIVE-HYPNOTIC) DRUGS[23]

Barbiturates

Barbiturates are nonselective CNS depressants because they can dull all excitable areas of the nervous system. They should be considered sedative-hypnotic–general anesthetics because graded doses of the compounds produce the same four stages of depression as seen with alcohol.

True barbiturates are derivatives of barbituric acid, a condensation of malonic acid and urea that was prepared by a German chemist in 1864. Over 2500 barbiturates were subsequently synthesized, 50 of which are in wide use today. Many barbiturate preparations are available commercially and approximately 300 tons of barbiturates are consumed in the United States each year.

Barbiturate intoxication is similar to that obtained with ethyl alcohol and involves motor impairment, dizziness, difficulty in thinking, slowness of comprehension and speech, emotional instability, and exaggeration of basic personality traits. Barbiturate use may lead to serious accidents because these drugs can impair coordination and performance while deluding users, as amphetamines do, into thinking their abilities are increased.

Many users become dependent on sedatives and sleeping pills and develop a tolerance that forces them to increase their dosages, resulting in severe physical symptoms when the drugs are withdrawn. As with amphetamines, the distinction between therapeutic use and the abuse of these chemicals is frequently blurred. The oral ingestion of a 100-milligram dose of short-acting barbiturates usually causes sleep if the drugs are used in an appropriate setting with that purpose in mind. But if sleep is neither achieved nor intended, individuals may show signs of euphoria and confusion, resembling alcohol intoxication. Many individuals take sleeping pills to induce this intoxication. The disinhibition characteristic of acute toxicity usually leads to sluggishness, slurring of speech, increased emotional lability, and nystagmus, an involuntary oscillation of the eyeballs. Excessive irritability and moroseness are also common, as are hostility and paranoia.

In large doses these drugs produce a state of deep anesthesia that is followed by respiratory and circulatory depression. Such overdosage is particularly frequent in those whose toxic confusion leads them to forget the extent of the drugs' effects and in those who use the chemicals singly and in combination to commit suicide. Acute barbiturate toxicity and overdosage have become major problems in most urban centers. Twenty percent of these attempted suicides succeed. Barbiturates and their equivalents in combination with alcohol figured in the deaths of Marilyn Monroe, Judy Garland, Alan Ladd, and a host of other celebrities.

An equally grave problem is chronic barbiturate toxicity, which resembles alcoholism. Its symptoms consist of extensive neurological damage, greatly impaired coordination and emotional lability, skin rashes, and malnutrition.

Repeated intoxication with the barbiturates produces true physical dependence, and abrupt withdrawal of the drug from a dependent individual can produce severe and dangerous symptoms. The abstinence syndrome varies considerably, depending on the duration and magnitude of barbiturate use. Some patients experience only weakness and anxiety; others exhibit hallucinations, delirium, and convulsions. Some patients who have seizures may then show improvement, but more than half of those reported proceed to a psychotic reaction that mimics the delirium tremens of withdrawal from alcohol or the paranoid-schizophrenic reaction associated with amphetamines. Anxiety mounts during this period, and frightening dreams may be followed by insomnia. Visual hallucinations, disorientation of time and space, and agitation may then lead to exhaustion, cardiovascular collapse, and death.

Acute and chronic barbiturate toxicity has increased dramatically at all levels of our society. Many of the barbiturate compounds are classified as dangerous drugs, the illicit manufacture, sale, or possession of which is prohibited by state and federal law. Yet they are widely available by ordinary medical prescriptions, which can be refilled repeatedly or obtained from more than one physician.

Alcohol[2]

The favorite drug of abuse in American society and the most toxic chemical is ethyl alcohol. This drug, which results from the fermentation by yeast of a sugar, was known to Paleolithic man and has been employed as an intoxicant by almost every culture in human history. It is classified pharmacologically as a nonselective CNS depressant because it can depress all excitable areas of the nervous system. Several experts have noted that alcohol should be considered a sedative-hypnotic–general anesthetic because graded doses of the compound produce the four discernible stages of CNS depression. These include sedation and the relief of anxiety; disinhibition, possible excitation, and hypnosis; general anesthesia; and complete respiratory and vasomotor depression.

Small amounts of alcohol also increase

Table 4-5. Barbiturates and barbiturate-like drugs

BRAND NAME	GENERIC NAME	SLANG NAME	USUAL SINGLE ADULT DOSE	DURATION OF ACTION
Amytal*	Amobarbital		15-100 mg tablets	4 hr
Amytal sodium*	Amobarbital sodium	Blues, blue dolls, blue bullets, blue devils, blue heavens	65 mg and 0.2 Gm capsules	4 hr
Alurate*	Aprobarbital		500 mg, 2.5 Gm, and 5.0 Gm ampules	4 hr
Brevital*	Methohexital sodium		500 mg, 2.5 Gm, and 5.0 Gm ampules	1 hr
Butisol sodium*	Butabarbital sodium		$\frac{1}{4}$-$\frac{1}{2}$ gr tablets and capsules	5 hr
Sombucaps*	Hexobarbital		250 mg tablets	1 hr
Gemonil*	Metharbital		100 mg tablets	5 hr
Nembutal*	Pentobarbital sodium	Nembies, yellows, yellow jackets, yellow bullets, yellow dolls	30-100 mg capsules	3 hr
Mebaral*	Mephobarbital		30-500 mg capsules	5 hr
Pentothal sodium*	Thiopental sodium		Ampules in various doses	1 hr
Tuinal*	50% Amytal sodium and 50% Seconal sodium	Double trouble, rainbows, blues and reds	$\frac{3}{4}$, 1$\frac{1}{2}$ and 3 gr capsules	4 hr
Seconal*	Secobarbital	Reds, red dolls, red devils, red bullets, red birds, pinks, seggy, seccy	$\frac{1}{2}$-1$\frac{1}{2}$ gr capsules	3 hr
Luminal*	Phenobarbital	Phennies	Varies	5 hr
Doriden	Glutethimide	Goofers	500 mg tablets and capsules	5 hr
Equanil	Meprobamate		400 mg tablets	4 hr
Miltown	Meprobamate		400 mg tablets	4 hr.
Librium	Chlordiazepoxide		5-10 mg capsules	5 hr
Somnos, Noctec, Lorinal	Chloral hydrate	Coral	500 mg capsules	5 hr

Method of administration—Swallowing capsules or tablets and I.V. injection
Legitimate medical uses (present and projected)—Treatment of insomnia and tension; induction of anesthesia
Potential for psychological dependence—High
Potential for tolerance leading to increased dosage—Yes

*Indicates true barbiturates.

Table 4-5. Barbiturates and barbiturate-like drugs—cont'd

Potential for physical dependence—Yes

Overall potential for abuse—High

Usual short term effects—CNS depressants; sleep induction; relaxation and sedation; sometimes euphoria; drowsiness; impaired judgment, reaction time, coordination, and emotional control; relief of anxiety-tension; muscle relaxation

Usual long-term effects—Irritability; weight loss; addiction with severe withdrawal illness (like D.T.'s); diversion of energy and money; habituation and addiction

Form of legal regulation and control—Available in large amounts by ordinary medical prescription that can be repeatedly refilled or obtained from more than one physician; widely advertised and "detailed" to doctors and pharmacists; other manufacture, sale and/or possession prohibited under federal drug abuse and similar state dangerous drug laws; moderate penalties; widespread illicit traffic.

---

the respiratory rate. This effect has led many to assume that the chemical has stimulative properties. More pronounced are alcohol's central effects, which are initially experienced as a lessening of inhibitions and a characteristic feeling of euphoria and self-confidence. These reactions are followed by increased sedation and an impairment of physical coordination. At a blood concentration of 0.2%, alcohol makes most drinkers comatose. If the drug's concentration increases further, drinkers may die of acute alcohol toxicity as their respiratory and cardiovascular functions are arrested.

Acute alcohol toxicity is quite common in our society and most urban communities must deal with dozens if not hundreds of cases daily. Even more common is chronic alcohol toxicity, or alcoholism, which ranks as one of America's most serious health problems. Alcohol is both psychologically habituating and physically addicting in high doses and can cause organic brain damage and personality change. It also has one of the highest abuse potentials known to man. Of the over 80 million people in the United States who use alcohol, at least 7 million are estimated to be alcoholics.

Alcoholism has no easy cure. Chronic alcohol toxicity is rightfully regarded as a behavioral disorder in our society and has been explained by a number of theories emphasizing that alcoholics, like other drug abusers, are dependent people who have difficulty forming interpersonal relationships and handling stress. Studies made of alcoholics reveal that most of them have parents who themselves abuse alcohol. But no one has found a completely effective way to help alcoholics.

Psychotherapy is one method of help, but few alcoholics have the motivation necessary to undergo complete treatment. Alcoholics Anonymous, which bases its appeal on group confession and catharsis and attempts to replace the alcoholic's dependence on drink with a dependence on the organization, is only moderately successful with confirmed drinkers. Drugs are also employed to treat alcoholism, especially in Europe. Some doctors have administered hallucinogenic agents to alcoholics, hoping to give them intense spiritual experiences. Others have used Antabuse, which inhibits the complete metabolism of alcohol and thereby floods the body with its toxic by-product, acetaldehyde. This agent is likely to deter people from drinking when it is taken with alcohol, but its use is generally restricted to highly motivated spree drinkers who are willing to risk suffering the sickening effects of Antabuse if they try some alcoholic beverage. Unmotivated alcoholics rarely request drug or nondrug treatment. In fact, they may not admit to having personal problems and may want to see abusers of other chemicals jailed.

Alcohol is socially sanctioned and retailed in this country at an annual rate of over 350 million gallons of hard liquor, in addition to several billion gallons of beer and wine. The companies responsible for this supply have never advertised the debilitating effects of their products, and few Americans even realize that alcohol is a dangerous drug. Fewer still are aware that alcohol is more harmful than heroin to the mind and body.

Because of this public ignorance, most people take their first drink in a social setting under pressure from their peer group to do so. Alcohol is used primarily as a social and medicinal agent, by adult and young Americans alike. Some drink beer

and wine at gatherings and rarely become intoxicated. Yet others begin to abuse the compound by drinking only to deaden their senses and cope with anxiety.

Inhalants—volatile hydrocarbons[9]

Substitutes for drugs that pose a serious threat to the health of young people are the halogenated and unhalogenated hydrocarbons found in petroleum distillates, including cleaning fluids, model airplane cement or glue, and carbon tetrachloride. If inhaled in sufficient quantities, these compounds can exert a sedative-hypnotic–general anesthetic effect by depressing the CNS. Their use can lead to liver damage, bronchial inflammation, chemical pneumonia, and potentially fatal illnesses such as aplastic anemia, a condition characterized by bone marrow depression with subsequent reduction in certain blood cells that results in tachycardia, excessive bleeding, and lassitude. The hydrocarbons can

Table 4-6. Alcohol

ALCOHOL SOURCE	GENERIC NAME	SLANG NAME	USUAL SINGLE ADULT DOSE	DURATION OF ACTION
Beer, ale, malt liquor	Ethyl alcohol	Suds, brew	12 oz	2-4 hr
Wine, champagne, wine drinks	Ethyl alcohol	Grapes	12 oz	2-4 hr
Whiskey, gin, "hard liquors," liqueurs	Ethyl alcohol	Booze, hard stuff, juice, hooch	1-1½ oz	2-4 hr
Wood or grain alcohol	Ethyl alcohol	Gut rot		

Method of administration—Swallowing liquid
Legitimate medical uses (present and projected)—Rare; sometimes used as a sedative for tension
Potential for psychological dependence—High
Potential for tolerance leading to increased dosage—Yes
Potential for physical dependence—Yes
Usual short-term effects—CNS depressant; relaxation (sedation); sometimes euphoria; impaired judgment, reaction time, coordination, and emotional control; frequent aggressive behavior; driving accidents
Usual long-term effects—Diversion of energy and money from creative and productive pursuits; habituation; possible obesity with chronic excessive use; irreversible damage to brain and liver; addiction with severe withdrawal illness (D.T.s)
Form of legal regulation and control—Available and advertised without limitation in many forms; only minimal regulation by age (18 or 21 years), hours of sale, location, taxation, driving laws, and ban on bootlegging; minimal penalties

also cause physical addiction, as evidenced by those recorded cases in which people have become addicted to gasoline.

GLUE. The most common glue sniffed is a form of plastic cement prepared for the construction of model airplanes and purchasable in most drug, novelty, hobby, and grocery stores throughout the country. Plastic cements vary in chemical composition, depending on the formula used by the manufacturer, but all contain volatile organic solvents such as hexane, benzene, acetone, toluene, carbon tetrachloride, chloroform, ethyl alcohol, and ethyl acetate—substances considered in industry to be relatively safe when inhaled in low vapor concentrations, but toxic when inhaled over a period of time in high concentrations.

The glue sniffer first experiences a tingling sensation in his head, a lightness, and an exhilaration known to him as a jag. If he continues to inhale the substance, he will experience a state comparable to alcoholic intoxication. He will feel dazed and may repeatedly lose contact with reality in periods he refers to as "blackouts" or "flash-outs." His speech will likely be slurred and his walk unsteady. If inhalation is prolonged after this stage, he may become disoriented, commit irresponsible acts, and ultimately lapse into a coma.

The solvents present in glue cause a temporary depression of the CNS and affect the mucous membranes of the nose and the throat, causing them to become swollen and inflamed. There is also evidence of the development of temporary blood abnormalities, including anemia, among glue sniffers.

Certain of the organic solvents present in plastic cements are capable of damaging the brain, of affecting liver and kidney action, and of interfering with the blood-forming function of the bone marrow. There is evidence that habitual glue sniffing leads to the development of tolerance and psychic dependence. Whereas one tube may suffice to produce a mild intoxication in the beginner, it may take several tubes to produce comparable results in the experienced sniffer who has developed a tolerance. In one case a 19-year-old youth admitted sniffing from 15 to 20 tubes a day. In the words of another glue sniffer, "Once you start, it's hard to lay off; you shake and shiver at night when you're off the stuff."

The extent of the practice of glue sniffing is difficult to determine. Glue is not classified as a narcotic or as a dangerous drug. Hence the statistics on narcotic and drug arrests do not include those of glue sniffing. Children who sniff glue to the point of acute intoxication are typically from lower socioeconomic groups and often show symptoms of emotional disturbance. Many youngsters apparently inhale fumes from paint, paint thinner, and lacquer, in addition to glue.

GASOLINE. The hydrocarbons in gasoline, notably butane, hexane, and pentane, affect the CNS, causing symptoms of intoxication that range from mild to severe, depending on the susceptibility of the individual and the volume of gasoline fumes inhaled. Mild symptoms resemble those of alcoholic intoxication; in extreme cases, delirium, coma, seizures, and death may occur. Symptoms appear rapidly and are exaggerated upon exposure to fresh air. The practice of gasoline sniffing in the cases reported appears not to have resulted in permanent organic damage, although some potentially serious initial symptoms were found. It is likely that prolonged sniffing can lead to permanent brain impairment.

Nonintoxicating solvents probably will eventually replace those now present in airplane glue. It is not likely, however, that the intoxicating volatile solvents will ever be eliminated from gasoline, kerosene, lighter fluid, paint and lacquer thinners, marking pencil fluid, and innumerable similar substances available to the general public. Injudicious use of any of these substances is potentially dangerous; deliberate misuse is an ever-present possibility.

Marijuana[18, 22]

Among all the current drugs of abuse, marijuana has drawn the most public attention. Endless controversy, much hysteria, and much plain misinformation have revolved around this substance. Nevertheless, the facts are largely known. The essential pharmacological and sociological findings arrived at by armies of researchers demonstrate that marijuana, by and large, is a mild drug.

Many persons believe that marijuana is, in fact, like LSD. We disagree with this grouping and concur with Dr. Frederick Meyers[14] that it is properly classified as a sedative-hypnotic. The closest pharmacological equivalent to marijuana would not be LSD or heroin, but rather nitrous oxide, or laughing gas.

Dr. Bertram Brown, director of the National Institute of Mental Health, has summed up the findings: "For the bulk of smokers, marijuana does not seem to be harmful—but it may be for some."[3] He cautioned that information is still unclear, especially about the long-term effects of marijuana.

The purpose of our discussion here is to try to provide for the health educator as reasonable an answer as can currently be framed to the question: what are the health implications of marijuana use? As we examine the drug in its various natural and synthetic forms, however, it becomes evident that this deceptively simple question is highly complex. Marijuana is not a single, simple substance of uniform type. It consists of varying mixtures of different parts of the plant *Cannabis sativa,* with psychoactive properties ranging from virtually nonexistent to decidedly hallucinogenic in its stronger forms and larger doses. Unfortunately much of the discussion in lay and scientific forums ignores this basic and important fact. The experience of most Americans has been limited to the widespread, relatively infrequent use of a weak form of marijuana. Early research dealing with the drug is inevitably faulted by the fact that it is difficult to be certain just what the potency of the material involved was, what the dose level was, and in what form the drug was consumed.

PATTERNS OF USE. The extent of marijuana use by schoolchildren has rapidly increased over the last few years. It is virtually certain that in some high schools and colleges a majority of students have tried it. By the end of 1970 about one college student in seven was using marijuana on a weekly or more frequent basis. A recent national survey indicated that 42% of the student population responding from cities of over 500,000 population have used marijuana. Although comparable data are not available for non-school attending youth, there is reason to believe that levels of use are at least comparable and for school dropouts are probably higher.

SUBJECTIVE EFFECTS. As is true of other drugs, the effects of marijuana are related to its amount and strength. There is general agreement that at the usual levels of social usage the typical subjective effects are alteration of time and space perception; sense of euphoria, relaxation, well-being, and disinhibition. At higher doses dulling of attention, fragmentation of thought, impaired immediate memory, an altered sense of identity, exaggerated laughter, and increased suggestibility may appear. Other less common effects are dizziness, a feeling of lightness, nausea, and hunger. At very high doses more pronounced thought distortions may occur, including a disrupted sense of one's own body, a sense of personal unreality, visual distortions, sometimes hallucinations, and paranoid thinking. The more marked distortions of reality or psychotic-like symptoms become increasingly common if the dosage used becomes extremely large.

In addition to the amount of the drug that is consumed, the set and setting of use are important factors in determining marijuana's subjective effects. Set refers to the attitudes, mood, expectations, and beliefs that the individual brings to the drug-using experience. A situation in which the individual is depressed or apprehensive about the drug's effects differs markedly from one in which the user is more sanguine and looks forward to the drug experience with eager anticipation. The degree of personality integration, psychological rigidity, and the presence or absence of psychopathology are all important contributors to one's subjective reactions to marijuana or other psychoactive drugs.

All of these psychological aspects also play a role in what is often referred to as the "placebo effect," that is, the response to the substance based not on its pharmacological activity but on the totality of *expectations* brought about by the set and setting of use.

Toxicity. We define a toxic reaction to marijuana as any effect that may result in physical or psychological damage unpleasant to the user, or that produces significant interference with his socioeconomic functioning. We specifically exclude the relaxed euphoric effect the user describes as being high or stoned from the definition of a toxic reaction. There is no evidence of physical damage with the use of marijuana, except for occasional cases of bronchial irritation in individuals who use the drug excessively, that is, from 2 to 10 marijuana cigarettes ("joints") per day. Almost all of these individuals also smoke tobacco cigarettes, so that it is impossible to determine the relative contribution of cannabis smoke inhalation to bronchial irritation.

Acute adverse psychological reactions do occur periodically with marijuana, as with any psychoactive drug. Their incidence ranged from approximately 8% in our study of college freshmen at a midwestern major university to 33% in the heavy drug-using population seen at the Haight-Ashbury Free Clinic.* By far the vast

majority of these reactions consisted of nausea, some dizziness, and occasional confusion. With experienced marijuana-using groups who had adopted the drug as their primary social agent, these adverse reactions were similar to those resulting from drinking too much alcohol. There was very little evidence of residual hangover or depression after these acute marijuana reactions. They seemed, in fact, to be less destructive to the individual than a similar alcohol overdose experience. This lack of "morning after" adversity seemed to be a significant factor in the adoption of marijuana as a social drug by many of the individuals interviewed. For example, one young adult said, "The reason I switched from alcohol to marijuana is that you don't have a hangover."

Effects of long-term chronic use and amotivational syndrome. Certain individuals, primarily adolescents and young adults, attempting to deal with both internal and external psychosocial confusion, use marijuana at high doses on a long-term daily basis. They smoke from 2 to 10 marijuana cigarettes a day and, as a consequence of excessive sedation and chronic intoxication, there is substantial deterioration in their performance and psychosocial functioning. Virtually all of these patients had adjustment problems prior to their heavy use of marijuana. When excessive use of marijuana was stopped, changes produced by the drug were, for the most part, reversed. Unfortunately the public and various professionals, in their determination to overstate the case against marijuana, have implied that even the experimental or social use of marijuana produces an impairment in motivation. It is the logical equivalent of saying that everybody who uses alcohol is an alcoholic. Nationally published statistics indicate that out of every 20 persons who use alcohol, one abuses it. Our data indicate that out of every 100 who use marijuana, only one abuses it. Thus, as marijuana is used in the United States, it has a lower potential for chronic abuse than does alcohol, the

---

*The primary setting for this research has been the Haight-Ashbury Free Clinic, which has seen over 100,000 patients in 4 years of operation, 79% of whom have had varying degrees of experience with marijuana. In addition, we have conducted surveys and interviews in the San Francisco Bay Area, with primary emphasis on high school students and students from selected college campuses across the country.

social drug whose patterns of use most closely approximate those of cannabis.

The vast majority of individuals who use marijuana do not develop psychopathology, nor do they perceive acute adverse marijuana reactions as a medically treatable condition. There is no question that we should have great concern about the use of psychoactive drugs by adolescents as they go through their crucial stages of adolescent maturation. However, it has not been demonstrated that making the use or the user of marijuana criminal will in any way prevent adolescent experimentation. In fact, it appears that more often than not just the opposite has happened. Our war on marijuana and the dishonest "killer weed" educational philosophy have tended to glamorize the drug and created the mystery of forbidden fruit in growing numbers of adolescents. Educators must recognize that the primary reasons most youth begin experimenting with marijuana are curiosity and peer-group pressure, and that by making the drug criminal we have helped create drug subcultures that are quite appealing to alienated youths who are going through identity crises.

BIRTH DEFECTS. A basic concern with any drug substance coming into wide use is the possibility that it may affect fetal mortality or fetal development (may be teratogenic) in such a way as to bring about abnormal offspring of pregnant users. It may also conceivably affect unborn generations by causing chromosomal changes (may be mutagenic) that persistently alter the genetic heritage. There is no evidence to suggest that marijuana use in humans affects fetal development. Despite the absence of such evidence, it is obviously unwise for anyone to use any drug of unknown teratogenic or mutagenic properties during the child-bearing years. Use during pregnancy is particularly unwise.

RELATIONSHIP TO DRUGS OF HIGHER ABUSE POTENTIAL. It is often stated that the primary reason to maintain the criminality of marijuana use in American society is that marijuana leads to more serious drugs of abuse, particularly to heroin. The origin of this argument seems to have come from heroin addicts who stated that they started on their road to heroin through the use of marijuana. One wonders why they picked marijuana as the first step of the often quoted stepping stone theory, when in fact studies have indicated that over 90% of those heroin addicts had their first psychoactive drug experience with alcohol.

It is generally conceded that marijuana use does not necessarily lead directly to the use of other drugs. On a worldwide basis there is little evidence of a progression from the use of marijuana to that of opiates or hallucinogens. However, those who study the use of other drug substances note that those drugs chosen may be popular among the peer group. These may include stronger hallucinogens, amphetamines, and the opiates. Although it is true that a high percentage of heroin addicts have used marijuana as well, most marijuana users both here and abroad do not appear to be attracted to the use of heroin.

What is the relationship between the marijuana and heroin? It is primarily a social relationship, in that marijuana and heroin coexist in the same criminal culture. Naive young marijuana users must enter into this criminal subculture to purchase their drug and are very often exposed to a variety of pressures to experiment with drugs of higher abuse potential. The only relationship of marijuana to heroin with a nonpsychopathological user is by association, and that link could be broken by removing marijuana from this criminal subculture.

SUMMARY AND SOCIAL POLICY RECOMMENDATIONS. The current policy of making the use of marijuana a criminal act has contributed substantially to the toxicity of the drug and has forged the only link between marijuana and drugs of higher abuse potential. However, despite the destructive contributions of existing social policy, it appears that marijuana, at worst, is no more harmful to the individual or to

Table 4-7. *Cannabis sativa**

CANNABIS DRUG TERMS	LOCATION	POTENCY	METHOD OF ADMINISTRATION	DURA- TION OF ACTION	ACTUAL CONTENT
Charas	India	Most potent form	Usually smoked	6-8 hr	Unadulterated resin
Ganja	India	Quite potent	Usually smoked; sometimes con- fections, bever- ages	4-6 hr	Top leaves, some resin
Bhang	India	Low potency	Usually beverage	4 hr	Top leaves, unculti- vated inferior plant
Hashish	Middle East	Most potent form	Usually smoked	6-8 hr	Powdered sifted form of Charas
Kif	N. Africa (Mor- occo)	Usually highly potent	Usually smoked	4-8 hr	Variable preparations
Dagga	S. Africa	Usually highly potent	Usually smoked	4-8 hr	Variable preparations
Marijuana	U. S., Latin America	Potent	Usually smoked	4-6 hr	Leaves, flowers, mostly dried

Legitimate medical uses (present and projected)—Treatment of depression, tensions, loss of appetite, sexual maladjustment, and narcotic addiction
Potential for psychological dependence—Moderate
Potential for tolerance leading to increased dosage—No
Potential for physical dependence—No
Overall potential for abuse—Moderate
Usual short-term effects—Relaxation; euphoria; increased appetite; some alteration of time percep- tion; possible impairment of judgment and coordination; probably CNS depressant; vomiting as side effect
Usual long-term effects—Usually none; possible diversion of energy and money
Forms of legal regulation and control—Unavailable (although permissible) for ordinary medical pre- scription; possession, sale, and cultivation prohibited by state and federal narcotic or marijuana laws; severe penalties; extensive illicit traffic

*Pharmacologically not a narcotic; obtained from flowering tops of female plants and resinous excretion from clusters and upper leaves.

society than its evolving social equivalent— alcohol. In addition, those of the emerging young generation who have adopted mari- juana as their new social drug perceive the marijuana laws to be arbitrary, hypo- critical, and discriminatory. Dishonest pre- sentations about marijuana have severely damaged the credibility of much-needed drug education and drug abuse prevention programs. The current policy of maintain- ing the criminality of marijuana use has contributed to the alienation of many

young persons from traditional social insti- tutions as well as from our system of gov- ernment.

PSYCHEDELIC DRUGS (HALLUCINOGENS)[19, 21]

The psychedelics are a number of com- pounds from different pharmacological classes that are able to disorganize nerve and ego functions and thereby induce a toxic psychosis or acute brain syndrome. The word "hallucinogenic" is most commonly used to describe their effects, but the terms "psychotomimetic" and "psychedelic" have also been employed.

The mechanism by which the psychedelics work is not clearly understood. Their effects are mostly indirect, releasing or inhibiting particular chemicals that in turn alter the transmission of neural impulses in the brain. This has an effect on the brain's screening and organizational processes.

LSD

LSD was isolated from the ergot fungus of rye in 1938 by Albert Hofmann, a chemist at Sandoz Laboratories in Switzerland. In 1943 he accidentally ingested some of the substance and took the first acid trip in history, which he later vividly described. LSD is an extremely potent substance, causing pharmacological effects in doses as low as 10 to 30 micrograms. By weight it is about 3 million times more potent than crude marijuana. It is postulated that LSD may act by blocking the effect of serotonin at the nerve synapse, but as yet its actual mechanism of action is unknown. As little as 100 micrograms of LSD can produce stimulative and hallucinogenic effects that are 300 times more powerful than those resulting from a much larger dose of mescaline.

As a sympathomimetic agent, LSD causes an increase in blood pressure, a dilation of the pupils, a relaxation of the bronchial muscles, and other peripheral actions. These effects last as long as 12 hours and serve as the prototype of the hallucinogenic or psychedelic drug experience.

Individuals under the influence of LSD may have vivid perceptual alterations, including illusions or auditory perceptions of musical compositions never before heard. Frequently there is a crossing of one sensory perception into another, called synesthesia. Music may be seen as colored lights, a pin prick becomes an explosion of light, or twinkling lights become tinkling bells.

Users rarely lose consciousness and can often recollect the entire content of their experience. But their thinking, their capacity for making judgments, and their coordination are likely to be impaired. Thoughts seem to move much faster during the hallucinogenic intoxication than they do under normal consciousness, and they appear in neither a logical nor a casual way. Phenomena that are usually perceived as being opposite can therefore suddenly coexist; good and bad may appear equal, and persons may feel light and heavy at the same moment. Most important, space and time orientations are frequently distorted much more than they are with marijuana, allowing past and future to merge with the present. Those using the drugs seem to desire this state of timelessness more than any other effect and prefer to avoid anything that detracts from its intensity. Many other individuals who take or have taken the drugs feel that they experience a form of protoplasmic consciousness that is so pronounced that they seem to lose their personal identities. This can produce the feeling of being an integral part of the universe, of being in union with the rest of the world and with whatever power exists behind the world, and of finally resolving all dichotomies. A feeling of rapture or ecstasy may occur. Conversely, the experience may result in paranoia, sensations of death or nonexistence, and the panic reactions of a bad trip.

Such dissolution can cause a terrifying feeling of unreality, with messianic delusions. It can also result in depression and periodic flashbacks or perceptual distortions months after the hallucinogenic experience. In certain cases individuals can be so panicked by these adverse reactions that they renounce the drug. In others, the toxic hallucinogenic psychoses seem to trigger more permanent disturbances. Adverse reactions are greatly dependent on the mood of the individual, the setting in which the drug is taken, and the availability of someone to give support and reality orientation to avert bad trips.

Table 4-8. Psychedelics

BRAND OR COMMON NAME	GENERIC NAME OR COMPONENTS	SLANG NAME	ADULT DOSE USUAL SINGLE	DURA- TION OF ACTION
LSD	d-Lysergic acid diethyla- mide	"A," acid	100 μg or greater	12 hr
Psilocybin		Magic mushroom	25 mg	8 hr
DET	Diethyltryptamine		0.7 mg/kg	
DMT	N,N-Dimethyltryptamine	The businessman's trip	0.7 mg/kg	½-2 hr
MDA	2,3-Methylenedioxyam- phetamine		100 mg	12 hr
STP	2,5-Dimethoxy-4-methyl- amphetamine	Serenity, tranquility, and peace	3.2-10.0 mg	6-24 hr
Peyote	Mescaline	Cactus	½-¾ oz or 6-12 buttons, 500- 800 mg	14 hr
Ditran, JB 329	N-Ethyl-3-piperidyl phe- nylcyclopentylglyco- late			
Sernyl (PCP)	Phencyclidine	Peace pill		
THC*	Tetrahydrocannabinol	Synthetic grass, "THC"		
K2,* "THC," hog	Benactyzine, Sernyl, vari- ous barbiturates			
Morning glory seeds	LSD-like components		300-400 seeds	
Baby wood rose seeds	Lysergic acid monoethyl- amide	Woodies	10-18 seeds	
Sominex†	Contains atropine-like compound			

Method of administration—Chewing plant; swallowing liquid, capsules, and pills; I.M. or I.V. injection
Legitimate medical uses (present and projected)—Experimental study of mind and brain function; treat-ment of alcoholism, neurosis, psychosis, psychosomatic disorders, and vomiting
Potential for psychological dependence—Minimal
Potential for tolerance leading to increased dosage—Yes (rare)
Potential for physical dependence—No
Overall potential for abuse—Moderate
Usual short-term effects—Production of visual imagery; increased sensory awareness; anxiety; nausea; impaired coordination; sometimes consciousness expansion
Usual long-term effects—Usually none; sometimes precipitates or intensifies an already existing psy-chosis; more commonly can produce a panic reaction when person is improperly prepared
Form of legal regulation and control—Available only to a few medical researchers or to members of the Native American Church; other manufacture, sale, or possession prohibited by state dangerous drug laws or federal drug laws; moderate to severe penalties, extensive illicit traffic

*Synthetically produced marijuana is presently being used in research in various parts of the country and supposedly is being sold on the streets. Preliminary analysis of samples of the "THC" being sold on the streets show it to be benactyzine, Sernyl, or a combination of several barbiturates. Sernyl was encountered in December 1967 in the form of the "peace pill." Market for this veterinary anesthetic was virtually destroyed in Haight-Ashbury by a one-page flier published by the clinic explaining its composition and lack of treatment. Now it and benactyzine are coming back under the names of Hog, THC, and K2. Presently no true THC is being sold on the street.
†Use of Sominex is currently on the rise. When used in dangerously high doses, hallucinations will occur. These are caused by the scopolamine found in Sominex. Sominex overdose should be treated in the same manner as an overdose of scopolamine, that being use of Librium and chloral hydrate.

Long-term LSD aftereffects may be seen, such as a recurrence of drug-related symptoms with anxiety or a paranoid feeling at times of stress. These are commonly called flashbacks and generally fade away as the use of hallucinogens is discontinued. There have been many reports concerning the potential of LSD to cause chromosomal breaks, perhaps leading to birth defects, but as yet this is unproved.

NARCOTIC DRUGS[8]

The natural alkaloids of opium and their derivatives are cassified pharmacologically as CNS modifiers because they manifest both depressant and excitory effects on the nervous system. They are categorized also as narcotics because they can induce sleep, and as narcotic analgesics because they are employed for the relief of pain.

Opium and heroin

Morphine, codeine, and some 20 other alkaloids occur naturally in the seed pods of the opium poppy, *Papaver somniferum,* which is indigenous to Asia Minor. The alkaloids are extracted from a gum that is exuded from the plants and then is used directly or modified to produce such semisynthetic derivatives as dihydromorphinone hydrochloride (Dilaudid) and dihydrohydroxycodeinone (Percodan) or converted by a simple and illegal process into heroin, which is approximately twice as potent as morphine in its central effects and is known chemically as diacetylmorphine.

The natural alkaloids and their equivalents have marked peripheral actions, the most immediately noticeable is a constriction of the pupils to pinpoint size. The drugs suppress coughing, cause a warm, flushed skin because of their dilating effect on surface blood vessels, and depress respiration and the heart rate in large doses. They also depress the secretion of gastric acid and liver bile, decrease urine flow, and reduce the propulsive contractions of the intestines, exerting a constipating effect.

More pronounced is the opiates' mixed stimulative and depressant effect on the CNS. Their essential central effect is to relieve pain not by blocking impulse transmission in the nervous system, but by altering the perception and psychological reaction to pain. This analgesia occurs before and often without sleep when the chemicals are administered in small or moderate doses, that is, in amounts from 5 to 10 milligrams. Pain is relieved regardless of its origin and intensity, and euphoria is frequently achieved.

Narcotics, more than any other drugs, can suppress those instinctual drives that usually motivate people to assuage hunger, seek sexual gratification, and respond to provocation with anger. They thus produce a state of drive satiation and a feeling of nurturance that is comparable to that enjoyed by fortunate children in early infancy. These compounds do not induce the sense of protoplasmic consciousness associated with hallucinogens, the general depression of barbiturates, the general stimulation of amphetamines, or the delirium of such parasympatholytic agents as atropine. But if taken intravenously, narcotics bring about an orgasmic rush that is as powerful as that of amphetamines. This feeling is followed by a toxic numbness and insulation that one addict has described as "death without permanence—life without pain."

The greatest danger from prolonged use or abuse of the opiates is the psychological dependence and physical addiction that occur because the drugs alter the body's chemistry in such a way that normal metabolic functioning becomes impossible if they are withdrawn. Two hundred thousand Americans were estimated to be addicted to legal and illegal narcotics in 1969. The number now may be as high as 500,000.

Experimental narcotics use usually begins by smoking opium, sniffing or snorting heroin, or taking heroin and other compounds orally. Users may proceed from this point to skin popping, in which they inject the drugs under the skin. The next step is intravenous injection, or "mainlining," which is alleged to be desirable both because of the attendant rush and because of the self-feeding implications of the needle. Most users are known as junkies at this point in their addiction. Others consider themselves "chippers," or occasional users, and insist, perhaps euphemistically, that they can regulate their consumption through self-control.

Such occasional use is complicated by the fact that tolerance to the effects of narcotics develops more rapidly and to a much greater extent than tolerance to other drugs. Persons given repeated and progressively larger doses over a 6- to 8-week period are soon able to tolerate many multiples of the original dose and may consume as much as 300 milligrams of morphine or heroin in several doses each day. In this process they develop a cross-tolerance to other narcotics.

For most addicts, then, the acquisition of opiates becomes an extremely expensive procedure. A kilogram of morphine costing $350 in Vietnam or Turkey is worth more than $250,000 after it is converted into heroin, passed through upper-level distributors, and sold on the street in fifteen-cent ($15) and quarter ($25) balloons or glassine bags containing from 300 to 400 milligrams of white or brown powder. The 30 to 40 milligrams of heroin in these containers is generally mixed with procaine, quinine, or milk sugar. Because of the small percentage of heroin (East coast heroin, 5% to 10%; West coast heroin, 3% to 5%) in its composition, many addicts develop such a tolerance to street smack that they are soon shooting from 3 to 15 quarter bags a day. Most become trapped in an addictive pattern that leads them to depend on opiate dealers, who are called connections, or pushers, as they might depend on a doctor for medical care. The addicts develop hustling skills to pay for their medication and engage in such criminal practices as petty theft, forgery, prostitution, and burglary.

Assuming that each of the 200,000 narcotics addicts in the United States had a $100-a-day habit, the total cost to society from their thefts, robberies, and related offenses exceeded $6 billion in 1969. This figure included relatively few crimes of violence, for opiate addicts are characteristically unaggressive, especially while stoned. Unlike amphetamines, barbiturates, and alcohol, narcotics per se seem to inhibit aggression; it is the need for them, rather than their pharmacological action, that motivates the user to criminality. The drugs also have few debilitating effects on the mind and body, so that addicts should be able to live as long as nonaddicts. The fact that they do not is related less to the chronic action of narcotics than to the drugs' illegality and to the dangers that accompany their abusers' lifestyle.

These dangers are comparable to, although more intense than, those associated with all underground drugs. Narcotics addicts run a regular risk of being poisoned if they have untrustworthy connections. They stand a good chance of being beaten up or arrested by the police or of being burned by competitors when they try to cop, or acquire, chemicals. They are subject to malnutrition because they rarely eat while intoxicated. They often overlook their physical condition because of the analgesia they experience from opiates. They are exposed to the high disease rates of their environment and are particularly prone to such problems as abscesses, septicemia, tetanus, bacterial infections, and serum hepatitis from unclean needles. They may die from acute opiate toxicity following an overdose. Overdose difficulties are sometimes related to impurities in street heroin, but are caused most often by uncommonly pure preparations that impose too great a demand on the user's constantly fluctuating tolerance.

The character and severity of withdrawal symptoms depend on several factors, including the kind and amount of opiates taken, the interval between doses, the duration of usage, the tolerance developed, and the health and personality of the patient involved. In cases of morphine or heroin addiction, withdrawal symptoms usually occur 6 or more hours after the final dose and persist for 48 hours or longer, the duration being shorter and more intense in the case of methadone.

The first withdrawal symptoms are anxiety and hyperexcitability; these occur shortly before the time of the next scheduled dose. Excessive yawning, sweating, tearfulness, and rhinorrhea, or nasal discharge begin at this point and may lead to a restless sleep known as the "yen," from which patients awake even more anxious than before. Their pupils then dilate widely, the hair on their skin stands up in a gooseflesh pattern, and the skin becomes cold, resembling that of a plucked turkey. This condition accounts for the term "cold turkey," applied to any form of abrupt or nonmedically assisted withdrawal.

Contractions may pass over the stomach a few hours after the onset of cold turkey, causing an explosive vomiting. Abdominal pain also increases as the intestines contract and the previously constipated bowels are suddenly voided. Weakness becomes prominent, the heart rate is elevated, and marked chilliness alternating with skin flushes and sweating may occur. So may the muscle spasms and kicking motions that are the basis of the often heard expression "kicking the habit." Convulsions and delirium tremens, however, do not occur.

As these conditions persist, patients usually become emaciated and dehydrated because they cannot eat or drink during withdrawal. They may improve, but they remain weak and often suffer from lingering diarrhea. These and other symptoms will disappear if narcotics are administered, so physicians often use methadone to ease the pain and remission rate of withdrawal.

Methadone—a chemical approach to heroin addiction[12, 13]

Methadone is a long-acting, orally administered narcotic possessing chemical characteristics that provide a blockage for the effects of heroin as well as eliminating the addicts' narcotic hunger. It compensates for the chemical imbalance created by long-term heroin usage.

Despite the fact that the use of methadone is substituting one drug dependency for another, experts are convinced that no other presently available therapy offers comparable promise for the many thousands of heroin addicts who are seeking help. The American Medical Association endorses methadone as the drug of choice for heroin withdrawal and detoxification.

The technique of methadone maintenance was developed and used with great success in New York by Dr. Vincent Dole and Dr. Marie Nyswander.[4] They have reported a heroin-free, crime-free, success rate of over 83% with 3000 hard-core addicts. Methadone has proved effective with some persons who had been addicted as long as 10 years and who had failed with other treatments.

The effectiveness of methadone as a type of immunization against further heroin usage results from its ability to block the euphoriant effects of heroin and to eliminate the craving for the opiate without heroin's deleterious physical and mental effects. Given as a tablet or predissolved in orange juice, the drug allows the patient to function with neither sedation nor euphoria, and with no impairment of vigilance, reaction time, or intellectual processes. This effect is specific for opiate-type drugs and does not help patients using other psychoactive drugs such as barbiturates, amphetamines, hallucinogens, or alcohol.

The dosage of methadone required by a patient to avoid abstinence symptoms during the initial treatment phase depends on how much heroin or other opiates he has been taking. Once on a regular methadone schedule, he returns to the hospital or clinic for a daily dose. He leaves a daily urine specimen for drug analysis. In many programs, supplementary social services such as vocational and social counseling are made available to him. The patient will continue receiving his daily dose as long as the attending physician considers it necessary. Social adjust-

Table 4-9. Narcotics

BRAND OR COMMON NAME	GENERIC NAME	SLANG NAME	USUAL SINGLE ADULT DOSE	METHOD OF ADMINISTRATION	DURA-TION OF ACTION
Opiates					
Opium		"O," op	1-2 "pipes" per single evening	Smoking, inhalation	5 hr
Heroin		"H," horse, Harry, hairy, joy power, smack, skag, junk, shit, jive	Spoon, bag, paper, or balloon of 5%-10% heroin	I.M. or I.V. injection	4 hr
Analgesics					
Dilaudid	Hydromorphone hydrochloride		2 mg	Swallowing pill, I.M. or I.V. injection	4 hr
Morphine	Morphine sulfate	Miss Emma, white stuff, MS	15 mg	Swallowing pill, I.M. or I.V. injection or subcutaneously	4 hr
Codeine	Codeine sulfate	Fours	30-65 mg	Swallowing pill, I.M. or I.V. injection	4 hr
Percodan	Oxycodone		1 tablet	Swallowing tablet	4 hr
Demerol hydrochloride	Meperidine hydrochloride		50-100 mg	Swallowing pill, I.M. or I.V. injection	4 hr
Dolophine hydrochloride	Methadone hydrochloride		5-10 mg	Swallowing pill, I.M. or I.V. injection	4 hr
Cough syrups Romilar, Robitussin A-C, terpin hydrate elixir, terpin hydrate with codeine, Cheracol, Hycodan			2-4 oz for euphoria; however, not recommended; 1 oz for cough	Swallowing liquid	2-4 hr

Legitimate medical uses (present and projected)—Treatment of severe pain, diarrhea, and cough; prevention of withdrawal symptoms

Potential for psychological dependence—High

Potential for tolerance leading to increased dosage—Yes

Potential for physical dependence—Yes

Overall potential for abuse—High

Usual short-term effects—CNS depressants; sedation; euphoria; relief of pain; impaired intellectual functioning and coordination

Usual long-term effects—Constipation; loss of weight and appetite; temporary impotency or sterility; habituation and addiction with unpleasant and painful withdrawal illness

Form of legal regulation and control—Available by special narcotics medical prescriptions; some (except opiates) available by ordinary prescription or over the counter; other manufacture, sale, or possession prohibited under state and federal narcotics laws; severe penalties; extensive illicit traffic ment and rehabilitation over a long period of time should permit the addict eventually to become drug-free. The advantages of administering a stabilization dose of methadone are that the patient has to receive only one dose daily, he feels no need to supplement the dose with heroin, he feels no narcotic hunger or euphoria, and he is able to work at a socially useful job or to go to school.

Narcotic antagonists[7]

A technique is now being tested to implant narcotic antagonists under the skin of the user. A narcotic antagonist is any drug such as nalorphine (Nalline) that antagonizes or blocks the effects of any narcotic. Such chemicals occupy sites in the brain cells and stop the action of heroin. If a narcotic user later takes a fix, he will feel no high. Research is being conducted on "second generation" antagonists that can be embedded in body tissue and released slowly and constantly over a period of days or weeks.

Investigation also is being carried on to develop viable immunization not only to heroin but to a variety of drugs of abuse. By coupling a psychoactive chemical molecule with certain proteins it may be possible to prepare vaccines whose action with respect to a specific drug or to a wide range of substances would be similar to a vaccination against measles. The body would release antibodies to destroy the drug before it acted in the brain centers.

NONCHEMICAL TREATMENT APPROACHES TO ADDICTION[1]

Groups for addicts, such as Synanon, that use no drugs are generally opposed to methadone (and other chemical blocking agents), which they claim are chemical crutches to carry a drug-dependent individual along without his having to deal with the inner person who craves such drugs. Despite the fact that methadone programs have high success rates, those of a more psychotherapeutic bent insist on changing the user's drug-using style of life, social environment, and ways of dealing with himself and others by nondrug means.

Many drug treatment specialists are convinced that Synanon and Synanon-like groups are the solution to drug addiction. Such programs typically offer a living-in community, such as "The Family" at Mendocino State Hospital in California. Treatment specialists often are ex-users themselves who insist on embarassingly frank personal intercommunications. Within the therapeutic community, there is intense verbal attacking of personal habits and character traits that are considered "drug oriented." To treat means to focus as a group on the habits, traits, and emotions that drive the addict to drugs.

Such "reality" type therapy is considered to reach the underlying motivational level that creates the need, the weakness, for drugs. Therapeutic communities have sprung up all over the United States and have become a major treatment modality, along with methadone. Unfortunately these projects usually receive very little financial support and are severely limited in capacity to handle the thousands of new, young addicts who are being created every week.

TRANQUILIZERS AND ANTIDEPRESSANT DRUGS

Tranquilizers are drugs useful in medicine for the treatment of people with psychosis. There are periodic cases of acute overdose and rare cases of chronic abuse.

Antidepressants are substances used by psychiatrists in the treatment of individuals with depression. There are occasional episodes of chronic abuse and overdose.

OVER-THE-COUNTER DRUGS

The discussion of these drugs will be found in Chapters 1 and 2. For more detailed information obtain the latest edition of *Handbook of Non-Prescription Drugs* by contacting:

American Pharmaceutical Association, 2215 Constitution Avenue, N. W., Washington, D. C. 20037.

Table 4-10. Tranquilizers

BRAND NAME	GENERIC NAME	USUAL SINGLE ADULT DOSE*	DURATION OF ACTION
Thorazine	Chlorpromazine hydrochloride	10-25 mg	4-6 hr
Compazine	Prochlorperazine dimaleate	10 mg	4-6 hr
Stelazine	Trifluoperazine dihydrochloride	2 mg	4-6 hr
Serpasil	Reserpine	1 mg	4-6 hr

Method of administration—Swallowing pill or liquid and sometimes I.M. and I.V. injection

Legitimate medical uses (present and projected)—Treatment of anxiety, tension, alcoholism, neurosis, psychosis, psychosomatic disorders, and vomiting

Potential for psychological dependence—Minimal

Potential for tolerance leading to increased dosage—No

Potential for physical dependence—No

Overall potential for abuse—Minimal

Usual short-term effects—Selective CNS depressants; relaxation, relief of anxiety-tension; suppression of hallucinations or delusions; improved functioning

Usual long-term effects—Sometimes drowsiness, dryness of mouth, blurring of vision, skin rash, tremor; occasionally jaundice, agranulocytosis

Form of legal regulation and control—Same as for the barbiturates except not usually included under the special federal or state drug law; negligible illicit traffic

*Institutional dose often greater.

Table 4-11. Antidepressants

BRAND NAME	GENERIC NAME	SLANG NAME	USUAL SINGLE ADULT DOSE	DURATION OF ACTION
Ritalin	Methylphenidate	Mood elevators, psychic energizers	10 mg	4-6 hr
Tofranil	Imipramine hydrochloride	Mood elevators	25 mg	4-6 hr
Flavil	Dibenzapine	Mood elevators	10 mg	4-6 hr
Nardil	Phenelzine		15 mg	4-6 hr
Parnate	Tranylcypromine		10 mg	4-6 hr

Method of administration—Swallowing pills or capsules

Legitimate medical uses (present and projected)—Treatment of moderate to severe depression

Potential for psychological dependence—Minimal

Potential for tolerance leading to increased dosage—No

Potential for physical dependence—No

Overall potential for abuse—Minimal

Usual short-term effects—Relief of depression (elevation of mood); stimulation

Form of legal regulation and control—Same as tranquilizers

GENERAL PHARMACOLOGICAL CLASSIFICATION OF DRUGS
CNS STIMULANTS

Amphetamines (Table 4-1)
 Benzedrine—amphetamine sulfate
 Dexedrine—dextroamphetamine sulfate
 Methedrine—methamphetamine hydrochloride
 Desoxyn—methamphetamine hydrochloride
Amphetamine equivalents
 Ritalin—methylphenidate
 Preludin—phenmetrazine
Cocaine—coca (Table 4-2)
Minor stimulants
 Nicotine—tobacco (Table 4-3)
 Caffeine—coffee, tea, cocoa, cola drinks (Table 4-4)

CNS DEPRESSANTS—SEDATIVE-HYPNOTICS, GENERAL ANESTHETICS

Alcohol—alcoholic beverages (Table 4-6)
Barbiturates (Table 4-5)
 Amytal—amobarbital
 Nembutal—pentobarbital sodium
 Luminal—phenobarbital
 Seconal—secobarbital
 Doriden—glutethimide
 Pentothal sodium—thiopental sodium
Nonbarbiturates (Table 4-5)
 Librium-chlordiazepoxide
 Valium—diazepam
 Miltown—meprobamate
Cannabis sativa—marijuana (Table 4-7)
Volatile hydrocarbons—inhalants, deliriants
 airplane glue—toluene
 gasoline, kerosine, paint thinner
Sernyl (PCP)—phencyclidine
Hog—benactyzine; antipsychotic tranquilizer
Nitrous oxide

PSYCHEDELICS—HALLUCINOGENS (Table 4-8)

Psychomimetic amphetamines—DOM, MDA, MMDA
LSD—d-lysergic acid diethylamide
DMT—mescaline-like substance
Peyote—mescaline
Psilocybin—magic mushrooms

NARCOTICS (Table 4-9)

Opiates—natural derivatives
 Opium
 Morphine
Semisynthetic opiates
 Heroin (from morphine)
 Codeine
 Dilaudid
Synthetic opiates
 Dolophine—methadone
 Demerol—meperidine

TRANQUILIZERS, ANTIDEPRESSANTS, AND MISCELLANEOUS PSYCHOACTIVE AGENTS (Table 4-10)

Major tranquilizers—phenothiazines
 Thorazine—chlorpromazine hydrochloride
 Compazine—prochlorperazine dimaleate
 Stelazine—trifluoperazine
Antidepressants (Table 4-11)
 Flavil
 Includes the category of amphetamines
Miscellaneous
 Atropine—scopolamine in Sominex, Compoz
 Jimson Weed—Dr. Shifman's Asmodor
 Loco-weed—atropine-like compound

OVER-THE-COUNTER DRUGS— NONPRESCRIPTION (Chapter 2)

Nonnarcotic analgesics (pain relief)
 Salicylates (in aspirin)
 Phenacetin
Sleep aids—Sominex
Sedatives—Compoz
Stimulants—NoDoz (caffeine)
Cold remedies—Contac, antihistamines

References

1. Batiste, C. G., and Yablonsky, L.: Synanon: a therapeutic life style, Calif. Med. 114:90-94, 1971.
2. Blum, R. H., et al.: Society and drugs, San Francisco, 1969, Jossey-Bass, Inc., Publishers.
3. Brown, B.: Statement made at press conference releasing Marihuana and health, second annual report, Washington, D. C., Feb. 11, 1972, Department of Health, Education and Welfare.
4. Dole, V., and Nyswander, M.: Speech presented at the fourth annual Methadone Maintenance Conference, San Francisco, Jan., 1972.
5. Goodman, L. S., and Gilman, A.: The pharmacological basis of therapeutics, ed. 4, London, 1971, The Macmillan Co.
6. Hammond, A. L.: Narcotic antagonists: new methods to treat heroin addiction, Science 173:503-506, 1971.
7. Hammond, E. C.: The scientific background: world costs of cigarette smoking in disease, disability, and death, World Conference on Smoking and Health, New York, 1967, National Interagency Council on Smoking and Health.
8. Harris, R. T., et al., editors: Drug dependence, 1970, University of Texas Press.
9. Kitzinger, A.: Narcotics and dangerous drugs: a manual of basic information for teachers, Sacramento, Calif., 1964, California State Department of Education.

10. Kumagai, H.: Drug abuse in Japan, Paper presented at the Conference on Psychotropic Drugs in Ottawa, Canada, Sept., 1971.
11. Lewin, L.: Phantastica: narcotic and stimulating drugs: their use and abuse, London, 1931, Kegan Paul, Trench, Trubner & Co.
12. Methadone in the management of heroin addiction, Med. letter on drugs and therapeutics 14:13-15, 1972.
13. Methadone, 1972, Connection, Jan.-Feb., 1972.
14. Meyers, F. H., and Smith, D. E.: Pharmacologic effects of marijuana, J. Psychedelic Drugs 2:31-36, 1968.
15. Public Health Service: Cigarette smoking and health characteristics, July 1964-June 1965, Washington, D. C., 1967, Public Health Service Publication no. 1000, series 10, no. 34, Government Printing Office.
16. Ray, O. S.: Drugs, society and human behavior, St. Louis, 1972, The C. V. Mosby Co.
17. Report on cigarette smoking, New York, 1971, American Cancer Society.
18. Smith, D. E., editor: Current marijuana issues, J. Psychedelic Drugs 2:1, 1968.
19. Smith, D. E., editor: Psychedelic drugs and religion, J. Psychedelic Drugs 1:2, 1967-68.
20. Smith, D. E., editor: Speed kills: a review of amphetamine abuse, J. Psychedelic Drugs 2:2, 1969.
21. Smith, D. E., editor: Drug abuse papers, ed. 2, San Francisco, 1969, University Extension, University of California at Berkeley.
22. Smith, D. E., and Bentel, D. J.: Drug Abuse Information Project, the fifth annual report to the legislature, San Francisco, 1971, University of California San Francisco Medical Center.
23. Smith, D. E., and Luce, J.: Love needs care, Boston, 1971, Little, Brown & Co.
24. Smoking and health facts, Washington, D. C., 1972, American Association for Health, Physical Education and Recreation.
25. Smoking and health, report of the Advisory Committee to the Surgeon General of the Public Health Service, Washington, D. C., 1964, Public Health Service.
26. U. S. Department of Health, Education and Welfare: Chartbook on smoking, tobacco, and health, Washington, D. C., 1969, Government Printing Office.
27. Wilder, J.: Paradox reactions to treatment, N. Y. State J. Med. 57:3348-3352, 1957.

CHAPTER 5

THE ROLE OF THE COMMUNITY IN THE DRUG PROBLEM

The magnitude of the drug problem is such that it does not limit itself to certain economic, social, educational, intellectual, or ethnic groups of people. Rather it involves the total community, including the home, school, church and religious groups, governmental and nongovernmental service, professional and voluntary organizations and agencies, and industry. All must participate in a variety of programs in terms of prevention, including education, control, rehabilitation, and treatment. There is need for different types of programs and approaches, many of which have not yet been developed. Without the multimodality concept approach and without community action on the part of a broad spectrum of individuals and groups in coordinated endeavors, the attack on the drug problem in society will be limited and probably ineffectual.

It is the purpose of this chapter to identify (1) the possible and current approaches to treatment and rehabilitation, (2) the governmental agencies developing leadership for action, (3) selected legal provisions for control, (4) illustrations of activities or programs, and (5) suggestions for community action. Occasional reference

only will be made to schools, since this book emphasizes the school's role. This information is not meant to be prescriptive nor all-inclusive, but merely illustrative. Many new approaches, activities, and programs are constantly emerging and being developed. The comments presented should not be construed as guidelines or models for community action, but rather as suggestions to receive consideration for local application.

TREATMENT AND REHABILITATION

In this discussion of treatment programs, we want the reader to be aware of the crucial difference between "civil commitment," forced commitment, and voluntary entry. To be helped away from drugs, the user must *want* very much to be helped, and he must want very much the *type* of help being offered. Our use of the term "voluntary" means just that—treatment without applying negative or criminal sanctions to encourage the user to volunteer for treatment.

For example, the prevailing law enforcement model of arresting the addict or drug user and forcing him into treatment must be seriously questioned. We believe that people create the market for drugs by demanding them in order to deal with both the *internal* and *external* chaos of their lives. Effective programs must not only be voluntary but must also help people to resolve their life problems.

Multimodality concept

We must first explain what we mean by a "multiple modality" approach to treatment, and why we feel this is important for the educator to understand. The causes of drug abuse and drug addiction are not well understood, and we are uncertain as to the *cures* of the problem as well. One likely reason for this uncertainty is that the term "drug abuse" embraces a wide variety of divergent behavior, and that, even in the narcotic addict population, there is marked heterogeny with many relevant variables.

Those who make up what is referred to as the "soft drug" or "hard drug" using populations as well as the multiple drug abusers exhibit widely differing reasons for initiating their use, engage in widely varying patterns of use, and are involved in widely differing psychosocial relationships, even within each population subgroup. Clearly a heterogenous group such as drug abusers requires a number of highly differentiated treatment and rehabilitative approaches. For example, Synanon[6] is a well-known treatment program for narcotic drug addicts. But the Chicano or Mexican-American addict typically adjusts poorly to Synanon-type programs because of the disjunction from the family to which he is traditionally tied. He often fails to develop a usable, new group identity. Other programs seem better suited to his needs.

Not only is the phenomenon we loosely refer to as drug abuse constantly in a state of flux (the only thing constant about drug abuse is constant change), but it also requires a number of treatment and rehabilitative approaches. There is also great diversity among the available resources of any one community. Therefore rather than selecting one program or approach to the exclusion of others, the multimodality treatment concept allows all community groups to participate.

Besides being heterogeneous, drug users also appear to have some common characteristics. A population of drug-involved or drug-dependent persons seems to generally be divided into a number of identifiable types and subgroups. Such divisions, as Van Dusen[16] observes, fall along age lines (teen-agers as against college-age youths), along racial lines, and include persons with particular life-styles who normally relate to each other exclusive of their drug involvement. Thus when a drug subgroup functions as a cultural entity, approaches to the group as a whole are possible as long as some treatment provision is *acceptable* to that group, and will be effectively utilized by it. However, the addict housewife or professional person who belongs to no drug subculture and may identify with no group must be treated individually.

Treatment for drug abusers today is in a state of monumental flux and transition, with new approaches still evolving. Mandell[7] draws the interesting analogy between drug treatment today and the treatment of pneumonia during the early part of this century. Before the discovery of antibiotics and modern chemotherapy, wide diversity of opinion existed among medical experts as to proper treatment—the appropriate temperature of the sick person's room, either regular or intermittent use of mustard plasters, etc. Such arguments are irrelevant and seem ridiculous in the light of our present knowledge, just as certain drug abuse treatment methods will seem ridiculous to future generations.

One may conclude, however, that whatever the evolution of medical treatment, spirited, antagonistic, and polarized positions as to the one appropriate strategy will always arise. Mandell states, "when human suffering combines with professional ignorance and the expectation of expertise by the patient, there inevitably arises superstitition and politicized organization of the so-called body of knowledge within which the delivery of health care . . . must go on."[7]

As viewed through the perspective of the medical model, drug abuse is a complex disease process. Presently, instead of a single expedient protocol, one must select among multiple treatment strategies—if they are available—and a community should utilize or provide as many as possible. A multimodality treatment system, if it is financially feasible, is the preferred choice. As Mandell states, a multimodality treatment system may be developed within a single administrative structure in order to reduce or eliminate entirely much of the inefficiency and destructive rivalries between various treatment programs. The multimodality concept, Mandell believes, is defensible; it brings together doctors, mental health professionals, indigenous groups, community organizations, and government in a potentially constructive way.

Procedures

To begin dealing with treatment requires that we first identify the three conventional treatment functions, that is, crisis intervention, detoxification, and aftercare. These are important because the first time the drug user interacts with the treatment facility, a crisis may result or may have resulted.

CRISIS INTERVENTION

Crisis intervention occurs either when a patient first arrives at a treatment facility, or, closer to the school situation (Chapter 8), when a student becomes ill or disturbed and needs assistance.[16]

In order to appropriately handle a crisis involving drug abuse, someone with *first-hand knowledge* must accurately assess the severity of the problem and make a diagnosis. This assessment is particularly important in such situations as handling the frantic phone calls from parents asking where they should take their youngster for treatment, or responding to the crisis created by an acutely disturbed student. No queries should be answered nor advice given until someone close to the problem has carefully assessed the nature of the youngster's drug-taking behavior.

The assessment of all significant persons involved in the crisis situation is important for the resolution of the problem. The attitudes, the behavior, the level of knowledge and sophistication about drugs and drug abuse, the communication skills, the degree of rapport with the youngster, and the maturity and emotional health of the parents must be considered in determining recommendations for the alleviation and elimination of the crisis.[3]

After disposition is made of the precipitating crisis, the severity of the individual's drug problem should be determined. The drug use per se may be the primary factor or even the cause of personality disturbances; here treatment must be directed at the drug use pattern or at the life-style of the individual involved. But it must be remembered that the *drug use* itself or the acute medical-psychiatric crisis that it has created may be *secondary factors,* and long-term treatment should be focused on the fundamental psychological difficulties that may be the source of the drug-using behavior.

THE "BAD TRIP." Arising out of an extremely complex drug scene involving multiple drugs, unknown compounds, adulteration, contamination, and some of the unknown potentials of "homegrown" psychedelic agents is the bad trip. All the reactions of all psychedelic drugs cannot ever be known, since an ever increasing list of new drugs leads to drug fads and indiscriminate usage as the popularity of one street drug gives way to another.

Threatening or moralizing approaches, although sincere, create stress at an inappropriate time and work detrimentally. They have no place in the short-term attack on the problem. The best aspects of a helped-helping relationship can be of value. This is highlighted by Dr. David E. Smith, Medical Director of the Haight-Ashbury Free Medical Clinic: ". . . remember that the patient has probably come reluctantly. To him, you represent the dominant culture that nearly all drug users—whether initiates or confirmed addicts—are somewhat at odds with, and he expects disapproval. *Try to make him feel as comfortable as possible. Show him by your manner as well as your words that you're concerned, that you're not just pumping him but trying to get information that will help you to help him.*"[11]

Protection of the individual from dangerous behavior to himself or to others should be of primary concern. The patient in a disturbed state should be provided with a quiet place, but *never* left entirely alone.

The comatose patient. Although the patient using psychedelic and other drugs and experiencing an acute toxic reaction ("freaking out") may appear to be a more difficult, demanding case, the comatose patient actually represents the most difficult of diagnostic and treatment problems. Whenever a student collapses into unconsciousness, you are dealing with a dangerous situation where prompt and *proper* therapy is essential and may be literally lifesaving.

The proper course of action in this case might seem obvious—call a school nurse or physician. However, many physicians are not familiar with drug overdose problems and will minister incorrectly. Time is also essential. If the emergency has to proceed through the administrative chain of command (student courier is sent to the vice-principal's office, where the school nurse is summoned, who then calls a doctor who must drive to the school from somewhere across town), precious minutes will be lost and the patient may suffer irrevocable damage or die. This has happened many times. An immediate response to this possibility should be planned with someone readily available who is experienced in handling such emergencies.

A school located in the inner city should establish specific procedures for overdose. Arrangements may be made with the county medical society or with a city hospital to have personnel other than a physician trained and available to intervene in a life-threatening situation. A paramedic who can give first aid to the drug victim may be a great asset to many schools. Schools should anticipate drug problems of a serious nature and make provisions for rapid, practical, and effective first aid and care (Chapter 8).

Freaking out. The other situation that we briefly mentioned earlier, freaking out, concerns the student who is disoriented and disturbed after taking psychedelic drugs.[2, 14] Behavior may range from aimlessness, incoherence, and unresponsiveness (being "spacey" or "spaced") to screaming hysteria ("freak out"). These reactions occur particularly with LSD; one moment the person is experiencing a pleasant or even exhilarating "dream" and the next instant, a horrifying nightmare. Both

situations can be unnerving to the teacher or administrator and can create considerable classroom disturbance. There are two important points to remember in dealing with these experiences: (1) do not become drawn into the person's hysteria and confusion and (2) remember that this situation is generally manageable through patience and comforting. With these two guidelines, the educator should be able to cope with either of the two extremes encountered in psychedelic drug use.

An hysterical, confused person seems to create confusion and hysteria in others. The educator must act calmly and confidently with the knowledge that he or she can handle the situation if certain procedures are followed. Otherwise the confusion is infectious and only amplifies an already stressful situation beyond all manageable limits.

Because freaking out *is* generally manageable, the person's bad trip can be turned into a good one by patient suggestion and comfort. The remedy typically applied by people experienced with this situation is *not medicinal.* The worst procedure is to forceably restrain the disturbed person and inject him with a tranquilizer. The results of this approach may include permanent psychic damage. The experienced approach is to lead the person calmly to a quiet room or a calm environment where paranoia, fear, and suspicion can be removed and the person talked down into a more relaxed frame of mind. The patient can usually be talked out of his bad trip and will calm himself to the point of becoming once again quite rational and cooperative. In his disoriented state the patient desperately needs a sympathetic, compassionate person to help him deal with his hysteria.

In most instances of freaking out *hospitalization will not be required,* since sympathetic reassurance, coupled with the appropriate use of medication, will tide the patient over the acute aspects of his experience. This is especially true when such aid can be given in a quiet room under adequate but subdued lighting, with no noise or extraneous stimuli, and in the presence of, or with the help of, a friend who can assist in establishing rapport with the patient. Physical contact, such as a reassuring arm around the shoulder, may be of help, but care must be taken to prevent misinterpretation by the patient, making him fearful of possible harm.

The successful use of verbal, nonpharmacological techniques to treat a bad trip requires qualities such as sympathy, empathy, and friendliness on the part of the therapist. Reassurance should be provided to abort spiraling anxiety and loss of control on the part of the patient. The simple use of the phrase, "This is just a bad drug reaction and the effects will soon be over," and the changing of the subject foremost in the patient's thoughts to a neutral or pleasant topic, such as music or an attractive object in his visual environment, can bring a patient back to reality (Chapter 8). Teachers who feel uncomfortable in such a role can utilize others for this purpose, and may learn how to do a "talkdown" from more experienced persons, often youths, who have mastered the technique. Friends of the patient may have a role here. Although controlled observations have not been reported, physicians who have treated bad trips generally concede that the patient's interests are best served by attempting a talkdown before considering the use of any drugs.

DETOXIFICATION

Although a modality such as detoxification is primarily medical and requires medical expertise, we want to include just enough specifics to provide the educator with guidelines and some familiarity with what is involved.

Detoxification is a technical-medical term that simply means the elimination of drug substance from the user's system. In most cases this involves nothing more than providing a drug-free environment where the user's body will metabolize and eliminate the foreign chemical without outside in-

tervention. While the person is under the influence of the drug, however, he may need sedation and talking down, including, in some cases, the use of other drugs that act as antagonists and diminish the effect of the drug presently in the user's system.

As an example, a patient acutely intoxicated with an overdose of heroin or a morphine base compound would be injected with Nalline, a chemical antagonist, to diminish the drug's effect or cancel it out. This, of course, is done only by a physician and is not without some danger. Most drug ingestion, like drunkenness, should be allowed to *run its course*. We expect to "sleep it off" and sober up after a night of heavy drinking. The drug user must be treated in much the same way. Pills, including sedatives and tranquilizers, and injections are too often administered to bad effect. The main exception to this, noted in this chapter, is the comatose or unconscious person. Here, drastic emergency measures may need to be taken.

Once the individual is drug free, he is ready for the next stage in his rehabilitation to a non-drug–dependent person, treatment, which may involve a variety of techniques and procedures.

AFTERCARE

When a narcotic addict has been detoxified (is drug free), the long, hard job of rehabilitation begins. Rehabilitation means many things to many people. Perhaps "aftercare" is a less ambiguous term. No doubt the most important factor here is what the term means to the ex-addict himself.

There are several rehabilitative approaches currently available to the addict who seeks—or who is compelled—to kick his habit. These include the classic psychiatric hospital approach offered at the federal hospitals at Lexington, Kentucky and Fort Worth, Texas, established in the late 1930s to provide continuity of treatment in an environment removed from the addict's old haunts and life-style; mutual help communities such as Synanon,

Daytop Village, Phoenix House, and Aware-ness House; religion-oriented programs such as Teen Challenge; narcotic antagonists therapy; and methadone maintenance. We shall briefly discuss each of these in turn to familiarize the educator with the barest essentials of the types of treatment.

Four approaches to drug abuse treat-ment, or aftercare, exist—the pharmaceu-tical, the psychiatric, the psychosocial, and the religious. Each is strikingly different and is supported by a highly vocal, dedi-cated group of treatment experts, each of whom claims that *his* treatment system is superior to the others.

Long-term treatment by chemicals, or synthetics, such as methadone and cycla-zocine is called the pharmaceutical ap-proach to addiction. This method of treat-ment is aimed primarily at the drug addict (narcotic drug user) and was found by the innovators of methadone treatment, Dr. Dole and Dr. Nyswander of New York.[12] The rationale is that addiction is not a moral or ethical issue but largely a *chemi-cal* one. The person's body chemistry has changed once he becomes addicted, they claim. The answer then, say Dole and Nyswander (and now thousands of other treaters), is to provide a *chemical substi-tute* until the user's own body chemistry can be changed back—a task requiring maybe 20 years.

In contrast to this position is the classi-cal psychiatric approach, which basically excludes the use of drugs in treatment and believes that only a long-term, fundamental restructuring of the patient's ego structure and outlook will alter his drug-using be-havior.

The therapeutic community approach be-lieves that drug use problems are largely incidental to problems of personal life-style and values. Many communities are modeled after a family with "big brothers and big sisters" who guide novices through the program. Such communities usually re-side in one house or dormitory and typical-ly insist that *no* drug of any kind, including coffee and cigarettes, be used. Later we shall discuss the therapeutic community approach to rehabilitation further and pro-vide two examples.

Finally, the religious approach involves, or invokes, reference to something, or some-one, supernatural or beyond the natural.

PHARMACEUTICAL APPROACHES. Within re-cent years, experimentation in the use of synthetic drugs to treat persons addicted to narcotics has been conducted in various institutions. The results of this experimen-tation have provided two techniques in particular—treatment with cyclazocine, a narcotic antagonist, and methadone—that have received the greatest amount of at-tention both in the literature and in their actual use.

Cyclazocine—a narcotic antagonist.[10] It has been proposed that the regular ad-ministration of cyclazocine, a long-acting narcotic antagonist, might be useful in the treatment of highly motivated, ambula-tory patients to avoid relapse to the com-pulsive use of narcotics. When cyclazocine is given in appropriate doses, it reduces the subjective and physiological effects of any morphinelike drug even when such a drug is used frequently. The regular use of cyclazocine reduces or prevents the de-velopment of physical dependency on mor-phinelike drugs, thereby stabilizing the patient and allowing the process of re-habilitation to be more rapid and efficient.

However, treatment through the use of cyclazocine does not appear to provide the patient with the opportunity to be com-pletely abstinent. The "narcotics hunger" still exists and the patient may stop taking the antagonist and return to narcotic use. Individuals may reduce their use of drugs from full addiction to occasional use and may resort to irregular shots of narcotics because they no longer fear the danger of addiction. Studies have shown that the use of cyclazocine alone is ineffective in the rehabilitation process and that individual and group helping services are needed as well.

Research for an additional drug that will have the same effect as cyclazocine but with longer lasting application is now being conducted. This new synthetic would last for 7 to 10 days and would alleviate the necessity for daily maintenance. In addition longer maintenance would remove the temptation on the part of the individual to use other drugs.

Methadone.[8, 9] The synthetic drug used for therapeutic purposes receiving the greatest amount of attention and generating the most controversy has been a synthetic addicting opiate called methadone. Research begun in 1964 by Dr. Vincent Dole and Dr. Marie Nyswander at Rockefeller University in New York indicates that methadone, when administered appropriately, blocks the action of heroin, eliminates the drug craving that drives many detoxified addicts to resume heroin use, and produces neither euphoria nor other distortions of behavior.

Methadone was brought to the United States from Germany after World War II. It was administered as a synthetic pain killer during the war when the Germans were in short supply of opiate derivatives. Since the war it has been used in Europe as an analgesic. The experimentation of Dole and Nyswander was among the first directed at employment of the drug in the treatment of heroin addiction.

THE METHADONE PROGRAM. Dole and Nyswander attribute drug addiction to a metabolic deficiency and tend to question psychological factors. They designed their experimental program into two phases. During phase 1 the patient undergoes an initial 6-week inpatient period during which oral doses of methadone dissolved in orange juice are administered. The doses are increased until a stabilizing dosage is reached. If the medication is given in proper doses, euphoria or undesirable side effects during the stabilization period should be nonexistent. In phase 2 of the program the patient is allowed to return to his community setting but is required to report to the clinic each day to take his supervised oral dose of methadone. Patients give daily urine samples to be analyzed for traces of illicit drugs. Eventually, if warranted by good conduct, patients are provided with several days' dosage at a time, and return once or twice a week for urine analysis and other tests.

Withdrawal from methadone is not, as of now, a part of the treatment process, except in a few experimental programs. Indications are that once withdrawn from methadone, patients experience a recurrence of the narcotic hunger and revert to the use of heroin. During each phase of the program, patients are provided with supportive services to aid in their rehabilitation. These supportive services are in the form of psychological, social, and vocational support. A wide array of therapists in each of these disciplines assist the patient.

OPPOSITION TO METHADONE. Despite the positive reaction regarding methadone maintenance in treating opiate drug addiction, there exists much opposition to its use on social, medical, and legal grounds. Former addicts who have chosen to become totally abstinent from the use of drugs via the cold turkey approach have voiced strong opposition to any treatment method that uses synthetic drugs to maintain an addict. These opponents see more worth in halfway houses such as Phoenix House, Synanon, and Daytop Village where, by living with other former addicts in a structured setting, one is kept drug free. They reason that addicts maintained on methadone will be deprived of the opportunity to ever be drug free.

It is also believed that the same modality of treatment is not desirable for all addicts. Those who were addicted to drugs but were rehabilitated with methadone should not be denied the right to choose the method of treatment best suited for them.

PSYCHIATRIC APPROACH. The psychiatric approach is characterized by individual counseling in a psychiatric hospital. Counseling involves an intense, long-term, personal, one-to-one dialogue with a psychiatrist. This means that whereas the addict picks up his methadone and goes home or to work, the patient of a classical psychiatrist is typically committed as an ambulatory or bed patient to a traditional psychiatric hospital. The cost of psychiatric treatment on the one-to-one model, with the "treater" playing "expert professional" and the patient acting as "passive submitter" to treatment, is therefore much higher than that of methadone, which can be administered cheaply to thousands of patients.

Clinical Research Center. The prototype of the psychiatric approach was the federal hospital for narcotics addiction treatment opened in 1935 in Lexington, Kentucky.[18] It was first called the United States Narcotics Farm, but within a year the name was changed to the United States Public Health Service Hospital. The institution was essentially a medical prison with barred windows and locked wards, "volunteer" admission being an alternative to an even longer sentence in a federal prison.

In 1967 the hospital joined the National Institute of Mental Health and became the Clinical Research Center; since then the Center has undergone changes in its treatment, philosophy, program procedures and rationales, operational structure, and physical facilities.

New patients receive physical examinations, undergo methadone detoxification, and then are assigned to wards. Individual and ward treatment teams consist of a physician, a social worker, and nurses. Most residents participate in group therapy; individual therapy is provided when it is both desirable and feasible. Patients engage in part-time work assignments related to maintaining the Center; residents who refuse to work are denied rewards and privileges. The education and training sections offer vocational training courses in bookbinding, shoe repair, alteration, dry cleaning and pressing of men's clothing, barbering, plastic laminating, auto ignition, microfilming, and the polishing, repairing, and waxing of dentures. Interested patients may also attend classes teaching paramedical or business-related subjects and Negro

history and culture. Charm, beauty culture, and fashion design courses are available in the Women's Service.

Patients are given opportunities to control their own behavior and improve their environment. Increased freedom, visits to the city, special social and recreational functions, choice of rooms, and vocational guidance opportunities are incentives for mature behavior, productivity, and progress in therapeutic activities. Male and female patients eat their meals together and attend social hours, picnics, dances, and religious services together. Patient government maintains an ethics committee and a representative council. Residents have been appointed to task forces to revamp the Center's structure and have surveyed the patient population to find areas of need and interest for future education.

To maintain a drug-free environment, the Center conducts routine random urine tests. Within each unit, residents who temporarily require restraint are given intensive therapy in a locked ward. Unacceptable behavior is dealt with therapeutically rather than punitively, in accordance with the goal of conveying knowledge and principles without dogmatism. As patients are released, the Center refers them to Narcotic Addicts Rehabilitation Act (NARA) aftercare agencies, the Salvation Army, Greenwich House Counseling Center, and welfare agencies.

PSYCHOSOCIOLOGICAL APPROACHES. The term "psychosociological" is applied to treatment methods and practitioners who do not believe maintenance with synthetic drugs is an effective means of treating drug addiction but who advocate instead the use of structured settings, specific therapeutic techniques, and other methods of treatment to effect the rehabilitation process.

There are those who contend that drug addicts suffer from *character disorders* that cause them to express their conflicts by behavioral manifestations. Individuals of this description present complex, enduring problems and an extreme degree of social pathology in all their familial and community relationships. In recognition of this, it has been suggested that only limited goals be set in the treatment and rehabilitation of addicts and that primary emphasis be placed on allowing the addict to develop the means for limiting and curing his acting-out behavior.

Therapeutic communities. An almost total-living alternative to the addict's or drug user's former street life is available. The therapeutic community is specifically designed to counter all the styles of personal interaction and hustling of the professional drug user with an acceptable alternative. Although such living communities do produce "graduates" who typically become outstanding treatment personnel, the number of those who complete the specified period of rehabilitation is small. Many novices are simply unable to adjust to the new life and "split" after a few days or a few weeks. Such treatment is not applicable to a large number of addicts. The programs themselves are not able to accommodate very many persons. Yet they represent an important innovation in drug treatment.

The expectation on entering a therapeutic community is prompt and complete renunciation of heroin. Traditionally this meant cold turkey, but many current therapeutic communities have somewhat relaxed their treatment ideology to permit detoxification with methadone or nonnarcotic therapeutic medication over the first 5 to 7 days of initial treatment.

One noticeable aspect of initiation into a therapeutic community is the benign nature of the withdrawal syndrome which, when occurring in a hostile setting, such as a jail or a hospital, can be severe. Passivity and regression, typically created in the patient by a more hostile setting, are not encouraged in the therapeutic community. The novice is nursed through his cold turkey or withdrawal, but at the same time expected to perform his share of the work. He is assigned housekeeping chores and is expected to actively participate in the social life of the house. The role expected of the new community member is

critical for future rehabilitation because psychological set and psychosocial reinforcement, or the lack of it, are always relevant variables in drug-related behavior.

A prospective patient must be able to live in the therapeutic community for 1 to 2 years of 24-hour a day, 7-day a week involvement with the "dynamics" of the house where he lives. All habits and relationships—past, present, and future—are subject to group inspection and evaluation. A patient has to prove his ability to be independent because a central part of the treatment philosophy of therapeutic communities is the view that the heroin addict is a dependent child who does not have the ability to be honest about property or feelings. Treatment is seen as a total resocialization process in which direct, honest communication is practiced with respect to all aspects of the addict's new life. If the addict can adjust to the experience (and it is clear that many cannot), he or she experiences tremendous support from his membership in the group.

Humor, tenderness, and affirmation begin to be felt as real experiences. The addict learns that negative feelings do not necessarily destroy the possibility of future warmth and he begins to learn effective social responses. These trusting and relating experiences are often totally contradictory to those experiences of his former life-style as a hustling street junkie.

One negative aspect is that the "reborn" addict may find himself as psychologically dependent on the new community as he was on the old. Most experts in the field of drug abuse treatment feel that therapeutic communities are of unquestioned value for some patients, but that such a community does not constitute an approach that is applicable to large numbers of persons. Charles Dederick, creator of the first therapeutic community (Synanon), is quoted as stating that he feels that his community was suitable for only one out of ten addicts.[1] The addict who is married, has children, and has a steady job is usually not disposed to want or to accept treatment in a therapeutic community. The single, more dependent, younger addict is more likely to want to do so.

Most therapeutic communities are organized around more or less identifiable steps in which increments of trust, status, and power in the group are acquired. These steps can be thought of as roughly similar to the various rites (such as confirmation or bar mitzvah) utilized by social groups in the "straight" world to mark various stages of maturation. Therapeutic communities have not institutionalized these basic steps, but the underlying process is the same.

SUBCOMMUNITY SETTINGS. The advent of structured community settings such as Daytop Village[4] and Synanon as a means for treating and rehabilitating drug addicts has come about as the result of the conviction that the most effective way to rid an individual of his addiction to drugs is through a combination of abstinence and supportive therapy. Control of the individual's behavior, including his use of drugs, is achieved by the fact that he lives within a subcommunity created for the exclusive purpose of treating and rehabilitating drug addicts. The use of any drug is forbidden while the individual is a member of the subcommunity and he may actually be excluded from the community if he does not abstain.

Supportive therapy in the treatment process is usually labeled "encounter therapy." In encounter therapy a specific treatment relationship is used to promote the personal growth of all the individuals involved. A definition of a treatment relationship has been offered by Casriel who has stated: "A treatment relationship is any situation in which two or more persons encounter each other as equal human beings with a sense of challenge, and with responsible concern rather than indulgence."[4] The need to submit to the comments of others regarding one's own behavior and to encounter or challenge the behavior of these others is a necessary ingredient of any therapeutic relationship if an individual is

to grow and understand his own behavior and eventually control it in more socially acceptable ways. Any treatment that evolves from sessions involving one or more persons demands a more human kind of involvement from the therapist and leads ideally to a fuller, more mature kind of growth for the individuals concerned.

Any person who accepts the responsibiilty for the treatment of drug addicts by means of encounter therapy must be willing to be open to challenges concerning changes in his own behavior. He must accept a relationship with drug addicts that reflects their dignity as human beings. He must not see their addiction or general behavior as a reflection of weakness, but must perceive the patient as an individual who is capable of achieving his aspirations and reducing his failures.

The success of these programs and their form of therapy has been questioned. The main consensus is that whatever success these methods may have achieved has been confined to the subcommunity setting in which the patient lives. Reintegration of the patient into the general community has not always been as successful.

SYNANON: PROTOTYPE OF A THERAPEUTIC LIFE-STYLE. Founded in California in 1958 by Charles E. Dederick, Synanon is the foremost therapeutic community in the country for drug rehabilitation. The organization has pioneered an alternative life-style involving thousands of people, most of whom have stopped their former drug use patterns. The Synanon model has been copied in many parts of the country, especially in New York.

Few people interested in the problem of drug abuse take neutral positions with regard to Synanon. Apart from Synanon's enormous direct impact in helping to solve the drug problem, the element of controversy about the organization and its life-style has evoked a considerable amount of highly significant and valuable dialogue.

The dictionary definition of Synanon, "a private organization assisting those who wish to be cured of drug addiction," refers to only one dimension of the overall Synanon system. The organization has steadily moved beyond the work of treating drug addiction and crime. Dederick, chairman of the Board of Regents at Synanon, has repeatedly stated that Synanon is not primarily interested in curing drug addiction, but that this seems to occur as a side effect of an individual's participation in Synanon's life-style.

Synanon's overall program encompasses (1) a new kind of group therapy; (2) an approach to racial integration; (3) a humane solution to some facets of bureaucratic organization; (4) a different way of being religious; (5) a humanistic method of encounter therapy; (6) an unusual kind of communication; and (7) an exciting, fresh approach to the cultural arts and to philosophy. One side effect of intense participation in these diverse human experiences is that those participants who were criminal addicts have found a new existence and now lead constructive lives.

A drug user with a past history of institutionalized treatment of another kind generally finds himself in a new situation in Synanon. In most standard treatment programs a patient or inmate subculture usually develops within the overall approach. This tends to produce a "we-they" conflict and a split between the professional personnel and the "clients." The "client society" tends to be underground and to develop norms, patterns of behavior, and goals different from and, more often than not, in conflict with the "treatment establishment." This is partly due to the fact that most clients have had severe difficulties with authority for a good part of their lives. Synanon does not have a "we-they" caste system where the client is relegated to a lower position in the organization. It provides instead an open-ended stratification situation. A full possibility for upward mobility is available in the organization. There is not only upward social mobility in Synanon, but healthy status seeking is encouraged.

Synanon assumes, with some supportive evidence, that a person's position in its hierarchy is a correlate of social maturity and mental health. An old Synanon adage is "character is the only rank." Since the development of character is related to success in the organization, certain behavior is encouraged, such as speaking out in a Synanon game when someone feels or observes a wrong. This is encouraged regardless of the wrongdoer's status in the organization. In fact, to be silent in the face of injustice carries with it the moral condemnation of the group. Unlike the code of the streets, "copping out" on each other for behavior that is either self-destructive or harmful to the group is both condoned and actively fostered. This does not occur in the usual institutional "we-they" atmosphere.

The most important widely and continually used group process in Synanon is "the game." All members participate in its process at least several times a week. In part it is an intimate group interaction situation in which a member can openly express his problems, fears, and hostilities to his fellow members. He can expect a response that enables him to see his personal truths in a new and exciting perspective. The game also enables members to express what they really think of each other without fear of retribution. Members can often solve the confusions and conflicts of their occupational and interpersonal relationships. A participant in a game can be as spontaneous, creative, rigid, angry, loud, or passive as he chooses with no authority rules save one, the proscription of physical violence.

The game frequently helps to regulate behavior in Synanon. Transgressions are often prevented by the knowledge that the next time the game is played a member's deviance will rapidly and necessarily be brought to the attention of the Synanon community. The participant is living in a community where others know about and, perhaps more importantly, care about his behavior.

Another major impact of the Synanon game is its ability to convey to each member a sense of responsibility and its corollary, a sense of personal value and significance. To persons who have suffered from chronic feelings of weakness or helplessness and who characteristically see themselves as victims, the game becomes very meaningful because they are shown that their behavior can have a direct effect on other people and that it is within their power to change the overall society in a positive way.

Some of the more recent activities of Synanon include (1) Synanon game group interaction sessions; (2) a challenging and involving educational system; (3) business activities that help finance the operation; (4) a human research and development center at Tomales Bay, California, where plans are being made for a model city; (5) a black social, cultural, and educational program; (6) a group program for the parents of residents; and (7) a continuing series of marathon trips (some lasting 24 and 48 hours) and educational and emotional experiences that have produced positive results.

DAYTOP VILLAGE.[5] The provision of a residential or community setting in which the addict can live in order to overcome his need for drugs and to be rehabilitated is also the premise on which Daytop Village functions. Originating in New York City, where three facilities are now able to help some 450 persons at a time, Trenton, New Jersey, has become the site of the first such "village" outside of New York City.

Anyone who shows a sincere desire to be helped is accepted. The only demands made are the following: no chemicals, drugs, or alcohol may be used and no violence or even threat of violence is allowed. An individual's degree of sincerity is measured by the staff, all ex-addicts, who feel they can tell when someone is insincere about wanting to be helped because they have been in that position themselves.

The process of treatment includes withdrawal, work, and therapy. Before an addict is accepted he must agree to free himself of drugs. When asked about the withdrawal process, Jim Halloram, the director of the program, has commented: "Withdrawal is not that bad. It's no worse than a case of the flu, and they go through it right here with everyone around them." Withdrawal is followed by a short period in which the prospective resident assists in maintaining the facility in which the center is located and participates in discussions. Once eligible for residency, the patient is accepted into one of the residential facilities.

During his tenure as a resident, usually about 20 months, the individual is assigned menial jobs initially, followed by other assignments as his degree of responsibility increases. During this time, therapy is provided by all enrolled in the program and by the staff through the means of periodic group sessions. Peer-group acceptance is emphasized at Daytop and with it the hope that each ex-addict will gain a sense of responsibility to himself and to others.

RELIGIOUS APPROACH. Last of all, the religious approach should be mentioned. The most effective examples that we have observed are fundamentalist groups called "Jesus freaks," who inculcate a whole Christian way of living and meaningful service to others. Some of these groups have almost no use of drugs among their teen-agers and have proved effective in turning off ordinarily nonreligious drug users. Usually these fundamentalist groups are closely knit and have a warm emotional interchange and a rewarding life of public service. Teen Challenge is one such organization. Young persons in these church groups are usually drug resistant in contrast to average teen-agers who have few or no mores against drugs.

Within the domain of what might be called spiritual or religious approaches to drug abuse treatment is the approach used by Alcoholics Anonymous. Emphasis in these groups is on testimonials from those who have struggled with a debilitating addiction, and who meet regularly to plan and discuss the importance of abstinence. AA relies on developing a quasi-religious community whose salvation is working together to lick their common affliction—

alcoholism. Many persons who for 20 or 30 years were not able to develop the will-power "to stay off alcoholic beverages" were able to do so for the first time after they joined AA. There is also a "Tobacco Anonymous."

National programs

There are thousands of treatment and rehabilitation programs[17] in the United States and its territories. They offer a variety of types of services that include the following: detoxification, methadone maintenance, crisis intervention, educational counseling, psychotherapy, family counseling, religious counseling, recreational counseling, social services, encounter groups, self-awareness groups, job placement, vocational preparation and guidance, and medical-surgical treatment.

GOVERNMENTAL PROGRAMS AND RESOURCES

The programs available to help combat the drug abuse problem at the federal, state, and local levels are numerous. This section will make brief reference to selected programs.

Drug dependence, a stubborn disease, calls for intensive and varied therapy for a prolonged period after withdrawal. Programs vary according to location and particular needs; they also have certain elements in common. One is the regular testing of urine for detection of any relapse to drugs. Others are self-help in the form of group therapy and the use of ex-addicts and former drug abusers as aides who participate in initial interviews and counseling, encourage self-help in group therapy sessions, help patients find jobs, and speak regularly to community groups on their own experiences with addiction and rehabilitation.

Federal level

The response of the federal government to recent increases in drug-taking and drug-abusing behavior has been traditional and conservative, focusing on the functional categories of implementing structure, service, training, education, research, and law enforcement. This increasing response has been largely reflected in the monies spent for national programs. In 1970 the federal investment in all drug abuse activities totaled $105 million. The proposed budget for fiscal year 1973 indicates expenditures may be between $500 and $700 million.

Research, treatment, rehabilitation, education, and prevention are concentrated within the federal structure, primarily within the National Institute of Mental Health of the Health, Education and Welfare Department. In a brief discussion of federal programs, we shall describe the President's Special Action Office, the National Institute of Mental Health, the National Clearinghouse for Drug Abuse Information, federal treatment efforts, and also the National Drug Education Training Program of the Office of Education. This latter program focuses on equipping school personnel, especially the teachers themselves, so they will be effective in the field of drug abuse education.

SPECIAL ACTION OFFICE OF DRUG ABUSE PREVENTION (SAODAP)

In a message to Congress in June 1971 the President called for the creation of the Special Action Office of Drug Abuse Prevention to coordinate the activities of the nine federal agencies already active in trying to control drugs. (This excludes certain Justice Department activities.) In both scope and power, its functions are unique; it is expected to develop overall federal strategy for drug programs in general, and specifically for those within the military. Among its responsibilities are major federal drug abuse prevention, education, treatment, rehabilitation, training, and research programs. The office is located within the Executive Office of the President under a director accountable to the President.

The President has established by executive order the position of Special Consultant to the President for Narcotics and Dangerous Drugs. Named to the post was

Dr. Jerome H. Jaffe, former director, Drug Abuse Programs, Illinois Department of Mental Health. Jaffe is an expert on methadone therapy for heroin addicts, a pioneer in the multimodality treatment approach to addiction, and a major figure in research on drug abuse.

The director of the Special Action Office prepares budget requests for all programs over which he has authority and determines funding priorities. He maintains general supervisory authority over the operations of such programs. He also coordinates research and information gathering and dispensing activities. He assumes overall responsibility for planning, evaluating, budgeting, selling policy, and establishing goals for all major non-law enforcement drug abuse programs, including those for prevention, education, treatment, rehabilitation, training, and research.

The President's programs in 1972 cost approximately $371 million. Of this, $105 million was earmarked for the treatment and rehabilitation of drug addicts and $10 million for drug abuse education. Another $14 million was allocated to support the expanded treatment programs in Veterans Administration facilities. It is expected that the total support in 1973 through 1974 will be $500 to $700 million for law enforcement, education and training, treatment and rehabilitation, and research evaluation and coordination.

The largest share of the funds is for the compulsory treatment and rehabilitation of addicted Vietnam veterans. Specifically this treatment and rehabilitation involves a massive drug detection program that subjects all American soldiers to urine tests before they return to the United States to ascertain whether they have been using heroin or amphetamines while overseas. Returning soldiers found to be on drugs are given a week of detoxification before they are sent home. They also receive an additional 3 weeks of mandatory therapy in one of 33 special Veterans Administration Drug Detoxification facilities scattered around the country.

NATIONAL INSTITUTE OF MENTAL HEALTH

The National Institute of Mental Health, by far the largest governmental institute to deal with the treatment of addicts, supports treatment programs under the Civil Commitment Program of the Narcotic Addicts Rehabilitation Act and under a grant program to establish community-based treatment centers. Of these centers, eighteen are now operating and another five have been funded and are getting underway. In addition, new legislation authorized the institute to fund individual treatment services such as detoxification centers, partial hospitalization, and emergency care.

The National Institute of Mental Health also engages in activities supplementing the establishment of centers to treat and rehabilitate drug addicts. As the result of a large-scale development program to meet the needs of school systems and other prevention efforts around the country, a wide range of professional training materials has been created for individuals who may not be able to participate in formal training activities at the various centers.

A series of single-concept films (each addressing itself to a single drug topic) have been produced for secondary school use. Topics run the gamut from drug culture and marijuana to volatile substances, narcotics, alcohol, and tobacco. Teachers are provided with a resource book and guide to further extend the information potential of these films. These materials and others are distributed through the National Clearinghouse for Drug Abuse Information. In addition, there are many drug addiction treatment, training, and research activities supported by grants from the Law Enforcement Assistance Administration of the Department of Justice. Experimental community addict rehabilitation programs are being funded through the Office of Economic Opportunity. The Veterans Administration and the Department of Defense are also providing medical and other treatment services to addicts under their care.

The National Institute of Mental Health is focusing primarily on research and the translation of research findings into information on education programs, training, and rehabilitation. Federally funded projects continue to expand, and the various nonfederal forces in the treatment field are addressing themselves more effectively to the problem. State and private agencies are exhibiting local initiative in developing a variety of low-cost treatment models.

NATIONAL CLEARINGHOUSE FOR DRUG ABUSE INFORMATION

After a national search for a focal point for accurate and reliable information about all aspects of drug abuse, the National Clearinghouse for Drug Abuse Information (NCDAI) was designated by the President as the central federal source for drug abuse information.

NCDAI operates as a main source for the collection and dissemination of drug abuse information within the federal government and serves as a coordinating information agency for groups throughout the country that are involved in drug abuse information. It is a *vital* resource for the educator. NCDAI distributes publications upon request and prepares materials for input into a computerized information retrieval system. The computer contains current and continually updated files on drug abuse programs throughout the country in addition to traditional materials on drug abuse in all media.

NCDAI distributes drug abuse information materials, answers mail and phone inquiries, refers specialized requests to appropriate government or private sources, periodically publishes secondary source reference materials and fact sheets, and operates on up-to-date and comprehensive computerized information storage and retrieval systems. NCDAI has developed an immense file of resource materials, including bibliographies, articles, speeches, program descriptions, published guidelines, and technical data in pharmacology, education, biochemistry, medicine, social work, and other disciplines. Cooperating information centers have access to these files

through the use of remote computer terminals that allow interaction between the main computer center at the National Institute of Mental Health and the searcher at his locale.

NCDAI has embarked on a new program called the Drug Abuse Communications Network (DRACON). This program will establish a group of satellite Drug Abuse Information Centers in the drug coordinator's office of each state. These centers will be allied with the NCDAI as "mini" clearinghouses and will provide the public and the schools ready access to current information and prepared materials distributed by the federal government. In addition, consultation in program development and special projects, and a 24-hour "hotline" for drug abuse information on a toll-free number will be available.

NEW DEVELOPMENTS IN THE OFFICE OF EDUCATION

Nearly 2 years have elapsed since the Office of Education's National Drug Education Program was inaugurated by a March 1970 presidential directive. During that period a grant program to states has been initiated, new authorization has been passed into law by Congress (the Drug Abuse Education Act of 1970, P.L. 91-527), and dozens of college and community based projects have been funded. Program experience to date indicates that two of the most basic needs of communities with drug problems are *trained leadership personnel*, and *continuing developmental assistance*.

To respond to these urgent needs, the Office of Education has developed a new "Help Communities Help Themselves" program. In February 1972, $5.2 million was allocated for this program. Part of this amount will be expended to establish and maintain eight regional training and support centers. The remainder will be awarded in the form of "mini-grants" to between 400 and 500 communities to defray the cost associated with training community teams at these centers.

Although the Office of Education's primary objective is to help communities develop the capacity to plan and implement comprehensive preventive drug education programs, it is, of course, assumed that no preventive program can operate in a vacuum, but must be closely coordinated with drug treatment and rehabilitation efforts. The Drug Abuse Education Act of 1970 authorizes the award of a grant to any organized public or private entity in a community or to a community itself. A community is defined loosely by the Office of Education as a set of people who have common needs and who should be able to effect decisions that will benefit them. The Office of Education selects communities that recognize their drug problems as being of a manageable geographical size and that have a representative group of persons who will respond to the need for a drug abuse program.

The training is planned in two phases of 1 week each and focuses on (1) developing understanding, capability, commitment, and team identity; (2) formulating specific strategies to deal with the problems of planning and implementing community drug programs; and (3) identifying and acquiring the necessary tools, skills, and information.

During phase 1, emphasis is placed on the aquisition by the participants of a basic understanding of drugs and of the current drug scene. Team building, that is, teaching participants to work together as a cohesive entity, to lead group discussions, and to facilitate group interaction, is also stressed.

The primary focus of phase 2 training is on the development of program planning, implementation skills, and community organization strategies. At the end of training, each team should be able to assess the drug problem in its own community, to develop a widespread community support base, to encourage the active participation of many diverse elements in the community (including the local power structures), and to provide the leadership to plan and oper-ate a comprehensive preventive drug program.

State level

Each state has its own organizational arrangement for handling drug problems. Generally a coordinator is attached to the governor's office and is responsible for coordinating the efforts of such departments as health, mental health, education, and law enforcement as well as other community activities in terms of prevention, control, treatment, and research. An advisory committee comprising a variety of community representatives may be appointed to render assistance and guidance. In addition, individual departments may employ specialists to deal with problems unique to that department. In line with President Nixon's policy of local autonomy in governmental matters, the administrative responsibility for allocating federal funds for drug programs has been shifted to the states. Henceforth all moneys appropriated through the Special Action Office of Drug Abuse Prevention (SAODAP) will no longer be categorized for educational, treatment, and other purposes. Instead individual states will be expected to distribute such funds probably through their coordinators.

CIVIL ADDICT PROGRAM. In 1961 California established the Civil Addict Program to provide compulsory inpatient and aftercare treatment and control for opiate users. Addicts are civilly committed by a California superior court. The proceedings under which the addict may be committed can be initiated in three ways: (1) The addict, a relative, or some other responsible person may approach the county district attorney, who may then petition the court for consideration of the addict's commitment. No criminal charge is involved. Where necessary, provisions are available to detain the alleged addict for medical examination. (2) If any person is convicted of any crime in a superior court of law and is believed by the judge to be an addict, the proceedings shall be adjourned or the judge may suspend the imposition of sentence. (3) Any person convicted of a felony (with certain exceptions) may, if the judge believes he is an addict, be referred to another superior court to determine the issue of his addiction after he is convicted and the original criminal proceedings are suspended.

All commitments are for the same technical and legal reason—addiction or "imminent danger" of addiction—regardless of the basis for referral. The criminal matter, if any, becomes irrelevant, remaining in suspended status with the court. Whether the addict is committed voluntarily or not, he is bound for a definite period of treatment. The law provides a maximum 2½-year commitment for volunteers and a 7-year commitment for others. This term is to include both inpatient and aftercare treatment. On an original commitment a minimum of 6-months' inpatient treatment is required; however, for a returnee there is no limit on length of stay for treatment.

Inpatient care consists of intensive interaction in community living groups, small group work, academic and vocational instruction, recreation, work therapy, physical fitness, and religious programs. The inpatient phase of the treatment process may be terminated after the minimum time has elapsed and when the professional staff of the institution feels that the person has made sufficient progress. The suggestion for termination is referred for certification to the Narcotic Addict Evaluation Authority, which acts in cases of release, return, and discharge. Upon transfer from the inpatient treatment center to the state-wide outpatient program, the individual is supervised by a specially trained field agent who works only with releasees from one of the centers.

The Civil Addict Program offers close supervision, antinarcotic testing, group therapy, job placement service, and halfway houses. Abstention from the use of narcotics for 3 consecutive years may permit the releasee to be discharged from his commitment and the criminal charges

against him, if any, may be dismissed by the judge.

Specific provisions of the program, compulsory inpatient treatment, close and continuing supervision in the community, and antinarcotic testing are means by which the former addict is forced to continue treatment. The results of these efforts have been fruitful.

Local level

Organizational patterns for handling drug problems in communities differ throughout the United States. These patterns probably relate to state level arrangements in which there may be an advisory committee and a coordinator. In California, recent legislation mandated drug coordinators at the county level.

LEGAL PERSPECTIVE
Federal laws regarding narcotics and drugs[14]

Since 1914 numerous federal laws have been passed concerning the distribution of narcotics and other drugs. The principal statutes are designed to ensure an adequate supply of narcotics for medical and scientific needs, and at the same time to curb the abuse of narcotic drugs and marijuana. What we consider to be the most important of these laws are summarized here and presented in chronological order.

HARRISON NARCOTIC ACT (1914). The Harrison Narcotic Act set up the machinery for the distribution of narcotic drugs within the country and initiated a policy that is still the basis of present drug control programs. Enacted as a revenue measure, the Treasury Department was designated as the enforcement agency. Under this law, all persons who imported, manufactured, produced, compounded, sold, dealt in, disposed of, or transferred narcotic drugs had to register annually and pay a graduated occupational tax of $1 to $24 per year. They were required to keep records, make them available to law officers, and file returns specified by the Secretary of the Treasury. The tax was placed on the following narcotic drugs:

opium, isonipecaine, coca leaves, and opiates; compounds, manufactures, salts, derivatives, or preparations of the foregoing; and substances chemically identical to the foregoing.

Traffic in narcotic drugs without registration was a separate offense, independent of failure to register. Thus the transportation of narcotic drugs in interstate commerce by persons not registered was prohibited except for employees and agents of registrants within the scope of their employment.

NARCOTIC DRUGS IMPORT AND EXPORT ACT (1922). The passage of the Narcotic Drugs Import and Export Act of 1922 extended the prohibition against opium imports (set in 1909) to other narcotics, including morphine, coca leaves, and their derivatives. The amount of narcotics that could be lawfully imported was limited to such amounts as the Commissioner of Narcotics found necessary for legitimate medical and scientific uses. Manufactured drugs and preparations could be exported under a rigid system of controls to assure that the drugs were used for medical needs only in the country of destination.

The penalty for unlawfully importing, receiving, facilitating transportation, or sale under this act was imprisonment for not less than 5 nor more than 20 years and a maximum fine of $20,000. Subsequent offenses were punishable by a minimum sentence of 10 years and a maximum sentence of 40 years, plus a $20,000 fine. A similar penalty was provided for smuggling marijuana.

MARIJUANA TAX ACT (1937). The Marijuana Tax Act required all persons who imported, manufactured, produced, compounded, sold, dealt in, dispensed, prescribed, administered, or gave away marijuana to register and pay a graduated occupational tax ranging from $1 to $24 per year. No commodity tax was imposed on this drug. Transfer of marijuana was limited to that made on the authority of official order forms.

A 1969 Supreme Court decision removed two of the federal government's major legal weapons against marijuana traffic in holding that the Marijuana Tax Act is unenforceable when the accused claims the Fifth Amendment privilege against self-incrimination. The Court also declared unreasonable the law's presumption that a person with marijuana in their possession knows that it was imported illegally, thus violating due process of law.

FEDERAL FOOD, DRUG, AND COSMETIC ACT (1938). The pertinent drug sections of the Federal Food, Drug, and Cosmetic Act of 1938 may be summarized as follows:

1. Proper labeling is required and the statement, "WARNING—May Be Habit Forming," must be attached to a drug that is for use by man and that contains any quantity of narcotic or hypnotic substance, alpha eucaine, barbituric acid, beta eucaine, bromal, cannabis, cabromal, chloral, coca, cocaine, codeine, heroin, marijuana, morphine, opium, paraldehyde, peyote, sulfonmethane, or chemical derivates of the foregoing.

2. Prescription is required for the dispensing of a drug intended for use by man that (a) contains certain narcotic or other substances designated by regulation as habit forming; (b) is not safe except under the supervision of a licensed practitioner because of its potentiality for harmful use; or (c) is limited to use under the professional supervision of a licensed practitioner under procedures for the introduction of new drugs into interstate commerce.

3. No new drugs may be introduced into interstate commerce unless an application filed with the Secretary of Health, Education and Welfare is in effect with respect to such drug.

4. Annual registration is required of establishments that manufacture, compound, or process drugs and that wholesale or distribute any depressant or stimulant drug. The 1962 Drug Act established registration requirements.

The depressant and stimulant drug registrations were added by the Drug Abuse Control Amendments of 1965, which established special federal controls over these and hallucinogenic drugs.

The Federal Food, Drug, and Cosmetic Act as amended in 1962 and 1965 enumerates prohibited acts as follows:

1. Introduction or delivery into interstate commerce of adulterated or misbranded foods, drugs, devices, or cosmetics
2. Their adulteration or misbranding in interstate commerce
3. Their receipt and delivery in adulterated or misbranded state
4. The introduction or delivery into interstate commerce of any article in violation of temporary permit controls (applicable to food) or in violation of procedures for the introduction of new drugs
5. Refusal to permit access to records of interstate shipments of food, drugs, devices, or cosmetics, or to make the records or reports required under procedures for the introduction of a new drug
6. Refusal to permit entry and inspection of certain establishments in which foods, drugs, devices, and cosmetics are manufactured or held
7. Manufacture of adulterated or misbranded foods, drugs, devices, and cosmetics
8. The giving of certain false guarantees regarding good faith in receiving or delivering such articles
9. Certain false use of identification devices required under law, doing of certain acts that cause a drug to be counterfeit, or the sale, dispensing, or holding for sale or dispensing of a counterfeit drug
10. Misuse of trade secret information
11. Certain acts resulting in adulteration or misbranding of foods, drugs, devices, or cosmetics in interstate commerce

12. Representing or suggesting in labeling or advertising that approval of a new drug application is in effect or that the drug complies with new drug introduction procedures
13. Violation of laws governing the coloring of margarine
14. The use in sales promotion of any reference to a report or analysis furnished under inspection procedures
15. In the case of prescription drugs, failure of the manufacturer, packer, or distributor to maintain or transmit to requesting practitioners true and correct copies of all printed matter required to be included in the drug package
16. Failure of drug manufacturers and processors and depressant or stimulant drug wholesalers, jobbers, or distributors to register with the Secretary of Health, Education and Welfare
17. Relative to stimulant or depressant drugs: manufacturing, processing, or compounding, except by registered drug firms for legal distribution; distributing such drugs to persons not licensed or authorized by law; failure to prepare, obtain, or keep required records and to permit inspection as authorized; and filling or refilling prescriptions for these drugs in violation of law

Imprisonment for not more than 1 year or a fine of not more than $1000 or both is the penalty for violation of any of these prohibitions. If the violation is committed after a previous conviction has become final, or is made with intent to defraud or mislead, the violator is subject to imprisonment for not more than 3 years or a fine of not more than $10,000 or both.

OPIUM POPPY CONTROL ACT (1942). Production of the opium poppy in the United States except under license of the Secretary of the Treasury, was prohibited by the Opium Poppy Control Act of 1942. No license has ever been issued under this statute.

HARRISON NARCOTIC ACT AMENDMENT (1946). This amendment to the 1914 Harrison Narcotic Act was made to include synthetic substances having addiction-forming or addiction-sustaining qualities similar to cocaine or morphine.

BOGGS AMENDMENT (1951). The 1951 legislation known popularly as the Boggs Amendment increased penalties for persons violating federal narcotic and marijuana laws, precluded suspension of sentence or probation on second and subsequent offenses, and made conspiracy to violate the narcotic laws a special offense. It substituted for the old maximum sentences a series of sentences for repeated offenders as follows:

First offense—not less than 2 nor more than 5 years
Second offense—not less than 5 nor more than 10 years with probation and suspension excluded
Subsequent offenses—not less than 10 nor more than 20 years with probation and suspension excluded

NARCOTIC CONTROL ACT (1956). As the result of 1955 congressional investigations of the illicit narcotic traffic, the Narcotic Control Act of 1956 increased and made more inflexible the penalties for narcotic offenders. Parole was excluded in cases of a selling offense and second or subsequent possession offenses. The penalties were as follows:

First possession offense—not less than 2 nor more than 10 years, with probation and parole permitted
Second possession or first selling of narcotics or marijuana—not less than 5 nor more than 20 years, with probation, suspension, and parole excluded
Third possession or second selling and subsequent offenses—not less than 10 nor more than 40 years with probation, suspension, and parole excluded

These penalties carried, in addition, a maximum $20,000 fine. Exclusion of drug offenders from federal parole laws means that they must serve two thirds of their sentence. Most other federal prisoners are eligible for release under supervision after serving one third of their sentences.

This act also banned the possession of heroin and required persons possessing heroin to surrender it to the Secretary of the Treasury within 120 days.

NARCOTICS MANUFACTURING ACT (1960). A system for licensing manufacturers to produce narcotic drugs was developed in the Narcotics Manufacturing Act of 1960. It also set manufacturing quotas for the basic classes of narcotic drugs, both natural and synthetic, ensuring that an adequate supply of each drug would be available for medicine and science.

Under this and other federal laws, the Secretary of the Treasury is the cabinet officer charged with responsibility for investigating offenses and regulating lawful imports and exports. He acts through the Commissioner of Narcotics, who is the chief officer of the Federal Bureau of Narcotics, and is required to cooperate with the states in the suppression of the abuse of narcotic drugs in their respective jurisdictions.

DRUG ABUSE CONTROL AMENDMENTS (1965). In January 1963 President Kennedy established a President's Advisory Commission on Narcotic and Drug Abuse. The Commission made 25 recommendations, the influence of these being reflected in the Drug Abuse Control Amendments of 1965.

Three groups of dangerous drugs—depressants, stimulants, and hallucinogens—are controlled by the Drug Abuse Control Amendments to the Federal Food, Drug, and Cosmetic Act passed in 1965 and amended in 1968. These amendments provide for stronger regulations in manufacture, distribution, delivery, and possession and strong criminal penalties against persons who deal in these drugs illegally. All registered manufacturers, processors, and their suppliers, wholesaler druggists, pharmacies, hospitals, clinics, public health agencies, and research laboratories must take an inventory, keep accurate records of receipts and sales of these drugs and make their records available to Bureau of Narcotics and Dangerous Drugs agents for examination. No prescription for a controlled drug older than 6 months can be filled nor can refills be made more than five times in the 6-month period.

The Drug Abuse Control Amendments of 1965 impose more stringent controls on stimulant, depressant, and hallucinogenic drugs. The new law, which became effective in 1966, begins with a declaration by Congress that these drugs need not move across state lines to be subject to its regulations. The law notes that "in order to make regulation and protection of interstate commerce in such drugs effective, regulation of intrastate commerce is also necessary" because of the difficulties of determining place of origin and consumption and because regulation of interstate but not intrastate commerce "would discriminate against and adversely affect interstate commerce in such drugs."

The amendments add to the body of law a definition of a depressant or stimulant drug as follows:

1. One that contains barbituric acid or its salts or a derivative therefrom which has been designated under federal law as habit forming
2. One that contains amphetamine or its salts or a substance designated as habit forming by the Secretary of Health, Education and Welfare because of its stimulant effect on the central nervous system
3. One containing a substance designated by regulations as having a "potential for abuse" because of its depressant or stimulant effect on the central nervous system or its hallucinogenic effect (Narcotic drugs are specifically excluded.)

Lysergic acid and lysergic acid amide are drugs covered by the amendments of 1965, along with mescaline and its salts, peyote, and psilocybin. The act also prohibits the possession of depressant or stimulant drugs except by seven classes of persons who can be generally described

as manufacturing or doing research upon the drug.

Further changes in the Drug Abuse Control Amendments to the Federal Food, Drug, and Cosmetic Act of 1965 were made in 1968. These changes increased the penalties for anyone who illegally produced, sold, or disposed of dangerous drugs, and imposed a misdemeanor penalty for possession.

NARCOTIC ADDICT REHABILITATION ACT (1966). A significant effort toward the treatment and rehabilitation of narcotic addicts was enacted in 1966 with the signing of the Narcotic Addict Rehabilitation Act. The legislation, effective February 1967, provided for civil commitment in lieu of prosecution (Chapter 4).

COMPREHENSIVE DRUG ABUSE PREVENTION AND CONTROL ACT (1970). In 1969 President Nixon delivered before Congress a ten-point message calling for a new federal drug law that would consolidate over 50 public drug-related laws promulgated by the federal government since 1914. On October 27, 1970, President Nixon signed into law the Comprehensive Drug Abuse Prevention and Control Act of 1970 (P.L. 91-513). Thus all federal dangerous drug, narcotic, and marijuana laws are consolidated into one comprehensive act designed to control the legitimate drug industry and to curtail importation and distribution of illicit drugs throughout the United States.

CONTROLLED SUBSTANCES ACT (1971). With the passage of the Controlled Substance Act, effective May 1, 1971, the control of narcotics and dangerous drugs was transferred from the Treasury Department, Internal Revenue Service, to the Department of Justice, Bureau of Narcotics and Dangerous Drugs (BNDD).

Many items not previously restricted are now included on the list of controlled substances, and stricter requirements for obtaining and handling such substances have been established. Five schedules of controlled substances have been defined.

Schedule 1 substances. Drugs in this schedule are those that have no *currently* accepted medical use in the United States.

Some examples are heroin, marijuana, LSD, peyote, mescaline, psilocybin, tetrahydrocannabinol, morphine, methylsulfonate, and nicocodeine.

Schedule II substances. The drugs in this schedule have a high abuse potential with severe psychic or physical dependence liability. Most Schedule II substances have been known in the past as Class A narcotic drugs. One nonnarcotic group is currently included in this schedule, the amphetamines, including methamphetamines (Syndrox, Desoxyn, Methedrine). Some examples of Schedule II narcotic substances are opium, morphine, codeine, dihydromorphinone (Dilaudid), methadone (Dolophine), pantopium (Pantopon), meperidine (Demerol), cocaine, and oxycodone (Percodan).

Schedule III substances. The drugs in this schedule have an abuse potential less than those in Schedules I and II and include those drugs formerly known as Class B narcotics, and, in addition, nonnarcotic drugs such as glutethimide (Doriden), phenmetrazine (Preludin), methyprylon (Noludar), methylphenidate (Ritalin), nalorphine, and barbiturates (except phenobarbital, methylphenobarbital, and barbital). Paregoric is now listed in this schedule.

Schedule IV substances. The drugs in this schedule have an abuse potential less than those listed in Schedule III and include barbital, phenobarbital, methylphenobarbital, chloral hydrate, ethchlorvynol (Placidyl), ethinamate (Valmid), and meprobamate (Equanil and Miltown).

Schedule V substances. The drugs in this schedule have an abuse potential less than those listed in Schedule IV and consist of those preparations formerly known as *exempt narcotics,* with the exception of paregoric (camphorated tincture of opium).

State laws
PRESIDENTIAL PROPOSAL

President Nixon also called for a *model state controlled substances act* designed to achieve uniformity among the laws of the various states and that of the federal government. This proposed state legislation was designed to complement the then pending federal narcotic and dangerous drug legislation and to provide an interlocking trellis of federal and state laws, thereby enabling government at all levels to control the drug abuse problem.

The main objective of this uniformity act is to create a coordinated and codified system of drug control, similar to that utilized at the federal level, classifying all narcotics, marijuana, and dangerous drugs subject to control into five schedules, each schedule having its own criteria for drug placement. This classification system enables the agency charged with implementation to add, delete, or reschedule substances based upon new scientific findings and the abuse potential of the substance.

Another objective of this act is to establish a regulatory system for the legitimate handlers of controlled drugs in order to curtail illicit drug diversion. This system will require that these individuals register with a designated state agency, maintain records, and make biennial inventories of all controlled drug stock.

The act sets out the prohibited activities in detail but leaves specific fines or sentences to the discretion of the individual state. It does provide innovative law enforcement tools to improve investigative efforts and provides for interim education and training programs relating to the drug abuse problem.

The model state controlled substances act updates existing state laws and ensures legislative and administrative flexibility to enable the states to cope with both present and future drug problems. It is recognized that law enforcement may not be the ultimate solution to the drug abuse problem. It is hoped that present research efforts will be continued and vigorously expanded, particularly as they relate to the development of rehabilitation, treatment, and educational programs for addicts, drug-dependent persons, and potential drug abusers.

Thirty-five states are presently considering passage of the Uniform Act in their legislatures. At this time, 16 states and 2 territories have enacted the Uniform Controlled Substances Act. They include Arkansas, Idaho, Iowa, Louisiana, Maryland, Mississippi, Nevada, New Jersey, North Dakota, Oklahoma, South Dakota, Tennessee, Utah, Virginia (which passed a modified version), West Virginia, Wyoming, Guam, and the Virgin Islands.

The act is at various stages of passage or consideration before the legislatures of the following states and territories: California, Delaware, the District of Columbia, Hawaii, Illinois, Kansas, Maine, Michigan, Minnesota, Missouri, Nebraska, New Mexico, North Carolina, South Carolina, Texas, Vermont, Washington, Wisconsin, Puerto Rico, and American Samoa.

CRIMINAL LAWS

Criminal penalties for the use of illegal drugs vary from state to state. Classifications of violation differ, as do the lengths of sentences for transporting, selling, or using different drugs, the laws affecting treatment, parole practices, and so on. The teacher or counselor whose responsibilities include working with drug users should know the laws as they apply in his particular state. Many municipalities also have specific ordinances regarding marijuana, narcotics, and dangerous drugs and these also may be consulted.

As an example of the laws applying in one particular state, California, there follows a summary prepared by Robert L. Blake, a past president of the Santa Clara County Bar Association, and used here with his permission.

CRIMINAL PENALTIES FOR UNLAWFUL DRUG USE IN THE STATE OF CALIFORNIA*

The criminal penalties are broken down into three major categories.

*Modified from Blake, R. L.: A short summary of drug laws, Santa Clara, Calif., 1971, Catholic Social Service.

1. The penalties for offenses in connection with narcotics
2. Offenses in connection with marijuana
3. Offenses in connection with dangerous drugs

In each of the three categories the punishment not only increases substantially with each subsequent offense, but the offenses themselves carry higher punishment as they move up from possession to possession for sale to actual sale, to furnishing transportation, and finally to the offense of an adult encouraging a minor to possess, sell, or use. Although many of the offenses can carry a maximum sentence of life imprisonment, the minimum, or, in the language of the street, the "must do" time, is generally more important. The first offense of possession of narcotics carries a maximum punishment of 10 years but probation is possible. A second conviction of the same offense, however, although only calling for a maximum of 20 years, requires a minimum of 5 years. A first offense of sale of narcotics and a second offense both call for a maximum of life imprisonment, but probation is possible on a first offense, and a 10-year minimum term is required on a second offense.

A first offense of possession of marijuana can be treated either as a misdemeanor, which would carry a maximum of 1 year in the county jail, or as a felony, which would carry a maximum of 10 years in prison. A second conviction of possession of marijuana calls for a maximum of 20 and a minimum of 2 years in prison.

Generally speaking, crimes involving dangerous drugs carry smaller penalties than narcotic offenses or marijuana offenses. In practice, however, the actual penalties imposed are usually greater in dangerous drug cases than in marijuana cases.

There are some miscellaneous offenses relating to all narcotics (including marijuana), such as possession of paraphernalia used for injecting or smoking a narcotic, visiting in a place where narcotics are being used, and maintaining a place for the furnishing or using of any narcotic. These are

Table 5-1. Statutory penalties[1] for illegal sale and possession of narcotics and restricted dangerous drugs*

DRUG	SALE			SALE TO MINORS			POSSESSION[2]			CALIFORNIA HEALTH AND SAFETY CODE SECTION
	First offense	Second[3] offense	Third offense	First offense	Second offense	Third offense	First offense	Second offense	Third offense	
Heroin, opium, morphine, codeine, Demerol, etc., cocaine	5 yr to life	10 yr to life	15 yr to life	10 yr to life	10 yr to life	15 yr to life	2 to 10 yr	5 to 20 yr	15 yr to life	11500 11501 11502
Marijuana	5 yr to life	5 yr to life	10 yr to life	10 yr to life	10 yr to life	15 yr to life	2 to 10 yr	5 to 15 yr	10 yr to life	11530.5 11531 11532
LSD, DMT Depressants Nembutal, Seconal, etc. (barbiturates) Miltown, Librium (tranquilizers) Stimulants Benzedrine (amphetamine), Methamphetamine (Desoxyn, etc.)	Jail[4] or 1 to 5 yr	2 to 10 yr		1 to 5 yr	2 to 10 yr		Fine or jail of maximum 1 yr	Jail or 1 to 5 yr		11910 11912 11913
Other prescription drugs (antibiotics, etc.)	Fine or jail of 1 yr maximum						Not restricted			26255, also B & P Code, Sec. 4227

*From California Health and Safety Code, 1965.
[1]The law also specifies minimal times that must be served prior to parole.
[2]Many of these drugs may be sold and possessed on the prescription of a physician.
[3]Second and third offenses include other violations of narcotic laws.
[4]A misdemeanor is a fine or jail sentence not to exceed 1 year. Any sentence over 1 year is a felony.

all misdemeanor offenses and provide for a maximum of 6 months to a year in the county jail, at least with regard to the first offense.

In addition to the jail penalties that can be imposed, there are other penalties that flow from most of these offenses. In general a felony conviction deprives an individual of most of his civil rights, including the right to vote. There are also provisions requiring a person who has been convicted of possessing marijuana or narcotics, or of any of the more serious crimes, to register with the chief of police of the city in which he resides.

In some situations a person who is addicted to narcotics can, after an appropriate hearing, be confined at a California rehabilitation center for treatment. If the individual satisfactorily completes a period of rehabilitation, no jail or prison penalty is normally imposed. The district attorney must consent to a so-called CRC commitment of an indivdual charged with one of the more serious offenses.

DRUG ABUSE TREATMENT AND THE LAWS OF THE STATE OF CALIFORNIA*

The legislature of this state has made the treatment of a narcotics addict by a physician in private practice extremely difficult, if not impossible. The law provides that no person shall treat an addict for addiction except in a county jail, state prison, state hospital, county hospital, county-operated mental health center, or an institution approved by the Board of Medical Examiners. In 1970 the legislature amended the law to provide that methadone in the continuing treatment of narcotic addiction shall be used only in those programs approved by the California Research Advisory Panel. The Research Advisory Panel was originally set up to encourage research into the nature and effects of marijuana and hallucinogenic drugs. Physicians are prohibited from issuing prescriptions to an addict or habitual user of narcotics, not in the normal course of professional treatment, but for the purpose of providing the user with narcotics sufficient to keep him comfortable by maintaining his customary use. A physician is also prohibited from prescribing, administering, or furnishing a narcotic to or for any person who is not under his treatment for a pathology or condition other than narcotic addiction. The requisites for addiction are as follows:

1. Emotional dependence on the drug in the sense that the user experiences a compulsive need to continue its use
2. A tolerance to its effects that leads the user to require larger and more potent doses
3. Physical dependence so that the user suffers withdrawal symptoms if he is deprived of his dosage.

There is an exception allowing the treatment of an addict by the use of narcotics

*Modified from Blake, R. L.: A short summary of drug laws, Santa Clara, Calif., 1971, Catholic Social Service.

during emergency treatment. No definition is given as to what "emergency treatment" covers.

COMMUNITY ACTION

It is often difficult for parents to admit that they may have a drug problem within their own family; a community may be equally reluctant to face up to its drug problem.

Too often the people in a community are unwilling to admit that there is a problem until something drastic happens. Resistance to a drug program occurs unless there already has been a serious drug confrontation in a community. For many "pillars of the community," it is much more convenient to sweep the problem under the rug or to pretend that it does not exist—not in *their* community! The truth is that even if only *one* child in the community is involved with drugs, that community has the beginning of a drug problem. Use by one child may be highly symptomatic of the approaching use by many others. There are going to be communities that are going to say that they really do not have a drug problem. Denial is the first line of defense for most communities, unfortunately, even when the situation is obvious to an outsider.

It is true that any search for a solution indicates that there is a problem. Once a community considers the possibility of a drug program, it is admitting the necessity for such a program or confessing that some of the area's residents are involved with drugs.

Once a community is able, calmly and objectively, to face the fact that drugs are now within its boundaries and affecting its citizens, what can be done? How, in detail, can responsible, concerned persons in the community take positive action? Admitting that there are no simplistic, overnight answers, *can* teachers and parents band together and accomplish much, if anything at all; can the segments of the community marshall their efforts toward a unified attack? *Yes*, if they go about it rationally. It is imperative, however, that community resources for prevention, control, and treatment be developed and coordinated for effective action.

Objectives

In general there is too much isolation and not enough mutual problem solving and sharing between families in any community. There has to be a much more interrelated and integrated approach. Programs must be a total community effort and should be based on the following objectives:

1. Research and community involvement to determine what the problem is and to set up the machinery to develop and coordinate a program
2. Education of children, parents, and teachers
3. Treatment via clinics, rehabilitation centers, hot lines, and therapy in school and by private professionals
4. Law enforcement to spell out the laws, to alert parents, and to locate drug sources

Coordination by a drug abuse council

Who takes the bull by the horns? Any responsible person in a community—a doctor, a teacher, a minister, a real-estate salesman, or a stockbroker—can take the first step. It simply means accepting the fact that there *is* a drug problem in the community and reaching the conclusion that *something* has to be done about it. Many communities have set up what are, in essence, drug advisory councils, composed of concerned, open-minded persons within the community who are attempting to set up antidrug programs tailored to the specific needs of their communities. The membership comprises a variety of community people; there is no set organizational pattern. Such councils, working closely with the schools, law enforcement, and governmental and nongovernmental agencies, are primarily concerned with how best to educate in a predrug abuse program and how to treat those who

are already abusers. It is their responsibility to enlist community support, coordinate the overall community program, and raise whatever funds are necessary.

It is also up to these councils to lead in an effort to educate the community. Their efforts can assist the teacher or school administrator. Some communities have initiated weekly town meetings during which area doctors, psychologists, law enforcement people, and the like discuss various aspects of the drug problem.

In some ways the job of educating the community has already begun. Representatives from various antidrug groups as well as former addicts are constantly speaking at community meetings. The National Institute of Mental Health has spot announcements on television to transmit information about drugs. It seems clear that all the tools—community groups, television, radio, literature, and local service agencies—should be utilized to spread the message in a steady, ongoing program.

In any community approach to drug abuse, some individuals feel that one of the major errors made is total *failure to get youth involved in the planning stage.* We have seen it happen over and over again. Community leaders all too often sit around, come to "meaningful" decisions, and pass them along to the young people. Although the decisions may be perfectly good ones, they will not have much meaning unless they are validated by young people. This kind of "we-they" thinking is not nearly as effective as a true dialogue.

Any valid, community-based approach must be a *balanced effort between law enforcement, research, education, and treatment,* even if this means confrontation and disagreement. The administration of such a program or series of programs cannot simply be turned over to health or education "professionals"; it has to have the active backing as well as the participation of the legal and educational establishment, influential citizens, and young people from the communities in which the problem first developed. Youth must be part of the solution rather than just part of the problem. Involving the youth is the key to success of any community.

One authority thinks that young people should have a right to be involved with designing programs that are going to have a direct relationship to them and their lives. Various people believe that many students are beginning to assume leadership when they are given the chance. They are striving to bring the school back into the total society, so that the school is an integral part of life and not just some place young people go for 6 or 7 hours before returning to the real world.

There is no doubt that students could be of value in helping to establish a drug education program merely by their aid in deciding what information should be furnished and how it should be presented. Some educators feel that young people could even take on some of the research themselves, such as determining how widespread the problem is in their own community. Such an evaluation has always been difficult to obtain, but perhaps the young people, talking to each other, could arrive at a more accurate estimate of the situation. On the basis of their findings a realistic program might emerge.

Another function of the drug advisory council should be the matter of locating financial support. Some communities have handled this particular concern by soliciting voluntary contributions. In other communities there is often local money available from such sources as state and local health departments and mental health departments.

Particularly important now is the massive federal funding through programs in the Office of Education and the National Institute of Mental Health. Many types of grants are available for counties and individual communities, even individual school districts, to support the development of training and educational programs.

It has been observed that the only communities in which the treatment, prevention, and educational programs achieved a substantial amount of success were those wherein all the elements worked together to seek mutual solutions for the betterment of their most valuable resource—their own children.

Such groups as constitute the community council should consist of two types of persons. First, community leaders who hopefully do not have a vested interest in any one modality should include minority groups, the city mayor and his council, business leaders, clergy, and students. The other group of persons consists of agency heads who do have vested interests and should include law enforcement officials, such as the chief of police; the head of a hospital, clinic, or local health service; local business heads; city and county administrators; city educators, superintendent of schools, etc.; researchers; government administrators (of program monies, etc.); and parents.

Such cooperating groups ought to include the *involved children themselves*. Too often such collaborations achieve merely escalated confrontation with those of school age rather than cooperation. An unhappy split occurs, separating the "we" from the "they" group.

There will always be differences of opinion as to just how such cooperative ventures should function and on whose terms. Drug abuse is intimately linked with human social values. About these values people differ strenuously. That which involves our social values touches upon the most sensitive part of the whole human social system. Certainly attitudes toward drugs center more around personal value systems than on one's knowledge of pharmacy. Large differences in educational emphasis, approach, and ideology, then, will occur from participant to participant, from school to school, and even from community to community.

Unfortunately such conflicts of values rapidly become translated into controversy —easily the most dreaded, threatening aspect of any group venture. A compromise is often achieved by importing a commercial "packaged" program that will hopefully serve the needs of everyone. Such commercially prefabricated efforts toward drug education show a great deal of resourcefulness on the part of their promoters and sometimes benefit from widespread public and private endorsement. They are likely, however, not to meet the needs of individuals involved in personal crises and of group processes unique to the various communities in which they occur. As has been stated before, drug abuse is not so much a problem of pharmacology as one of human needs and values. No single program will meet the needs of all. Drug use, its nature, and the life-style of its different types of users vary widely from city to city and even within the communities of a single city.

Certainly some basic information on the psychopharmacology of drugs as well as the peculiarities of their various uses is a practical and necessary adjunct to any comprehensive educational curriculum. Beyond that the peculiar abuse pattern of each area, modified by the conditions unique to that area, must be dealt with by a concerned public at that time and place. Styles and habits of use are in constant flux. Ambitious programs geared to one style of abuse may rapidly become obsolete.

Role of law enforcement

Our experience has demonstrated that, whatever problem is contemplated for a community, it is essential to bring the police in at the *planning stage*. Do not wait until the program is set up and trouble develops. Ensuring the cooperation, even the *neutrality*, of local law enforcement in the operation of a drug program is vital to its success. If law enforcement personnel are ignored, their hostility to any drug program can almost be guaranteed, and as a consequence of that alone, the program may be doomed to failure.

Community programs and facilities

We need to look at community programs and how they can best be utilized. Basically there are two types of programs: (1) an urban or ghetto-type program and (2) a small town or suburban program. In each case the needs, although similar in some respects, must be approached differently. One stresses treatment; the other is concerned with prevention. One operates with the isolated individual; the other considers him as part of the family unit.

HAIGHT-ASHBURY FREE MEDICAL CLINIC

In the various urban programs available, one of the most common resources is the free clinic, such as the Haight-Ashbury Free Clinic in San Francisco. In Haight-Ashbury, as in certain sections of other cities, a drug culture has evolved, the young people have been totally alienated from their parents, and drug problems tend to be much more severe than in suburban areas. Here drug prevention education is not the major issue, although a task force of workers may spread out through the district to try and steer experimenters away from heavy drug involvement. For the most part, these young people are not concerned with the decision of *whether* to use drugs, but rather with the question of "what kind of drugs will it be this time?"

Let us sidetrack for a moment and take a closer look at the purpose and operation of the Haight-Ashbury Free Clinic. Clearly no one type of clinic is useful for every community but the Haight-Ashbury clinic has for years been the number one touchstone for new national drug abuse patterns. The clinic is a prototype for hundreds now in operation all over the country.

Young persons are viewed as candidates for medical treatment rather than as drug abusers. At the clinic there is a medical section, a dental section, a drug section, and a psychiatric section. The medical section staff deals with general adolescent medicine—abscesses, hepatitis, malnutrition, infections, breakdown of blood vessels, etc. The drug section is equipped to deal with acute drug detoxification and heroin withdrawal. The dental clinic is important because so many drug abusers have poor oral hygiene. Dental pain is one of the reasons people return to heroin use. The psychiatric section works with those patients who have "flipped" or who require long-term therapy.

The Haight-Ashbury Free Clinic is a comprehensive medical facility for drug abusers. A commune health section was recently added to work with the health problems of commune dwellers. In 3 years of operation the clinic has seen over 50,000 patients, the basic focus being acute treatment, crisis intervention, diagnosis, and referral, if possible. Seeing a large number of patients means that most can be worked with for only a short period of time. An attempt is then made to refer them to other programs that have long-term treatment modalities, such as methadone maintenance programs or a therapeutic community. A certain number of patients are kept in long-term treatment using the multiple modality approach and trying a variety of different techniques with different persons.

Extensive use is made of ex-addicts in working with the more compulsive drug users. An outpatient psychiatric clinic works with the psychological problems of the individuals on a one-to-one basis. There is vocational counseling and, at the present time, a small residential facility. There are, in fact, many young drug abusers in long-term treatment, but the majority of the work is short-term crisis intervention, diagnosis, and referral, since about 150 patients are seen each day.

The phases of treatment are outlined in the following.

PHASE 1: DETOXIFICATION. The patient is provided with medication, supportive counseling, and housing while going through withdrawal. Referrals may be made to other existing drug treatment facilities such as those at Mendocino State Hospital, Langley-Porter Neuropsychiatric Institute, and Napa State Hospital, all California facilities, or for intensive medical treatment for drug-related illnesses. The detoxification center will accommodate twenty individuals, a dietician, and staff members and will be housed in the same facilities as the operational headquarters and the officers of the director and his assistant. This phase includes a 24-hour emergency drug information and referral service.

PHASE 2: GROUP HOUSE—SELF-HELP PROGRAM. Certain patients who have passed through detoxification will be admitted to one of the six group residence homes for a stay of 3 to 6 months, as needed. Each residence will be limited to a maximum of ten persons. In a homelike atmosphere, members will share responsibilities for operating and supporting the house and remaining drug free. Therapy will be provided through encounter groups, sensitivity training, and weekly meetings, as well as through special activities designed to expand social and personal experiences.

PHASE 3: GROUP TREATMENT. Group treatment will be provided on a regular weekly basis.

PHASE 4: JOB COUNSELING AND PLACEMENT. Since this is a most important aspect of rehabilitation, a full-time employment counselor provides personal guidance and referrals for testing, training, and placing individuals in temporary, part-time, and full-time work. The intention is to expand job placement relations with community businesses in addition to working through the usual community agencies. Contact is made with vocational training programs as well as with the Department of Rehabilitation, the State Department of Employment, and other job placement and training agencies.

PHASE 5: STREET WORKERS. A mobile team of four ex-users is employed to circulate freely with the street people and provide assistance and guidance if needed.

PHASE 6: THE OUTPOST. A rehabilitation center in the country, when funded, will provide the following: (1) an assembly place for ex-users for group treatment, sensitivity training, creative activities, and special programs and (2) a conference center for staff planning, training, and evaluation.

PHASE 7: FAMILY AND COMMUNITY EDUCATION. This phase provides a crucial bridge between the users, their families, and the community. It will involve (1) group sensitivity training for parents of users and other interested individuals; (2) community education and lecture series; and (3) publication of drug-related literature.

PRESENT SERVICES OFFERED BY THE DRUG TREATMENT PROGRAM. At present the Drug Treatment Program of the Haight-Ashbury Medical Clinic is one of the only drug treatment programs in the city of San Francisco that is effectively helping drug abusers to kick their habits. Approximately 350 users visit on an outpatient basis, 12 on an inpatient basis, and between 30 and 50 new persons come each week.

TEEN OR DROP-IN CENTER

Community resources can be utilized in the development of a teen or drop-in center on campus or off campus. Within this framework the school can be innovative and develop its own approach. For example, the school might provide an open clubroom or locale where students can sit around and talk, or the community may provide such a service and make it available to schools (Chapter 8).

Teen-agers will *come* to a place with a relaxing atmosphere that allows them to be themselves. Pot smoking or drugs might become problems, but they are already problems. An on-campus teen center where students make their own rules to keep drugs out is likely to have more effect in shaping the nucleus of an antidrug culture than strict surveillance by the school.

Such a locale might also be a place where the bad tripper can be cared for. The availability of quick emergency care from a staff of volunteer ex-drug users with clinic medical support as an available backup seems an ideal situation.

As an example, emergency clinics staffed by a nurse, a psychiatric technician, and student aides have been established in four San Francisco high schools. Called "crash pads," these emergency clinics have been set up to care for students. Officially the clinics have been established as part of an experimental project that has three goals:

(1) to save the lives of students overcome by drugs; (2) to preserve and promote the health of students misusing or about to misuse drugs; and (3) to redirect students to seek alternatives to drug use. Specifically the clinics have been looked upon as filling the need for a rap center where young persons can get accurate drug information with no moralizing and relatively little judging and can talk about personal problems with other students, social workers, or teachers—and feel safe doing it.

The point we are trying to make is that the services, including the school health service, existing on the campus should be *made more responsive to student needs* (Chapter 8). Make the school respond to the need and be relevant in its educational approach is the slogan that might express this position.

COMMUNITY FACILITIES

Let us again briefly touch upon the question of facilities and personnel available to communities or already there. The particular treatment facility established must of necessity depend on the community involved. The urban approach can stress prevention as well as different treatment programs. Urban treatment centers often have to deal with hard-core addiction, whereas suburbia is concerned with soft drug abuse. Basically, however, these treatment facilities may be categorized as follows:

1. Crisis centers. These may be part of a clinic, part of a college medical group, or a special section of a hospital. The main purpose of a crisis center is to provide immediate onsite help and long-range support for the drug abuser as well as treatment of acute drug toxicity.

2. Clinics. In addition to being able to handle acute drug toxicity, the clinics concentrate on overall medical treatment, including deleterious drug-caused side effects and long-term therapy.

3. Hot lines. In many parts of the country, groups of young persons, often ex-drug abusers or addicts, are manning round-the-

clock hot lines to answer calls from either curious or drug-disturbed youngsters. Often, under the guidance of a psychologist or other drug expert, these anonymous counselors can provide information, talk down a bad trip on LSD, inform medical authorities of dangerous symptoms, and provide a full range of therapeutic resources and emergency medical treatment centers.

4. Ongoing groups. Informal meetings should be held where adolescents have an opportunity to participate in honest discussions without fear of being arrested. One example is the Fort Bragg Awareness House, an off-campus meeting place for youth where counselors, psychologists, and ex-users are available to answer any and all questions.

5. Self-help groups. One of the most hopeful treatment methods revolves around the so-called "self-help" groups. Usually staffed for the most part by ex-addicts and abusers and operating out of storefronts, offices, or coffeehouses, these rehabilitation centers are springing up around the country. They document the increasing public awareness of the need for alternative health care systems.

AN EXAMPLE OF COOPERATIVE, UNIFIED COMMUNITY ACTION. Guidelines and support from local, state, and federal sources may provide vital initiative. However, drug abuse is specific for any given area and should be handled at its source. The following is an example of how one bay area commuity discovered and solved its drug problem.

Awareness on the part of Center City citizens (ficticious) of the chronic use of drugs by their children came about several years ago almost accidently with the publishing of a series of articles in the local newspaper. Two reporters had been routinely assigned to cover the local marijuana situation because big news had been lagging for several days. They found that a great deal more than marijuana, was being distributed and consumed by local high school and junior high school children.

The reporters spent several days talking with students and collected a large sample of assorted stimulants and depressants, including LSD, DMT, and some mysterious unknowns. They even engaged two local college students to make a study of local drug use, including a sample poll of the attitudes of young persons of various communities in the city toward drug use.

The reporters found additionally that, although the drugs were easily attainable and many of the students had developed serious habits of use, the local, flourishing drug scene had very *low visibility* to both adults and police. Increasing incidents of students falling asleep in class were explained by teachers as due to the all-night beer busts and other social gatherings of students excited because summer and graduation were only a month away. Clearly most of the adult community was out of touch with its youth.

But students, once queried about what was happening, were extremely candid about their drug use. They said that for just a couple of bucks you could buy handfuls of assorted pills from just about anybody. It seemed to be true. Everybody was using just about everything, they said, and everything about the drug business was "kind of loose."

The city was shocked by these disclosures. Over the next several months, community interest and concern, as well as the expected hysteria, slowly mounted. Local response, though, was more or less fractionated. Various concerned citizen groups joined together for discussion and local law enforcement activity against drug users and sellers mounted sharply. Law officers began to pose as local hippies to infiltrate the local scene. Almost immediately children from some of Center City's most respected families were arrested. The community became galvanized into action almost overnight. There was a drug crisis in Center City. Something had to be done and done soon.

The Center City police department, which had reported only 38 total arrests of youth and adults on drug charges during the past year and only one arrest during the previous year, now reported that 44 youths had been arrested in the past 3 months.

These reports culminated in a mass meeting on November 17. Over 1000 people from the community attended the meeting, held in the high school auditorium, to hear a panel discussion on the local drug problem. The panel included a speaker from Synanon, a police sergeant, a probation officer, a doctor, a judge, a high school teacher, several self-confessed users, and the student body president of the local high school.

The mood of the meeting was serious but not vindictive. Everyone agreed that there was a serious drug problem among all the school-age youth and that some kind of substantial action had to be taken. As one might expect, opinions on what to do ranged from "harsh laws won't solve the problem" (judge), "we can't handle every kind of problem here in our classes" (one teacher), to "if you see someone using drugs, you're really saving a life when you snitch on him" (Synanon speaker).

But the idea of community unity, of cooperation without factionalism in educating both the students and the community at large to the problem of youth and drugs easily carried the day. On that point there was almost unanimous agreement. The specific projects and programs that were a result of this meeting clearly reflected the community's orientation; education for the total community is the real key to solving the "November drug crisis."

Residents opened a drug information center on January 20 to provide information to the general public about the danger of drugs, their use, and their effects. Films, literature, and lists of prominent speakers were solicited from the state and other communities to round out the program. These materials were made available at cost to all contingents of the city. Other salient features of the new community

drug center included a 24-hour a day referral service, a "troubled parents" talk session, and a regular teen-age rap session.

A second, dovetailing program was being run at the same time by the local high schools. High school students were selected and sent to the elementary and junior high schools to speak to younger students. The emphasis was on what was really happening, not on how young persons should behave. In short, the youth-to-youth programs were totally reality oriented; or, as they put it, "where it's really at with drugs." Although admittedly the programs may have lacked something in sophistication and even in total accuracy of presentation, the difference was more than made up for by the fact that the students themselves were doing their own program and were personally involved in its outcome.

A third aspect of the community's action response to drug use was also educationally oriented. It involved talks with industrial employees at Center City companies. Local industry requested this service because their own employees had developed a drug problem that started with the night shift crews taking pep pills to stay awake.

A final program, and perhaps the most innovative and helpful in this community, was the "Our Family" halfway house rehabilitation project. The program was a continuation of an innovative state hospital rehabilitation program for narcotic addicts. The halfway house established in Center City was a final, decisive step in an almost totally integrated program, insomuch as one is possible in any large urban center. It provided the needed transition for ex-drug users returning to a useful life as part of the community.

The halfway house served two functions. First, it provided rehabilitated addicts with work at the center or at an outside job, returning them to community life. Second, the center provided its own drug abuse information and education program. It recruited its own rehabilitated addicts to give presentations in Center City and other adjacent communities.

The "Our Family" project offered free weekly counseling for concerned parents and weekly open house meetings where insiders and guests could discuss their handicaps and hang-ups about drugs. Counseling was also scheduled on an individual basis. The Center City Police Department had taken a supporting role and assumed responsibility for the program.

At a recent meeting in a continuing series of the Center City Citizens Committee on Drug Abuse, everyone agreed that things had improved considerably. Where they had not, at least the prospects for the future looked considerably brighter. The name Center City is fictional. But the community and its services really exist.

SUMMARY

This brief and sketchy description of the role of the community in the drug abuse problem should provide information and suggestions about the community resources available for action programs. Programs of treatment, rehabilitation, control, and education should be initiated and carried out on local levels using guidelines and models developed elsewhere, but modified to fit the particular needs of the locale where they are put to use.

Community action includes coordination at all levels of all agencies and organizations, including the schools, for an effective attack on the drug problem.

References

1. Batiste, C. G., and Yablonsky, L.: Synanon: a therapeutic life style, Calif. Med. 114:90, 1971.
2. Benforado, J. M.: A guide to the medical management of acute mind-altering drug reactions, ed. 2, Madison, Wis., 1972, Charitable, Educational and Scientific Foundation of the State Medical Society of Wisconsin.
3. Berman, R.: An introduction to crisis counseling: making the best use of the "dangerous opportunity," Los Angeles, 1970, Los Angeles County Superintendent of Schools Office.
4. Casriel, D. H.: The family physician and the narcotics addict, Panorama, Feb., 1970.
5. Drug abuse: escape to nowhere, Philadelphia, 1969, Smith, Kline & French Laboratories.
6. Garrett, D. L.: Synanon: the communiversity, Humanist 25:184-189, 1965.
7. Mandell, A. J.: The sociology of a multi-modality strategy in the treatment of narcotics addicts. In Blackly, P., editor: Drug abuse, Springfield, Ill., 1971, Charles C Thomas, Publisher.
8. Methadone in the management of heroin addiction, Med. Letter Drugs Ther. 14:13-14, 1972.
9. Methadone, 1972, Connection, Jan.-Feb., 1972.
10. Narcotic antagonists: new methods to treat heroin addiction, Science 173:503-506, 1971.
11. Smith, D. E.: Speech at Michigan Physicians' Conference, Ann Arbor, Mich., Nov., 1970.
12. Smith, D. E., and Bentel, D. J.: Drug Abuse Information Project, The third annual report to the legislature, San Francisco, 1969, University of California San Francisco Medical Center.
13. Smith, D. E., and Bentel, D. J.: Drug Abuse Information Project, the fourth and fifth reports to the legislature, San Francisco, 1970 and 1971, University of California San Francisco Medical Center.
14. Smith, D. E., and Gay, G. R.: Office and emergency room care of the new drug scene, Unpublished paper, San Francisco, 1971, Haight-Ashbury Free Medical Clinic.
15. Taylor, R. L., et al.: Management of "bad trips" in an evolving drug scene, J.A.M.A. 213:422, 1970.
16. Van Dusen, W.: Treatment approaches to drug subcultures, Unpublished monograph, Fort Bragg, Colo., 1969.
17. Watson, D.: National directory of drug abuse treatment programs, Washington, D. C., 1972, National Clearinghouse for Drug Abuse Information.
18. Watson, D., and Sells, G. B.: Directory of narcotic addiction treatment agencies in the United States, Fort Worth, Tex., June 15, 1970, National Institute of Mental Health.

PART III · THE ROLE OF
THE SCHOOL

CHAPTER 6

THE SCHOOL DRUG PROGRAM

Law enforcement, education and science have all failed to come up with a good program of drug abuse prevention.

JOHN FINLATER[10]

At present there is no standard or widely accepted model for planning an effective drug education program. This is an area that urgently needs research, development and demonstration.

. . . There are no recipes for effective drug education programs.

HELEN NOWLIS[15]

Efforts continue in the areas of law enforcement, rehabilitation, and treatment to control and reduce the drug abuse problem, but the realization exists that such efforts by themselves are not adequate, do not reach people at the most appropriate times, nor are they sufficient in themselves to prevent or reduce the problem. Society is turning to educational institutions for help, and the emphasis is being placed on a preventive approach to the problem. The school is expected to act as society's officially designated primary educational agent despite the lack of appropriate guidelines and model programs.

Much confusion exists regarding the role of the school in the drug misuse and abuse problem in the United States. It has been mentioned that this dilemma is due to a number of factors: (1) the lack of clarity in definitions of drug education and drug prevention, (2) the lack of understanding of the nature and extent of drug use and nonuse, (3) the belief that the school's responsibility is solely educational and can be developed and conducted in isolation from the social problems of young people and the community, (4) the confusion as to whether or not educational objectives should solely emphasize turning off students to drug use, and (5) the objection to the sordid image of the addict, the street pusher, and the youthful abuser (long hair, dirty, lazy), stereotypes that some people believe relate to student drug experimentation and drug abuse, among other forms of deviance. Thus drug education has been labeled as a controversial subject for inclusion in the curriculum. In addition, the information available today does not provide simple or complete answers to the drug problem. Nor are there easy or single solutions. Adequate ways for schools to help solve the problem do not exist despite the many excellent efforts that have occurred in recent years and that are now taking place. Schools have been, and are, active in developing fragmentary, superficial, "crash," incomplete, and uncoordinated programs that frequently produce ineffectual results.

Schools alone cannot solve the drug problem now confronting society. However, they have a unique and special role to play in its resolution. The conclusion has been reached that there is no one best, effective school program in operation today. Nor has anyone attempted to define or identify the nature of an adequate or complete program. Is it any wonder that schools are criticized for ineffective programs? The forces in society tell schools to take action and yet the schools must explore and experiment with a variety of ways to find solutions because they are not provided with the needed parameters. When schools fail in their efforts, they are subject to criticisms that are often unjustified. This book has been prepared in order to help in this dilemma. We are attempting to provide guidelines that will give the clarity and direction that schools so desperately need. We do not mean to be prescriptive, since there is no single model or single program that is usable, or useful, in all schools. Each school or school district must devise and determine its own program to meet local needs. Programs in ghetto areas may have different emphases than those in middle-class communities. The material contained in this book will provide directions and practical suggestions that can be utilized in developing suitable and appropriate school programs. There is sufficient diversity so that schools can be innovative and creative in resolving local problems.

Before identifying the conceptual model of the school drug program there are important fundamental principles with which the reader must be acquainted.

PRINCIPLES

An effective preventive school drug program must give consideration to the following basic principles:

1. The nature and extent of the drug problem (Chapter 1) in each school and school district must be identified, and attention must be given to the variety of physical, psychological, social, and spiritual needs of the users and nonusers of drugs. Although the majority of pupils are nonusers of the illegal drugs, there are a substantial number who are experimenters, a considerably smaller number of periodic and infrequent users, and a very small group of so-called compulsive users. This student distribution may vary according to area and to type of drug.

2. The school program must include more than just education. Students who are periodic, compulsive, and relapse users and abusers of drugs will need special counseling, guidance, and assistance that cannot be provided in the usual educational program.

3. Drug misuse and abuse must be viewed as symptomatic in nature and as illustrative behavior. Drug use provides alternatives that help young persons satisfy such needs as excitement or thrills, avoidance of pressures, escape from boredom, escape from certain environmental conditions, attainment of identity, definition of self-image, development of values, success experiences, security, peer challenge, affection, independence, and equality of opportunity. Drug abuse unquestionably is related to such social and spiritual factors as war, violence and destruction, bias and prejudice, stress on materialism, dichotomies in values and morals in terms of beliefs as opposed to practices, the search for life's meaning, and the influence of the mass media. Thus the basic deterrents to drug misuse and abuse appear not to be directly concerned with drugs themselves but with (a) social environment, (b) provision for a variety of necessary social and spiritual considerations and arrangements, and (c) encouragement and improvement of communications between youth and adults. These factors provide some of the basic elements needed for student guidance and curriculum development. Such considerations will aid students in the development of more effective ways of handling problems rather than seeking solutions through the risk-taking use of drugs.

4. The established goals of the program should be behaviorally centered. Although

factual, nonbiased information about drugs is necessary, such understandings by themselves usually do not have much effect on the life-styles of the young. The didactic, authoritative, teacher-centered, "scare" approaches to learning will have little if any impact on most students. Students need to be involved attitudinally and engaged actively in discussions, explorations, discoveries, and other activities that relate directly to the social context in which they are living if practices in the use and abuse of drugs are to be affected.

5. The school atmosphere should focus on the improvement of the quality of human interaction and human relatedness, especially between teachers and students. This approach is usually referred to as the humanistic approach, or the humanistic emphasis. Schools, and especially teachers, need to be more concerned with pupils than with the content they teach. The drug problem is a human problem.

6. School activities must be related to and coordinated with those efforts taking place outside the school and should involve the participation of the community, including parents. The support of the community and its resources is most important for effective programs. Drysdale indicates this need in this statement: ". . . it is a partnership of State agencies that must be joined with a partnership of community agencies in each locality if we are to make a comprehensive and effective effort to combat the critical problem of youthful drug abuse."[9] By the same token, schools can encourage and motivate communities to develop and make available a variety of services that are useful to the young persons attending their institutions. The need for parental help must not be overlooked for effective results. A parent educational program could be one method of parental participation.

7. The educational program should be graded and sequential in order to reach all students. It should begin in kindergarten, although it could start earlier in districts that have preschool programs. Many authorities believe the most effective edu-cational program to be one that reaches children and youth at the earliest age that they start to be involved in the use of drugs and especially before they start experimenting with illegal drugs. Primary prevention is thought to be of the greatest importance in reducing the drug problem.

8. Student involvement in the planning, management, and implementation of the drug program is essential. Although the manner and extent of pupil participation is not clear and is in need of identification, and although the degree of effectiveness of such involvement is not known, the action is logically and defensibly sound. Areas in which the use of young persons has been tried by schools include the following: determining student needs, conducting surveys, program planning, peer-group education, ex-addict presentations, developing teaching materials, teacher and parent education, and evaluation.

9. Teachers, counselors, and other school personnel involved in the guidance of students with special drug problems must not only be academically competent and qualified, but must be able to communicate effectively with young persons.

These basic fundamentals clearly identify the need for a multidimensional, multiphased school program to implement the principles outlined. Therefore, as a result of an exploration of activities now occurring in schools in many of the states, together with an extensive review of the literature and of suggestions by a variety of authorities in education, pharmacology, medicine, and other fields, and in the light of our varied experiences in the drug scene and in educational circles, a conceptual model of a school drug program has been developed. It is based on a philosophical approach to the school drug problem and includes education as a part of a broader program. It needs to be tried and tested.

THE PROGRAM

The school drug program model that has been designed includes the following four distinctive phases: (1) education, (2) services, (3) school atmosphere, or climate, and (4) coordination. These phases, however, cannot be developed without the consideration of certain administrative problems, which will be introduced in later chapters.

The following details outline the parts of a school drug program that will receive extensive coverage in the succeeding chapters.

I. Drug education
  A. Students
    1. Formal education
      a. Patterns of instructional organization
      b. Curriculum development
        (1) Scope and sequence
        (2) Curriculum guide
          (a) Concept approach
          (b) Objectives
          (c) Content
          (d) Methods
          (e) Resources
          (f) Evaluation
    2. Informal education
    3. Resource centers
    4. Factors in need of consideration for program implementation
  B. Parents
    1. Formal education
    2. Informal education
II. Drug services
  A. Identification of abuse drugs
  B. Identification of drug users and abusers
  C. Assistance for users and abusers
  D. Follow-up procedures
    1. Counseling and guidance
    2. Use of community resources
    3. Adjustment of school programs
III. School atmosphere
  A. Student alienation and unrest
  B. Physical and psychological needs of students
  C. Creating humaneness in schools
IV. Coordination of the program
  A. Administration organization
    1. Leadership
    2. Advisory drug committee
  B. Policies and procedures
  C. Role of personnel
  D. Finance
  E. In-service preparation
  F. Evaluation

References

1. Alsever, W. D.: An evaluation of marihuana for school physicians, nurses and educators, J. Sch. Health 38:629-638, 1968.
2. American School Health Association: Teaching about drugs: a curriculum guide, K-12, ed. 2, Kent, Ohio, 1971, Association Press.
3. Barrins, P. C.: How to face up to drug abuse in your schools and your community, Am. Sch. Board J. 158:17-20, 1970.
4. Bureau of Narcotics and Dangerous Drugs, United States Department of Justice: Guidelines for drug abuse prevention education, Washington, D. C., 1970, Government Printing Office.
5. Cohen, S.: The drug dilemma: a partial solution. In Resource book for drug abuse education, Washington, D. C., 1969, National Clearinghouse for Mental Health Information.
6. Drug education handbook, Denver, 1970, Alcohol and Drug Dependence Division, Colorado State Department of Public Health.
7. Cornacchia, H. J.: Teaching in difficult areas in health, J. Sch. Health 41:193-196, 1971.
8. Demos, G. D., and Bennett, J. C., editors: Drug abuse and what we can do about it., Springfield, Ill., 1970, Charles C Thomas, Publisher.
9. Drysdale, E. J.: Youthful drug abuse: the problem and program, J. Drug Educ. 1: 93-99, 1971.
10. Finlator, J.: The drug scene: the scope of the problem faced by the schools. In American School Health Association: Teaching about drugs: a curriculum guide, K-12, Kent, Ohio, 1970, Association Press.
11. Greenberg, J. S.: Drug abuse and the schools, J. Drug Educ. 1:171-175, 1971.
12. Lewis, D. C.: How the schools can prevent drug abuse, N.A.S.S.P. Bull. 54:43-51, 1970.
13. Miller, T. J.: Drug abuse: schools find some answers, Sch. Manage. pp. 27-31, 1970.
14. National School Public Relations Association: Drug crisis: schools fight back with innovative programs, Washington, D. C., 1971, Association Press.
15. Nowlis, H.: Drugs on the college campus, Garden City, N. Y., 1969, Anchor Books.
16. Ochberg, F. M.: Drug problems and the high school principal, N.A.S.S.P. Bull. 54:52-59, 1970.
17. Petrillo, R. F.: Comprehensive action model to combat drug abuse in high school, J. Sch. Psychol. 8:226-230, 1970.
18. Prettyman, R. L., et al.: Drug abuse and the school scene, Sci. Teacher 37:45-47, 1970.
19. Report of the Ad Hoc Committee on Drug Abuse, Dallas, 1970, Superintendent of Schools, Dallas Independent School District.
20. Taylor, R. M., and Rackers, J.: How Missouri high school principals deal with student use of tobacco, alcohol, narcotics and drugs, Sch. and Country 56:7, 1970.
21. A teacher resource guide for drug use and abuse for Michigan schools, Lansing, 1970, Michigan State Department of Education.

CHAPTER 7

DRUG EDUCATION

The capacity of this society to learn to live wisely in a world in which chemicals and chemical change will be increasingly significant will depend, in very large measure, on the understanding our citizens have of both themselves and the effects, dangerous and beneficial, of an ever-growing list of chemical compounds. In this context, the necessity for effective drug education is paramount.

. . . We believe that the purpose (of education) must be to provide the basis for informed and wise personal choice. The ultimate effect that we would hope for is reasonable control and even overall reduction in the non-medical use of drugs.

LE DAIN COMMISSION INTERIM REPORT[49a]

Making drug education an integral part of the preventive phase of a school drug program has been widely advocated by Yolles,[94] Langer,[48] Lewis,[52] and Mikeal and Smith,[58] among others. These sources indicate that had adequate programs been available to children before they started using drugs, in fact, if such programs were now operative, the drug problem could be measurably reduced.

The quality of present drug education programs is perhaps best expressed by Halleck[32] in the title of his article, "The Great Education Hoax." He concludes that present programs may be encouraging rather than discouraging drug usage. Halleck does not question the need for education, but believes that present programs are too narrowly focused and fail to include an emphasis on the larger social and ethical issues. He claims that instruction must deal with the basic causes of human despair; otherwise the programs are nothing more than cop-outs. We agree, adding that psychological and spiritual matters must also be part of any educational program. These matters will be discussed later in this chapter.

Yolles indicates that educational efforts must be appropriate for specific population groups and should have the best educational and scientific bases available. The omission or lack of consideration of these points, in addition to the numerous crash, fragmented, and incomplete efforts that are under way in schools, are sufficient reasons to suspect the quality of many programs today.

The comments of authorities indicate that drug education programs may have value, but that those now operating may not be preventive. They may not be turning youth off drugs; they may not be helping youth to identify alternatives to drugs or to establish values. Apparently better understanding by school personnel and new approaches are needed if education is to have any significant impact on young people. This chapter provides information that will be useful to administrators, teachers, and others not only in defining a complete approach to the situation but also in developing and conducting quality drug education programs. It will address itself to the criticisms about education introduced in Chapter 1 as well as to numerous other points. It will attempt to offer positive suggestions for the improvement of present educational offerings.

Essentially the material that follows considers both student and parent educational programs. Such complementary efforts are necessary for permanent and lasting results with young people. The student phase includes (1) formal education, that is, patterns of instructional organization and curriculum, (2) informal education, (3) resource centers, and (4) personnel needed for program implementation—teachers, counselors, nurses, students, and the community. The parent phase will give consideration to both formal and informal education.

DRUG EDUCATION FOR STUDENTS

Instructional programs must give attention to the variety of student drug users—the nonusers, the experimenters, and the periodic, the compulsive, and the relapse users. To adequately meet these needs it is necessary to integrate the drug education program with all phases of the school curriculum. Whatever occurs within the school will have implications for drug education because the drug problem is a "people problem." In addition, both formal and informal drug education programs must be provided. The formal phase will more effectively reach the majority of young people who are nonusers and experimenters in the regular classroom setting. The informal phase, which usually occurs in various settings outside the classroom, is generally more appropriate for the periodic, compulsive, and relapse users of drugs. No program, however complete, can ever be designed to meet the needs of all students at all times. Nevertheless if the broad spectrum of educational offerings includes both formal and informal aspects and is inte-

grated throughout the school program, the chances will be greatest not only of reaching but also of positively influencing many of the young people in school.

Student formal education

Numerous authorities agree that a comprehensive, sequential program of drug education should be provided in schools at all grade levels from K through 12. We need to reach students before they start using illegal drugs so that hopefully they will not want to begin. We need to help young people use all drugs wisely. This is the primary preventive approach. Few programs now in operation are so broadly developed, although many are now emerging that could achieve such a goal if they continue to be financially supported for a minimum of 3 to 5 years and have qualified leadership. However, there are no model programs to direct schools, and there are only a few attempts at illustrative programs from which schools may seek guidance, although programs are becoming more numerous. Many curriculum guides have been developed, but most need considerable improvement. School personnel in need of help should find this chapter useful and practical. The material on curriculum should be of special assistance.

Where to put drug education in the curriculum is a frequent administrative problem. Should drug education be a separate, self-contained subject, or should it be a unit or a segment in another course or area? There does not seem to be any support for the separate subject status and the latter approach is the one most widely used. However, a further question can be asked, should drug education be a part of health education, science, social science, English, physical education, biology, chemistry, government, or some other subject? It actually has relationships to all of these subject fields and might well be included in any or all of them. Would it perhaps be simpler to conduct one or two large assembly programs with all students in attendance and not be concerned about where to place drug education in the curriculum? These questions all relate to the patterns of instructional organization for drug education. How best to organize the instructional program to accommodate drug education is a significant question for administrators.

PATTERNS OF INSTRUCTION

No one organizational arrangement for drug education has been demonstrated to be the most effective in schools to date. Philosophically, it would be ideal to have a totally integrated instructional approach. Thus wherever formal education is offered, not only would the direct and correlated patterns exist, but they would be related to informal education and with all the other phases of the school drug program. Although efforts should be made to achieve such a goal, realistically it may not be possible. The complexity of operating such a system, the limitations in funds, and other restrictions imposed on schools are the main obstacles inhibiting such a program.

Nationally, schools do not appear to be making efforts to move forward and provide the integrated arrangement. At this stage many schools are struggling merely to include formal education in their curriculum, which is evidenced by the sporadic, piecemeal, and crash programs that are emerging. Some administrators believe that a simple solution to drug education is to have an assembly with all students present, bring in a few speakers, and give students the facts. In other situations students participate in a special day- or week-long program in which the drug problem is emphasized. These approaches are questionable practices that have little impact on students. Quite often they act as substitutes for other, more appropriate educational arrangements.

The organizational patterns of formal drug education usually refer to the direct and correlated patterns of instruction. The direct pattern includes drug education as part of a subject that usually deals with a variety of health problems and seeks changes in the health behavior of students; this occurs in health education. The correlated pattern means that instruction is co-related to other subjects in the curriculum that generally do not focus on health matters or practices, as in social studies or biology. In health education, attitudes and behaviors are oriented toward health and are people centered; in other curriculum areas the purposes are more likely to focus on cognitive objectives. Cognitive ends by themselves usually have little or no impact on healthful living.

In the secondary schools the direct and correlated patterns of instruction are easily distinguished. However, it is more complex at the elementary level. In elementary schools using the direct arrangement one might find drug education as a part of a subject area such as health education. Thus drug education would have status with other subjects such as language arts or social studies. The direct pattern could also refer to specific drug units that may be part of health education or entirely separated as distinct areas of instruction, provided time is allowed in the curriculum. The direct arrangement could also mean that the drug education program is related to social studies and science. In such instances drug education could be said to be co-related but often is said to be integrated into the curriculum. At the elementary level the words "correlated" and "integrated" are frequently used synonymously. Perhaps the distinction can be made that if elementary students are exposed to only one teacher daily, as in the self-contained classroom, a subject may be said to be integrated into the curriculum, whereas if students experience a variety of teachers daily in differing subject areas, a subject is said to be correlated into the curriculum.

Both the direct and the correlated patterns of instruction present problems and difficulties that need to be resolved in order to achieve the greatest degree of effectiveness. The correlated pattern is probably more complex and less likely to effect changes in the health behavior of students. The direct approach is believed to offer the best promise for providing the most effective drug education at both the elementary and secondary levels. Support for this position will be presented shortly.

The correlated organizational pattern of drug education seems to be the one most frequently used in schools today. However, a growing number of developing programs use the direct pattern. Perhaps administrative ease is the primary reason for selecting the correlation arrangement. It is relatively simple to decide to put new content and new social problems or matters into already existing curriculum subjects, especially if no subject such as health education is offered.

Drug education may be correlated with numerous subject matters. In each area drug education is approached through different methods to achieve various objectives. Examples of this correlation with the major subject areas might include the following:

Biology	Effects of drugs on the circulatory, respiratory, nervous, and other systems of the body; possible chromosomal and brain damage; other drug-induced organ damage
Chemistry	Chemical properties of alcohol, tobacco, and drugs; effects of smoking on chemical exchange of oxygen and carbon dioxide in the lungs; process of alcohol breakdown in the liver; percentage of alcohol in the blood
English	Preparation of essays, themes, poems, and speeches; reading and interpreting popular magazine articles, books, and pamphlets; analyzing themes of rock music
Driver education and safety	Effects of alcohol and drugs on accidents; cigarettes and fires
Government	Manufacturing, processing, distribution, sales, and taxes on the economics of the nation; role in the control of sale and distribution of drugs; prevention, rehabilitation, and treatment of addicts
History	Use of drugs by man throughout the ages; opium in Chinese settlements; morphine addiction of U. S. soldiers in the Civil War; the frontier and drugs; foreign, national, and state laws
Physical education	Drugs and their relationships to fitness and performance in athletics
Mathematics	A statistical information analysis of costs, profits, taxes, and other economic factors related to alcohol, tobacco, and drugs; percentages, graphs, budgets, and charts
Psychology	Motivational research in advertising; how to change attitudes and behaviors toward drugs; why people use drugs
Social studies	Incidence of drug use in society; foreign, national, state, and local laws; drugs in the culture and society; drugs and crime, poverty, and inequalities; student unrest and alienation

The following conditions should be operative if drug education is to be correlated into the curriculum:

1. Curriculum materials should be available that identify the specific content for each subject area with clearly stated goals to be achieved.
2. Teachers should be selected who are interested, or willing to become interested, in including drug information in their subject fields.
3. Provision is made for appropriate in-service preparation of teachers with supportive help from resource teachers when desired to maintain interest and obtain current information.
4. Responsible school personnel should be administratively assigned to (a) coordinate the correlation efforts, (b) help keep teachers up to date and interested, and (c) periodically evaluate the program.
5. It should be included as part of a broader, integrated, school drug program as outlined herein. It should be a segment of a formal and informal, comprehensive drug education program that also includes the direct approach.

The primary advantage of the correlated approach may be the fact that the drug problem needs a multidisciplinary educational attack. Drugs relate to people in all phases of life. If the topic is placed in any one area, such as science or social studies, the goal of a multidisciplinary program may not be achieved. If drug education is placed in several subject areas, problems of coordination immediately need to be resolved.

All too frequently when new content areas are proposed for school curricula, administrators are prone to use only the correlated approach because of the organizational ease of making it operational. It is a simple solution that quickly resolves the dilemma of where to place the topic in the school curriculum. Unfortunately when such action has occurred in the past, little or no consideration was given to the correlation problems previously identified. Neither was much if any thought given to the goals to be achieved or to the quality of the educational program. Such action and lack of concern could well be the main difficulties with present drug education programs and the reason for their ineffectiveness.

Additional problems with the correlated approach support the need to consider a different way to present drug education in the curriculum. Frequently the objectives in these programs are not behavior or even health centered; some teachers may not wish to introduce other content into their crowded subject areas; no one may be available to coordinate the program. Therefore drug programs are dumped into the curriculum by administrative edict, and teachers are not always enthusiastically receptive. In addition, many teachers will not be interested or will not feel qualified to teach about drugs. Thus although the initial effort in launching a correlated program may meet with some success, it is doomed to failure or disappearance within a relatively short time because of the difficulties outlined. This will be especially true if no one periodically rejuvenates the program, motivates teachers,

and occasionally assesses results. A few individual, dedicated teachers will continue their efforts, but when it becomes apparent that administrative support has waned, and when other matters of greater importance need attention, drug education will be pushed aside in order to take care of more pressing problems.

The logical, probably more natural, and perhaps most effective way of organizing the formal instructional program for drug education places this social health problem in a course or subject area that deals with all student health problems. Health education would be such a subject area. This pattern of instruction is the direct pattern because the content relates better with health problems, including venereal disease, communicable and chronic diseases, mental health, smoking, nutrition, and family health. Health education is gaining wide acceptance by students because it provides meaningful, relevant, and useful information.

The advantages of presenting drug education as part of health education include the following:

1. Curriculum materials in health education have been developed over the years and would continue to be developed with drugs included as one important area. A sequential, comprehensive drug program throughout the grades is more easily and more effectively achieved through an ongoing program of health education.

2. The concept approach to the teaching of health education, including drug education, identifies behaviorally centered objectives. This is the philosophical concept under which current health education curricula are developed and operated.

3. The teachers of established health education programs in junior and senior high schools are interested, generally well qualified, and desire to add drug education to the health program. It is easier for these teachers to maintain this interest, to become knowledgeable, and to become familiar with current information.

4. Teachers of health education are usually concerned not only with the acquisi-

tion of information—cognitive domain—but also with the modification of attitudes and practices. Thus goals are more apt to be established accordingly.

5. Drug education as part of health education programs has been endorsed and promoted by at least 13 state departments of education, including California, Colorado, Delaware, Illinois, Maine, Maryland, Michigan, Nebraska, New Jersey, New York, Pennsylvania, Utah, and Washington.

6. Drug education can more easily be evaluated and adapted to changing conditions and local community problems if it is included in health education.

The main problem with including drug education in health education is that vast numbers of schools do not yet include this subject in their curricula. Although many schools are adding this subject, many others are still in need of a health education program. Related to this problem is an auxiliary one. In a few schools where health education is provided, it is a weak and poorly taught area. These problems may be due to a variety of reasons, including insufficient administrative support and recognition of the subject; ineffective teaching, primarily due to poorly qualified and uninterested instructors; and the absence of a responsible administrative coordinator to oversee the program. These situations can be rather easily resolved.

If the fragmented, piecemeal approach to drug education is to be modified to provide an instructional program with impact on young people, such a program must include a formal education component that incorporates both the direct and correlated instructional patterns outlined herein. However, if only one such arrangement is possible, we believe that the program more likely to be ongoing, continually improved, and effective in the lives of young persons will present drug education as a part of health education.

CURRICULUM

To provide continuity with a minimum of overlapping and duplication of content, a scope and sequence should be developed that indicates the nature of the drug content and the grade or grade levels at which this material is to be introduced in each school or school district. This local approach is necessary to develop a curriculum that is relevant to any given community. The student drug needs and interests survey (p. 148) and Tables 7-7 to 7-10 offer specific help in local scope and sequence preparation.

Upon the completion of the scope and sequence material, a teacher's curriculum guide should be prepared for use at all grade levels where drug education is to be included. Such a guide may be developed locally, obtained from another school district, or adapted from state guidelines. The content should be locally relevant.

A curriculum guide could include the scope and sequence, consideration of the direct or correlated patterns of instruction, a statement of philosophy, and a variety of appropriate units prepared for the various grades. These units should include behavioral objectives, content, teaching activities, teaching aids, and practical procedures for evaluation. Material in this book will aid in general preparation as well as helping teachers who wish to develop their own guide.

CONCEPT APPROACH.* The current philosophical ideal used in health education and applicable to drug education is the concept approach to curriculum. It emphasizes the learning of comprehensive ideas rather than mere factual information. Concepts are identified as ideas, generalizations, or conclusions that in simple form may be sensory perceptions of external objects or events (sight, smell, accident, eating) or in more complex form are high-level abstractions. (Drugs may result in health and safety problems for individuals.) Concepts cannot be taught directly but rather

---

*Adapted from Health education approach to curriculum design, School health education study, St. Paul, Minn., 1967, 3M Company.

are the result of learning. What students learn, therefore, are not unrelated, isolated facts, but rather understandings and attitudes that enable them to form conclusions and make intelligent decisions about drugs. Thus the most effective teaching must be directed toward conceptual development.

The conceptual approach refers to the organization of various levels of abstractions, or generalizations, about drugs into a framework, or hierarchy, of concepts basic to the drug education curriculum. The essential categories of concepts that form the philosophical foundation for the drug education curriculum are the following: (1) definition of health applied to drug education; (2) values in the curriculum; (3) key concepts, the unifying threads of the curriculum; and (4) basic drug education concepts. These are the fundamental principles to be used in curriculum development and should receive major consideration by teachers in drug instruction programs.

Definition of health applied to drug education. Health has frequently been defined as a state of physical, mental, and social well-being and not merely the absence of disease or infirmity for effective living. Positive health involves a multidimensional state of the organism that helps a person to function better or to adapt and adjust more easily to his society. This definition of health identifies man as a composite of interrelated segments that act independently or collectively to affect the individual's well-being.

When applied to drug education, and more specifically to adequate and effective teaching, a fourth dimension, the spiritual phase, must be added to this definition in order to identify the interrelationships of the physical, social, and mental aspects in a more meaningful manner. In drug education programs to date the focus of attention has been on the physiological or pharmacological effects of drugs on the human body. This emphasis alone provides an important clue to the probable

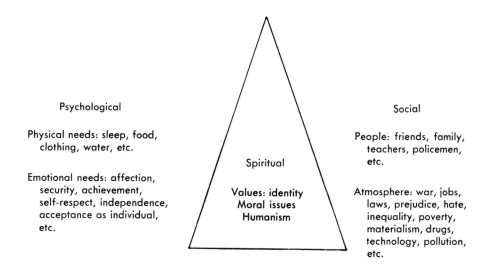

Psychological

Physical needs: sleep, food, clothing, water, etc.

Emotional needs: affection, security, achievement, self-respect, independence, acceptance as individual, etc.

Spiritual

Values: identity
Moral issues
Humanism

Social

People: friends, family, teachers, policemen, etc.

Atmosphere: war, jobs, laws, prejudice, hate, inequality, poverty, materialism, drugs, technology, pollution, etc.

Physical

Effect on human organism in function, work, life, play

FIG. 6
Health dimension emphasis in drug education.

ineffectiveness of numerous programs. The need is for greater emphasis on the psychological, social, and spiritual aspects of the educational program. These phases have been limited or ignored in drug education programs. Greater attention to these aspects will provide more opportunities for the achievement of goals in the affective and action domains.

Fig. 6 is an isosceles triangle representing graphically the degrees of emphasis that the various dimensions of health as applied to drug education should receive in the instructional program. It should be noted that the physical phase is basic but is of lesser importance than the equally significant psychological and social aspects. However, the spiritual aspect is the core or the action director. This configuration emphasizes that man, as a result of his values, his moral principles, and his physical and emotional needs, not only influences, or is influenced by, the social atmosphere in which he lives and survives but also helps to determine his own behavior.

Psychological or social factors bring about the physical health of the individual. If a man has an unfulfilled need and seeks an escape, he may find in his environment the appropriate drug to change his mood or feelings and achieve his goal. By the same token the television commercial or the peer-group influence may help an individual find the drug to satisfy an emotional need. A person with good psychological or social health is perhaps more likely to enjoy good physical health. Such a person may be better able to adjust to society and have less desire to seek drugs that may affect his body. However, it is not necessarily true that a person with good physical health has good psychological or social health, or that a person with poor physical health has poor psychological or social health. The individual and his interrelationships with his environment basically control the status of the human organism. In arriving at decisions affecting one's physical body, the individual is guided by his values and moral principles, or by his lack of them, and by their application to other individuals.

The highest level of psychological health results from the individual's fulfillment of a variety of physical and emotional needs, which shape behavior. Failure to acquire adequate food, housing, and health together with lack of affection, achievement, and self-respect may affect one's physical health. Such omissions may be important causal factors in drug misuse and abuse.

Social health results from the interaction of individuals with their environment. This means not only influencing society but also being influenced by it. Man is physically affected by many hazardous and harmful substances and materials—alcohol, tobacco, and drugs—that he creates, develops, or promotes in the world. By the same token television encourages us to drink more beer and use more aspirin. The speed in our world and the rapid changes in technology may be creating personal anxieties that demand an escape from the world through drugs. If the drug abuse problem is to be reduced, greater concern and emphasis must be given to the psychological and social aspects of health in the drug education program.

Probably the most important influence on health, yet the one most frequently overlooked or omitted in teaching, is the spiritual aspect. The decisions individuals must make about health are dependent upon the values and moral codes by which these individuals live and their concerns for their fellowmen (the humanistic aspect). The emphasis on greed, avarice, prejudice, hate, destruction, inequality, and racism should be removed from the world and replaced with concern for people. It has been said quite frequently that the drug problem is a people problem. This concern for humanism must be brought into the drug education program. One way this can be achieved is by helping young persons to find their identities and to find meaningfulness in life. The achievement of spiritual health and the emphasis on moral issues and values can only occur if education focuses on the learner as a person. The teacher must realize and accept his role as not solely a specialist in subject matter but as an expert in knowing and understanding children. He must be able to communicate with students, to make learning relevant, to respect the dignity of individuals regardless of race, color, and creed, to give students a share of the power, and to allow the freedom to make choices but in so doing he should provide a variety of alternatives.

Values in the curriculum. Social turmoils with numerous dichotomies, confusing and conflicting occurrences, are creating difficulties in the establishment of values by children and young persons. Factors related to these difficulties include the following:

1. Family changes—mothers working and not home, broken homes
2. Influence of communication media—radio, TV, movies, publications
3. Technological innovations—cars, jets, computers, satallite communication
4. Less influence of church on growing child and on people in general
5. World events—violence and destruction, impoverished and hungry people, war
6. Value conflict of peace and war in society
7. Teacher emphasis on factual teaching only
8. Conflict of conformity and self-reliance, independency
9. Dichotomies of values—good and bad, moral and immoral, wealth and poverty
10. Affluence—emphasis on materialism, secularism
11. Existence of unemployment, hunger, inequality, prejudice
12. Conflict of authoritarianism and democracy
13. Pressures exerted for high academic performance—grades, courses
14. Dehumanization of schools

15. Extensive exciting stimuli that create a psychological numbness in students

As a result of these factors, a sizable number of young persons are questioning the values of society. These youth seem less secure and are searching for the ultimate meaning of life. They are asking such questions as: Who am I? What am I? Why am I here? What really matters? Thus a variety of different patterns of behavioral problems are appearing in schools among a sizable number of students. These problems include apathy (not being involved); inconsistent behaviors (flighty interests, uncertainty about choices, fluctuating achievements); drifting (no plans); drop-outs (dissent through negative action); overconformers (lack of purpose leading to bandwagon behavior); overdissenters (radical activists); and role-playing (cover for lack of clarity of direction).

Freud and the mental health movement indicated that the uncertainty about, or the lack of, values may be added to the explanations for children's behavior problems. Raths et al.[72] discovered that when children with certain behavioral problems were exposed to particular value experiences, these problems were often eased in intensity, or frequency, or both. Maslow,[53] Frankl,[24] and Keniston[45] further indicate that individuals need a sense of purpose and belief. People actively search for meaningfulness and identity in life as guides to good mental health.

There are indications that the use of drugs is closely related to the factors just identified. Young people are searching for ways to break out of the shell and the numbness in which society has placed them. Perhaps they are using drugs as one means of breaking through, of escaping. Youths are seeking immediate pleasure and satisfaction rather than deferring gratification and enjoyment. They are testing new, experimental values such as responsiveness, genuineness, spontaneity, and sensation in order to find meaningfulness in life. Although the vast majority of students do not seek meaning and experience primarily via psychoactive compounds, many are uncertain, unclear, and in need of help in understanding their purposes in life. Thus the need for learning about values and developing a value system becomes apparent.

No one clear, accepted definition of values exists; however, values manifest how a person decides to use his life. Values give direction to life and hence may be considered the determiners of behavior. Schools have been emphasizing intellectual values, but it is evident that facts alone are an insufficient basis for learning because they have relevance only in the context of human experience.

Values may be seen as goals that can be learned in the educational process. Such objectives have particular reference to the use, misuse, and abuse of drugs in the affective or attitudinal domain and in the experiential realm. Attitudes themselves have a multiplicity of understandings. Suffice it to say that attitudes refer to learned predispositions to action or behavior that may have varying effects on individuals. The degree and intensity of an attitude determine the potential and extent of the behavior or action. Table

7-1 presents a hierarchy of attitudes illustrating this concept.

There is no consensus regarding how to categorize values. Rucker et al.[79] offer the following list as a possible guideline:

1. Affection—congenial human relationships, love, friendship, and emotional security
2. Respect—use of individual talents, self-esteem assured
3. Skill—develop individual talents to potential limits
4. Enlightenment—respect for scholarship, seeking truths, student solves own problems; present both sides of issue
5. Power—student involvement in classroom decisions, democracy in action
6. Wealth—guide student to produce wealth in form of services and materials himself
7. Well-being—foster good physical and mental health for each student
8. Rectitude—student to develop moral responsibility and standards for own behavior; sharing of values

Another authority, Fraenkel,[23] indicates the diversity of values that exists in the following catalogue:

1. Intelligent use of forces of nature

Table 7-1. Hierarchy of attitudes*

	ATTITUDE	DEFINITIONS	BEHAVIORAL MANIFESTATIONS
Overt action	1. Interest	Emotional responses to stimuli; feelings	1. Attention, awareness, appreciation by listening, talking, reading, writing, and other ways
	2. Opinion		2. Verbal or written expression
Internalization	3. Belief	Emotional acceptance of a concept, proposition, or doctrine; a preference; a decision about something; a conviction to or about something	3. Willingness to be identified with a proposition, or concept; self-expression with verbal, written, or performance action
	4. Value	A high, deep, and long-lasting degree of emotional acceptance and commitment to a concept, proposition, or doctrine; to cherish or prize; a faith; a potential goal	4. Pursues, seeks, and wants; takes action in satisfying ways through participation—convincing others, spending time, effort, and funds

*Modified from Rosser, J. M.: J. Sch. Health **41**:386-390, 1971.

2. Recognition of the worth and dignity of the individual

3. Use of intelligence to improve human living

4. Increasing effectiveness of the family as a basic social institution

5. Effective development of moral and spiritual values

6. Intelligent and responsible sharing of power in order to attain justice

7. Cooperative interest in peace and welfare

8. Widening and deepening the ability to live more richly

9. Recognition and understanding of world interdependence

10. Intelligent acceptance by individuals and groups of the responsibility for achieving democratic social action

11. Intelligent utilization of scarce resources to attain modest general well-being

Young persons learn values through exposure to a variety of meaningful experiences and through interaction with the environment. Therefore the sources of their attitudes are adults, peer culture, the family, the church, the communication media, the school, and friends and social groups who influence their decisions.

The school has a role to play as one source of value development but Simon states, "It is values, ultimately, which give a man the stars by which he steers his life; yet the schools are doing almost nothing to help young people make sense out of the clamoring and bewildering appeals rampant in these baffling times."[81] Thus old "shall nots" may be irrelevant today.

The teaching of values should be included in the school curriculum because the drug problem is a people problem; values can be significant aids in helping individuals with their search for meaning in life and with solving behavioral problems. One promising approach to value teaching is offered by Raths et al.[72] who state that value-clarification involves a series of strategies or methods for helping students to learn values. Specific methods will be found later in this chapter, and in the book by Raths et al.[72]

A value must meet these seven criteria:

Choosing 1. Choosing freely—individual should not be coerced and should have freedom of selection.

2. Choosing from alternatives—a variety of alternatives must be provided.

3. Choosing thoughtfully—consideration should be given to the consequences of each alternative.

Prizing 4. Prizing and cherishing—choice has a positive tone and is held in high esteem.

5. Affirming—when something is cherished it is publicly and verbally supported; doing something.

Action 6. Acting upon choices—life is affected through reading, spending money, and budgeting time.

7. Repeating—persistency and endurance become a pattern of life.

Application of the criteria identified should make it obvious that most individuals will have few values. However, so-called value indicators, or potential values, may be evidenced in a variety of ways through such expressions as goals or purposes, aspirations, attitudes, interests, feelings, beliefs, activities, worries, and problems.

The inclusion of the value approach in the curriculum, except for the efforts of Raths et al.[72] and Rucker et al.,[79] has been limited. In the drug area the Coronado Unified School District, Coronado, California, attempted an innovative approach using values with the help of a grant acquired through the Elementary and Secondary Education Act, Title III, U. S. Office of Education. More such efforts need to be made in schools if effective attempts to reduce the drug problem are to take place. Such methods will hopefully guide students to alternative routes to attain valid goals rather than using drugs to reach these goals. The value approach will help students realize that how one chooses to live one's life, how and where one hopes to seek experiences, and how one searches for meaning are important. Knowing that there are better and more lasting ways to experience the fullness, depth, and richness of life than through ingesting drugs should aid young persons in reaching their own decisions. Thus energies will be focused on the causes of drug misuse and abuse rather than the symptoms.

Key concepts. In organizing the hierarchy of concepts basic to the drug education curriculum, certain key concepts are applicable to all individuals and therefore are essential understandings not only in curriculum development but more importantly in the instructional program. We have chosen three key concepts that serve as unifying threads and that should permeate the entire drug education curriculum.

1. Every person is a growing, and developing organism born with certain hereditary factors. In the growth process each individual develops some characteristics common to all individuals, but shares certain traits with fewer individuals, and maintains other attributes that are distinctly his own. Although everyone usually has two arms, two legs, and two eyes, everyone does not have white skin or black skin; each person has his own features and his own personality that identify him in a unique way. With regard to the drug problem, students have different physical and psychological needs that must receive attention. Drug education programs in schools therefore must include consideration of the diverse characteristics of students as well as the types and extent of drugs each individual uses or abuses. Byler's and Berlow's questions on pp. 148 and 150 provide indications of such needs.

2. The growing, developing organism, the individual, is constantly affected by and in turn affects certain biological, social, psychological, economic, cultural, and physical forces in the environment. Racism, prejudice, war, destruction, peer groups, the family, the school, and other social factors have varying degrees of impact on individuals. However, action can be taken to modify these environmental conditions. Applied to the drug field, television and newspapers continually try to influence people to use tobacco and alcohol. If all or many individuals suddenly decided to stop smoking cigarettes or drinking alcoholic beverages, such action could have considerable economic effect on the tobacco and alcohol industries.

3. People must make their own decisions about whether or not to use drugs. In the educational process, all the alternatives, both positive and negative, must be presented to students so that they will have the best opportunity for free and intelligent choices. The instructional program must be one of education and not indoctrination.

In summarizing, it can be stated that growing, developing young persons can be affected by the pressures of their peers to use drugs. In turn they can partially affect the social climate by not associating with such peer groups or by refusing to use the drugs. However, the decision to participate must be made by the students themselves and not by the teacher, the parent, or another adult. This concept is extremely important in the drug education program. Many teachers today are still using the "scare" approach or are imposing their own value systems on young people when teaching about drugs. Such approaches have not been successful, nor will they be.

Basic drug education concepts. The application of the definition of health to drug education together with knowledge of the drug use, misuse, and abuse problem in society and other material presented in this chapter lays the groundwork for the formulation of the basic concepts found in Table 7-2. These concepts are the foundation for the entire drug education curriculum. They are the main generalizations, or conclusions, that should be learned in the educational program. Some schools and teachers may desire, or find it advisable, to develop subconcepts for specific grade level groups or for individual grades. This is an acceptable practice and may enable such individuals to focus more easily on the concepts to be achieved.

OBJECTIVES. The fundamental concepts for drug education previously described

Table 7-2. Basic drug education concepts

NUMBER	CONCEPT	APPLICATION OF DEFINITION OF HEALTH
I	Drugs differ in kind and degree; they have multiple uses with a variety of effects on individuals.	Physical
II	Proper use of drugs may be beneficial to individuals, the family, and the community.	Physical
III	Improper use of drugs may result in health and safety problems to individuals, the family, and the community.	Physical
IV	Numerous factors and forces influence the availability as well as the use and misuse of legal and illegal drugs by individuals and the community.	Psychological-social
V	The individual, the family, and the community have interrelated and reciprocal responsibilities to help control the availability, to prevent the misuse and abuse, and to assist individuals who become misusers and abusers of drugs in society.	Social
VI	The use and misuse of drugs by individuals involve moral principles and issues, and are related to one's sense of values as well as to the humane and just treatment of all people in society.	Spiritual-philosophical

serve as the bases for developing the objectives desired in the instructional program. Objectives are necessary, since they give direction to teaching and learning. They identify the *why* of teaching and form the basis for the evaluation to determine the effectiveness of the educational program. Objectives enable teachers and other school personnel to determine the quality of the instructional offering. The objectives should be written so that they give clues to the teacher and are useful in the evaluation process.

Goals, specifically identified as objectives later in this chapter, should stress behavioral changes and be written in behavioral terms. They should include purposes of a cognitive (understanding and knowledge), affective (attitude), and action (practice) nature. These behaviors should stress preventive drug education. Thus the formal educational program can aid in secondary and in primary prevention.

Many drug education programs have had little impact on young persons because school personnel have not been sure of their direction. Goals have been inadequately defined. Purposes need to be written behaviorally, stated clearly and concisely, formulated for use in the evaluation procedures, and considered from the psychological, social, and spiritual emphases previously described. Application of these principles to the drug education goals at a variety of grade levels will be found later in this chapter.

STUDENT DRUG NEEDS AND INTERESTS. To prepare objectives that are appropriate for local communities, whether predominantly ghetto areas or suburbs, to make the instructional program meaningful, and to involve students in curriculum development, drug interests and needs should be identified. Insight and guidance as to the diversity and extent of objectives and guidelines for content can be determined from such data. A variety of procedures may be used to obtain this information but only two will be described herein. Teachers and school districts will want to conduct their own needs-interests survey for use in instructional programs. Byler[8] and Berlow[4] provide information for use in constructing survey instruments. The evaluation devices in Chapter 11 will also be helpful.

Byler[8] recently completed an extensive study of the health education needs and interests of over 5000 students in Connecticut. The excerpted data about drugs are presented in the question form the students used and are organized into grade level groupings around the following categories:

1. Classification of drugs
2. Physical and pharmacological effects of drugs
3. Psychological reasons why drugs are used
4. Social considerations
5. Spiritual values

STUDENT NEEDS AND INTERESTS*

GRADES K TO 2
Drugs

Physical. Are hospitals where they help us? Do dentists help you? Do they give shots so it will not hurt? Will it hurt to have my tonsils out?

GRADES 3 AND 4
Alcohol

Physical. What does alcohol have in it? If you drink wine or booze, will you get drunk? Could you die from too much alcohol? What would happen if I should drink some whiskey?

Psychological. Why do people drink so much? Do people drink things with alcohol because they like them?

Drugs

Physical. What is LSD? Is marijuana dangerous? How do they affect you? What does glue sniffing do to you? Why might people who take dope have a deformed child?

Psychological. Why do so many people take shots of marijuana, STP, LSD, "snow," and "speed?" Why do people smoke pot?

Social. Why do people make drugs when they know drugs can cause bad health and death? Why were these drugs invented and why are people bringing them to America?

Tobacco

Physical. Does smoking cause lung cancer? How many more smokers get heart attacks than nonsmokers? Will one cigarette a day hurt you? Twenty packs? Is smoking more of a hazard to young people than to older people? My father smokes a lot and he bought these pills. How could they help him stop smoking?

---

*Adapted from Byler, R.: Teach us what we want to know, New York, 1969, Mental Health Materials Center, Inc.

Psychological. Why do so many people smoke? Is it hard to give up smoking?

Social. Why do people continue to make cigarettes?

Mental health

Psychological and social. If you worry to much, will you become sick? My mother and father do not love each other anymore; which one shall I love? Why am I so lonely? Why do humans always fight with one another? Why do I not have any friends? Why do I hate my sister? My brother?

GRADES 5 TO 6
Drugs

Physical. What do drugs do to you? What are drugs and the differences between drugs and drugstores? How does it feel to get high on LSD? If a girl takes LSD and has a baby, will the baby be deformed?

Psychological. Why do people take drugs? Why can't people stop taking overdoses of drugs? Can anyone ever break the drug habit?

Social. How are different drugs made? How do people start taking "dopejuice"? My brother takes dope; what shall I do?

Spiritual. If we had a better sense of values would there be a need to take LSD?

Tobacco

Physical. What pleasures do people derive from smoking?

Psychological. Why do people want to smoke? Why do high school students want to smoke? Why do adults think they can't give up smoking?

Social. Why do they sell cigarettes?

Mental health

Psychological. Why do I act happy, sad, and angry? Why don't people like me? Why do I lose control of my temper? Why do I sometimes hate everybody? Why am I afraid of darkness, ghosts, etc.? Why are Negroes treated differently than white people? Why do my problems sometimes overcome me?

Social. What is a real friend? Why can I not get along with my brother? My sister? Why do people marry if they do not love each other? What are the different races of people?

Spiritual. Who am I? What is life? What makes me tick?

GRADES 7 TO 8
Alcohol

Physical. What is alcohol? How does alcohol get into the bloodstream? What emotional reaction is caused by drinking? Can alcohol cause brain damage to the unborn child if the mother drinks during pregnancy? What are the effects of alcohol on the body and mind?

Psychological. Why do people drink? Why do people become alcoholics?

Social. What is an alcoholic? Why is alcohol on the market? How can young people drink without parents knowing it when stores do not sell alcohol to people under 21 years of age?

Drugs

Physical. What are drugs? Are drugs habit forming? Could dope ever be properly used? Is dope a drug? Is it liquid? A cigar? A cigarette? What is a "trip"? What are the effects of marijuana and LSD on the body and brain? Does LSD affect the unborn child if the father uses it? If the mother uses it? Which medicines are good or bad? What do narcotics look like "so I can protect myself against pushers"?

Psychological. Why do people like to "trip-out" on drugs? Why do some teen-agers use drugs? Do hippies use drugs? How can a person stop using drugs?

Social. How many people use drugs? Which drugs are useful and which are not? How can we help people who use drugs? If someone offers you LSD should you tell your parents or someone older? Why do high school students sell marijuana? Why does the government not stop the sale of drugs? Why do newspapers make so much of drugs that young people want to try them?

Tobacco

Physical. Does smoking produce cancer? Does smoking affect the heart? Lungs? Brain? Does smoking stop tension?

Psychological. Why do people smoke? How can people stop smoking?

Social. Why are cigarettes made? Why do men in Vietnam receive free cigarettes if smoking is not good for people?

Mental health

Psychological. Why do people rob, murder, and commit suicide?

Social. Why do Negroes not have the right to live as whites do? Why do young persons drop out of school? What makes slums? How do you get rid of slums?

GRADE 9
Alcohol

Physical. How does alcohol make a person drunk? What are the effects of alcohol on the body and brain?

Psychological. Why do people drink? What causes alcoholism?

Drugs

Physical. Is there such a thing as a safe drug? Are drugs as harmful as people say?

Psychological. Why do people use drugs? How does a person become addicted?

Social. Should marijuana be made legal? What is the extent of the drug problem?

Tobacco

Physical. Is it certain that you can get cancer from smoking cigarettes? How dangerous is smoking? What substance in tobacco causes cancer?

Social. Why do stores continue to sell tobacco to youngsters?

Spiritual. Is it right or wrong for stores to sell tobacco to youngsters?

GRADE 10
Alcohol

Physical. What are the effects of drinking on health? What is the difference between sensible and unwise drinking? What are the results of excessive drinking? When under the influence, is a person able to make a decision to benefit himself?

Psychological. Is there harm in drinking if you are not an alcoholic?

Social. What are the dangers of drinking and driving? If alcohol is injurious, why is it so easy to buy?

Drugs

Physical. What are the dangers of taking drugs during pregnancy? What are the effects of drugs on offspring? Are drugs as enjoyable as they sound? How many times must you take drugs in order to get hooked?

Psychological. Are there any common factors in the background of drug addicts? Why should I not try drugs if everybody else does?

Social. Why are some drugs that are not habit forming made illegal?

Spiritual. What and who is God? How does he feel about love, sex, etc.? What is right? What is wrong? How are values established? How can I be more considerate, more helpful, and less critical? Why am I here?

Tobacco

Physical. What are the pleasures of smoking? What are the dangers to health?

Psychological. How can I achieve happiness?

Social. If cigarettes are dangerous, why are they easy to buy? How do you get along with people of your own age? How can we get along better with our parents?

GRADE 11
Alcohol

Physical. What are the real hazards of drinking? What are the effects of drinking on the body? On the mind? How does drinking affect athletic performance?

Psychological. Why are young persons drinking more hard liquor and less beer?

Social. Can teen-agers be taught to control social drinking and alcohol consumption?

Drugs

Physical. Who should you believe about drugs —the users, the experts, or the "slanting" press? What should teen-agers know about stimulants and drugs?

Psychological. Why do most teen-agers on drugs have a weary outlook, and why do they think it is "cool" to use drugs? How does a person become addicted? What are the psychological effects of drugs?

Social. What legal problems can drug users and pushers face?

GRADE 12
Alcohol

Psychological. If adults drink, why can't students?

Social. Why not lower the drinking age?

Drugs

Psychological. How can students be helped who have problems at home, school, and with friends and who want to get away from problems? How can students be helped to face reality?

Berlow,[4] a member of the staff of the School of Pharmacy, University of North Carolina, compiled a list of questions about drugs from discussion groups conducted by selected advanced pharmacy students in schools; it is reproduced in part here. Although they do not indicate grade levels, these questions can be utilized for teacher preparation, for developing tests for the student to give himself, for use in problem-solving experiences, for the preparation of survey inventories to determine local student interest, and in a variety of other ways. The questions focus on the following general areas: classification and nature of drugs, physical or pharmacological effects of drugs, psychological reasons why people take drugs, and social considerations.

A COLLECTION OF QUESTIONS
ABOUT DRUGS*
WHY DO PEOPLE TAKE DRUGS?

Why do people think drugs are the solution to their problems?

Why do most people think that teen-agers will eventually resort to drugs? We are not all alike.

---

*Excerpted from Berlow, L.: Kids 'n drugs, Chapel Hill, N. C., 1971, University of North Carolina, School of Pharmacy.

Why is it important to stay off drugs?

Do you become sexually aroused if you take LSD or marijuana?

Can the will power of a person keep him from using drugs?

Why do hippies mostly take drugs?

Why do people take drugs and say they did not?

Do you think the commercials on TV urge students and adults to try drugs?

If I myself believe that drugs are not harmful and I am all for drugs, do you think that I am wrong in feeling this way?

Is it a fact that many rock music groups use LSD to produce their music?

WHO TAKES DRUGS?

If you know a person who is taking drugs, should you associate with him? Will he try to slip you some?

How many people in the United States take drugs?

What is the percentage of drug use in Vietnam?

What percent of black people and what percent of white people are hooked on drugs?

Are drugs as prevalent in the other countries of the world as in the United States?

What are the ages of most people who take drugs?

At what age do kids start taking drugs?

Suppose someone were to drug your food, how would you know?

WHERE DO DRUGS COME FROM?

How did drugs first come about?

Do the people who try to push drugs take them?

Where do the pushers get the drugs?

What plants do the different drugs come from?

How do drugs get in the country if they are against the law?

Can you spot a pusher?

WHAT CAN DRUGS DO TO ME?

Why do drugs kill a person?

Do drugs really change a person's personality?

How long would you have to stay on drugs before they completely destroyed your body?

Can smoking stunt your growth? Can it cause lung cancer?

What long-range effects on hormones, genes, mental and physical abilities come from the use of drugs?

If an expectant mother is physically dependent on heroin, will her baby be?

Is it true that some drugs damage the chromosomes?

How does a person look when he has been taking drugs?

Approximately how long does it take for drugs to enter the bloodstream?

What are the effects produced by pot, pep pills, LSD, and heroin?

If you take drugs will it affect your parents' and friends' emotions toward you?

If you were 15 years old and were caught with drugs, what would happen to you?

Can drugs cause any well-known diseases?

What effect does the drug have on the person when it wears off?

How dangerous can an afterflash be?

CAN I GET HOOKED ON DRUGS?

Do you think it is true that you use drugs once and you are hooked?

What do you do if you are hooked and scared to tell anybody but you want to get off drugs?

What do you do if someone in the family is on dope and you do not want to get them into trouble but you want to help them?

Could people get unhooked on drugs?

What drug is the hardest to stop taking?

How do you know when you are actually hooked?

Can speed or heroin become a day-to-day necessity after just injecting it for the first time? If not, how many times does it take to get hooked?

Why is it so hard to keep getting drugs after you are hooked?

What is the average age of a drug addict?

Can you become physically or psychologically dependent on legal amphetamines such as Vivarin or No-Doz?

Why does it make you go crazy if you stop taking dope?

If you take drugs today, years from now will they still be affecting you?

If you would just smoke one cigarette, would it harm you? Also, would it lead to worse drugs?

CAN I GET INTO TROUBLE TAKING DRUGS?

Is it true that if you are caught with drugs you can lose your right to vote?

What is the penalty for pushing heroin?

If you are caught while on probation where do you go or what kind of sentence do you get?

If you know a person who shoots drugs and know people who sell drugs, should you report them?

How many people use and are caught using drugs each year?

Are drugs illegal in other countries?

If you are riding in a car with guys who are drinking and are stopped, can the police do anything with you if you are not drinking?

WHAT ABOUT . . . ?

Can you smell drugs?

If you are on two different drugs, what will happen?

What does THC mean?

What is the most popular kind of drug?

Does cough medicine hurt you besides making you drunk?

How much do drugs cost?

What different kinds of drugs do truck drivers use to stay awake on the job?

What is the difference between marijuana and LSD?

Can you take drugs without their becoming a habit?

Could water injected into the body have any effect on a person?

How do parents find out that their child is taking drugs?

Can you inject the blood from one person who was high into another to get the same effect?

Which is the most dangerous drug among opiates, sedatives, tranquilizers, cocaine, stimulants, hallucinogens, and marijuana?

When a person injects a drug could you take this drug out the same way you put it in?

How many aspirin can you take to get high?

Which drugs have no medical uses?

Can a boy or girl my age take a drug and really not know about it?

Is it possible that drugs can also be used as medicine?

Can an overdose of aspirin affect you?

How can coffee or tea act as drugs?

What is the difference between ups and downs?

MARIJUANA

Can marijuana kill you?

How does inhaling marijuana through the nose affect the body?

If I take grass once can I stop?

How is marijuana sold? How much? What prices?

If there has been no proof of the harm of marijuana, why is the penalty so harsh?

What would happen if you were caught in possession of marijuana?

Is marijuana intoxicating?

Do you think that eventually marijuana will be or should be legalized like alcohol?

If grass is growing in your backyard and you do not know it can you be put in jail?

Can you have a bad trip on marijuana?

Why do people call marijuana mary jane, pot, grass, etc.? What is the sticky substance on the marijuana plant?

Is the withdrawal process of marijuana severe?

Has it been proved that marijuana is habit forming, and does it lead to harder drugs?

If you know where marijuana grows, should you tell the cops?

Would a person get more effect from ground hash or unground hash?

Which is worse, smoking grass or chewing it?

LSD

Can LSD cause chromosome damage?

How long do you have to stay on LSD before you are addicted to it?

What would happen to someone if he got caught for pushing LSD?

What part of the body does LSD affect?

What causes a bad trip?

If your brother is on LSD and you are locked in the room with him, what can you do?

What is acid? What can it do to a person who takes it?

Is it true that an LSD trip can recur as much as a year after taking LSD?

Can people put LSD on food and take it?

How many forms does LSD come in?

How long does it take for a drug to take effect and how long does a trip last?

If a pregnant woman takes LSD only one time, can it have any effects on the baby?

GLUE SNIFFING

Does sniffing glue harm your body?

Does glue sniffing cause drug abuse?

Can you be sent to prison for sniffing glue?

Is glue sniffing dangerous and does it lead to harder drugs?

NARCOTICS

What illnesses need narcotics and drugs?

Can there be physical dependence with codeine?

If a doctor prescribed something with a narcotic in it, could someone become addicted?

What cough syrups containing narcotics such as codeine can be bought without a prescription?

What is the name of the dope that is taken by needle?

MORPHINE AND HEROIN

What would happen if you drank alcohol and took heroin at the same time?

If a child were born to a heroin addict, would this child also be an addict?

How much of an overdose of heroin would it take to kill you?

How much heroin can you buy for $100?

Why do you have to inject heroin in a vein or under the skin?

Why do people take heroin?

Which is the most dangerous drug, LSD or heroin?

Can heroin kill you instantly?

What effects do heroin and morphine have on the body?

Are heroin and morphine used for medical purposes? Is this legal?

STIMULANTS

Do diet pills really work or is it in your mind?

Is cocaine a very deadly drug?

If you take an overdose of stimulants will it affect you later in life?

What are pep pills? Why are pep pills habit forming?

I know someone who takes an aspirin every night before going to bed. Is this good or bad?

DEPRESSANTS

Are tranquilizers dangerous if you become addicted to them?

What are yellow jackets?

What are some necessary precautions to take in the use of sleeping pills?

How many sleeping pills does it take to kill somebody?

Do you think young people should take sleeping pills?

Can you get hooked on sleeping pills? How?

AND WHAT ABOUT ALCOHOL?

What is the best treatment for alcoholism?

Is it true that the day after you drink alcohol you have a headache and a hangover?

What happens when alcohol and drugs mix?

What effects can cough syrup with alcohol in it have on your mind and your body?

I am an alcoholic. What should I do?

Can a small amount of alcohol hurt the body?

I know a person who drinks beer and liquor, and he is always complaining about seeing a devil in the middle of the road while driving. Would this be a sign that he is an alcoholic?

HOW CAN PEOPLE ON DRUGS GET HELP?

What could you do if a friend admitted to you that he or she was taking drugs?

Can drug addicts be cured?

How do you stop someone from taking drugs when you know it is dangerous? How do you get though to him?

What are the chances for an addict to be treated successfully?

Is it possible for addicts to get help without being turned in?

DRUG EDUCATION OBJECTIVES. One of the major problems in drug education programs is the lack of clearly defined, reasonably achieved, and adequately covered drug education objectives. In the numerous curriculum guides and other resource materials we reviewed, there were many diverse approaches. Therefore, in an attempt to bring consistency and clarity to this matter, the broad perspective of objectives identified in Tables 7-3 to 7-6 have been assembled in grade level groupings. They should provide guidance and assistance to teachers and curriculum directors. These objectives have been prepared using the basic philosophical concepts previously outlined.

In addition to the cognitive, affective, and action domain classification of goals, further clarity is attempted by identification of those goals that may not be observable in the classroom or that may have delayed achievement in the action domain. Any attempt to evaluate the accomplishment of such nonobservable and delayed purposes may be difficult, if not impossible.

DRUG EDUCATION CONTENT. The degree of emphasis to be placed on the physiological, psychological, sociological, and spiritual aspects of drugs at the various grade levels is not known at this time. Such factors as the community, the level of sophistication of the students, and the teacher's knowledge of drugs must be given consideration. However, it is believed that at the primary grades the major emphasis should be on the physiological or pharmacological aspects, with some minimal reference to the other areas. In the middle grades there will probably be the need for an increase in the psychological and sociological phases, with

Table 7-3. Drug education objectives, grades K to 2*

DOMAIN	OBJECTIVES FOR STUDENTS	BASIC CONCEPTS†
Cognitive	1. Identifies drugs commonly used	I
	2. Illustrates ways common drugs are used by individuals	I
	3. Lists beneficial effects of drugs	II
	4. Identifies substances that can be harmful or misused	III
	5. Lists responsible people who can help when medicines are needed	II, III
	6. Explains why medicines should be taken under supervision of parent as prescribed or recommended by a physician or dentist	IV
	7. States conditions under which individuals show lack of responsibility when using medicine	V
	8. Cites ways in which individual shows respect for drugs	V
Affective	9. Is aware of differences between alcohol and other drugs and of their usage by individuals	I, IV
	10. Displays interest in learning about the beneficial as well as harmful effects of drugs	II, III
	11. Desires to use drugs in useful and responsible ways	IV, V
	12. Shows interest in discovering people who can help when medicines are needed	V
Action (nonobservable or delayed)	13. Uses only substances that aid in proper growth and development	II
	14. Takes medicines and drugs only under responsible supervision	III
	15. Refuses to accept substances from strangers	III, IV, V
	16. Limits or refrains from use of drugs, except medicines prescribed and recommended, until grown-up	III, V

*Adapted from California State Department of Education: Framework for health instruction in California public schools, K-12, Sacramento, Calif., 1970, State Printing Office; and Health education: a conceptual approach to curriculum design, School health education study, St. Paul, Minn., 1967, 3M Company.
†Roman numerals refer to basic concepts in Table 7-2.

Table 7-4. Drug education objectives, grades 3 to 6*

DOMAIN	OBJECTIVES FOR STUDENTS	BASIC CONCEPTS†
Cognitive	1. Identifies varieties of drugs used by individuals	I
	2. Lists reasons for drugs in society	III
	3. Explains medical uses of commonly used drugs	II
	4. Explains physiological effects of some of the commonly used drugs	I
	5. Lists reasons persons react differently to chemicals contained in drugs	I
	6. Cites examples of misuse and abuse of drugs	III, IV
	7. Identifies difficulties or possible problems from misuse and abuse of drugs	III
	8. Explains why misuse and abuse of drugs may start early in life	IV
	9. Lists ways society tries to protect individuals from abuse of drugs	IV
	10. Identifies ways to protect self against misuse and abuse of drugs	III, IV
	11. Starts to analyze information about drugs on television, in newspapers and magazines	IV, V
Affective	12. Displays interest in learning about varieties of drugs and their effects on the body	I, II, III
	13. Asks questions about problems involved with misuse or abuse of drugs	III, V
	14. Seeks further information about community efforts to help people who misuse and abuse drugs	V
	15. Discusses ways to protect self against misuse and abuse of drugs	V, VI
	16. Expresses desire to use drugs responsibly and usefully	II, VI
Action (nonobservable or delayed)	17. Uses only substances that aid in proper growth and development	II
	18. Takes medicines and drugs only under responsible supervision	III
	19. Limits or refrains from use of drugs, except medicines prescribed or recommended, until grown-up	III
	20. Refuses to use illegal drugs	III, IV
	21. Starts to develop own practices and habit patterns to protect self against abuse of drugs	III, V

*Adapted from California State Department of Education: Framework for health instruction in California public schools, K-12, Sacramento, Calif., 1970, State Printing Office; and Health education: a conceptual approach to curriculum design, School health education study, St. Paul, Minn., 1967, 3M Company.
†Roman numerals refer to basic concepts in Table 7-2.

Table 7-5. Drug education objectives, grades 7 to 9*

DOMAIN	OBJECTIVES FOR STUDENTS	BASIC CONCEPTS†
Cognitive	1. Recalls varieties of drugs used by people	I
	2. Describes how medicines can be used to benefit individual	II
	3. Lists variety of individual and social factors that influence misuse and abuse of drugs	IV
	4. Interprets role of business and advertising in sale of drugs	IV, V
	5. Identifies differing effects of variety of drugs on the body	I, IV
	6. Compares benefits of smoking, drinking, and using drugs with possible detrimental effects	II, III
	7. Identifies reasons why people do and do not use, misuse, and abuse drugs	IV
	8. Illustrates ways to cope with social and emotional pressures of life other than through use of drugs	IV, V
	9. States procedures used by community to control availability and sale and use of drugs	V
	10. Discusses need for development of a value system	VI
	11. Recalls signs and symptoms of drug misusers and abusers	
Affective	12. Is attentive to information presented on varieties of drugs used by people, their benefits, their hazards, and their differing physiological effects	I, II, III
	13. Shows interest in comparisons of benefits and detrimental effects of alcohol, tobacco, and drugs on individuals and society	II, III
	14. Gives opinions regarding role of business and advertising in sale and availability of drugs	II, III, V
	15. Asks questions about alternatives to drug use	IV, V
	16. Displays interest in developing a value system	VI
	17. Is aware and discusses long-term results from frequent and regular misuse and abuse of drugs	IV, V
Action (observable)	18. Makes judgments about drugs and drug users after reviewing all aspects of problem	IV, V, VI
	19. Seeks to discover one's own identity and purposes in life	VI
	20. Participates in a school education-information program	V
	21. Seeks help from school personnel if having a drug problem	IV, V
Action (nonobservable or delayed)	22. Refrains from regular use of drugs that may lead to dependency, disease, or disability	III, IV, V, VI
	23. Avoids use of drugs that may affect ability to think clearly and react normally	III, IV, V, VI
	24. Refuses to use illegal drugs	III, IV, V, VI

*Adapted from California State Department of Education: Framework for health instruction in California public schools, K-12, Sacramento, Calif., 1970, State Printing Office; and Health education: a conceptual approach to curriculum design, School health education study, St. Paul, Minn., 1967, 3M Company.
†Roman numerals refer to basic concepts in Table 7-2.

Table 7-6. Drug education objectives, grades 10 to 12*

DOMAIN	OBJECTIVES FOR STUDENTS	BASIC CONCEPTS†
Cognitive	1. Analyzes nature and content of prescription and nonprescription as well as legal and illegal drugs	I
	2. Reviews physiological effects of alcohol, tobacco, and drugs	I
	3. Compares beneficial and harmful effects of drugs on the body	II, III
	4. Interprets reasons why people use, misuse, and abuse drugs	IV
	5. Identifies various alternatives to use, misuse, and abuse of drugs	IV, V
	6. Identifies predisposing characteristics of potential drug abusers	IV, V
	7. Compares patterns of drug use and abuse in children, youth, and adults in religious, racial, and social situations	IV, V
	8. Summarizes nature and extent of legal and illegal drug use and abuse in children, youth, and adults	IV, V
	9. Lists individual and social problems that result from misuse and abuse of alcohol, tobacco, and drugs	III, IV, V
	10. Identifies society's contributions to use, misuse, and abuse of drugs	IV, V
	11. Suggests ways individual, family, and society can reduce use, misuse, and abuse of alcohol, tobacco, and drugs	III, IV, V
	12. Identifies social situation or conditions when individuals may be apt to use, misuse, or abuse drugs with suggested ways to avoid or to handle such occasions	IV, V
	13. Analyzes effects of laws on use, misuse, and abuse of legal and illegal drugs	IV, V
	14. Lists resources available in school and community where individuals or families with drug problems may obtain help	V
	15. Discusses rightness and wrongness of use, misuse, and abuse of drugs by individuals and their relations to right of individuals to make their own decisions	VI
	16. Recalls historical use of drugs by man	I
	17. Identifies procedures to help drug abusers in emergencies and crisis	I, III
Affective	18. Asks questions about nature, content, and physiological and beneficial and harmful effects of drugs and other related matters	I, II, III
	19. Gives opinions about reasons persons use drugs	IV
	20. Talks about problems of use, misuse, and abuse of drugs	III, IV
	21. Displays interest in wanting society to resolve the drug problem	V
	22. Expresses desire to help individuals and society solve the problem of drugs	IV, V, VI
	23. Reacts to laws and law enforcement aspects of the drug problem	V
	24. Is interested in developing an individual value system	VI
	25. Is concerned with fair and just treatment of all individuals in schools and in community	VI

*Adapted from California State Department of Education: Framework for health instruction in California public schools, K-12, Sacramento, Calif., 1970, State Printing Office; and Health education: a conceptual approach to curriculum design, School health education study, St. Paul, Minn., 1967, 3M Company.
†Roman numerals refer to basic concepts in Table 7-2.

Table 7-6. Drug education objectives, grades 10 to 12—cont'd

DOMAIN	OBJECTIVES FOR STUDENTS	BASIC CONCEPTS
Action (observable and nonobservable)	26. Makes judgments about drugs and drug users after reviewing all aspects of the problem	VI
	27. Seeks to discover one's own identity and purposes in life	VI
	28. Attempts to develop an individual value system appropriate to one's potential, interests, and abilities	VI
	29. Voluntarily participates in activities and agencies or organizations attempting to rehabilitate drug abusers	V
	30. Helps organize or participate in school or community educational-information programs for students and others to aid those in need of help or with drug problems	V
	31. Shows tolerance and respect for other's views and opinions	VI
	32. Seeks help if he has a drug problem	V, VI
	33. Is able to provide guidance and help to individuals in crisis situations	V
	34. Seeks alternative behaviors to drug use and abuse	IV, V
Action (nonobservable or delayed)	35. Refuses to use illegal drugs	IV, V
	36. Refrains from use of drugs in situations that may be unsafe or hazardous to health	III, V
	37. Avoids use of drugs that may reduce ability to think clearly and act normally	III, IV
	38. Refrains from use of drugs that may lead to dependency or habit-formation	III, IV, V

some introduction of the spiritual side. At the junior and senior high school levels the focus should be on the psychological, sociological, and spiritual aspects, with limited concern for the physiological. This philosophical approach will need exploration and experimentation in the instructional program.

The content of drug education to be presented was developed from the objectives already discussed. Tables 7-7 to 7-10 are not meant to be all-inclusive but rather illustrative in nature. Additional material may be necessary to achieve the established goals.

Tables 7-7 to 7-10 follow.

Table 7-7. Drug education content, grades K to 2

QUESTION-ANSWER APPLICATION OF CONCEPTS AND OBJECTIVES	OBJECTIVES*
What are drugs? Substances, other than food, that affect body structure and function	1

In what form are the commonly used drugs taken?
Medicines:
    Pills—aspirin; injections—penicillin; liquid—cough medicine; capsule—anti-
      histamine; ointment—zinc oxide or menthol
Others:
    Liquids—whiskey, beer, wine, coffee, tea, gasoline, kerosene, airplane glue;
      smoking—cigarettes, cigars, pipes
	1, 2, 9

What are the beneficial effects of medicines? Prevent infection Relieve pain Control coughs Ease upset stomach	3, 10, 11
What substances can be harmful if misused? Cola drinks Coffee and tea Alcohol, beer, wine Medicines—aspirin, vitamins, diet pills, antibiotics, and antihistamines Glue	4, 10, 13
Who are the responsible people who can help when medicines are needed? Parents, nurses, doctors, dentists, pharmacists	5, 6, 14
Why should medicines be taken under a parent's or responsible person's supervision? To ensure correct drug for illness To ensure proper dosage To ensure proper frequency of use	6, 11, 14
What are the conditions under which a person may take a wrong medicine? Not reading the label Taking in the dark Accepting substances from strangers Using another person's medicine Taking more than the prescribed dose Taking medicine from an unlabeled bottle	7, 11, 13, 14
How may a person show respect for drugs? Use only when necessary Take only in recommended amounts and at recommended times Take only under supervision Do not accept substances from strangers	8, 11, 15, 16

*Numbers refer to behavioral objectives found in Table 7-4.

Table 7-8. Drug education content, grades 3 to 6

QUESTION-ANSWER APPLICATION OF CONCEPTS AND OBJECTIVES	OBJECTIVES*

What are the various types of drugs used by people?
  General classifications: stimulants, depressants, hallucinogens, psychedelic tranquilizers, and narcotics
  Legal: prescription and nonprescription (over the counter); alcohol, tobacco, coffee, tea, cola drinks, aspirin, vitamins, laxatives, cough depressants, diet control items, oral antiseptics
  Illegal: marijuana, heroin, LSD
	1, 10, 13

Why are drugs needed by man?
  To control disease
  Relieve pain and suffering
  Escape from reality
  Relaxation and relief from tension
	2, 3, 10, 12

What are the medical uses of some of the commonly used drugs?
  Alcohol—antiseptic, diet stimulant
  Tobacco—emetic (nicotine)
  Marijuana—none
  Amphetamines—control appetite, relieve mild depression, weight control
  Barbiturates—relieve high blood pressure, epilepsy, hyperthyroidism, sleep
  Narcotics (morphine)—pain relief, euphoria
  Tranquilizers—relieve anxiety and tension
  Hallucinogens—possible treatment in mental and emotional illness and alcoholism
	1, 2, 3, 12, 17, 18

What are the effects of some of the commonly used drugs on the body?
  Stimulants—relieve fatigue, alertness, activeness
  Depressants—relaxation, sleep, tension escape
  Sedative-hypnotics—euphoria, relaxation, anxiety reduction, sense alteration
  Hallucinogens—distortion of senses, consciousness expansion, exhilaration
  Narcotics—euphoria, escape, pain relief
  Tranquilizers—anxiety and tension reductions
  Inhalants—get "high," intoxication
	1, 4, 10, 13

Why do people react differently to drugs?
  Body size
  Rate of metabolism
  Dosage or amount taken
  Amount of time elapsed while taking drug
  Sensitivity
	1, 2, 5, 10, 12, 13, 19

What are illustrative ways drugs can be misused or abused?
  Use medicines prescribed for someone else
  Take more than the recommended or prescribed amount
  Do not follow prescribed or recommended time table
  Use nonprescription drugs unwisely
  Take drugs for kicks
	2, 3, 4, 6, 10, 12, 13, 19, 20

What problems may arise when drugs are misused or abused?
  May become physiologically or psychologically dependent
  May cause organic damage
  May cause death
  May develop drug-reaction sensitivity
  May lose incentive for school, work, play, appearance, friends
	4, 5, 6, 7, 10, 12, 13, 19

*Numbers refer to behavioral objectives found in Table 7-5.

Continued.

Table 7-8. Drug education content, grades 3 to 6—cont'd

QUESTION-ANSWER APPLICATION OF CONCEPTS AND OBJECTIVES	OBJECTIVES
Why does the misuse and abuse of drugs possibly start early in life? Curiosity Imitating adult use of drugs Using accidentally Peer influence Acting on a dare Experimentation Boredom	8, 12, 13, 19, 20
What does the community do to help protect individuals from the abuse of drugs? Federal, state, and local laws control sale and distribution of legal and illegal drugs Law enforcement agencies implement laws Establishes courts to penalize breakers of the laws Provides rehabilitation and treatment services Provides educational programs	4, 6, 7, 9, 11, 13, 14, 20
What can an individual do to protect himself against the abuse of drugs? Develop a healthy body Follow the suggestions outlined herein Learn to get along with all persons and to treat all persons equally Decide upon values and goals in life and seek to achieve them Know sources of help should you need it Seek alternatives through play, sports, camping, fishing, hobbies, work Learn to make intelligent decisions Critically analyze information on television, in newspapers, and in magazines	10, 11, 13, 15, 16, 19, 20, 21

METHODS OF TEACHING

The teaching techniques selected for the formal program should help achieve the established behavioral goals. Although the process for modifying behavior, especially drug misuse and abuse behavior, is not known, a variety of guidelines and principles of learning exist that teachers in drug education programs will find useful.

GUIDELINES. Some important guidelines are as follows:

1. Know your students and the community in which they live. Try to become familiar with their values, culture, and ethnic backgrounds. Attempt to understand their feelings about life, the world, the school, and other psychological and social matters. Be familiar with community attitudes toward drug use, including that of alcohol.

2. Present the positive as well as the negative side of the drug abuse problem, including the dichotomies that exist between these two extremes. Some drugs for some people, and other drugs for many people, are beneficial, pleasant, and useful.

3. Be well informed about drugs, including the broad spectrum of concepts presented herein. Try to build trust in your students through truth.

Untruths, exaggeration, sensationalism and moralizing kill the effectiveness of drug education. If 20% of the students in a classroom of 50 have used a drug, there are at least ten students carefully measuring the teacher's word against empirical knowledge. At least 30 students will know the ten users and be briefed by them. With 40 of the audience of 50 in a good position to judge the accuracy of the teacher's statements about a drug he has never tried, any discrepancies will

Text continued p. 166.

Table 7-9. Drug education content, grades 7 to 9

QUESTION-ANSWER APPLICATION OF CONCEPTS AND OBJECTIVES	OBJECTIVES*
What are drugs?	1

Substances, other than food, that affect body structure and function

What are the common varieties of drugs used by people?	1, 2, 12

Stimulants
Depressants
Sedative-hypnotics
Hallucinogens
Inhalants
Narcotics

What are ways that drugs can be beneficial to people?	2, 12

Prevent infection
Prevent premature deaths
Prevent epidemics
Weight control
Decrease infant and maternity mortality rates
Ease pain and suffering
Aid in surgery
Sleep and relaxation
Control of chronic diseases and disorders—heart, cancer, diabetes, epilepsy

What are the individual and social factors that may influence the misuse of drugs?	3, 13

Self-medication
Attempts to escape reality
Discovery of new drugs
Activity of criminal element
Ease of transportation of drugs
Advertising
Ineffective law enforcement
Inadequate law enforcement
Widespread use of drugs
Ease of obtaining and purchasing drugs
Business profit motive
Excess leisure time
Nonrelevant school programs
Discrimination and inequality in schooling, housing, jobs

What are the effects of drugs on the body?	5, 12, 16, 22, 23

Effects from tobacco:
   Immediate—cardiovascular stimulation; mucous membrane, minor drying effect and irritation with acute use, subsequent production of secretions with chronic use; may improve short-term human performance; blood chemistry, chronic use may cause some impairment of interchange of O_2, CO, and CO_2
   Long-range—heart disease, lung cancer, emphysema, other circulatory disorders
Effects from alcohol:
   Immediate—intoxication; reaction time slowed; sense organs, disinhibition and relaxation at low dosages and dulling effect at high dosages; blood chemistry, alcohol in blood supply affects bodily functions; neuromuscular coordination may be impaired
   Long-range—alcoholism, liver malfunction, brain damage

*Numbers refer to behavioral objectives found in Table 7-6.

Continued.

Table 7-9. Drug education content, grades 7 to 9—cont'd

QUESTION-ANSWER APPLICATION OF CONCEPTS AND OBJECTIVES	OBJECTIVES

Effects from other stimulants, depressants, or hallucinogens:
Immediate—stimulation or depression of nervous or circulatory system, hallu-cinations, distortion of senses, death caused by overdose
Long-range—dependence, chromosomal change, mental disorder, shortening of life expectancy
Synergistic effects (result of combination of drugs): Death, masked symptoms

What are some of the beneficial and detrimental effects of the use and misuse of drugs? — 6, 11, 12, 16, 22, 23, 24
Benefits: relaxation, stimulation, acceptance by peer group, social value, sign of adulthood, satisfies curiosity, possible pleasure, escape from reality
Detriments: organic effects, possibility of death, economic cost high, possible loss of inhibitions, danger of dependency, loss of friends, loved ones, and job

What are the reasons why people do, or do not, use or misuse drugs? — 7, 15, 18, 23
Do's: stay awake, sleep and relaxation, ease pain, feel different, escape from reality, rebellion, curiosity, pleasure, group acceptance, social need
Don't's: fear of dependency, feel secure and emotionally mature, have success experiences, accepted as individuals without bias and prejudice, have equality of opportunities, have viable alternatives to drug use, enjoy school, have friends among teen-agers and adults

What are some of the viable alternatives to the use of drugs? — 8, 13, 15, 16, 20, 22, 24
Establish realistic goals
Seek success in school
Remain in school
Develop and participate in leisure time activities—hiking, camping, fishing, art, music, drama, writing, sports, travel, reading, helping others
Make intelligent decisions
Acquire appropriate social relationships
Develop a value system
Participate in activities to help change injustices, inequities, and the like

What does the community do to protect against the abuse of drugs? — 4, 5, 9, 18, 21, 22, 23, 24
Establishes laws and law enforcement agencies
Provides educational programs
Establishes public and private agencies and organizations authorized to im-plement laws, to control business and advertising, and other things
Provides rehabilitation and treatment services

Why should an individual develop a value system? — 10, 16, 19, 21, 22, 24
To identify his purpose in life
To determine realistic goals in life
To decide ways to achieve goals
To assess his potential, abilities, and skills
To develop independence, security, acceptance as an individual, recognition, status, and peace with the world

What can the teen-ager do to help solve the drug problem? — 6, 7, 12, 14, 16, 18, 19, 21, 22, 24
Learn facts about drugs
Use necessary drugs carefully
Avoid unnecessary drug use
Resist peer pressure to experiment
Help others learn about drugs
Develop wide interests
Recognize early signs of personal inadequacy in dealing with problems and seek help

Table 7-10. Drug education content, grades 10 to 12

QUESTION-ANSWER APPLICATION OF CONCEPTS AND OBJECTIVES	OBJECTIVES
What is the nature and content of drugs? (See Chapter 4)	1

Legal
- a. Prescription:
  Stimulants—amphetamines (Benzedrine, Methedrine)
  Sedative-hypnotics—barbiturates (Nembutal, Seconal)
  Narcotic—morphine
- b. Nonprescription (over-the-counter): sleeping aids, cough depressants, nasal decongestants, alcohol

Illegal
- a. Stimulants—cocaine (also prescribed as local anesthetic for mucous membranes)
- b. Sedative-hypnotic—marijuana
- c. Narcotic—heroin
- d. Psychedelics—LSD

What are the physiological effects of drugs on the body? (Refer to Table 7-9)	2, 3, 17
What are the beneficial and harmful effects of drugs on the body? (Refer to Table 7-9)	13, 19, 25, 34, 35, 36
What are the reasons why people use and abuse drugs? (Refer to Table 7-9)	4, 6, 11, 18, 26, 34
What are the alternatives to the use and abuse of drugs? (Refer to Table 7-9)	5, 25, 31, 34
	4, 6, 19, 22

What are the characteristics of potential drug misusers and abusers?
- Little tolerance for frustration
- Difficulty in coping with stress
- Tensions and conflict in family situation
- Alienation with community and family
- High levels of energy and poor impulse control

What are the patterns of drug use and abuse found in society?	7, 17

Types: nonusers, experimenters, periodic, compulsive, and relapse users; also social, ritualistic-religious, and instrumental—for valid medical reasons

What is the nature and extent of drug use and abuse?	8

Children and youth:
- Alcohol, 60% to 90%
- Tobacco, 40% to 60%
- Marijuana, 6% to 40%
- Amphetamines, 5% to 15%
- Barbiturates, 2% to 15%
- Solvents, 2% to 12%
- Heroin, 1% to 3%

Adults:
- 7 million experimenters, 5 million moderate, and 3 million chronic users of illegal drugs

Prescription and nonprescription drugs—used daily by most individuals in some form; 202 million prescriptions in 1970 for stimulants, sedatives, tranquilizers, and antidepressants; billions of dollars spent yearly on alcohol, tobacco, cough syrups, laxatives

*Numbers refer to behavioral objectives found in Table 7-7.

Continued.

Table 7-10. Drug education content, grades 10 to 12—cont'd

QUESTION-ANSWER APPLICATION OF CONCEPTS AND OBJECTIVES	OBJECTIVES

What are the individual and social problems that result from the misuse of drugs? — 9
Crime
Accidents
Prostitution
Suicides
Deaths from overdose
Dependency necessitating rehabilitation and treatment services
Work absenteeism
Cost of rehabilitation and treatment services
Personal and family relations problems
Loss of job

What are the hazards from the use of drugs in driving an automobile and in sports? — 3, 11, 34, 35
Accidents, poor performance, organic damage

What are the social factors that contribute to drug misuse? — 10
Stress brought on by personal and adult pressures, technological change, Vietnam war, discrimination, inequality and lack of consideration for humaneness, need for success in school and elsewhere, emphasis on materialism, dichotomy of principles and practice regarding morals and others (Also refer to Table 7-9)

What can be done to reduce the misuse of drugs? — 11, 14, 17, 19, 20, 21, 30, 31, 32, 37
Individuals:
Learn about drugs
Make intell gent decisions about use of unnecessary drugs
Resist peer pressures to experiment and use
Develop a variety of interests and behaviors that foster emotional maturity
Accept responsibilities
Establish attainable goals
Extend help to others
Seek help if abusing drugs

What can be done to reduce the misuse of drugs? — 14, 16, 20, 22, 25
Community:
Support community efforts to control drugs and rehabilitate users
Support law enforcement
Establish reasonable laws
Educate public

What social situations may cause individuals to misuse drugs and how might they be handled? — 12, 20, 32, 34, 35
Situations: invitation to party; social meeting with unknown people; peer group pressures; friends who encourage experimentation; excessive free time and nothing to do; few, if any, friends and family members; failure at school; loss of job; lack of job opportunity; availability of drugs at school or elsewhere, etc.
Possible actions: eat food before attending party; be selective in choice of friends; be able to refuse drugs graciously and stand firm in decisions; weigh carefully all the alternatives; try to increase circle of friends—try to be friendly; have varied interests including recreational; ask for help when unsuccessful at school; try to get along with others

Table 7-10. Drug education content, grades 10 to 12—cont'd

QUESTION-ANSWER APPLICATION OF CONCEPTS AND OBJECTIVES	OBJECTIVES
What effects do laws have on the use and misuse of drugs? 　Some drugs legal and easy to get 　Controls the age of purchaser of alcohol and tobacco 　Prevents the availability of illegal drugs 　Some may be too harsh on penalties and make mere possession of marijuana a felony 　Help to deter use and misuse of illegal drugs 　May cause large expenditures of funds for enforcement and prosecution of offenders	13, 20, 22, 32
Should all drugs be legalized? 　Yes: 　　Reduces crime 　　Reduces cost of law enforcement and prosecution 　　Reduces number of teen-age criminals 　　Right of individual to make own decisions 　No: 　　Easy availability of dependent drugs may create greater health hazards and deaths and other problems 　　Business and social groups might apply greater pressures to experiment 　　People should learn to solve problems without chemicals	13, 20, 22, 32
What community resources are available to help people with drug problems? 　School counselor, nurse, physicians, psychiatrists, clergy, and others; free clinics, "drop-in" centers, short- and long-term rehabilitation and treatment modalities—hospitals, Synanon, Gateway House, Reality House	14, 17, 21, 28, 29, 30, 34
How should one go about developing a value system? 　Determine who you are and why you are here 　Decide what you would like to do or to be 　Set reasonable, attainable goals 　Seek help from counselors, friends, teachers, clergy, parents, and others	15, 23, 24, 30, 31, 33

be quickly noted and used to breach distrust of the total situation.°

4. Present a variety of alternatives to behavior for decision making. To be able to make intelligent, rational decisions, all viewpoints and all sides of the picture must be presented openly, clearly, and with the opportunity for freedom of expression.

5. Utilize the community in your educational program in a variety of ways, including the following: field trips, discussions with ex-addicts, and interviews with and presentations by experts and parents.

6. Keep the lines of communication with students open regardless of attitudes and feelings that may arise. Avoid student stereotypes because of appearance, language, or other factors. Prevent personal, critical, and moral judgments from ending discussions. Explore opportunities to increase and improve communication. Be a good listener.

7. Involve students through critical thinking, discussion, problem solving, analysis, development of responsibility, and in other ways. Opportunities for self-direction should be provided, encouraged, and supported.

PRINCIPLES OF LEARNING.[12] Motivation is essential to learning and depends on the following factors:

1. The individual's readiness to learn is related to the meaningfulness of the material presented. The drug needs and interests introduced earlier will be helpful in selecting goals and content.

2. The experiences and environment to which individuals are exposed affect learning. Many of the teaching techniques provided in this chapter as well as consideration of the environmental factors (Chapter 8) will be invaluable.

3. Guidance is necessary for the most effective learning. Although learning takes place within the student, teachers should select experiences, create the atmosphere in the classroom, and extend opportunities for individualized, self-directed learning. The amount of help needed and provided should differ with the individual student.

4. Learning is a self-active process. Students must talk, interact, do, and be actively involved in numerous aspects of the drug problem. This may necessitate going outside the classroom and even outside the school for the greatest learning to occur.

5. Much learning is soon forgotten and only a fraction is ultimately remembered. Thus the stress on attitudes, practices, behavior, and on the conceptual approach to drug education becomes imperative. The generalizations, conclusions, and attitudes about drugs will be more likely to remain than will the informational details.

6. The ability to solve problems, to reason, and to think reflectively involves training and must be learned. All the factors previously mentioned are related to this one. If helping students with drug problems is to be effective, the experiences must be meaningful, must be relevant, must involve students, and must provide the direction and guidance of teachers and other school personnel.

TEACHING TECHNIQUES. The teaching techniques supplied here are practical applications of the guidelines and principles of learning already introduced. These techniques have been grouped into four categories for easy reference: alcohol, drugs, tobacco, and psychic-social-spiritual.

Text continued p. 187.

°Guidelines for drug abuse prevention, Washington, D. C., 1970, Bureau of Narcotics and Dangerous Drugs, U. S. Department of Justice.

ALCOHOL

	GRADES*
Advertisements	
Students bring ads to class for analysis.	J,S
Bulletin board	
Students illustrate some commercial or medical uses of alcohol.	I,J
Students post a variety of ads with analysis statement.	I,J
Buzz group	
Why do people drink alcoholic beverages?	J,S
Why do young people experiment with alcoholic beverages?	J
Chart	
Students construct a chart illustrating level of alcohol in blood, number of drinks consumed, and effect on the body.	S
Debate	
Drinking alcoholic beverages is a hazardous practice.	J,S
To drink or not to drink.	
Demonstration	
Place a small (3-inch) goldfish in a solution of ½ ounce of alcohol in ¾ pint of water (the amount in a 12-ounce bottle of beer). In almost 20 minutes the fish will be "under the influence" (floating to the surface). When the effect of the alcohol can be seen, remove the fish and place him in fresh water to revive him.	I
Discussion	
Effects on the body.	I,J,S
Explain: "Action of alcohol starts at the highest brain centers and works progressively to the lowest brain centers as the blood level increases."	J,S
Medical, industrial, social, religious uses.	I,J,S
Compare nutritive values of foods and alcoholic beverages—wine, whiskey, beer.	J,S
Auto accidents and drinking alcoholic beverages.	S
Safe and unsafe alcohol.	J,S
Should I drink alcoholic beverages?	I,J,S
Why do teen-agers start to drink?	J,S
Why do adults drink alcoholic beverages?	J,S
Why do some teen-agers not drink?	J,S
At what age should one be permitted to drink?	J,S
Effect of advertising media on teen-age drinking.	S
Why do hangovers occur?	S
Differing attitudes toward drinking in your community.	J,S
Nature, types, and methods of production of alcoholic beverages.	I,J,S
Oxidizing rate of alcohol in the body.	J,S
Personality characteristics of alcoholics.	J,S
Predisposing factors to alcoholism.	J,S
Laws relating to alcohol use.	J,S
Extent of and attitudes toward alcoholism in society.	S
Differing effects of alcohol on individuals.	J,S
The economics of alcohol and industry.	S
Rehabilitation and treatment services in the community.	S
Effects of problem drinking on families.	J,S

*Letters refer to suggested grade level for which the activity is appropriate. P = primary, I = intermediate, J = junior high school, and S = senior high school.

Continued.

GRADES

Ways to alleviate drinking problems in the home. | J,S

Types of drinkers: social, occasional, problem. | J,S

Exhibit

Display beer, whiskey, and wine glasses with caption: "Each contains same amount of alcohol?" Why are they different sizes? | J,S

Field trip

Visit Alcoholics Anonymous or an alcoholic treatment center or clinic. | J,S

Interview

Policeman regarding auto accidents and alcohol. Physician or psychiatrist regarding methods of treatment of alcoholics. Counselor regarding problems relating to alcoholics and the famliy, alcoholism in industry, etc. | J,S

Opinionnaire

Prepare an opinionnaire and use as a motivating device to discuss drinking, drunkenness, and alcoholism as follows: | J,S

	AGREE	DISAGREE	DON'T KNOW
A user of alcohol is one who:			
1. Takes one drink before dinner always.	_____	_____	_____
2. Takes one drink after dinner always.	_____	_____	_____
3. Takes one or two drinks periodically.	_____	_____	_____
4. Takes alcohol at a religious ceremony.	_____	_____	_____
A misuser of alcohol is one who:			
1. Gets drunk occasionally.	_____	_____	_____
2. Always gets drunk at socials where alcohol is served.	_____	_____	_____
3. Takes a drink before or after dinner.	_____	_____	_____
4. Gets drunk after 2 to 3 drinks.	_____	_____	_____
5. Takes alcohol at a religious ceremony.	_____	_____	_____
An abuser of alcohol is one who:			
1. Is addicted.	_____	_____	_____
2. Gets drunk only on weekends.	_____	_____	_____
3. Gets drunk after 2 to 3 drinks.	_____	_____	_____

Pretest

Prepare pretest about alcohol and its effect on body systems. (Chapter 11) | J,S

Problem solving

You know three people: one drinks excessively, one drinks moderately, one abstains. Compare their personal traits, ambitions, appearance, popularity, and other appropriate characteristics. | J,S

Reports

Cultural and religious uses of alcohol throughout history. | J,S

Effectiveness of Alateen and Alanon programs. | J,S

Relation of alcohol to nutritional problems. | J,S

Golin's "Robber of Five Million Brains" in *Journal of American Medical Association* (**167**:1496, 1958). | S

State alcohol use and control laws. | J,S

Tests to determine intoxication: alcoholometer, Breath Alyzer, drunkometer, blood tests, etc. | S

ALCOHOL—cont'd

	GRADES
Alcoholism and home and family relations.	S
Differentiation between drinking, drunkenness, and alcoholism.	S
Role of Alcoholics Anonymous in the rehabilitation of alcoholics.	S
Effects of alcohol on the body.	I,J,S
Government and private agencies involved in problem of alcoholism.	J,S
Extent of alcohol use in the United States.	S

Research

Ingredients, manufacturing techniques, and alcoholic content of beer, wine, whiskey, vodka, gin, and rum.	J,S
The economic factors of alcohol in society.	S
Why some people drink alcoholic beverages and others do not.	J,S
Uses of alcohol in food, medicine, beverages, cosmetics, and other products.	J,S
Various state legal standards defining intoxication as a percentage of alcohol in blood.	J,S
Alcohol and its effects on the brain.	J,S
Comparison of effects of alcohol with those of other drugs.	J,S

Resource person

Invite a member of Alcoholics Anonymous to speak to the class.	S
Invite a social worker or family guidance counselor to discuss alcoholism and home and family problems.	S
Policeman to demonstrate alcohol intoxication tests used.	J,S
Pharmacologist to discuss effects on body.	J,S

Role play

Saying "No" when offered an alcoholic beverage.	J,S
Pressures to consume alcoholic beverages by peer group in social situation.	J,S

Survey

Students identify types and amounts of alcoholic beverages consumed by classmates.	S
Student attitudes about use of alcoholic beverages.	S

Tape recording

"Man-in-the-street" interview as to attitudes toward use of alcohol.	J,S
Interview ex-alcoholic about his attitude and reaction to use of alcoholic beverages.	J,S
Interview physician, pharmacologist, guidance counselor, and others about any aspect of alcohol and alcoholism.	J,S
Collect TV and radio commercials for class analysis.	J,S

GRADES*

Action group

Students participate in community and school action groups designed to help   S
resolve drug problem.

Advertisements

Students study radio and TV ads on drugs and prepare reports on product   S
name and type, program seen with, time of day, length of commercial,
appeal used, and group appeal directed toward.

Collect ads for discussion, analysis, evaluation, preparation of scrapbook and   I,J,S
displays, and reports.

Collect ads from different magazines and newspapers over a period of months.   S
Categorize by magazine, type of drug, frequency of appearance, space
allocation, and analysis of information provided.

Brainstorming

Ways students can contribute to drug control in the school and community.   J,S
Values held by students and significance in own lives.   J,S

Bulletin board

Students post current newspaper and magazine articles as well as appropriate   I,J,S
pictures and ads. Might be titled "The Chemical Cop-Out" or "The Choice
is Yours." May be organized around specific drugs, music, law enforcement, research, and the like. Use to stimulate class discussion.

Students prepare reports (also useful for school newspaper) titled "To Smoke   J,S
or Not to Smoke"; "Pot's a Put-On"; "Are We a Drug-Taking Society?";
"Watch Out for 'Con' Men"; "To Drink or Not to Drink"; "How to Say No";
etc.

Buzz group

Discuss these questions on how to make your own decisions about drug use: I
    1. Me, drugs, and my future.   J,S
    2. Should marijuana be legalized?   J,S
    3. Is marijuana no worse than alcohol or tobacco?   J,S
    4. Do marijuana and LSD always make you happy and like other people?   J,S
    5. Is there a drug problem at school? In the community?   J,S
    6. Is there influence from the university students on the drug problems at   S
       high school?
    7. What factors contribute to drug abuse?   J,S
    8. What should you do if you learn your classmates are using illegal drugs?   J,S
    9. What needs to be done to resolve the drug problem at school? In the   J,S
       community?

Cartoons

Have talented students prepare cartoons on various aspects of drug use in   I,J,S
society: medical use, religious use, abuse, etc.

Chart

A committee of students could be assigned to research a variety of drugs and   I,J,S
cooperatively prepare a chart for classroom or school display that contains
broad classifications and specific drug names, form, dosage, source, legal
or illegal, effects on body, and others. Younger students may wish to limit
this to common household medicines.

Debate

Questions for debate include:
    1. Is the antiestablishment feeling of some young people a factor in the   S
       teen-age drug abuse problem?

*Letters refer to suggested grade level for which the activity is appropriate. P = primary, I = intermediate, J = junior
high school, and S = senior high school.

	GRADES
2. Should narcotic or drug addicts be treated as criminals or as sick people?	S
3. Should marijuana be legalized?	J,S
4. To smoke or not to smoke.	J,S
5. To drink or not to drink.	J,S
6. To use or not to use drugs.	J,S
7. Should the British system of legally providing narcotics to addicts be adopted in the United States?	S
8. Does the U. S. government have the right and the duty to control the availability and use of drugs?	S
9. Have "rock music" and "rock music festivals" contributed to the greater use of drugs by young people?	J,S

Demonstration

Burn some Lipton tea leaves. Odor similar to the burning of marijuana.	J,S
Administer tranquilizers or barbiturates and amphetamine drugs to Daphnia (minute freshwater crustaceans) to observe effects.	J,S
Pharmacologist at local medical center may be willing to illustrate effects of certain drugs on small animals.	J,S

Discussion

Read warning labels on containers and discuss meaning of the skull and cross-bones sign.	P,I
The family medicine cabinet.	P,I
Medicines: Why take them? How do they help? How much do you take? Who decides when and what to take? Why? Why is prescription needed for some and not others?	P,I
What are drugs? Medicines? Why are they available?	P,I
What to do if you feel sick or dizzy after taking a drug or medicine with or without supervision.	P
What to do if no responsible person is available and an emergency exists.	P,I
Difference between tattling and responsible reporting if stranger offers candy; if older child dares someone to use a drug; if you think someone is abusing drugs.	P,I
Ways to help someone in need.	P,I
Who do you discuss a serious problem with? (See *That's What Friends Are For* by Sylvia Van Chief and Florence Heidi.)	P,I
What made you feel sad or glad at times? (See *The Sorely Trying Day* by Russel and Lillian Hoben.)	P,I
Keeping confidences. (See *A Friend Is Someone Who Likes You* by Joan Anglund.)	P
Meaning of use, misuse, abuse, addiction, physical and psychological dependence, habituation, and tolerance.	I,J
Categories and types of drugs, including coffee, tea, and cola drinks.	I,J,S
Effect of drugs on the body, including habit-forming aspect.	P,I,J
Why do people take drugs? What are the alternatives?	P,I,J,S
Differences between over-the-counter and prescription drugs.	I,J,S
Drugs and allergies, infections, and malnutrition.	I,J,S
First aid procedures for poisoning or for overdose of drugs.	I,J,S
Peer pressure and drug use; "taking a dare."	I,J,S
Laws and penalties regarding illegal drugs.	I,J,S
Impact of advertising on sale and use of drugs.	I,J
Dangers of self-medication.	J,S
Ways to relieve worry, tension, and frustration.	I,J,S
The drug-oriented society and patterns of drug use.	J,S
Ways to solve a problem with drugs; ways to solve any problem.	J,S
Drugs and autos, athletes, studying, housewives.	J,S
Psychological and sociological effects of drugs.	J,S

Continued.

	GRADES
All drugs may be dangerous to ingest.	P,I,J,S
Why do some people not use drugs?	I,J,S
Hazards of potentiation with, for example, alcohol and barbiturates.	J,S
Economics of drugs.	J,S
Government control of use and sale of drugs. Relate to freedom and independence.	J,S
Attitudes of people toward addicts, drug abusers, hippies, etc.	J,S
Community resources available for drug abusers.	J,S
Marijuana is the new social drug.	S
Influence of propaganda and motivational research control on individual's decisions.	S
Personalities of drug abusers.	J,S
Methods of rehabilitation and treatment of drug abusers.	S
History of drugs.	J,S
Drugs and social problems: war, crime, poverty, racism, inequalities, etc.	S
Potential drug abusers: risk personalities, risk behaviors, risk environments.	J,S
Legalization of marijuana.	J,S
Physical and psychological needs of people.	J,S
Improving interpersonal relations.	I,J,S
Student alienation and unrest.	S
Values and their meaning in life.	I,J,S
Is it right or wrong to use, misuse, and abuse drugs?	J,S
Role of the school, home, church, community, and individual in drug problem.	J,S

Dramatization

Characters illustrate sadness, depression, happiness, joy, fear, anger, and other emotions. Students discuss ways to help.	P
Making an emergency telephone call.	P
Ways to ask for help when in need.	P
Student urged to take a dare. Discuss consequence. Have students prepare several different endings and discuss.	P
Teacher reads story to pupils, then they act out the parts. Choose different children to play each episode. Pantomime may be used without props. Such simple objects as a toy telephone, bottle, or spoon may be used.	P

Story:

Dennis has a little sister named Prue. One day Prue got sick. Mother took her temperature. Then Mother went to phone the doctor.

The Doctor came to see Prue. He said Prue must have some medicine. He wrote out a prescription.

Dennis went with his father to the drug store to have the prescription filled. His father gave the prescription to the pharmacist. The pharmacist read the prescription. Then he mixed the medicine in a dish and poured it into a bottle.

"This medicine is meant for Prue," the druggist said. "It is not good for anyone else. It might even make another child sick." "I will not touch it," Dennis promised. "You must never touch any medicine, even if it was mixed especially for you, unless Mother or Father are with you," the druggist said. Then the druggist put a label on the bottle to tell just how much medicine Prue should take and when she should take it.

When Dennis and his father reached home, Mother looked at the bottle of medicine very carefully before she opened it. "I must be careful to give Prue just the amount it says on the label," Mother said. "Will you get me a clean teaspoon, Dennis?"

GRADES

Dennis gave his mother a clean teaspoon. She measured the medicine and gave it to Prue. Prue made a face but she swallowed it because she knew it would make her well.

Mother looked at the clock. "The label says I should give Prue some more medicine in 1 hour. It is 2 o'clock now." She held up two fingers. "When will it be time to give Prue her medicine again?" Dennis held up three fingers. "At 3 o'clock," he said. "I will watch the clock and tell you. May I put the medicine away?" "No," said Mother. "It is good of you to offer but children should *never* touch medicine. I will put it in the medicine cabinet where it belongs and lock it up until we need it again." And she did.

At 3 o'clock Dennis called Mother and she took the medicine out of the cabinet and gave Prue another spoonful. Just then the telephone rang. Mother heard the phone but did not pay any attention to it. Instead, she put the medicine in the cabinet and locked it up before answering. "It is most important to put the medicine away before answering the phone," she said. "Dennis, would you answer the phone for me?" Dennis answered the phone, saying, "Mother will come in a minute; she is putting the medicine away."

As soon as Prue was well, Mother took her medicine and poured what was left of it into the toilet. Then she flushed the bowl, washed the bottle carefully, and put it in the trash can. "Why did you do that?" asked Dennis. "There was some left. I could have used it if I got sick." "Oh, no," said Mother. "You will have your own medicine if you are sick. It is not safe for one person to take another person's medicine." Then she hugged Dennis. "But we hope you will never be sick," she said. Dennis hoped so, too.

Drawings

Students make drawings and pictures of beneficial effects of medicine and substances that can be harmful if misused.   P

Students prepare illustrations of how specific mood-modifying substances affect people physically, socially, and psychologically.   I

Exhibit

Display labels and containers of over-the-counter drugs and others for student examination and discussion.   P,I

Display a variety of pamphlets, books, and other items in class, in the library, or elsewhere for review.   J,S

Students participate in a classroom or school "Drug Fair." A variety of displays are prepared: bulletin boards, charts, posters, pamphlets, books, films, filmstrips, reports, oral presentations, a question corner. Parents, the community, and teachers may be invited.   I,J

Field trip

Visit local jail to discuss drug law violations with officials and see interior.   I,J,S

Attend court in session on illegal drug case.   J,S

Tour community rehabilitation and treatment agencies such as Teen Challenge, Synanon, Damien House.   J,S

Visit the street drug scene to meet and talk with drug users and abusers.   J,S

Interview

Pharmacist to discuss common nonprescription drugs.   I

Addicts and ex-addicts about their involvement, attitudes, and feelings.   J,S

Physician or pharmacologist about the use and effects of drugs.   I,J,S

Police to discover what happens when a drug abuser is arrested, especially a minor.   J,S

Continued.

GRADES

Friends and neighbors about attitudes toward drug use and abuse.   J,S
Judge regarding his views on the drug problem.   J,S

Magazine and newspaper articles

Collect articles for scrapbook, current information reports and summaries,   I,J,S
class presentations, motivation.

Map

Prepare world map indicating the sources, distribution, processing, and market-   J,S
ing of legal and illegal drugs.

Mural

Students make a mural depicting all the people responsible for controlling   P,I
drugs and tracing the route of a drug from producer to consumer.

Music

Expose students to various types of music depicting people's moods—rock   I,J,S
music, ballads, classical, and country—and relate the music to drug scene.
When words to songs are available, lyrics could be analyzed.

Opinionnaire

Place a check in the appropriate space on the right.   J,S

	AGREE	DISAGREE	DON'T KNOW
A drug user is one who uses drugs:			
1. Once and stops.	____	____	____
2. Ten times and stops.	____	____	____
3. More than ten times and stops.	____	____	____
4. Once a week but not every week.	____	____	____
5. Occasionally and can stop when so desires.	____	____	____
A drug misuser is one who uses a drug:			
1. Once every week and stops after several weeks.	____	____	____
2. Ten times and stops.	____	____	____
3. Daily for several months and stops.	____	____	____
4. Takes overdose, almost dies, and stops.	____	____	____
A drug abuser is one who uses a drug:			
1. Once every week.	____	____	____
2. Once every day.	____	____	____
3. Several times most days.	____	____	____
4. All the time and must steal to sustain the habit.	____	____	____
5. Because is addicted.	____	____	____
6. And can buy whatever drugs needed.	____	____	____

Panel discussion

Topics for consideration include:
1. Are we a drug-oriented society?   J,S
2. What can a teen-ager do to help solve the drug problem in school? In the community?   J,S
3. What drug laws need changing?   J,S
4. How can young people achieve emotional maturity?   J,S
5. What are the alternatives to drug use and abuse?   J,S
6. How can a drug abuser get help in school? In the community?   J,S

	GRADES

Parent involvement

Invite parents to a presentation on drugs given by a physician, pharmacologist, or other qualified person.   I,J,S

Conduct a program with a variety of speakers covering a broad spectrum of drug topics.   I,J,S

Arrange for sessions of student-parent discussions about drugs. Have specialists on hand to assist.   J,S

Students prepare programs for parents followed by question and answer period.   I,J,S

Peer group

Students prepare program on drugs for presentation to other classes.   I,J

Students conduct survey among students, "What can we do about the school drug problem?"   J,S

Establish a volunteer speakers bureau comprising teams of two to four speakers to visit fifth, sixth, seventh, or eighth grade classes in nearby schools to discuss drugs.   J,S

Posters

Students prepare posters to be used in school anti-drug abuse program.   J,S

Pretest

Prepare pretest (also use as posttest) to discover student knowledge, attitudes, and practices regarding drugs. (See Chapter 11 for illustrative questions.)   I,J,S

Problem solving

Students respond to these statements by checking on the right: J,S

	AGREE	DISAGREE	DON'T KNOW
1. It is my life and I can do with it as I please.	———	———	———
2. My responsibility is to myself and no one else.	———	———	———
3. If you experiment with drugs, that is your problem, not mine.	———	———	———
4. If you have a pain or a problem just pop in a pill; it is the shortest trip to joy.	———	———	———

Pupils respond orally to these questions: P
1. Who can help you if you misuse a medicine?
2. What should you do?
3. Whom should you tell?
4. Whom should you call?
5. If you found a box of pills or an open bottle of medicine at home what would you do? Why?
6. If a friend offered you something to eat or drink and you were not sure what it was, what would you do? Why?

If you discovered that your brother, sister, or friend was experimenting with drugs, what would you do?   J,S

What are the consequences of being discovered at a party where illegal drugs are being used or in a car where they are found? What effect might this discovery have on your life? What could you do to prevent this occurrence?   J,S

Project

Organize students into teams to prepare a special edition of the school newspaper about drugs. Students should work on topics or sections of their choice. Some talented young people may do the art work; others may be organizers; most should have research and writing responsibilities.   J,S

Continued.

GRADES

Publicity campaign

Conduct a school-wide, student-run drug use information campaign using   J,S
the school newspaper, student-made signs, materials, displays, assemblies,
films, and outside speakers or resource persons.

Puppets

Students use prepared puppets or make them out of paper bags and other   P
materials to depict dramatically a variety of situations for discussion, such
as something I could not have, loss of a pet dog, dislike of a neighbor.

Questions

Students bring to class written questions about drugs that they have pre-   I,J,S
pared or others have asked them to have answered. Time is set aside for
a question and answer session.

A question box for anonymous questions or concerns is provided.   J,S

Students raise questions about drugs and list them on the chalkboard. As-   J,S
signments are made individually or by group to research the answers
and make reports to class.

Reports—oral or written

The nature of community resources available and the services they provide.	J,S
The effects of drugs on the body.	I,J,S
Students select drugs to research and prepare material on medical use, effects, dosage, form sold, hazards, and other information.	J,S
Health problems related to drug abuse—malnutrition, VD, infectious diseases, etc.	J,S
Legal responsibility of the school in regard to drugs.	J,S
Drug laws pertaining to minors.	J,S
Having the courage of my convictions.	J,S
The importance of maintaining freedom of choice.	J,S
How students can help in the school drug program.	J,S
Legal, financial, physiological, psychological, and familial problems of the narcotic addict.	J,S
Driving and drugs.	S
Cost and problems of maintaining a heroin habit.	S
Where would I like to be 10 years from now and what would I be doing?	J,S
Addicted mothers and their unborn children.	J,S
The American vs. the British system of dealing with narcotic addicts.	J,S
Comparison of various types of drug withdrawal symptoms.	J,S
Several case histories of drug abusers.	S
Describe a friend with a well-balanced personality and give reasons why so well-adjusted.	S
My philosophy of life.	S
How to say "No" to drugs.	J,S
The school drug problem.	J,S
Precautions to follow when using drugs.	J,S
Physical, psychological, and social aspects of drugs.	J,S
Why students use drugs.	J,S
How can parents help students with drug problems? Or how could they have have helped to prevent the problem?	J,S
How I feel about using drugs.	J,S
Alternatives to drug use.	I,J,S
Peer pressure and drug abuse.	J,S
Prescription and nonprescription drugs.	J,S
The law and drugs.	S
My school and its likes and dislikes.	S

	GRADES
My friends and their likes and dislikes.	S
My family and its effect on my life.	S
What are my values in life? What attitudes have the greatest meaning and influence on my life?	S
Is there rightness and wrongness in this world?	S
Who am I? Why am I here? Where am I going?	S
The story of drug abusers such as Judy Garland, Janis Joplin, Jimi Hendrix, Bill Stern.	S
What makes me sad, happy, angry?	I,J

Research

Role of the World Health Organization in drug control.	J,S
Federal and state drug laws.	J,S
Historical development of drugs.	J,S
Current information about various drugs.	J,S
Illegal heroin and marijuana traffic and efforts to control it.	J,S
Cultural and religious use of drugs.	J,S
Properties of marijuana, including strength, varying strength, effects on body, and other current information.	J,S
Functions and responsibilities of government agencies involved in the standardization, purity, and safety of drugs.	J,S
Route of legal drugs to illegal markets.	S
International control of illegal drugs.	S
Current status of methadone in treatment of addicts.	J,S
Addiction in pregnant women and resultant fetal problems.	S
Services rendered by community rehabilitation and treatment centers for youth and how adequate they are.	S
Tests to determine whether a person is under the influence of drugs (nalline, urinalysis, chromatography).	S
Personality characteristics of drug abusers.	S
Treatment modalities for addicts.	S

Resource and information center

Students conduct programs for peers, parents, and others, with pamphlets, information, speakers, and rapping. May also have hot-line if school funds available.	J,S
Students obtain books, pamphlets, and other materials for use in classroom.	I,J,S

Resource person

A variety of community and school personnel may be invited to meet with students and discuss numerous topics. Some of these individuals are pharmacists, pharmacologists, physicians, psychologists, psychiatrists, policemen, attorneys, district attorneys, judges, probation officers, narcotic squad officers, treatment center representatives, counselors, drug abusers, and ex-addicts.	I,J,S

Role play

These situations can be dramatized:

1. A parent giving medicine to a sick child.	P
2. Mother takes sick child to doctor who prescribes medicine later obtained at drug store. Mother takes child home and gives exact amount.	P
3. Adolescent who feels his problems can only be resolved by escaping through drugs.	I,J
4. Refusal to accept the offer of a marijuana cigarette.	I,J
5. Different moods or emotions of people with discussion of meaning and action to take—anger, happiness, anxiety, fear, etc.	P,I
6. A friend offers his friend a pill that he has been taking in an attempt to help the second person who is complaining of a minor ailment. The friend refuses the pill and indicates the possible problems in accepting medicine from unauthorized individuals.	P,I

Continued.

GRADES

7. Teen-ager is caught with illegal drugs in his possession.   J,S
8. Student admits to parents he is using drugs.   J,S
9. Clergyman speaks to teen-age drug abuser about youth's involvement   J,S
in drugs.
10. A girl is at a party and a "joint" is passed around.   J,S
11. A man is employed and has a good position but is dependent on   S
heroin. His employer discovers the problem.

School newspaper

Provide column in each publication for questions to be answered by student   J,S
researchers.

Periodic articles on drugs written by students should be included.   J,S

An entire edition might be devoted to a variety of articles on drugs as part   J,S
of an antidrug campaign or drug education week.

School program

Organize school into a series of committees to control and prevent the spread   S
of drug abuse. Students should be actively involved in the planning and execution of the program. A plan of action that would not be solely educational could evolve and include parent and community participation.

Scrapbook

Students collect newspaper and magazine articles, advertisements, pictures,   I
and other appropriate materials and organize in a useful manner. Could
become part of school or classroom resource and information center or
be taken home for parent reference.

Self-test

Ask students to verbally identify the person responsible for: P
1. Making safe drugs.
2. Writing prescriptions.
3. Choosing drugs to be used.
4. Filling prescriptions correctly.
5. Choosing over-the-counter drugs.
6. Reading labels and following directions.
7. Keeping drugs in a safe place.
8. Helping younger children.
9. Taking drugs only under supervision.

Show and tell

Students describe experiences with medicines and identify what they con-   P
sider to be ways to act responsibly.

Show pictures of medicines taken in the home such as aspirin, laxatives, and   P
cough syrups. Have students respond to these questions:
1. How should they be taken?
2. Who should give them?
3. Where should drugs be stored at home?

Cut out pictures of people representing different emotions—fear, pain, anger,   P,I
joy, hate. Place them on the bulletin board with possible caption: "These
people feel," or "How do you think these people feel?" Have children
view pictures and explain why the people in the pictures acted as they did.

Songs

Students analyze and discuss the lyrics of popular songs that refer to drugs.   J,S

Story

Teacher prepares unfinished story wherein students can supply answers to   P
appropriate questions in regard to proper use of medicines. For example,
Jane's mother was given a prescription to get some medicine_____

Questions:

1. Who would give her the prescription? Why?
2. Where would she take it? Why?
3. What would be on the label? Why?

Teacher may read this story or duplicate it so that students may read it.   P
Afterward, children may complete it with verbal conclusions or write an
ending.

Grandma Periwinckle has not been feeling too well lately. She went to
see her doctor. He wrote a prescription which she took to the pharmacist
at the drug store. She went back to the pharmacy a few hours later and
picked up the pills. She read the label, which said, "Take two every four
hours." Also printed on the label was "CAUTION: KEEP OUT OF REACH
OF CHILDREN." Grandma Periwinckle put the pills in her purse and went
home. Just as she arrived at the door, her little grandson, Jeffrey, came
around the corner with his mother. Grandma Periwinckle went into the
bedroom where she took off her coat and put it, along with her purse,
on the bed. She then returned to the living room to talk to Jeffrey's mother.
Usually Grandma Periwinckle is very careful to keep all her medicines
and household products on high shelves because, even though she has no
small children of her own, Jeffrey and his friends visit her quite often.
She always warns the children never to put anything into their mouths
without asking first. But this time she forgot that purses containing medicines
should also be put out of children's reach. As she was talking in the living
room, little Jeffrey walked into the bedroom and emptied her purse. Along
with her cosmetics, her change, and her handkerchief, he found the bottle
of pills.

Tell what happened then.

Survey

Conduct anonymous, open-ended survey of students regarding their ex-   I,J,S
periences in the use of drugs—types, frequency, reasons.

Students prepare survey form to be used in class or schoolwide to determine   I,J,S
incidence and type of drug abuse in school.

Teacher asks students to identify interests and concerns in drugs. Use to de-   I,J,S
termine content of material to be presented to students.

Students identify substances in home medicine cabinets that can be classified   I
as drugs.

Students survey adults for reasons why they use such drugs as alcohol, to-   I,J
bacco, and aspirin.

Students prepare in class a list of benefits of marijuana as revealed by drug   J,S
abusers. They then research the topic and compare findings.

Prepare survey form with yes or no answers to these questions. Do you: J,S

1. Drink coffee every morning?
2. Take more than three aspirin a week?
3. Participate in extracurricular activities?
4. Participate in sports?
5. Enjoy dancing?
6. Use sleeping pills often?
7. Drink milk every day?
8. Eat hamburgers frequently?
9. Use stay-awake pills?

Continued.

GRADES

    10. Use pep pills?
    11. Take diet pills?
    12. Have regular physical examinations?
    13. Drink alcoholic beverages?
    14. Use cold remedies frequently?
    15. Feel sick often?
    16. Like school?
    17. Have hobbies?

Visit local pharmacies seeking answers to these questions: J,S
    1. What drugs are in greatest demand? What are they used for?
    2. Do any of the nonprescription drugs contain dependency-producing substances?

Survey drug section of a shopping center and list the various medicines J,S
available.

Survey the community resources where individuals with drug problems are J,S
helped.

Survey the social and recreational activities available to teen-agers in the S
school, church, and community.

Tape recording

Interview a physician for answers to questions raised in class about drugs. I,J
Radio and TV ads for class discussion. J,S

Volunteer student services

Students volunteer to spend time helping at the various rehabilitation and S
treatment centers in the community. Later they report their experiences to
the class for discussion.

	GRADES*

Advertisements

Bring newspaper and magazine ads to class for analysis regarding accuracy and further research.   I,J,S

Tape radio commercials and discuss in class.   J,S

Students prepare reports analyzing ads in terms of appeal and factual aspects, misleading or deceptive.   J,S

Brainstorming

Students raise relevant questions about tobacco and health; these are placed on blackboard. Individuals or groups conduct research and report findings in class.   I,J,S

Buzz group

Discuss such questions as: Should you smoke? Why do people smoke? Do people learn to smoke in groups or alone? Why do some people not smoke? Are school smoking regulations necessary? Why is it difficult to stop smoking?   J,S

Cartoon and picture collecting

Collect cartoon characters or pictures of people who are smoking from newspapers and magazines. Remove captions. Have students place their own captions under each cartoon or picture. (Student attitudes toward smoking may be revealed.)   I,J

Chart

Students prepare chart or charts illustrating death rates, life-expectancy rates, incidence of lung cancer, heart disease, and respiratory problems of heavy smokers, moderate smokers, and nonsmokers.   J,S

Debate

To smoke or not to smoke. Are school smoking regulations necessary? Should cigarette advertising be banned? Is cigarette advertising deceptive and misleading?   J,S

Demonstration

Use a smoking machine (American Cancer Society) to demonstrate the residue found in cigarettes and discuss implications.   I,J,S

Take pulse rates before and after smoking a cigarette and discuss reasons for difference.   J,S

Diagram

Diagram and describe on chalkboard the effect of tobacco smoke on respiratory system.   J,S

Discussion

Effects of smoking on the circulatory, respiratory, and digestive systems, on athletic performance, and on other areas.   I,J,S

Advantages and disadvantages of smoking.   I,J,S

Why young people begin to smoke.   I,J

Effect of smoking on others at social functions, in public places, and in other situations.   J,S

Effectiveness of cigarette filters.   J,S

Relationships between use of alcohol, tobacco, and drugs.   J,S

Difficulty in breaking smoking habit.   I,J,S

Cultural and sociological influences on the attitudes and habits of smokers.   J,S

Use of tobacco by society.   J,S

*Letters refer to suggested grade level for which the activity is appropriate. P = primary, I = intermediate, J = junior high school, and S = senior high school.

Continued.

	GRADES
Laws relating to tobacco.	J,S
Effect of antismoking campaign.	I,J,S

Dramatization

| A 10-year-old child is encouraged by his friends to smoke a cigarette. | I |
| Prepare skits or puppet shows satirizing smoking ads. | I |

Exhibit

Models of cancerous and noncancerous lung tissue (American Cancer Society).	I,J,S
Microscopic lung tissue from smoker, nonsmoker, and ex-smoker. (See pathologist at local hospital.)	I,J,S
Charts, graphs, and other statistics (American Cancer Society).	J,S
Variety of filters in cigarettes.	J,S

Field trip

| Visit local health department, hospital, and voluntary health agencies to discuss smoking and health. | J,S |

Forum

| Students conduct discussions, debates, and programs in classrooms, assemblies, and other places; letters to the editor, pro and con column in newspaper. | J,S |

Health fair

| Students plan and conduct variety of activities, including health agency exhibits, student-prepared exhibits, presentations, films, filmstrips, and pamphlet distribution. | J,S |

Notebook

| Include a collection of ads with student analysis resulting from research. | I,J |
| Current newspaper and magazine articles with brief summaries. | I,J |

Parents' day

| Parents attend classroom or school display of student activities such as fact gathering, experiments, contacts with health agencies, survey results, conclusions, and summary of individual work. | I,J |

Parodies

| Develop parodies, satires, and singing commercials on cigarette ad slogans such as "Why filter springtime?" and "Don't smoke. The life you save may be your own." | J,S |

Posters

| Effects of tobacco on the body. | I,J |
| For school, home, or community antismoking campaign. | J,S |

Pretest

| Conduct a pretest on tobacco and health. | I,J,S |

Problem solving

| Conduct research on a problem using following procedure: (1) collect data, (2) analyze data, and (3) draw conclusion. | I,J,S |

Publicity campaign

| Prepare posters, buttons, and newspaper articles to discourage smoking. | I,J,S |

Reports—individual or group

Examine materials received from agency contacted and report to class.	I,J
Reasons for decision to smoke or not to smoke.	I,J,S
In-depth study of advertising based on motivational research.	J,S

TOBACCO—cont'd

	GRADES
Analysis of current newspaper and magazine articles.	I,J,S
Development of a safe cigarette.	J,S
Effects of tobacco on body.	I,J,S
Laws against sale to minors.	J,S
Economic cost of smoking one package of cigarettes a day for a week, a month, a year, a lifetime.	I,J,S

Resource person

Invite nurse, physician, representative from voluntary health agency, and others to discuss smoking and health.	I,J
Invite members of local withdrawal clinic to speak.	S

Role play

How to refuse a cigarette offered.	J,S
A home situation where teen-ager announces that he has started smoking.	J,S
Disciplinary action of principal against three students caught smoking at school.	J,S
A group of students discussing whether or not to smoke.	I,J

Survey

Extent of student smoking.	J,S
Extent of parent smoking.	I,J
Why students or adults started smoking.	I,J
Attitudes of students, parents, coaches, and other people toward smoking.	I,J
People who have tried to stop smoking and the results.	J,S
Most popular brand of cigarettes sold in a few stores.	J,S

Write

Request materials from voluntary health agencies about smoking and health.	I,J

GRADES*

Attitude questionnaire

Complete short answers to: I,J

1. Happiness is _____.
2. Sadness is _____.
3. I am fearful of _____.
4. I am angry when _____.

Conduct discussion when completed.

Have students complete open-ended questions such as: J,S
1. If I could go any place in the world on an all-expense paid vacation, would go to _____.
2. If I could be any person in the world, I would be _____.
3. If I could make one change in the school program it would be _____ _____.
4. I believe the three most important things in life are _____, _____, and _____.

Have discussion of choices after completion.

Brainstorming

Students prepare list of problems they consider important and develop plans   I,J
to resolve them.

Bulletin board

Students prepare a display of pictures that expose a variety of emotions such   I,J
as anger, fear, love, and happiness. Title might be "Emotions We Live With."
Students display pictures, advertisements, and cut-outs to help make decisions   I,J
about drugs with captions and selections such as:

DRINK **DON'T DRINK** **SMOKE** **DON'T SMOKE** **USE DRUGS** **ABUSE DRUGS**
☐   ☐   ☐   ☐   ☐   ☐

Buzz group

Involve students in answering these questions: J,S
1. What is reality?
2. How do you make your own decisions to be a good leader and a sensible follower?
3. Does having the courage of one's convictions mean one is stubborn?
4. Does "everybody's doing it" mean everyone should do it?

Chart/posters

Illustrate in writing, pictures, or drawings ways to handle upset feelings,   I,J
anger, hate, and other emotions.

Checklist

Students prepare a checklist of personal or family values and discuss bases for   S
them.

Construction

Have students make life-size outline of self on butcher paper. Have them   P,I
color as desired, cut out with scissors, and display around the room. Students may need to help one another to make the outlines (a way to get
to "know myself").

Debate

How do value systems affect behavior patterns of individuals? Cover positive   S
and negative aspects relating to persistence in completing a job, cheating,
and premarital pregnancy.

*Letters refer to suggested grade level for which the activity is appropriate. P = primary, I = intermediate, J = junior
high school. and S = senior high school.

	GRADES
Discussion	
What causes quarrels? How can they be prevented?	P,I
Ways feelings were hurt and how hurt was overcome.	P,I
Emotional needs and how they can be satisfied.	J,S
Constructive and destructive criticism.	J,S
Hate and inherent dangers.	P,I,J
Wholesome outlets for anger.	P,I,J
"He or she has no personality."	J,S
Causes of conflicts and frustrations and how to handle.	J,S
Who besides our family can help us—doctors, teachers, nurses, policemen, friends?	P,I
How can we make friends? Why are friends necessary?	P,I,J
Should you discuss problems with your parents?	P,I,J
How negative moods and feelings (anger, jealousy, rage, fear, worry, etc.) can produce anxiety and stress. What can be done?	P,I,J
Why is it frequently difficult to do what is right? What factors influence decision making?	I,J,S
How illness, lack of rest, and lack of food can affect feelings and cause irritability.	I,J
How anxiety affects learning and doing what we enjoy.	I,J
How talking with someone may help with problems.	P,I,J
Prepare list of what "turns kids on" and "turns kids off." Then prepare list of human needs—physical, social, etc.—and compare to determine relationships.	I,J
Prepare list of values and spend time determining if they are values or merely interests. Draw conclusions.	I,J
Meaning of "growing up."	I,J
Fears—of earthquakes, illness, war—and reasons why they develop.	I,J,S
Control of emotions.	P,I,J
Process to follow in making decisions (relate to drugs).	I,J,S
What are desirable and undesirable factors of belonging to a clique or gang?	J,S
Do parents, teachers, and other adults belong to cliques or groups?	J,S
Why do people join a clique or group? Are dress, behavior, appearance, and attitudes related to acceptance in the group?	J,S
Several races and cultures of people in society.	I,J,S
Cultural deprivation.	S
Drawings	
Express feelings and emotions in drawings, paintings, clay modeling, and other self-expressive activities.	P,I
Exhibit	
Prepare display of materials of different faiths, races, and countries and discuss.	I,J
Problem solving	
Children prepare short, anonymous paragraphs of realistic problem situations to be read or dramatized in class with follow-up discussion in problem-solving techniques.	I,J
Reports—individual or group	
When I wanted something I could not have.	I
"Me as I see myself" or "Me as I would like to be."	I,J
How brothers, sisters, or friends react to emotional situations.	I
Committee prepares list of recreational and social opportunities in school and neighborhood and discusses in class.	J,S
Characteristics necessary to get along with others.	I,J

Continued.

GRADES

Committees analyze propaganda methods and motivational researchers' ways to try to influence people—alcohol and tobacco industries and others. S

Research

Students investigate how emotions affect the endocrine, digestive, respiratory, and circulatory systems. I,J

Resource person

Advertising agency representative to describe techniques used to sell products. S

Psychologist or psychiatrist from local treatment center to discuss relationship between emotional stability and drug dependence. J,S

Nurse to discuss emotions and the body functions. I

Counselors, clergy, social workers, and others to discuss how they can help students. J,S

Role play

Feelings of difference in terms of race, religion, cultural customs, ethnic origin, and others followed by discussion. I,J,S

Negative emotional behavior. I,J

How to make new friends. P,I

How to help an unhappy person or one with hurt feelings. P,I

How to say "No" if someone offers you a marijuana cigarette. J,S

How to say "No." I,J

Approached by a stranger and offered a ride home. P

Someone you do not know offers you some candy. P

Story

Introduce group of pictures representing anger, sadness, hate, love, and joy and develop stories relating to why each emotion is expressed. P,I

Obtain books containing stories about emotions for students to read and discuss. I

Share stories and poems that create different moods. I

Value analysis

Ask students series of questions and after responses ask "Why?" J,S
1. What aspect of health do you value most?
2. If you had to give up one of your senses, which one would it be?
3. If you had 6 months to live, what would you do?
4. What do you like about yourself?
5. If you could make one telephone call anywhere in the world, who would you call?

Value challenges*

Teacher consistently and regularly raises value issues with students by introducing provocative, controversial statements found in newspapers, magazines, books, and on radio, or TV. These should be duplicated for student reading and accompanied by a series of teacher questions that might include: What is your reaction to the statement? Would you be proud of this action? Does it make you want to change your life? J,S

Value questionnaire*

Prepare a series of questions for student response and discussion purposes. Illustrative questions might include the following: J,S
1. What do you most like to do with your free time?
2. What adult qualities do you admire?
3. Where will you be and what will you be doing in 10 years?

*Adapted from Simon, S. B.: Promoting the search for values, Sch. Health Rev. 2:21-24, 1971. Also review Raths, L. E., et al.: Values and teaching, Columbus, Ohio, 1966, Charles E. Merrill Publishing Co.

PSYCHIC-SOCIAL-SPIRITUAL—cont'd

GRADES

    4. What injustices exist in the community?
    5. How do you feel about money and material possessions?
    6. Will you marry outside your race or religion?

Value report card*

    Students anonymously turn in 4 × 6 value cards on which they describe things   J,S
    they care about deeply or value highly. One card is turned in each week
    and contains one value. Some cards are read and discussed in class periodic-
    ally.

Value time diary*

    Students maintain a time diary for 1 week—a daily chart divided into ½   J,S
    hour time blocks. Actual uses of time are listed. These should be personal
    and not viewed by teachers or others. An attempt is made to help students
    locate those things they most like to do, to discover wasted time, to identify
    inconsistencies, and to focus on the difference between what one says and
    what one does. After tabulation by students and clarification of activities,
    efforts are made individually to determine what students really value.

Inventory of risk-taking behaviors and rewards. Distribute copies of the inventory shown in Fig. 7 to all students. Have them complete this and use it as a basis for discussion. The inventory may also be collected at the end of class if it is completed anonymously. Results could be tabulated and findings reported to the class for use in further discussions.

DRUG EDUCATION RESOURCE MATERIALS

Printed materials such as textbooks, pamphlets, and leaflets and visual items, including films, filmstrips, cassettes, transparencies, and posters, are teaching aids, or resource materials, that are helpful in drug education programs. They have a multiplicity of uses and frequently can provide direct experiences obtainable in no other way. They are often referred to as the tools of education.

Literally thousands of items (many of which are not well prepared) are available; the problem is one of selection. Hammond[32a] states that of the 800 posters, charts, giveaways, pamphlets, and other items received by the National Coordinating Council on Drug Education, perhaps only 30 will be recommended. There-

fore any materials for the instructional program should be carefully screened as to appropriateness and suitability. Chapter 11 includes several instruments for the evaluation of resource materials.

Special consideration should be given to items available from the National Clearinghouse for Drug Abuse Information and the National Coordinating Council on Drug Education because these agencies are probably two of the best sources for drug education materials. Their addresses may be found on p. 189.

The National Clearinghouse for Drug Abuse Information is a federal agency that operates as a central source for the collection and dissemination of drug abuse information as well as a coordinating information agency for groups throughout the country. Its major activities include the distribution of drug abuse information materials, the answering of mail and phone inquiries, the referral of specialized requests to appropriate government and private sources, the publication of periodical secondary source reference materials and fact sheets, and the operation of an up-to-date and computerized information storage and retrieval system. It is developing

| Type of Risk | Degree of Risk | | Degree of Reward |
	To Individual Lowest Highest 1 2 3 4 5	To Society Lowest Highest 1 2 3 4 5	To Individual Lowest Highest 1 2 3 4 5
Smoking cigarettes			
Lack of affection			
Drinking beer			
Use of "pep" pills			
Marriage			
Stealing			
Drinking alcohol and driving			
Lack of success experiences			
Smoking cigars			
Drinking wine			
Lack of identity			
Use of heroin			
Sexual intercourse			
Use of marijuana			
Smoking pipes			
Drinking whiskey			
Use of sleeping pills			
Inequality of opportunity			
Abortion			
Use of coffee, tea, cola			
Self-medication			
Use other's prescrip- tion drugs			
Pushing drugs			
Lack of job			
Fighting			
Arguing with friends, with parents			
Sniffing glue			
Inadequate housing			
Use of contraceptives			
Cheating or lying			
Use of aspirin			
Destruction of property			
Mainlining drugs			
Racial, ethnic prejudice			

List your three most important risks. Why are they risks?   What are the rewards?

FIG. 7

Risk-taking behaviors and rewards inventory. Students insert most appropriate number (1 to 5) in columns and spaces. (Adapted from Carney, R. E.: Risk-taking behavior questionnaire. In Report on feasibility of using risk-taking attitudes as a basis for programs to control and predict drug abuse, Coronado Unified School District, California, 1970.)

"mini" clearinghouses (DRACON, Chapter 5) in each state so that information will be more readily available. The National Clearinghouse for Drug Abuse Information has developed an immense file of resource materials, including bibliographies, articles, speeches, program descriptions, published guidelines, and technical data in pharmacology, sociology, biochemistry, medicine, social work, and other disciplines. In the main, the Clearinghouse features the following resources:

1. National Inventory of Drug Abuse Programs—a comprehensive file describing federal and federally supported programs, voluntary action, and state, regional, county, and local drug abuse programs throughout the country

2. Drug Abuse Information Resources and Material Files—a comprehensive file of technical and resource materials in the drug abuse area, including abstracts of curriculum guides, pamphlets, journal articles, books, and descriptions of audiovisual materials.

3. Drug Abuse Current Awareness System—a comprehensive file of the latest materials in the scientific, technical, and professional literature that will supplement the overall resources and materials file

The National Coordinating Council on Drug Education is a private, nonprofit organization that has worked to promote rational approaches to all drug-related issues. Its membership is extended to any interdisciplinary regional, state, or local organization whose function is drug education as well as to any national organization with an interest in the Council's purposes. It is supported by a number of foundations, by the National Institute of Mental Health, and by the contributions of its over 100 members. The Council has prepared the following nominally priced materials and services that are available upon request:

Common Sense Lives Here—a step-by-step guide to community drug abuse organization

Drug Abuse Films, ed. 2– an evaluative report on over 110 films and audiovisual materials

Drug Abuse Bibliography —an extensive bibliography with each publication categorized according to subject

Drug Abuse Directory—a compilation of information about the Council's 124 members

National Drug Reporter—a monthly newsletter on the latest developments in drug abuse education, treatment, and enforcement

Grassroots—a comprehensive drug abuse information service offering monthly supplements for up-to-the-minute revisions of 20 categories of information

Marijuana and Health, a report to Congress, January 31, 1971—the introduction and summary of the report from the Secretary of Health, Education and Welfare

The references that follow include sources of drug materials, including books, curriculum guides, films and filmstrips, library sources, newsletters, professional journals, textbooks, and other materials usable in the instructional program. It is recommended that local and state resources also be identified and located when seeking instructional materials. It should be noted that the cost and availability of items listed by agencies and organizations may, on occasion, change rather rapidly.

BOOKS

The wide variety of available references makes it impossible to provide a comprehensive list of books, pamphlets, and magazine articles. It is suggested that the following publications be obtained for more complete lists:

Drug Dependence and Abuse: A Selected Bibliography, National Clearinghouse for Drug Abuse Information, 1971
Order from: Superintendent of Documents
U. S. Government Printing Office
Washington, D. C. 20402 (60¢)
Drug Education Bibliography, 1970-1971
Order from: National Coordinating Council on Drug Education
Suite 212
1211 Connecticut Ave., N. W.
Washington, D. C. 20036 ($5)

The following books, selected from the bibliographies previously identified, will serve as introductory and reference volumes to the drug scene:

Aaronson, B., and Osmond, H.: Psychedelics: the uses and implications of hallucinogenic drugs, Garden City, N. Y., 1970, Doubleday & Co., Inc.

Aberle, D. P.: The peyote religion among the Navajo, Chicago, 1966, Aldine-Atherton, Inc.

Answers to the most frequently asked questions about drug abuse, Chevy Chase, Md., 1970, National Clearinghouse for Drug Abuse Information.

Bell, J. C., and Chambers, C. D.: The epidemiology of opiate addiction in the United States, Springfield, Ill., 1970, Charles C Thomas, Publisher.

Barber, B.: Drugs and society, New York, 1967, Russell Sage Foundation.

Beggs, L.: Huckleberry's for runaways, New York, 1969, Ballantine Books, Inc.

Bloomquist, E. R.: Marijuana: the second trip, Beverly Hills, Calif., 1971, Glencoe Press.

Blum, R. H.: Drugs I: society and drugs. Drugs II: students and drugs, San Francisco, 1969, Jossey-Bass, Inc., Publishers.

Blum, R. H., et al.: The utopiates: the use and users of LSD-25, New York, 1964, Aldine-Atherton Press, Inc.

Brown, D.: The milder hallucinogens: nutmeg, morning glory seeds and marijuana, London, 1965, Westmount Press.

Bureau of Narcotics and Dangerous Drugs: Drugs of abuse, Washington, D. C., 1970, Government Printing Office.

Burroughs, W., Jr.: Speed, New York, 1970, The Olympia Press, Inc.

Cahalan, D., et al.: American drinking practices, New Brunswick, N. J., 1969, Rutgers Center for Alcohol Studies.

Cain, A. H.: Young people and drugs, New York, 1969, The John Day Co., Inc.

Clark, W. H.: Chemical ecstasy: psychedelic drugs and religion, New York, 1969, Sheed & Ward, Inc.

Clinebell, H. J., Jr.: Understanding and counseling the alcoholic through religion and psychology, Nashville, Tenn., 1968, Abingdon Press.

Cohen, S.: The beyond within: the LSD story, New York, 1967, Atheneum Publishers.

Conley, P. C., and Sorensen, A. A.: The staggering steeple; the story of alcoholism and the churches, Philadelphia, 1971, Pilgrim Press.

Creekmore, H.: Daffodils are dangerous: the poisonous plants in your garden, New York, 1966, Walker & Co.

DeBold, R. C., and Leaf, R. C.: LSD, man and society, Middletown, Conn., 1967, Wesleyan University Press.

DeRopp, R. S.: Drugs and the mind, New York, 1957, Grove Press, Inc.

Diehl, H. J.: Tobacco and your health: the smoking controversy, New York, 1969, McGraw-Hill Book Co., Inc.

Duncan, T. L.: Understanding and helping the narcotic addict, Philadelphia, 1965, Fortress Press.

Einstein, S.: The use and misuse of drugs, Belmont, Calif., 1970, Wadsworth Publishing Co., Inc.

Fiddle, S.: Portraits from a shooting gallery: life styles from the drug addict world, New York, 1967, Harper & Row, Publishers.

Fort, J.: The pleasure seekers: the drug crisis, youth and society, New York, 1969, Grove Press, Inc.

Gillespie, D. G., editor: Drug abuse and law enforcement, St. Louis, 1970, Law Enforcement Study Center, Social Science Institute, Washington University.

Goode, E., editor: Marijuana, New York, 1969, Aldine-Atherton Press.

Irwin, S.: An introduction to their actions and potential hazards, Beloit, Wis., 1970, The Student Association for the Study of Hallucinogens.

Kaplan, J.: Marijuana—the new prohibition, Cleveland, 1970, World Publishing Co.

Kron, Y. J., and Brown, E. M.: Mainline to nowhere: the making of a heroin addict, Cleveland, 1967, Meridian Books.

Laurie, P.: Drugs: medical, psychological and social facts, Baltimore, 1967, Penguin Books, Inc.

Lindesmith, A. R.: The addict and the law, Bloomington, Ind., 1965, Indiana University Press.

Lingeman, R. R.: Drugs from A to Z: a dictionary, New York, 1969, McGraw-Hill Book Co., Inc.

Loennecken, S. J.: Acute barbiturate poisoning, London, 1967, John Wright & Sons, Ltd.

Louria, D. B.: The drug scene, 1970, Bantam Books, Inc.

Margolis, J. S., and Clorfene, R.: A child's garden of grass: the official handbook of marijuana users, New York, 1969, Pocket Books.

Marijuana: a signal of misunderstanding, first report of the National Commission on Marijuana and Drug Abuse, Washington, D. C., 1972, Government Printing Office.

Marijuana and health, a report to the Congress from the Secretary, Department of Health, Education and Welfare, Washington, D. C., 1971, Government Printing Office.

Marin, P., and Cohen, A.: Understanding drug use: an adult's guide to drugs and the young, New York, 1970, Harper & Row, Publishers.

Masters, R. F. L., and Houston, J.: The varieties of psychedelic experience, New York, 1966, Dell Publishing Co., Inc.

Nowlis, H. H.: Drugs on the college campus, New York, 1969, Anchor Books.

Plaut, F. F. A.: Alcohol problems: a report to

the nation by the Cooperative Commission on the Study of Alcoholism, New York, 1967, Oxford University Press, Inc.

President's Commission on Law Enforcement and Administration of Justice: Task force report: narcotics and drug abuse, Washington, D. C., 1967, Government Printing Office.

Price, T. E.: Putting the pieces together: drug education resource book, Cincinnati, Ohio, 1970, United Methodist Board of Christian Social Concerns and Missions.

Ray, O. S.: Drugs, society and human behavior, St. Louis, 1972, The C. V. Mosby Co.

Resource book for drug abuse education, ed. 2, Chevy Chase, Md., 1972, National Clearinghouse for Drug Abuse Information.

Richards, L. G., et al.: LSD-25: a factual account, Washington, D. C., 1969, Bureau of Narcotics and Dangerous Drugs, Superintendent of Documents, Government Printing Office.

Roszak, T.: Making of a counter culture, New York, 1969, Doubleday & Co., Inc.

Russo, J. R., editor: Amphetamine abuse, Springfield, Ill., 1968, Charles C Thomas, Publisher.

Schur, E. M.: Narcotic addiction in Britain and America: the impact of public policy, Bloomington, Ind., 1962, Indiana University Press.

Scott, J. M.: The white poppy: a history of opium, New York, 1969, Funk & Wagnalls, Inc.

Simmons, J. L., and Winograd, B.: It's happening: a portrait of the youth scene today, Santa Barbara, Calif., 1966, Marc-Laird Publications.

Slotkin, J. S.: The peyote religion, New York, 1956, The Free Press.

Smith, D. E., editor: The new social drug: cultural, medical and legal perspectives on marijuana, New Jersey, 1970, Prentice-Hall, Inc.

Smith, D. E., Bentel, D., and Schwartz, J.: The free clinic: a community approach to health care and drug abuse, Beloit, Wis., 1971, Stash Press.

Smith, D. E., and Gay, G. R.: It's so good, don't even try it once: heroin in perspective, Englewood Cliffs, N. J., 1972, Prentice-Hall, Inc.

Solomon, D., editor: The marihuana papers, New York, 1966, Signet Books.

U. S. Department of Health, Education and Welfare, Public Health Service: The health consequences of smoking, a report to the Surgeon General, Washington, D. C., 1971, Government Printing Office.

Wilkinson, R.: The prevention of drinking problems: alcohol control and cultural influences, New York, 1970, Oxford University Press, Inc.

Winick, C., and Goldstein, J.: The glue sniffing problem, New York, 1965, American Social Health Association.

Yablonsky, L.: Synanon: the tunnel back, Baltimore, 1969, Penguin Books, Inc.

Yablonsky, L.: The hippie trip, New York, 1968, Pegasus.

CURRICULUM GUIDES

Numerous drug education curriculum guides have been prepared and are available from state departments of education and local school districts. If such references are desired, it is recommended that state directors of drug education be contacted for information and assistance.

FILMS AND FILMSTRIPS

The films and filmstrips listed below were selected from the Film Directory prepared by the National Coordinating Council on Drug Education, whose address was previously listed. This publication contains over 100 films and filmstrips that have been evaluated by qualified authorities. Note that materials are categorized as "recommended" and "others." The recommended items are those chosen by authorities. The others are usable for discussion purposes but may have weaknesses or flaws that prevent their being placed in the recommended category.

FILMS

Marijuana

Recommended

Marijuana Carousel Films, Inc., 1501 Broadway, New York, N. Y. 10036, 52 min., B/W sd., Jr. & Sr. High, 1969 ($25 rental).

This CBS documentary surveys the controversy over the social and legal aspects of marijuana use.

Weed Encyclopaedia Britannica Educational Corporation, 425 N. Michigan Ave., Chicago, Ill., 60611, 24 min., color, sd., Jr. & Sr. High, 1971 ($15 rental for 3 days).

A potpourri of information on the legal, historical, physical, and sociological aspects of marijuana.

Others

Marijuana BFA Educ. Media, 2211 Michigan Ave., Santa Monica, Calif., 90404, 34 min., color, sd., Jr. & Sr. High, 1968 ($25 rental).

Arguments for and against smoking marijuana and advice to make own decisions.

Marijuana: the great escape BFA Educ. Media, 2211 Michigan Ave., Santa Monica, Calif. 90404, 20 min., color, sd., Jr. & Sr. High, 1970 ($15 rental).

Dramatization of what happens to a teen-ager who experiments with marijuana.

Research report: THC—the chemistry of marijuana Audiovisual Center, Indiana University, Bloomington, Ind. 47401, 20 min., B/W, sd., Sr. High, 1968 ($5.50 rental).

An experiment at the Palo Alto Veterans Hospital exploring the physiological and psychological effects of marijuana on a volunteer subject.

World of the weed Audiovisual Center, Indiana University, Bloomington, Ind. 47401, 21 min., B/W, sd., Jr. & Sr. High, 1968 ($5.50 rental).

Historical background and biological facts, capsule history of legislation and medical studies of marijuana.

Depressants

Other

Up pill, down pill BFA Educ. Media, 2211 Michigan Ave., Santa Monica, Calif. 90404, 23 min., color, sd., Interm., Jr. & Sr. High, 1970 ($15 rental).

Drama of the different life-styles of Roger, a teen-age dropout who uses pills to escape the boredom of his life, and Charlie, an old man who directs his energy toward rebuilding an old boat.

Stimulants

Recommended

Speedscene: the problem of amphetamine abuse BFA Educ. Media, 2211 Michigan Ave., Santa Monica, Calif. 90404, 17 min., color, sd., Jr. & Sr. High, 1969 ($15 rental).

Interviews with speed users and statements of medical authorities about physical dangers and psychological problems with use of speed.

Hallucinogens

Others

Acid Encyclopaedia Britannica Educational Corporation, 425 N. Michigan Ave., Chicago, Ill. 60611, 26 min., color, sd., Jr. & Sr. High, 1971 ($15 rental for 3 days).

Superstitions about LSD, medical research, personal descriptions of trips, legal issues, and the quality of black market acid are included.

Beyond LSD BFA Educ. Media, 2211 Michigan Ave., Santa Monica, Calif. 90404, 25 min., color, sd., parents & teen-agers, 1968 ($20 rental).

Dramatization of a medical doctor's discussion with neighborhood parents who are concerned that teen-agers' long hair, dress, and music styles may indicate involvement with LSD.

The hippie temptation McGraw-Hill Films, Highstown, N. J. 08520, 2 pts., 51 min., color, sd., Sr. High, 1967 ($40 rental).

Harry Reasoner of CBS visits the hippie haven in San Francisco's Haight-Ashbury district to find out "who and what" the hippies are, how they dress, where and how they live, and why they chose their life-style.

LSD: the Spring Grove experiment McGraw-Hill Films, Highstown, N. J. 08520, 2 pts., 54 min., B/W, sd. Sr. High, 1966 ($25 rental).

This CBS documentary film records a highly controlled experiment at the Spring Grove State Hospital in Baltimore, Maryland, involving two patients in LSD-assisted psychotherapy.

LSD-25 Professional Arts, Inc., P.O. Box 8484, Universal City, Calif. 91608, 27 min., color, sd., Jr. & Sr. High, 1967 ($27.50 rental for 3 days plus postage).

Film emphasizes drug's unpredictability and unknown properties, including potential dangers from use of illegally purchased drugs, bad trips, possible chromosomal damage, self-injury under the influence, and recurring effects.

Narcotics

Recommended

Darkness, darkness Haight-Ashbury Films, 1559 19th Ave., San Francisco, Calif. 94122; See Saw Films, P.O. Box 262, Palo Alto, Calif. 94302, 36 min., color, sd., Sr. High, 1970 ($60 rental for 3 days).

The film records conversations of a dozen people, all middle-class whites, whose lives in some way have been touched by heroin.

Junkies are people Haight-Ashbury Films, 1559 19th Ave., San Francisco, Calif. 94122, 26 min., color, sd., Sr. High, 1970 ($60 rental for 3 days).

The film presents four different heroin treatment programs, including methadone maintenance, Marin Open House, Haight-Ashbury Free Medical Clinic, and Walden House, a therapeutic community.

Scag Encyclopaedia Britannica Educational Corporation, 425 N. Michigan Ave., Chicago, Ill. 60611, 26 min., color, sd., Interm., Jr. & Sr. High, 1970 ($15 rental for 3 days).

The film relates the experiences of two heroin addicts—a middle-class white male and an inner-city black girl.

Skezag Soho Cinema Ltd., 508 Broadway, New York, N. Y. 10012, 73 min., color, sd., Jr. & Sr. High, 1970 (rental on request).

Documentary film about a 21-year-old black living in New York City who talks about a variety of topics, including the Vietnam war, his use of heroin, why he will not become addicted, and his attitude toward his mother, his friends, and the white race.

Others

A day in the death of Donny B. National Audiovisual Center, NIMH, Washington, D. C. 20409, 14 min., B/W, sd., Interm., Jr. & Sr. High, 1970 (free).

The film portrays what could be a typical day in the life of a heroin addict in a ghetto slum. Donny, a young black, is shown in his search for means to support his habit.

Three Benchmark Films, 145 Scarborough Rd., Briarcliff Manor, N. Y. 10510, 52 min., B/W, sd., Sr. High, 1968 ($30 rental).

Three people meet in a New York state rehabilitation program for drug addicts where, in group therapy sessions, they relate individual experiences of heroin addiction.

Psychology

Recommended
Darkness, darkness Refer to "Narcotics."

Sociocultural aspects of drug use in the ghetto

Recommended
Skezag Refer to "Narcotics."

Other
A day in the death of Donny B. Refer to "Narcotics."

Sociocultural aspects of drug use in middle and upper classes

Recommended

Almost everyone does Wombat Productions Inc., 87 Main St., Hasting-on-Hudson, N. Y. 10706, 14½ min., color, sd., Interm., Jr. & Sr. High, 1970 ($18, $25, & $40 for 1 day, 3 days, and 1 week, respectively).

Film emphasizes that all people have feelings, both good and bad, and focuses on how people learn to deal with their feelings by drinking a martini, smoking cigarettes, talking to a neighbor, and taking a pill to relax. Alternatives to eliminating bad feelings without taking a drug are explored.

Grooving Benchmark Films Inc., 145 Scarborough Rd., Briarcliff, N. Y. 10510, 31 min., color, sd., Interm., Jr. & Sr. High, 1970 ($40 rental).

A group of teen-agers, drug users, nonusers, and ex-users talk about reasons for trying various drugs and their individual experiences with drugs.

A nice kid like you Extension Media Center, University of California, Berkeley, Calif. 94720, 38 min., B/W, sd., Sr. High, 1969 ($17.50 rental).

Students from two unidentified eastern colleges reveal their feelings about drugs, sex, parents, the educational system, and American society in general.

Others

The distant drummer National Audiovisual Center (GSA), Washington, D. C. 20409, 45 min., color, sd., Sr. High, 1968 (free).

Includes an historical perspective of the origin of opium, importation route into the United States, several rehabilitation techniques, and the use of drugs by young, rebellious, middle-class Americans.

Escape to nowhere Professional Arts, Inc., P.O. Box 8484, Universal City, Calif. 91608, 25 min., color, sd., Jr. & Sr. High, 1968 ($27.50 rental for 3 days plus postage).

This film tells the real-life story of Debbie, a teen-ager, who describes her attitudes and feelings, and the role drugs play in her life.

Rapping Filmfair Communications, 10946 Ventura Blvd., Studio City, Calif. 91604, 15 min., color, sd., Jr. & Sr. High, 1970 ($20 rental).

In an idyllic setting a small group of teen-agers, some of them drug-users, considers why teen-agers use drugs and why they stop.

Tripping Filmfair Communications, 10946 Ventura Blvd., Studio City, Calif. 91604, 15 min., color, sd., Jr. & Sr. High, 1970 ($20 rental).

Students attempt to find some "positive alternatives" to drug use through communication with each other.

Treatment and rehabilitation

Recommended

Help Concept Films, Suite 312, 1155 15th St., N. W., Washington, D. C. 20005, 25½ min., color, sd., Jr. & Sr. High, 1970 (rental not available).

Live scenes filmed at a hot-line crisis center in Philadelphia portray the staff in action as they offer telephone counseling, give medical examinations, and trace potential suicide calls.

Others

The circle McGraw-Hill Films, Highstown, N. J. 08520, 2 pts, 57 min., B/W, sd., Sr. High, 1967 ($25 rental).

Film portrays the rehabilitation process of drug addicts at Daytop Village by focusing on one individual from his first day until the time he is ready to leave.

Here's help National Audiovisual Center (GSA), Washington, D. C. 20409, 28 min., color, sd., Jr. & Sr. High, 1970 (free).

Film centers on a variety of rehabilitation procedures and centers, including Lexington, Kentucky, Teen Challenge, Samaritan Halfway Society, and a methadone program.

FILMSTRIPS

Recommended

Narcotics° (1970)—Jr. & Sr. High

Identifies drugs in the narcotic family; focuses on the life-style of the heroin addict; ex-addict describes how he kicked the habit.

Psychedelics° (1970)—Sr. High

Names various types of psychedelics; young couples' experience with LSD and physicians' and psychologists' comments; effects on personality; and "flashback" problems.

Sedatives° (1970)—Jr. & Sr. High

Covers broad range from caffeine and nicotine to cocaine, amphetamines, and methamphetamine (speed), but concentrates on speed.

Drugs: friend or foe? Marsh Film Enterprises, Inc., 7900 Rosewood Dr., Shawnee Mission, Kan. 66208, grades K to 3, $15 with record; $18.50 with cassette, teaching guide accompanies filmstrip, 1970.

R. E. Davis, M. D., leads a discussion on drugs with a group of elementary children. Designed to create awareness of the benefits of proper drug use and knowledge of the dangers of drug misuse.

Let's talk about drugs Multi-Media Productions, Inc., P.O. Box 5097, Stanford, Calif. 94305, grades 4 to 5, $49.50, includes sound records with teaching guide.

Program centered around these questions: What is a drug? Why are drugs different from other substances taken into the body? What kinds of drugs are there? Why do people take drugs? What do drugs do?

Marijuana: what can you believe Guidance Associates, 41 Washington Ave., Pleasantville, N. Y. 10570, Sr. High, $35.00 with records; $39.00 with cassettes and discussion guide.

Part I: D. E. Smith, M.D., defines marijuana use as a political-legal-cultural problem rather than a major health issue. He also explores the relationship to other drugs and a variety of other matters.

Part II: Five teen-agers relate some of their experiences with marijuana and other drugs.

LIBRARY SOURCES AND REFERENCE WORKS

Anti-depressant drug studies, 1955-1956: bibliography and selected abstracts, Washington, D. C., 1969, National Institute of Mental Health.

_____

°These filmstrips are part of the Drug Information Service. They may be ordered from: Guidance Associates, 41 Washington Ave., Pleasantville, N. Y. 10570. Purchase: $18.00 with record; $20 with cassette and discussion guide.

Bibliography on drug dependence and abuse, 1928-1966, Washington, D. C., 1969, National Clearinghouse for Mental Health Information.

Drugs in current use and new drugs, New York, 1967, Springer Publishing Co., Inc. (annual).

Interaction of alcohol and other drugs; an annotated bibliography, Toronto, Ontario, 1970, Addiction Research Foundation.

International bibliography of studies on alcohol, 1901-1950, New Brunswick, N. J., 1966, Rutgers Center of Alcohol Studies (2 vols.).

Keller, M., and McCormick, M.: Dictionary of words about alcohol, New Brunswick, N. J., 1968, Rutgers Center of Alcohol Studies.

Lingeman, R. R.: Drugs from A to Z, a dictionary, New York, 1969, McGraw-Hill Book Co., Inc.

ABSTRACTS AND INDEXES

Abstracts for social workers, New York, 1965 to date, National Association of Social Workers (quarterly).

Behavior and physiology index, Kansas City, 1967 to date, Science Search Associates (monthly).

Crime and delinquency abstracts, Bethesda, Md., 1963 to date, National Clearinghouse for Mental Health Information.

Education index, New York, 1929 to date, The H. W. Wilson Co. (monthly).

Educational administration abstracts, Columbus, Ohio, 1966 to date, University Council for Education Administration (3 a year).

Psychological abstracts, Washington, D. C., 1927 to date, American Psychological Association (monthly).

Psychopharmacology abstracts, Washington, D. C., 1961 to date, Government Printing Office (monthly).

Research in education (ERIC), Washington, D. C., 1966 to date, Educational Resources Information Center, U. S. Office of Education (monthly).

Sociological abstracts, New York, 1952 to date, (8 a year).

NEWSLETTERS

Addict Report and Drug Abuse (monthly)
Grafton Publications, Inc.
667 Madison Ave.
New York, N. Y. 10021
Cost: about $20 yearly

Catalyst (quarterly)
North Conway Institute
8 Newbury St.
Boston, Mass. 02116

National Drug Reporter (monthly)
National Coordinating Council on Drug Education
Suite 212
1211 Connecticut Ave., N. W.
Washington, D. C. 20036
Cost: $18 yearly

Drugs and Drug Abuse Education Newsletter
Scope Publications, Inc.
1120 National Press Building
Washington, D. C.
Cost: about $25 yearly

Grassroots (periodic)
National Coordinating Council on Drug Education
Suite 212
1211 Connecticut Ave., N. W.
Washington, D. C. 20036
Cost: $95 yearly

The Journal (monthly)
Addiction Research Foundation of Ontario
33 Russell St.
Toronto 179, Ontario
Cost: about $8 yearly

Stash Capsules (quarterly)
The Student Association for the Study of Hallucinogens, Inc.
638 Pleasant St.
Beloit, Wisc. 53511
Cost: $5 yearly contribution

Smoking and Health Bulletin (periodic)
National Clearinghouse for Smoking and Health
Health, Education and Welfare Department
Rockville, Md. 20852
or
P.O. Box 3654
Central Station
Arlington, Va. 22203
Cost: free on request

Smoking and Health Newsletter (periodic)
National Interagency Council on Smoking and Health
419 Paris Ave., South
New York, N. Y. 10016
Cost: free on request

PROFESSIONAL JOURNALS

Addictions (quarterly)
Alcoholism and Drug Addiction Research Foundation
33 Russell St.
Toronto 179, Ontario
Cost: free on request

British Journal of Addiction (semi-annually)
Society for the Study of Addiction to Alcohol and Drugs
Bedford, England
New York: Pergamon Press, Inc.

Bulletin on narcotics (quarterly)
Division of Narcotic Drugs
Geneva, Switzerland
United Nations (also New York)

Mental Health Digest (monthly)
National Clearinghouse for Mental Health Information
Superintendent of Documents
U. S. Government Printing Office
Washington, D. C. 20402
Subscription: $3.50 yearly

Drug Dependence (irregular)
National Clearinghouse for Mental Health Information
Westwood Towers
5401 Westbard Ave.
Washington, D. C. 20016

Drug Forum (quarterly)
Baywood Publishing Company, Inc.
1 Northwest Dr.
Farmingdale, N. Y. 11735
Subscription: $25 yearly

International Journal of Addictions (quarterly)
Marcel Dekker, Inc.
95 Madison Ave.
New York, N. Y. 10002
Subscription: $25 yearly

Journal of Alcoholism (quarterly)
Medical Council on Alcoholism
London, England

Journal of Drug Education (quarterly)
Baywood Publishing Company, Inc.
1 Northwest Dr.
Farmingdale, N. Y. 11735
Subscription: $25 yearly

Journal of Psychedelic Drugs (semi-annually)
P.O. Box 27278
San Francisco, Calif. 94127

Oil, Paint and Drug Reporter
Schnell Publishing Company
100 Church St.
New York, N. Y. 10007

Psychedelic Information Bulletin
Lisa Bieberman
26 Boylston St.
Boston, Mass. 02138

Psychedelic Review
Box 498
Peter Stuyvesant Station
New York, N. Y. 10009

Quarterly Journal of Studies on Alcohol
Yale Center of Alcohol Studies
Yale University
New Haven, Conn. 06525

TEXTBOOKS

Schools can obtain textbooks from the following sources:

Allyn & Bacon, Inc.
Grades 4 to 8: *What you should know about drugs,* Donald A. Read, 1970

Barron's Educational Series Inc.
Junior high: *You,* Pearl Roam, 1964

Fearon Publishers
Grades 6 to 8: *Going places with your personality,* Charles Kahn and Robert Tong, 1971
Grades 4 to 8: *About drugs,* Haskell L. Bowen and Les Landin, 1971

George A. Pflaum, Publisher, Dimensions in Personality Series, Walter J. Limbacher, series editor
Grade 4: *Here I am,* 1970
Grade 5: *I'm not alone,* 1970
Grade 6: *Becoming myself,* 1970

Ginn and Company
Grades 7 to 8: *Youth and the drug problem,* Henry T. Van Dyke, 1970

Harcourt Brace Jovanovich, Inc.
Grades 6 to 8: *Drugs and people,* Charles W. Gorodetsky and Samuel T. Christian, 1968

J. B. Lippincott Company
Grades 4 to 6: *The good drug and the bad drug,* John S. Marr, 1970

Julian Messner
Grades 4 to 6: *Drugs and you,* Arnold Madison, 1971

Laidlaw Brothers
Grades 4 to 8: *Basic concepts of tobacco and smoking,* Richard H. Needle, 1970

Oxford Book Co., Inc.
Grade 8: *Drugs and you,* Hal W. Chauncey and Laurence A. Kirkpatrick, 1970

Ramapo House
Elementary: *The play is yours: you and drugs,* Lawrence S. Finkel and Ruth Drawitz, 1971
It's really up to you: you and smoking, Diane Gess, 1970
It's really up to you: you and alcohol, George Patterson, 1971
Junior high: *It's your decision: you and narcotics,* Ronald Berg, 1971
It's your decision: you and smoking, John Curran, 1971
It's your decision: you and alcohol, Jean Patterson, 1971
Senior high: *You and narcotics: choose for yourself,* Gilbert Shevlin, 1970
You and smoking: choose for yourself, Robert Spillane, 1970
You and alcohol: choose for yourself, Maurice Ames, 1970

Scholastic Book Services
Grade 1: *What you must know about drugs,* Harvey R. Greenberg, 1970

Science Research Associates, Inc.
Grades 6 to 8: *What you should know about smoking and drinking,* W. W. Bauer, and Donald D. Dukelow, 1971
Grades 7 to 8: *Facts about narcotics and other dangerous drugs,* V. H. Vogel and V. E. Vogel, 1971
Grades 7 to 8: *Facts about smoking and health,* E. J. Salber, 1968

Scott, Foresman and Company
Grades 5 to 8: *About you and smoking,* Norman W. Houser et al., 1971
Grades 6 to 8: *Drugs: facts on their use and abuse,* Norman W. Houser et al., 1971

Steck-Vaughn Company, The Human Value Series
Grades 1 to 6:
Our values, 1969
Values to live by, 1967
Values to share, 1967
V. Clyde Arnspiger, James A. Brill, and W. Ray Rucker
Myself, 1970
Myself, and others, 1970
V. Clyde Arnspiger, James A. Brill, W. Ray Rucker, and Zelda Beth Blanchette

SELECTED SOURCES OF OTHER DRUG EDUCATION MATERIALS
COMMERCIAL*

AIDE, Action in Drug Education, Inc.
P.O. Box 186
Orange, N. J. 07051
(drug I.D. wheel and slide rule, large display wheel)

Allied Youth, Inc.
1901 Fort Myer Dr.
Suite 1011
Rosslyn, Va. 22209
(pamphlets, booklets)

American Guidance Services, Inc.
Publisher's Bldg.
Circle Pines, Minn. 55014
(pamphlets)

Associated Press
Room 601
50 Rockefeller Plaza
New York, N. Y. 10020
(booklet)

CCM: American School, Inc.
P.O. Box 568
Monterey Park, Calif. 91754
(films, cassettes, guides, scripts)

---

*Unless otherwise indicated, there is a charge for some or all of the materials.

Channing L. Bete Co., Inc.
45 Federal St.
Greenfield, Mass. 01301
(booklets)

Center for Mass Communication
562 W. 113th St.
New York, N. Y. 10025
(films, audiotape)

Chronicle Guidance Publications, Inc.
Moravia, N. Y. 13118
(booklet, poster, reprints)

Creative Learning Group
145 Portland St.
Cambridge, Mass. 02139
(multimedia package—cassettes, filmstrip, games, etc.)

Creative Visuals Guidance Dept.
Box 1911 G
Big Spring, Tex. 79720
(programs)

DARR Publishing, Inc.
717 Loma Verde
Palo Alto, Calif. 94303
(booklets)

DCA Educational Products, Inc.
4865 Stenton Ave.
Philadelphia, Pa. 19144
(transparencies, annotated film catalogue)

Denoyer- Geppart Times Mirror
5235 Ravenswood Ave.
Chicago, Ill. 60640
(filmstrips, transparencies, annotated catalogue)

Drug Abuse Information Service, Inc.
1190 Lincoln Ave.
San Jose, Calif. 95125
(pamphlet for parents)

Educational Aids of Long Beach
P.O. Box 4242
Long Beach, Calif. 90804
(visual aids, booklet)

Educational Progress Corporation
8538 East 41st St.
Tulsa, Okla. 74145
(audio program, drug I.D. kit)

Educational Resources, Inc.
47 W. 13th St.
New York, N. Y. 10011
(complete program; cassettes, filmstrips, tapes, chart, etc.)

Eli Lilly and Company
Indianapolis, Ind. 46206
(films, drug abuse information kit)

Educational Summaries, Inc.
P.O. Bin 14
Pasadena, Calif. 91109
(film, brochures)

Eye Gate House, Inc.
146-01 Archer Ave.
Jamaica, N. Y. 11435
(filmstrips, cassettes, tapes)

Family Life Publications, Inc.
Box 6725
Durham, N. C. 27708
(test, drug knowledge inventory)

Fawcett Publications, Inc.
Education Department
Greenwich, Conn. 06830
(paperback books)

Gamco Industries, Inc.
Box 1911
Big Spring, Tex. 79720
(transparencies)

Guidance Associates
Pleasantville, N. Y. 10570
(filmstrips, cassettes, records, slides)

Henk Newenhouse, Inc.
1825 Willow Rd.
Northfield, Ill. 60093
(films with record and study guides)

IDEA
C. F. Kettering Foundation
P.O. Box 446
Melbourne, Fla. 32901
(films and publications)

Imagination, Inc.
1821 University Ave.
St. Paul, Minn. 55104
(leaflets)

Information Materials Press
25 W. 45th St.
New York, N. Y. 10036
(comic-style booklet)

Instructor Publications, Inc.
2730 Lafayette Dr.
Sacramento, Calif. 95821
(dial-a-drug wheel, mechanical smoker)

International Education & Training, Inc.
1776 New Highway
Farmingdale, N. Y. 11735
(books, tapes, transparencies)

Jam Handy Productions
2821 E. Grand Blvd.
Detroit, Mich. 48211
(film, filmstrips, record, cassette)

Kemper Insurance
4750 Sheridan Rd.
Chicago, Ill. 60640
(booklets)

KNOW

A Visual Educational Service
262 Orinoco Dr.

Brightwaters, N. Y. 11718
(posters)

Love Publishing Company
6635 E. Villanove Pl.
Denver, Colo. 80222
(booklet)

Marsh Fil Enterprises, Inc.
7900 Rosewood Dr.
Shawnee Mission, Kan. 66208
(filmstrip, record, teacher's guide)

Media Medica, Inc.
555 Fifth Ave.
New York, N. Y. 10017
(records)

Media Publishers, Inc.
200 N. W. 65th Terrace
Kansas City, Mo. 64118
(pamphlets, bibliography)

Medical Economics, Inc.
Book Division
Oradell, N. J. 07649
(drug I.D. guide, reprints)

Methods and Materials Press
P.O. Box 162
Springfield, N. J. 07081
(booklet, socio-drama playlet)

Modern Merchandising Company
440 Brannan St.
San Francisco, Calif. 94107
(drug I.D. and abuse charts)

Multi-Media Education, Inc.
11 W. 42nd St.
New York, N. Y. 10036
(cassette lecture)

National Instructional Television
Field Service
Box A
Bloomington, Ind. 47401
(videotapes)

National Leadership Method
500 W. 13th St.
Austin, Tex. 78701
(booklet)

Pacifica Tape Library & Affiliate Station
2217 Shattuck Ave.
Berkeley, Calif. 94704
(audiotape)

Professional Arts, Inc.
P.O. Box 8484
Universal City, Calif. 91608
(films, multimedia drug education programs)

Psychedelic Information Center
26 Boylston St.
Cambridge, Mass. 02138
(bulletins, leaflets, manual)

Q-ED Productions
Division of Cathedral Films, Inc.
2921 W. Alameda Ave.
Burbank, Calif. 91505
(filmstrips, records, cassettes)

Raytheon Learning Systems Company
Raytheon Educational Company
475 South Dean St.
Englewood, N. J. 07631
(record, filmstrip, teacher's guide)

Reader's Digest Services, Inc.
Educational Division
Pleasantville, N. Y. 10570
(booklet and bibliography)

Stanford Press
Educational Development Corporation
Palo Alto, Calif.
(self-enhancing education materials)

Schering Corporation
Galloping Hill Rd.
Kenilworth, N. J. 07033
(booklet, source list)

Scholastic Magazines, Inc.
Englewood Cliffs, N. J. 07637
(brochure, books, posters, multimedia units)

School Health Education Study
3M Visual Products Division
St. Paul, Minn. 55101
(teacher's guide, transparencies)

School Health Supply Company
300 Lombard Rd.
Addison, Ill. 60101
(tapes, L.P. record, book)

Science Research Associates, Inc.
259 E. Erie St.
Chicago, Ill. 60611
(booklets)

Scott, Foresman & Company
855 California Ave.
Palo Alto, Calif. 94304
(books)

Signal Press
1730 Chicago Ave.
Evanston, Ill.
(films, teaching packets)

Society for Visual Education, Inc.
1345 Diversey Parkway
Chicago, Ill. 60614
(filmstrips, records, cassettes)

Smart Set International, Inc.
1680 N. Vine St.
Hollywood, Calif. 90028
(kits, posters, stickers, reprints, newsletters, tape)

Smith, Kline & French Laboratories
1500 Spring Garden St.

Philadelphia, Pa. 19101
(booklets, book on drug abuse, drug abuse products chart)

Spenco Corporation
P.O. Box 6322
Salt Lake City, Utah 84106
(drug wheel, buttons, badges, pamphlets)

Sufism Reoriented, Inc.
1290 Sutter St.
San Francisco, Calif. 94109
(booklet)

Systemedics, Inc.
Princeton Air Research Park
Box 449
Princeton, N. J. 08540
(booklet)

Tane Press
2814 Oak Lawn
Dallas, Tex. 75219
(booklets, charts, filmstrips, etc.)

Time Education Program
Time & Life Bldg.
New York, N. Y. 10020
(booklet)

Trend House Publications
P.O. Box 2350
1306 W. Kennedy Blvd.
Tampa, Fla. 33601
(handbook—abused drugs)

Tripping Out
Box 285
Sylvania, Ohio 43560
(teaching kit)

Winston Products for Education
P.O. Box 12219
San Diego, Calif. 92112
(drug I.D. kit, flipchart, slides, poster sets, marijuana awareness packet)

GOVERNMENTAL*

Addiction Services Agency
Human Resources Administration
71 Worth St.
New York, N. Y. 10013
(brochure; free)

Campbell Union High School District
3235 Union Ave.
San Jose, Calif. 95124
(resource materials)

Department of National Health and Welfare
Ottawa, Ontario
(biography, book reviews, booklets, films, filmstrips)

Federal Food and Drug Administration
200 C St., S. W.
Washington, D. C. 20204
(pamphlets, booklets; free)

Mendocino State Hospital
Talmadge, Calif. 95481
(pamphlet, handbook; free)

Mental Health Planning Committee of Milwaukee County
8855 W. Watertown Plank Rd.
Milwaukee, Wisc. 53266
(booklets, program directory)

Pennsylvania Department of Health
P.O. Box 90
Harrisburg, Pa. 17120
(pamphlets, booklets, teacher resource guide)

National Archives and Records Service
National Audio-Visual Center
Washington, D. C. 20409
(films, slide-kit, annotated catalogue)

National Clearinghouse for Drug Abuse Information
5454 Wisconsin Ave.
Chevy Chase, Md. 20015
(pamphlets, booklets, etc.)

National Institute of Mental Health
5454 Wisconsin Ave.
Chevy Chase, Md. 20015
(pamphlets, films, source book, etc.)

National Institute of Mental Health
Clinical Research Center
Lexington, Ky. 40507
(bibliography, leaflets)

Office of Economic Opportunity
Washington, D. C. 20506
(pamphlets; free)

U. S. Department of Justice
Bureau of Narcotics and Dangerous Drugs
1405 I St.
Washington, D. C. 20405
(booklets, leaflets, pamphlets)

PROFESSIONAL*

American Academy of Pediatrics
1801 Hinman Ave.
Evanston, Ill. 60204
(monograph, reprints)

American Association for Health, Physical Education & Recreation
1201 16th St., N. W.
Washington, D. C. 20036
(booklets, film)

*Unless otherwise indicated, there is a charge for some or all of the materials.

*Unless otherwise indicated, there is a charge for some or all of the materials.

American Bar Association
1155 East 60th St.
Chicago, Ill. 60637
(handbook, resource kit; free)

American Correctional Association
Woolbridge Station
P.O. Box 10176
Washington, D. C. 20018
(reprints; free)

American Medical Association
535 N. Dearborn St.
Chicago, Ill. 60610
(pamphlets, booklets, articles)

American Nurses' Association
10 Columbus Circle
New York, N. Y. 10019
(pamphlets)

American Pharmaceutical Association
2216 Constitution Ave., N. W.
Washington, D. C. 20037
(newsletter, over-the-counter drugs booklet)

American School Health Association
P.O. Box 416
107 S. Depeyster St.
Kent, Ohio 44240
(articles, drug education teachers' guide)

American Social Health Association
1240 Broadway
New York, N. Y. 10019
(pamphlets, newsletter)

International Narcotic Enforcement Officers Association
178 Washington Ave.
Albany, N. Y. 12210
(newsletter, pamphlets; free)

National Council for Prevention of Drug Abuse
959 South Van Ness Ave.
San Francisco, Calif. 94110
(parents' handbook; free)

National Council for the Social Studies
1201 16th St., N. W.
Washington, D. C. 20036
(booklet)

National District Attorneys Association
211 E. Chicago Ave.
Chicago, Ill. 60611
(book)

National Education Association
1201 16th St., N. W.
Washington, D. C. 20036
(pamphlets, articles)

The Proprietary Association
1700 Pennsylvania Ave., N. W.
Washington, D. C. 20006
(booklets; free)

PUBLIC SERVICE*

Addiction Research Foundation
33 Russell St.
Toronto 4, Ontario
(book, booklets, newsletter)

Aerosol Education Bureau
300 E. 44th St.
New York, N. Y. 10017
(leaflets)

Al-Anon Family Group Headquarters, Inc.
P.O. Box 182
Madison Square Station
New York, N. Y. 10010
(pamphlets; free)

American Council on Alcohol Problems
119 Constitution Ave., N. E.
Washington, D. C. 20002
(pamphlets, leaflets)

B'Nai B'Rith Youth Organization
1640 Rhode Island Ave., N. W.
Washington, D. C. 20036
(pamphlets)

Board of Social Ministry
Lutheran Church in America
231 Madison Ave.
New York, N. Y. 10016
(booklet, filmstrip, resources)

Boy Scouts of America
Health and Safety Service
North Brunswick, N. J. 08902
(reprints)

Brain Research Institute and Biomedical Library
University of California
Los Angeles, Calif. 90024
(selected bibliography on marijuana; free)

Child Study Association of America, Inc.
9 East 89th St.
New York, N. Y. 10028
(book)

Christian Social Concerns
United Methodist Church
100 Maryland Ave., N. E.
Washington, D. C. 20002
(drug education packet, resource book, films, pamphlets)

Cleveland Health Museum and Education Center
8911 Euclid Ave.
Cleveland, Ohio 44106
(drugs, smoking, alcohol education kits)

Committee for Effective Drug Abuse Legislation
Box 572

---

*Unless otherwise indicated, there is a charge for some or all of the materials.

1629 K St., N. W.
Washington, D. C. 20006
(leaflet; free)

Committee for Psychedelic Drug Information
P.O. Box 851
Berkeley, Calif. 94701
(fact sheets, pamphlets)

Connecticut Mutual Life Insurance Co.
140 Garden St.
Hartford, Conn. 06115
(reprints; free)

DARE
c/o The Neuropsychiatric Institute
UCLA Center for the Health Sciences
Los Angeles, Calif. 90024
(kit on drug information, reprints, leaflets)

Health Education Service
P.O. Box 7283
Albany, N. Y. 12224
(book: desk reference on drug abuse)

DO IT NOW FOUNDATION
P.O. Box 3573
Hollywood, Calif. 90028
(pamphlets, records, leaflets)

Family Service Association of America
44 E. 23rd St.
New York, N. Y. 10010
(bibliography; free)

Kiwanis International
101 E. Erie St.
Chicago, Ill. 60611
(pamphlets, booklet, bibliography)

Licensed Beverage Industries, Inc.
155 E. 44th St.
New York, N. Y. 10017
(book, booklets, leaflets; free)

Loma Linda University
Department of Health Education
School of Health
Loma Linda, Calif. 92354
(cartoon booklet, grades 6 to 8 teachers' guide)

Lutheran Church in America
231 Madison Ave.
New York, N. Y. 10016
(booklet; free)

Lutheran Church Supply Store
2900 Queen Lane
Philadelphia, Pa. 19129
(drug program)

Narcotic Education Bureau
National Women's Christian Temperance Union
1730 Chicago Ave.
Evanston, Ill. 60201
(dial-a-drug wheel, booklets, films, filmstrips)

Narcotic Educational Foundation of America
5055 Sunset Blvd.
Los Angeles, Calif. 90027
(pamphlets, film, etc.)

Narcotics Education, Inc.
6830 Laurel St., N. W.
Box 4390
Washington, D. C. 20012
(films, booklets, pamphlets)

National Coordinating Council on Drug Abuse Education
Suite 212
1211 Connecticut Ave., N. W.
Washington, D. C. 20036
(newsletter, booklets, bibliographies)

National Alcoholic Beverage Control Association, Inc.
Suite 1610
5454 Wisconsin Ave., N. W.
Washington, D. C. 20015
(comic-style booklet)

National Association of Blue Shield Plans
720 California St.
San Francisco, Calif. 94119
(booklet, film)

The National Association of Mental Health
10 Columbus Circle
New York, N. Y. 10019
(resource list, booklets, leaflets)

National Association of Retail Druggists
One E. Wacker Dr.
Chicago, Ill. 60601
(leaflet, reprints; free)

National Congress of Parents & Teachers
700 N. Rush St.
Chicago, Ill. 60611
(reprints; free)

National Council on Alcoholism, Inc.
2 Park Ave.
New York, N. Y. 10016
(pamphlets, reprints, books, slides, etc.)

National Council of Churches of Christ
475 Riverside Dr.
New York, N. Y. 10027
(booklet, pamphlets)

National Safety Council
425 N. Michigan Ave.
Chicago, Ill. 60611
(pamphlets, booklets)

North Conway Institute
8 Newbury St.
Boston, Mass. 02116
(pamphlets, resource book, newsletter, etc.)

Optimist International
4494 Lindell Blvd.

St. Louis, Mo. 63108
(drug abuse information program; free)

Pennsylvania State University
Psychological Cinema Register
Audio-visual Services
6 Willard Bldg.
University Park, Pa. 16802
(newsletter, catalogue; free)

Pharmaceutical Manufacturers' Association
1155 15th St., N. W.
Washington, D. C. 20005
(pamphlet, drug abuse products reference; free)

Public Affairs Committee, Inc.
381 Park Ave., South
New York, N. Y. 10016
(pamphlets)

Rutgers Center of Alcoholic Studies
Rutgers University
New Brunswick, N. J. 08903
(books, pamphlets, reprints)

Student Association for the Study of Hallucinogens, Inc.
638 Pleasant St.
Beloit, Wisc. 53511
(pamphlets, symposium proceedings)

Synanon Foundation, Inc.
110 Lombard St.
San Francisco, Calif. 94111
(reprints, pamphlets; free)

TAR
National TAR Headquarters
359 National Press Bldg.
Washington, D. C. 20004
(drug abuse information kit)

The National Sex and Drug Forums
Glide Urban Center
330 Ellis St.
San Francisco, Calif. 94102
(pamphlets, leaflets, reprints)

The U. S. Jaycees
Box 7
Tulsa, Okla. 74102
(booklets, parents' guide; free)

Union of American Hebrew Congregations
Publications Department
838 Fifth Ave.
New York, N. Y. 10021
(resource guide, cassette, poster set, articles)

University of Michigan
Audio-Visual Education Center
416 Fourth St.
Ann Arbor, Mich. 48103
(annotated film catalogue; free)

University of Oregon Medical School
Department of Psychiatry

3181 S. W. Sam Jackson Park Rd.
Portland, Ore. 97201
(reprints; free)

Western Electric Service
Division West-Central Region
3800 Golf Rd.
Rolling Meadows, Ill. 60008
(parent's' guide on marijuana, pamphlet; free)

World Health Organization
Public Inquiries Unit
United Nations
New York, N. Y. 10017
(booklet, magazine, reprints)

EVALUATION

The effectiveness of the formal education program will need to be evaluated by teachers and other school personnel. Consideration should be given to short-range and long-range procedures. A comprehensive discussion of evaluation is contained in Chapter 11; therefore no attempt will be made to duplicate that material. Instead time will be spent in trying to assist the teacher in terms of general functional procedures for the classroom.

The classroom teacher should perhaps give consideration to assessing these four areas: (1) the curriculum or curricula materials provided in drug education, (2) the course, or unit, on drug education when completed, (3) the achievement of established objectives, and (4) the resource materials provided. These items may be realistically evaluated by the teacher on a short-range basis. The long-range program should be planned by a committee of representative teachers.

The procedures for evaluation have to be determined by the teacher and by the material to be evaluated. Procedures might include subjective observations by teachers, parents, and nurses, the use of teacher-made tests on a pretest-posttest arrangement, checklists, and inventories.

Subjective teacher impressions as to completeness, serviceability, organization, and other related matters may form the basis for the evaluation of the curriculum. The drug course or unit itself might necessitate a device adopted from one in the in-service preparation part of Chapter 11.

The objectives probably should be assessed on a pretest-posttest basis, with the appropriate questionnaire or test prepared by the teacher. Chapter 11 has illustrative knowledge (cognitive) questions that may be adapted for any given classroom. It also contains suggested attitudinal questions for use in developing an inventory and several practice surveys for use on a pretest-posttest basis.

Resource materials may be evaluated by using the instruments found in Chapter 11.

These suggestions on evaluation are not meant to be comprehensive. They serve to illustrate possibilities for the teacher's assessment of the drug education program on a short-range basis.

Student informal education

The informal educational approach is a program of information, counseling, and guidance that is nondirective, voluntary, and generally has little structure. This latter aspect may not be quite true if young persons express a need for assistance, in which case some regularized, partially formal program may be necessary and established. The informal educational approach can be extremely helpful for some drug experimenters in school but can probably be most productive with periodic, compulsive, or relapse users. Empirical evidence indicates the formal educational program to have little impact on the experienced misusers and abusers of drugs, whereas the informal approach has possibilities for success if the individual wants help.

The informal educational program must be complementary to the formal program. Both must be operative concurrently if drug education is to be truly preventive and reach all students effectively.

Informal learning occurs in diverse forms, in many places, under varying circumstances, and involves all kinds of people. This type of education lends itself to the involvement of peer groups. Schools must seriously consider the opportunity for student participation in such a service capacity of the drug program.

The organization of the informal educational program has not been established. Informal education perhaps functions best if a resourse person is provided to whom individuals can turn for help. This could be a teacher, counselor, student, psychologist, nurse, ex-addict, or anyone who is capable of effective communication with people. Some schools are hiring specialists for the position of drug counselor or drug coordinator. Informal education could take place anywhere—in a classroom, in a hall, on the street, in the schoolyard, on the way home, or in a drop-in center in or outside the school. It basically occurs when a person reaches out to someone else for information, guidance, or help, and it takes place wherever these people happen to be at the time. Informal learning could occur in a partially structured arrangement, such as a small group discussion in or out of school where attendance or participation is voluntary. Such sessions are often referred to as rap sessions.

Two popular organizational patterns for rap sessions are drop-in centers and hot-lines. The drop-in center is a place to meet and rap with an individual or a group. It may be located inside or outside the school. The drop-in center may be under school, community, or their combined supervision. These centers may employ specialized personnel who are capable of assisting with rehabilitation and treatment as well as providing crisis intervention and parent education. These centers should be initiated and operated with the cooperation of local police departments.

The hot-line is a telephone service, usually manned by students, or ex-addicts, or both, that provides information and guidance to young persons, parents, and others desiring assistance.

ILLUSTRATIVE PROGRAMS

A number of illustrative programs are presented in Chapter 8, but others will be introduced at this time.

GLEN COVE, NEW YORK. With community help the Glen Cove schools started a storefront drug counseling center during the summer to provide continuity with the school year programs.

NEW HYDE PARK, NEW YORK. A community grant of $19,000 enabled the schools of New Hyde Park to hire two full-time staff workers and five part-time group leaders who had backgrounds in drug involvement (were not ex-addicts) to staff a "walk-in" center open 7 days a week. The child guidance center in town provided a social worker to meet informally with students. Parent meetings and education programs were conducted. The center's purpose was to respond to emergencies, to work with the police, and to provide psychological help, among other services.

In the Herrick Public Schools, a group of teen-agers who had received training in group dynamics conducted student rap sessions under the supervision of the school psychologist. These young people actively engaged in planning the program, selecting personnel to participate therein, and leading discussions in the formal educational program.

MEDFORD, NEW JERSEY. A high school in Medford sponsored a series of encounter sessions for eight students, most of whom had been arrested for narcotics offenses. They were conducted by a guidance counselor and met weekly in his home.

DO IT NOW FOUNDATION, HOLLYWOOD, CALIFORNIA. A nonprofit organization largely staffed by ex-users works closely with schools. The Do It Now Foundation provides literature and uses the medium of rock music to reach students. They operate a 24-hour hot-line service for emergencies and counseling.

SMART SET INTERNATIONAL, LOS ANGELES, CALIFORNIA. Combining the efforts of young adults, parents, teachers, and others, the Smart Set International endeavors to stamp out drugs. Their trade mark is SOS ("Stamp Out Stupidity"). The peer-group organization in school is called *Smarteens,* and it participates in and conducts a number of activities: rallies, poster contests, news-papers, assemblies, a drug reference library, and Smart Set Smarteen posters located in strategic places in the school and community.

TEEN CHALLENGE, LOS ANGELES, CALIFORNIA. Teen Challenge was started by a group of former drug addicts who dropped out of high school. They became interested in attacking drug use through a spiritual approach, and now present lectures at assemblies, go to classrooms, and speak with students informally.

KINGSTON, MASSACHUSETTS. Students were permitted to sign up voluntarily for small discussion groups of 15 students each. These groups met at various times during the day and the discussion leader of each was a drug-experienced youth. This approach consisted primarily of a question and answer session with freedom of expression encouraged.

Resource centers

Resource centers for drug education at federal, state, and possibly county or large school district levels are necessary if school drug education programs are to receive the necessary supplementary support to operate effective programs. Several hundred governmental and nongovernmental sources, including many commercial companies, organizations, and agencies, are developing, distributing, and selling a variety of materials. These items include books, magazines, pamphlets, folders, films, filmstrips, tape cassettes, transparencies, drug kits, and numerous other teacher aids for use in community, teacher, student, and parent educational programs. In addition, new materials are being developed and made available. It is conservatively estimated that there are available for purchase or distribution:

1000 to 2000 books on drugs
3.5 million magazine and reference articles from hundreds of periodicals
10 to 15 newsletters and other special publications
100 to 200 films
50 to 100 curriculum guides
2000 to 3000 pamphlets, folders, and other printed materials

200 to 300 catalogues of items
Also numerous filmstrips, cassettes, transparencies, and other aids

The quality of these items varies from poor to excellent. The mammoth problem confronting educators is not only to know what and where these materials are, but, more importantly, how good they are. These complications added to the emergence of new research data make keeping up to date and knowledgeable about drugs and suitable drug education materials an impossible task to manage for the teacher, the local school administrator, and other school personnel.

It is therefore recommended that state departments of education, through their drug coordinators' offices, establish resource centers where all materials related to drugs can be catalogued and evaluated, and where a variety of information and help can be made available to teachers and schools upon request. It is further suggested that a newsletter be periodically distributed to school districts within the state of disseminate new information, new materials, and new ideas for school drug education programs.

At the federal level the National Clearinghouse for Drug Abuse Information has served as a coordinating agency, making numerous materials and services available. However, it has not provided the evaluation process so vital to educational programs, nor has it made known the items available from commercial and nonvoluntary sources. The National Coordinating Council on Drug Abuse Education has evaluated films, provided a bibliography, a drug education directory, a monthly newsletter, and other valuable aids, and is about to assess pamphlets, posters, and other items. However, their services are also limited. These two organizations have provided excellent and useful services, although a statewide service is needed to coordinate the efforts and materials of all the agencies and organizations. A resource center could effectively accomplish this goal. The establishment of state "mini" clearinghouses

(DRACON, Chapter 5) is a step in this direction.

Such a center could also have regional satellite offices if the state is sufficiently large and ample funds are forthcoming. The larger school districts may wish to develop their own informational offices.

There is no model for the nature or conduct of the proposed drug resource center. The experience of school audio-visual centers could be useful in organization and operation. However, the services needed and proposed for drug education extend beyond the usual assistance made available by such offices in the past.

Whether or not resource centers become a reality unquestionably depends on the allocation of the necessary financial support. However, after the completion of the initial awareness and in-service educational programs now underway, such a center would provide efficient, effective, and economic in-service help at nominal cost.

Roles of school and community resource personnel

For an educational program to function effectively, the personnel involved must have their roles and responsibilities clearly identified, efforts must be cordinated, and any anticipated problems must receive appropriate attention. The purpose of this section is to outline briefly the roles of drug coordinators, teachers, counselors, nurses, students, and community resource personnel.

DRUG COORDINATOR

Chapter 11 covers coordination and qualifications, so we will refer to the functions of the drug coordinator only briefly. Some schools or school districts may not wish to designate one individual as responsible for the total school drug program, nor to use the title indicated. Other schools may wish to coordinate only the educational phase or only the service phase of the program. In any event, someone must be delegated with administrative responsibility for the program if it is to function efficiently and effectively, in part or in its totality. The title of this position and the nature of the responsibilities must be determined at the local school level. In small districts some administrative help may be forthcoming at the next echelon of school organization, perhaps the county level.

TEACHERS

The teacher's responsibility for formal and informal education will differ, depending on the grade level taught and the assignments provided by local schools and school districts. At the elementary level, formal education may be expected of teachers in all grades. Informally, every teacher becomes a counselor at some time. However, the specific function of the teacher when such help is needed may be to refer the student to someone else, such as the nurse or drug coordinator. At the secondary level, formal education may be organized into the direct or correlated pattern, and teacher responsibilities would become clear. At both elementary and secondary levels some teachers may be needed as drug education resource individuals for their respective schools. All teachers will need to be aware of student drug problems and be able to recognize signs and symptoms so they can identify and refer those individuals needing help to those who can assist them. At all grade levels, teachers should be concerned with the material contained in Chapter 9 regarding the school atmosphere and make efforts to utilize these suggestions in their classrooms.

COUNSELORS

Counselors will most likely be primarily responsible for informal educational services. Their specific activities are discussed in Chapter 8, but many of the comments in Chapter 9 are also appropriate for counselor implementation.

NURSES

The school nurse may act as a resource person in the formal educational program, as an occasional speaker to make classroom presentations, and she may also provide help in curriculum development. Informally, she has always been a health counselor and undoubtedly should extend this role to include the drug problem. The information and guidance that the nurse may provide for both students and parents is outlined in Chapter 8.

PHYSICIANS

The physician could provide services similar to those of the nurse, although perhaps at a higher administrative level. In addition he may serve as a liaison with the community.

STUDENTS

It is axiomatic that students have an important role to play in the educational program. The students involved might include ex-addicts, drug users, former users, and "straights." Although the specifics still need clarification, the following are responsibilities that have been assigned to students in a number of schools:

1. Develop, administer, and tabulate questionnaires to determine the extent of drug use in the school.
2. Aid in curriculum development by helping to (a) identify needs and interests in drugs and (b) suggest course content.
3. Hold membership on school or school district drug advisory committee.
4. Speak or participate as a panelist, debater, or presenter in class and at parent and community meetings.
5. Review and evaluate drug education resource materials to be used in school.
6. Act as discussion leader for small groups of students in elementary schools (fifth and sixth grades) and junior high schools.
7. Provide information, guidance, and counseling in rap centers and other places.
8. Participate in the operation of hotlines.
9. Develop recommendations for drug

intervention and prevention activities in school.

COMMUNITY RESOURCE PEOPLE

There are numerous speakers, experts, and helpers, such as physicians, pharmacologists, psychiatrists, parents, and ex-addicts, who are available to assist in educational programs. This source of assistance should be utilized by school districts in those capacities outlined in this chapter. One thought about ex-addicts reported by Miller needs consideration:

The advantage of using an ex-addict is that he can often establish rapport with students who tend to reject counseling attempts by teachers or law enforcement officials. But a word of caution: attempts to do 'the right thing' by hiring ex-addicts to run drug programs has made some schoolmen fair game for the flimflam man. A district in New Jersey was embarrassed last year when it discovered the chief of its drug prevention efforts, supposedly an ex-addict with a hatful of ideas for curbing narcotics abuse among teen-agers was, in fact, still an addict. He was supporting his habit with the money the district paid him to run the program. Local or state narcotic officials can confirm whether someone is actually an ex-addict.*

DRUG EDUCATION FOR PARENTS

Schools must provide or stimulate community agencies to provide both formal and informal educational programs for parents. The drug abuse problems among young persons cannot be resolved without the help and support of parents. Such action, however, may demand community support and coordination with society's many educational sources outside the school. The purposes of such instructional programs may be to help parents in the following ways:

1. Obtain understandings about children and youth
2. Improve communication between parents and young persons
3. Become aware of drug abuse as a social problem and particularly as a youth problem

4. Understand reasons why drugs are misused and abused
5. Understand the effects of drugs on the body
6. Identify the signs and symptoms of drug misuse and abuse
7. Become acquainted with sources of help for youth involved with drugs
8. Become aware of the laws relating to drugs
9. Recognize the parents' role in prevention
10. Understand the role of the school in the drug program and the parental support needed

Parent formal education

Planned sessions, seminars, study groups, or courses conducted for interested parents are all involved in parent formal education. These programs may be repeated if desired in an attempt to reach a broader segment of the adult population. They should be conducted at convenient times for parents and may tie in with existing adult organizatinons, such as the Parent-Teacher Association or Rotary Club.

The types of programs and the manner in which they are conducted should be dependent on such factors as the nature, size, diversity, needs, and locale of the audience. The programs might include speakers; panels; debate presentations involving knowledgeable and acceptable community leaders or representatives; group discussions with opportunity for free expression, including questions and answers; opportunities to meet and talk with young persons in the drug scene as well as ex-addicts; parent-student informal discussions; use of a television series prepared with school-community cooperation and sponsorship; field trips to rehabilitation and treatment resources; and student presentations and discussions.

Parent education is difficult and time consuming, especially if schools try to conduct a program alone. Therefore schools may wish to coordinate their efforts through one or more community groups who might

*Miller, T. J.: Drug abuse: schools find some answers, Sch. Manage. p. 30, April, 1970.

be in a better position to reach the adult community. These community groups may be able to assume the primary leadership in this enterprise. Such action may be particularly necessary in ghetto areas where parental communication may be more difficult to achieve. Schools working with community action groups may be in a better position to reach parents.

In attempting to help parents, the following preventive action should be introduced in educational programs:

1. Seek your child's trust and trust your child.
2. Get to know your child, encourage him to discuss his feelings, and try to understand them.
3. Help him to understand your feelings.
4. Take an honest interest in your child and his activities, his friends, and his friends' parents.
5. Help your child establish goals for himself.
6. Spend time together as a family.
7. Be firm, fair, consistent, and honest.
8. Maintain parental control and establish fair limits.
9. Help your child to understand that parental discipline is a form of concern and love.

Parent informal education

No guidelines or procedures have been established for conducting informal parent educational programs. Someone in each school or school district should act as a source of information and guidance upon parents' request. In any event, procedures should be established to provide this assistance.

Some suggested ways of helping are as follows:

1. Have a hot-line available for crisis intervention and emergencies. In some areas, this may be better provided by a community agency or organization.
2. Be knowledgeable about community resources to which parents can turn for assistance and guidance.
3. Prepare informational booklets or pamphlets about drugs and drug prevention for distribution to parents.
4. Utilize the mass communication media to disseminate information to parents about the services available to help youthful drug abusers.

References

1. Arnold, M. R.: The trouble in drug education, Natl. Observer 10:16, 1971.
2. Association for Supervision and Curriculum Development: Yearbook: perceiving, behaving, becoming, Washington, D. C., 1962, Association Press.
3. Bedworth, A., and D'Elia, J. A.: Guidelines for programs in drug education, J. Drug Educ. 1:1-4, 1971.
4. Berlow, L.: Kids 'n drugs, Chapel Hill, N. C., 1971, School of Pharmacy, University of North Carolina.
5. Bland, H. B.: Problems related to teaching about drugs, J. Sch. Health 39:117-119, 1969.
6. Blavat, H., and Flocco, W.: A survey of a workable drug abuse program, Phi Delta Kappan 52:532-533, 1971.
7. Brayer, H. O., and Carney, R. E.: Program for preventive drug abuse education using the concept of values and risk-taking, Coronado, Calif., 1969, Coronado Unified School District.
8. Byler, R.: Teach us what we want to know, New York, 1969, Mental Health Materials Center, Inc.
9. Carney, R. E.: Application of the RTAQ approach to a value-oriented drug abuse curriculum, Coronado, Calif., 1970, Coronado Unified School District.
10. Carney, R. E.: A report on the feasibility of using risk-taking attitudes as a basis for programs to control and predict drug abuse, Coronado, Calif., 1970, Coronado Unified School District.
11. Conceptual guidelines for school health programs in Pennsylvania, Harrisburg, Pa., 1970, Bureau of General and Academic Education, Pennsylvania Department of Education.
12. Cornacchia, H. J., et al.: Health in elementary schools, ed. 3, St. Louis, 1970, The C. V. Mosby Co.
13. Cwalina, G. E.: Drug use on high school and college campuses, J. Sch. Health 38:638-646, 1968.
14. Daniels, R. M.: Drug education begins before kindergarten: the Glen Cove, New York pilot program, J. Sch. Health 40:242-248, 1970.
15. Dearden, M. H., and Tekal, J. F.: A pilot program in high school drug education utilizing nondirective techniques and sensitivity training, J. Sch. Health 41:118-124, 1971.

16. Dezelsky, T., and Toohey, J. V.: Are you listening to the lyrics? J. Sch. Health **40**: 40-42, 1970.

17. Drug abuse: escape to nowhere, a guide for educators, Philadelphia, 1967, American Association for Health, Physical Education, and Recreation, and Smith, Kline & French Laboratories.

18. Drug education in Maine, Augusta, 1970, Maine State Department of Education.

19. Eiseman, S.: Education about narcotics and dangerous drugs—a challenge to our schools, J. Drug Educ. **1**:177-185, 1971.

20. Emery, R. C.: Existentialism in the classroom, J. Teacher Educ. **22**:5-9, 1971.

21. Farias, H., Jr.: Mexican-American values and attitudes toward education, Phi Delta Kappan **52**:602-604, 1971.

22. Feinglass, S. J.: Drug abuse education in Marin County—basic considerations, Calif. Sch. Health **4**:21-23, 1968.

23. Fraenkel, J. R.: Value education in the social studies, Phi Delta Kappan **50**:457-461, 1969.

24. Frankl, V. E.: Man's search for meaning: an introduction to logotherapy, Boston, 1963, Beacon Press.

25. Freedman, M., et al.: Utilizing drug education programs: Silver Lake Regional High School, Kingston, Massachusetts, N.A.S.S.P. Bull. **53**:45-51, 1969.

26. Fromm, E.: Man for himself, New York, 1947, Rinehart & Co.

27. Glaser, F. B.: Misinformation about drugs: a problem for drug abuse education, Int. J. Addictions **5**:595-609, 1970.

28. Globetti, G.: Alcohol education in the schools, J. Drug Educ. **1**:241-248, 1971.

29. Goldstein, R., editor: The poetry of rock, New York, 1969, Bantam Books, Inc.

30. Guidelines for drug abuse prevention, Washington, D. C., 1970, Bureau of Narcotics and Dangerous Drugs, U. S. Department of Justice.

31. Guidelines for the prevention of drug abuse problems through education, interim report, Milwaukee, Wisc., 1971, Mental Health Planning Committee of Milwaukee County, Wisconsin.

32. Halleck, S. L.: The great drug education hoax, The Progressive **34**:30-33, 1970.

32a. Hammond, P. G., Executive Director, National Coordinating Council on Drug Education: Why drug abuse education is failing in America, Speech given at thirtieth International Congress on Alcoholism and Drug Dependence, Amsterdam, Sept., 1972.

33. Hill, P. J., and Kitzinger, A.: A study of more effective education relative to narcotics, other harmful drugs, and hallucinogenic substances, Calif. Sch. Health **4**:27-31, 1968.

34. Hochbaum, G. M.: Behavior modification, Sch. Health Rev. **2**:5-11, 1971.

35. Hochbaum, G. M.: Changing health behavior in youth, Sch. Health Rev. pp. 15-19, Sept., 1969.

36. Hochbaum, G. M.: Effecting health behavior, Presented at the annual meeting of the New York State Public Health Association, Buffalo, N. Y., May 23, 1967.

37. Hochbaum, G. M.: How can we teach adolescents about smoking, drinking and drug abuse? In Resource book for drug abuse education, Washington, D. C., 1969, National Institute of Mental Health, National Clearinghouse for Mental Health Information.

38. Hochbaum, G. M.: Learning and behavior—alcohol education for what? In U. S. Department of Health, Education and Welfare: Alcohol Education Conference proceedings, Washington, D. C., 1966, Government Printing Office.

39. Hochbaum, G. M.: The problem of abuse of stimulants and depressants. In Hafen, B. Q, editor: Readings in drug use and abuse, Provo, Utah, 1970, Brigham Young University Press.

40. Hunt, M. P.: Some views on situational morality, Phi Delta Kappan **50**:452-456, 1969.

41. Imhof, J. E.: Drug education for teachers and parents, New York, 1970, William H. Sadlier, Inc.

42. Jacobsen, J.: Drug abuse and learning effects, Educ. Horizons **4**:97-104, 1970.

43. Jordan, C. W.: Drug abuse project, J. Sch. Health **38**:692-695, 1968.

44. Junell, J. S.: Can our schools teach moral commitment? Phi Delta Kappan **50**:446-451, 1969.

45. Keniston, K.: Drug use and student values. In Resource book for drug abuse education, Washington, D. C., 1969, National Institute of Mental Health, National Clearinghouse for Mental Health Information.

46. Kitzinger, A., and Hill, P. J.: Drug abuse: A source book and guide for teachers, Sacramento, 1967, California State Department of Education.

47. KQED Educational Services: Drugs the children are choosing, Fadiman, J., instructor, a supplementary manual for teachers and parents for KQED Education Services, San Francisco, 1969.

48. Langer, J. H.: Educational approaches for drug abuse prevention. In Guidelines for drug abuse prevention education, Washington, D. C., 1970, Bureau of Narcotics and Dangerous Drugs, U. S. Department of Justice.

49. Lawler, J. T.: Peer group approach to drug education, J. Drug Educ. **1**:63-76, 1971.

49a. Le Dain, G., chairman, Interim report of the Commission of Inquiry into the Non-medical Use of Drugs, Ottawa, 1970, Crown Copyrights.

50. Levy, M. R.: Background considerations for drug programs. In Resource book for drug abuse education, Washington, D. C., 1969, National Institute of Mental Health, National Clearinghouse for Mental Health Information.

51. Lewis, D. C.: Drug education, N. A. S. S. P. Bull. 53:87-98, 1969.

52. Lewis, D. C.: How the schools can prevent drug abuse, N. A. S. S. P. Bull. 54:43-51, 1970.

53. Maslow, A. H.: Toward a psychology of being, New York, 1962, Van Nostrand Reinhold Co.

54. May, R., editor: Existential psychology, New York, 1961, Random House, Inc.

55. Means, R. K.: Drug abuse education: many hands of help, J. Alcohol Educ. 16:20-27, 1970.

56. Meeds, L.: Education: key to the drug problem, Soc. Educ. 33:664-666, 1969.

57. Merki, D. J.: What we need before drug abuse education, J. Sch. Health 39:656-657, 1968.

58. Mikeal, R. L., and Smith, M. C.: A positive approach to drug education, J. Sch. Health 40:450-453, 1970.

59. Miller, M.: Drug education: a re-evaluation, J. Drug Educ. 1:15-24, 1971.

60. Miller, T. J.: Drug abuse: schools find some answers, Sch. Manage. pp. 23-31, April, 1970.

61. Mullin, L. S.: Alcohol education: the school's responsibility, J. Sch. Health 38:518-522, 1968.

62. Nagel, C. A.: Behavioral objectives approach to health instruction, J. Sch. Health 40:255-257, 1970.

63. National Clearinghouse for Smoking and Health, National Center for Chronic Disease Control, U. S. Public Health Service: Classroom tested techniques for teaching about smoking, Washington, D. C., 1968, Government Printing Office.

64. National Conference on Public Education in Drug Abuse: Drug abuse education: a guide for the professions, Washington, D. C., 1968, American Pharmaceutical Association.

65. National School Public Relations Association: Drug crisis: schools fight back with innovative programs, Washington, D. C., 1971, Association Press.

66. New York State Department of Education: Drug education: a positive paper, J. Drug Educ. 1:123-126, 1971.

67. Nowlis, H. H.: Communicating about drugs. In Resource book for drug abuse education, Washington, D. C., 1969, National Institute of Mental Health, National Clearinghouse for Mental Health Information.

68. Nowlis, H. H.: Drugs on the college campus, Garden City, N. Y., 1969, Anchor Books.

69. Petersen, R. C.: Suggestions for educators. In Resource book for drug abuse education, Washington, D. C., 1969, National Institute of Mental Health, National Clearinghouse for Mental Health Information.

70. Pertz, R.: Drug education and the law, J. Drug Educ. 1:157-170, 1971.

71. Plesent, E.: A community and its school's efforts to understand and deal with drug abuse, J. Drug Educ. 1:85-91, 1971.

72. Raths, L. E., et al.: Values and teaching: working with values in the classroom, Columbus, Ohio, 1966, Charles E. Merrill Publishing Co.

73. Rees, F. D.: Teaching values through health education, Sch. Health Rev. 1:14-17, 1970.

74. Resource book for drug abuse education, Washington, D. C., 1969, National Institute of Mental Health, National Clearinghouse for Mental Health Information.

75. Richards, L.: Psychological sophistication in current drug abuse education, Presented at the Rutgers Symposium on Communications and Drug Abuse, Oct. 14, 1969.

76. Richardson, C. E.: Drug education: some insights and some analysis of a conceptual approach, J. Alcohol Educ. 16:1-7, 1970.

77. Rogers, C. R.: On becoming a person, Boston, 1961, Houghton Mifflin Co.

78. Rosser, J. M.: Values and health, J. Sch. Health 41:386-390, 1971.

79. Rucker, W. R., et al.: Human values in education, Dubuque, Iowa, 1969, Kendall-Hunt Publishing Co.

80. Russell, R. D.: Some important ideas relating to the future of substances that modify mood and behavior, J. Alcohol Educ. 16:8-9, 1970.

81. Simon, S. B.: Promoting the search for values, Sch. Health Rev. 2:21-24, 1971.

82. Sinacore, J. S.: Drug education—better late than never, J. Drug Educ. 1:9-14, 1971.

83. Suchman, E. A.: The hang-loose ethic and the spirit of drug use, J. Health Soc. Behav. 9:146-155, 1968.

84. Todd, F.: The school's role in alcohol education, Calif. Sch. Health 2:11-15, 1966.

85. Toohey, J. V.: Beatle lyrics can help adolescents identify and understand their emotional health problems, J. Sch. Health 40:295-296, 1970.

86. Ungerleider, J. T., and Bowers, H. L.: Drug abuse and the schools, Am. J. Psychiatry 125:1691-1697, 1969.

87. U. S. Department of Health, Education and Welfare: Alcohol Education Conference pro-

ceedings, Washington, D. C., 1966, Government Printing Office.

88. University of Nevada: A drug abuse prevention program for students, grades 4-6, project developed by the Research and Educational Planning Center, College of Education, Jan., 1971.

89. Vincent, R. J.: Selected instructional and behavioral objectives for a tenth grade drug education program, J. Sch. Health 41:310-313, 1971.

90. Vincent, R. J.: A ten month comparison of the incidence of smoking marihuana at a midwestern university, J. Alcohol Educ. 15:25-34, 1970.

91. Wheelis, A.: The quest for identity, New York, 1958, W. W. Norton & Co., Inc.

92. Wolk, D. J.: Youth and drugs: guidelines for teachers, Soc. Educ. 33:667-674, 1969.

93. Yolles, S. F.: Prescription for drug abuse education, J. Drug Educ. 1:101-113, 1971.

94. Yolles, S. F.: Prevention of drug abuse. In Resource book for drug abuse education, Washington, D. C., 1969, National Institute of Mental Health, National Clearinghouse for Mental Health Information.

CHAPTER 8

DRUG SERVICES

School drug programs must include secondary prevention of drug misuse and abuse as well as provide guidance toward tertiary prevention. Students participating in the drug scene and using drugs should receive aid that will interrupt the development of more serious problems or help to solve existing difficulties. Students may need someone to talk with, to turn to in an emergency, or to ask about community resources. This assistance is identified as the drug services phase of the school program. It includes procedures and personnel necessary to (1) identify students using drugs, (2) give attention to crisis and other situations when students are under the influence of drugs, and (3) provide follow-up activities to help young drug users and abusers.

Previously evidence was presented indicating that a sizable segment of the student population was involved to varying degrees with an assortment of drugs. This data further revealed that the extent of drug usage was dependent on the drug selected. Although the reliability and validity of some of this information may be open to question, the data show that young people in school are using drugs. Some students have no problems, fewer have minor problems, and a still smaller number have more serious problems. This chapter, therefore, is devoted to those drug users who are in school, and special consideration will be given to those who are misusers and abusers. The information herein should help identify the various types of drug users so

that they can receive counseling and guidance. It should also indicate where abusers can obtain treatment and, if necessary, rehabilitation. It is expected that such services, if provided, would not only have considerable impact in reducing the number of drug misusers and abusers in schools but would also help pupils find viable behavioral alternatives.

Participation of the schools in the drug services program identified herein is not meant to usurp the role of the home or of the community but rather to supplement and complement such efforts. In many areas of the nation, parents undoubtedly are looking to the school for such assistance. In addition, numerous community agencies can provide help that neither parents nor the schools can make available to pupils.

IDENTIFICATION OF DRUGS OF ABUSE

Brief attention will be given to the question frequently raised by teachers, administrators, and other school personnel: How can I identify drugs of abuse? Many school personnel feel that such information will help them protect students from using such drugs or aid in identifying drug users. Actually such drugs cannot be effectively identified by sight, taste, or smell because all drugs except marijuana can be found in tablet, capsule, powder, or liquid form and in varying colors and shapes. Even marijuana, which is usually smoked, can be found in candy, cookies, and tea. Identifying the drugs used by individuals is a difficult and complex problem. Most drugs can be correctly identified only by trained technicians using complicated laboratory techniques. Such qualified experts may be found in clinical laboratories, in medical schools, or in police departments. School personnel who feel these services are needed should seek out such resources in their own communities. In the event that, drugs, or alleged drugs, are found on campus and it is necessary to determine if they are drugs of abuse, technical help should be solicited.

IDENTIFICATION OF DRUG USERS AND ABUSERS

Few tests exist that physicians or clinical specialists can use to detect drug use and abuse, but such procedures are normally not conducted in schools. Therefore, if schools are to aid young people, less exacting methods will be needed to identify drug misusers and abusers, particularly potential hard-core addicts. Secondary techniques can be used by school personnel to identify students using drugs and to guide these pupils to counseling services and rehabilitation or treatment assistance.

Some of the ways school employees may participate in locating drug misusers include the following:

1. Observe (a) signs and symptoms of the effects of drugs on student behavior, (b) personality characteristics of potential users, and (c) tell-tale evidence of use
2. Identify students taking prescribed medications at school
3. Self-identification of drug abusers
4. Peer identification
5. Clinical tests (for example, urine test for drugs)

Observable signs and symptoms
EFFECTS OF DRUGS ON BEHAVIOR

The most useful and perhaps the best way for school personnel to spot drug users, unless the students turn themselves in, is by observing behavioral signs and symptoms. *This method combined with the other procedures found herein will at best only give clues or suspicions of drug use.* Actually, some symptomatic characteristics that are identified may not be due to drugs but to illness or depression resulting from emotional reaction. Drowsiness, apparent intoxication, and loss of appetite are symptoms of many diseases. Also the normal adolescent occasionally becomes moody, changes interests abruptly, loses interest in the opposite sex, skips school, and still may not be involved in the use of drugs. *There should be significant and recurrent behavioral and physical changes before suspicions are aroused.*

Unless students identify themselves as users or misusers, are subjected to the few clinical tests available, or are examined by clinical experts, *there is no accurate way of knowing whether a person is on drugs.* The pupil using drugs will usually endeavor to conceal the fact. He will generally, although not always, confine his involvement to after-school hours and weekends or absent himself from school. He may be evasive of questions. These factors complicate the identification process for schools.

School personnel should not be quick to draw conclusions about student drug use from observations of symptomatic behavior because of (1) the possible irreparable alienation that may result and (2) the hazard of infringement on the rights of pupils. Caution is the best advice to the observer.

Regardless of the procedure, or combination of procedures used, the matter of diagnosis is not within the capability or responsibility of teachers, nurses, or other school personnel. *Diagnosis should be left to physicians and clinical experts who are thoroughly familiar with the pharmacology of drugs and with the drug scene.* However, the observation of signs or symptoms of deviant behavior is within the capability of all school personnel.

GENERAL SIGNS AND SYMPTOMS. The general behavioral signs to look for in students who are drug abusers include the following:

1. Immediate observations
   a. Changes in attendance, discipline, academic performance, interest, legibility, neatness, caliber of homework, attention; loss of interest in sports; failing memory
   b. Display of unusual degrees of activity—excitement, boundless energy, excessive laughter, unusual talkativeness
   c. Display of unusual inactivity—moodiness, depression, apathy due to questioning of values, drowsiness, lethargy
   d. Deterioration of personal appearance and of concern for health habits—dress, loss of appetite and rapid weight loss, sudden increase in appetite
   e. Unpredictable outbreaks of temper and

Table 8-1. Specific physical and behavioral signs and symptoms

DRUG	PHYSICAL	BEHAVIORAL
Depressants* Barbiturates (reds, redbirds, downers, goofballs), e.g., phenobarbital, Seconal, pentobarbital; tranquilizers	Signs of alcoholic intoxication, no odor of alcohol on breath; unsteady, stumbling gait; slurred speech; possible mental confusion, delirium, convulsions	Loss of interest in usual activities—school, family, etc.; quarrelsome disposition; drowsiness or sleeping in class; may appear disoriented; coma or deep sleep; if only small amount, relaxed, sociable, in good humor
Hallucinogens† LSD (acid, cubes, STP, DMT) psilocybin, mescaline, peyote, nutmeg, morning glory seeds	Sit or recline in dreamlike trance; distortion of time and sense perceptions—sight, hearing, touch; increased heart rate and blood pressure, dilated pupils, "goosebumps"; not always euphoric; unpredictable flashback episodes possible	Sit or recline in dreamlike trance; may experience fear, terror, grotesque distortion of visual and auditory stimuli and self-image ("bad trip"); hallucinations; may try to escape from group; may be anxious to relate experiences and "insights"; less apt to hide involvement
Marijuana‡ (pot, weed, grass, tea, hay, mary jane, hemp, hash)	Red, watery eyes; dilated pupils; odor on breath or clothing similar to burnt rope; fingers show burns from smoking; increased appetite and desire for sweets	Behavior dependent on dose, psychological set of individual, and social setting in which the drug is taken; at lower doses—mild disinhibition; behavior patterns inconsistent, variable, and difficult to discern; at higher doses—behavior patterns more consistent, such as laughter, animation, drowsiness, possibly stupor, lack of coordination, impaired sense of time and distance, confusion
Narcotics Heroin (H, horse, smack, junk, snow), morphine, Demerol, codeine	Needle marks or scars over veins of inner surface of arm (mainlining) or over other parts of body; constricted pupils, does not respond to light; flushed face, red, watery eyes; redness and rawness of nostrils—sniffing heroin; loss of weight, appears emaciated; lack of pain	Lethargy, drowsiness, sleep, stupor, coma (deep intoxication); generally antisocial, shuns friends, classmates; may disappear from group; euphoria; hiding syringes, needles, bent spoons in locker
Solvents§ Glue, gasoline, lighter fluid, paint thinner, freon (pressurized cans), marker fluid, liquid shoe polish, tire patch cement	Runny nose and watery eyes (mucous membrane irritation); pungent odor of substance inhaled remaining on clothes and breath; nausea, poor appetite, weight loss (frequent user);	Drowsiness or unconsciousness after excess use; concealing rags, plastic or paper bags containing dried glue, model cement, or other solvents in student's belongings

*Usually taken in the form of pills.
†Usually taken orally on impregnated sugar cubes, cookies, or crackers and in a group setting under special conditions to enhance effect; not usually in school.
‡Smoked rolled in cigarette paper (reefers, joints, sticks) or in Oriental-style water pipe, or pipe; cooked in brownies or cookies; unless under influence at observation, difficult to recognize; infrequent users may not show general symptoms.
§Usually inhaled by putting head in cellophane or paper bag.

Table 8-1. Specific physical and behavioral signs and symptoms—cont'd

DRUG	PHYSICAL	BEHAVIORAL
	poor muscular control; may appear intoxicated; may complain of double vision, ringing in ears, hallucinations	
Stimulants Amphetamines (bennies, speed, dexies, uppers, drivers, pep pills), cocaine (crystal)	Dilated pupils; tremor, unsteady hands; dryness of mouth and nose, bad breath (onion, garlic, alcohol), licks lips frequently; flushing, excessive sweating; prolonged periods without eating or sleeping (frequent user); enlarged pupils	Exessive activity, difficult sitting still, nervous, chain smoking; euphoria, liveliness, talkativeness followed by depressed mood and irritability, restlessness, argumentativeness; exaggerated self-confidence

flareups—nervousness, irritability, argumentativeness

2. Long-term observations
   a. Wearing sunglasses at inappropriate times to conceal redness of eyes, constriction or dilation of pupils
   b. Constantly wearing long-sleeved shirts or blouses to hide needle marks
   c. Borrowing frequently from others or stealing to obtain money required to purchase drugs
   d. Appearing frequently in out-of-the-way areas, such as closets, storage areas, or rest rooms; furtive behavior; fear of discovery
   e. Association with known or possible drug users; evasive answers when questioned about nocturnal activities
   f. Appearance of intoxication but no smell of alcohol, indicates possible involvement with marijuana or barbiturates
   g. Adoption of use of "odd" words; different vocabulary

SPECIFIC SIGNS AND SYMPTOMS. Table 8-1 shows the specific physical and behavioral signs and symptoms of the commonly abused drugs. School personnel should be alert to observe these signs in pupils.

PERSONALITY CHARACTERISTICS OF POTENTIAL USERS

The literature does not reveal a great deal of information that would be useful or particularly helpful for predictive purposes. However, several references provide useful clues. Helm,[13] when speaking about the predisposition to alcoholism, says that most alcoholics share the following characteristics:

1. Little tolerance for frustration
2. Difficulty in coping with stress or withstanding anxiety
3. Emotional tensions and conflicts, especially in family relations
4. Strong feeling of alienation from their community or family
5. High energy levels but poor impulse control

Raskin[31] has indentified the following personality characteristics of drug users:

1. Passively dependent
2. Withdrawn
3. Rigidly compulsive
4. Anxious-insecure
5. Depressed
6. Distrustful
7. Aggressive
8. Emotionally unstable
9. Antisocial
10. Hypochondrical
11. Attention-seeking
12. Symptoms of psychosomatic illness

Blum[1] claims that high-risk youth are behavioral problems at school, have mild conduct disorders, and lack self-confidence. In addition, they may be self-centered and self-indulgent, which may not impair their ability to work or achieve.

With the limited data presented, it would be impossible to draw valid conclusions on which to make predictions. Perhaps an assumption or two, however, might be in order. It appears that drug abusers have various adjustment problems that most likely have bearing on their exhibited behavior toward drugs. Teachers, nurses, counselors, and other school personnel need to be alert to the signs and symptoms of deviant behavior resulting from the failure of students to have their physical and psychological needs satisfied. These signs and symptoms may provide clues about potential drug users and abusers among children and youth. It has also been shown that schools may be able to help with these adjustment problems. Perhaps assisting students in finding their own identities and their own meaningfulness in life would be helpful. Chapter 9 provides further guidance and help.

TELL-TALE EVIDENCE OF USE

Tell-tale evidence refers to those objects that indicate the presence of drugs. These objects serve merely as additional clues to be assembled in attempting to identify drug users and misusers in school. The following list of tell-tale evidence is not all-inclusive but merely illustrative of the possible materials that may be found in the possession of students, in lockers, and in other places on the school grounds:

1. Hypodermic syringe, needle, or equipment
2. Blackened or charred spoon
3. Eyedropper syringe (makeshift)
4. Cellophane, plastic, or paper bag with dried glue
5. Unprescribed pills and cough medicine
6. Solvents, especially glue
7. Special cigarette papers or pipes with odors other than tobacco
8. Purchase of expensive articles and unexplained possession of large sums of money

Taking prescribed medicines at school

Permitting students who need medication, even though prescribed, to come to school creates a variety of problems that have not always been easily resolved. Whether a teacher, nurse, or other school official should be responsible for remembering to administer the substance, or for reminding the student to do so, has been the biggest hassle created. Students who come to school with such conditions as anemia, coughs, diabetes, hyper- or hypothyroidism, allergy, or epilepsy are usually readily identified. Parents generally inform schools of their children's conditions and seek the school's assistance with prescribed medications. Due to the legal complications involved, many school districts have developed general policies and procedures for handling such situations. When an emergency arises, such as a diabetic coma, and schools have been informed as to the student's condition, they are better able to cope with the situation.

One issue that has received considerable newspaper publicity recently is whether amphetamines should be used to calm hyperactive, or hyperkinetic, children despite their prescription and the general consensus of medical people as to their value. This controversy came to light in June 1970 when it was reported that 5% to 10% of the elementary schoolchildren in Omaha, Nebraska, received such treatment. Someone then concluded that apparently some 500,000 pupils in grades 1 to 6 in the United States were receiving amphetamines. With the present drug problem in society, a variety of people, including legislators, began to question this use of amphetamines because it added further complexities to a major social problem. The matter became more involved when additional individuals challenged physicians' diagnoses and still others made claims that children were being unnecessarily quieted when the real problem was that they were bored with their classes.

It is not the purpose of this book to take a stand for or against the use of amphetamines or stimulants for hyperactive children. We wish rather to indicate the complexity of the drug problem faced by schools even when certain drug users have been identified. A second purpose is to provide understanding about the hyperkinetic child.

Laufer[19] states that medication for hyperactive students has been used quite often in recent years. The condition itself (generally referred to as "cerebral dysfunction") is associated with the abnormal functioning of the part of the brain that controls automatic, involuntary processes. It is believed to have many possible causes, including genetic factors, birth process difficulties, illness, hemorrhage, emotional problems, and delay in maturation. The symptoms of this condition are overactivity, distractibility, impulsiveness, variability, unpredictability, emotional sensitivity, explosive irritability, and repetition of the active behavior. Hyperactivity causes problems in learning and may be extremely upsetting to other students and teachers. Stimulating drugs, including Dexedrine, Benzedrine, Ritalin, and Tofranil, have been prescribed for treatment, and in clinical experience the medications have had desirable effects on the hyperkinetic condition.

Peer identification

Occasionally students who are concerned about their friends and their friends' drug habits will give teachers and other school personnel information revealing that these friends are taking drugs. This information should be turned over to the individual in school who is best qualified to communicate with such students in an effort to provide assistance and guidance.

Peer identification should be looked upon as a means of helping students with problems and not for any other purpose. In addition, information received should be held in strict confidence and young people who provide it should understand that it will be treated this way.

Self-identification of drug abusers

A fourth, and unquestionably the best, procedure for locating drug users is to motivate users to identify themselves. As stated earlier, observations or other methods for discovering drug-involved students may not be reliable and at best are only indicators. Therefore, if young people could be stimulated to seek help on their own, the possibility of combating the drug problem would be greatly improved. To accomplish such a goal is no easy task; some of the methods used will be discussed later. At the moment it is sufficient to say that every school will need someone with whom students feel they can communicate. Whether this is a teacher, nurse, counselor, or someone else, such an individual must not only be well informed about the drug scene and knowledgeable about youth and their problems but also should be easily, readily, and frequently available when requested to rap with students. He should be willing to render aid when called upon for help. Some schools have delegated one person to serve in the capacity of an ombudsman—a kind of mediator for student problems and a counselor for students involved with drugs. Ungerleider and Bowen[33] recommend the ombudsman approach and have reported its successful use in the Campbell Union High School District, San Jose, California. Numerous schools have since employed such individuals.

Should school personnel wish to motivate drug-using students to make their own decisions about the need for help, a list of considerations prepared by Dr. Allen Y. Cohen[2] might be made available. Dr. Cohen states that if students wish to find out if the danger line has been crossed, they might use the following checklist:

1. Increase in concentration problems
2. A failing memory
3. Decrease in mathematical ability
4. Creeping paranoia, feelings of persecution, or thinking that certain people or institutions are becoming hostile toward you
5. Exaggerated feelings of self-confidence or increased underlying feelings of inferiority
6. Passivity, loss of energy, or lack of desire to do anything except "lie back and groove"

7. Difficulty in speech; feeling you cannot form thoughts into words
8. Increasing hang-ups in close relationships, especially with parents and with the opposite sex
9. Greater impressionability; flying off the handle easily
10. Feelings of futility about life and hopelessness about your own future
11. A total denial on your part that drugs might be harmful for you

Clinical tests

Although blood tests may be used to locate drug abusers, urine testing is the current clinical procedure to determine if drugs are present in the body. Heroin, amphetamines, barbiturates, and other drugs, except marijuana and LSD, are tested in this manner. Currently there are no adequate tests to identify these latter two drugs if present in the biological fluids of the body.

Technical help is necessary to analyze urine. Samples are collected and sent to a laboratory where two procedures may be used. The thin-layer chromatography test is less expensive and less sensitive but will also produce fewer false positives. The free radical analyzation test (FRAT) is more expensive and more sensitive but provides a high incidence of false positive results.

The presence of alcohol can be detected in two ways. A rough but simple method is the breath, or balloon, test, which determines the percentage of alcohol present. A more accurate method is to analyze the blood, but this involves clinical help.

Clinical testing information is discussed because a few individuals have advocated its use in the school program. We disagree with such a proposal for these reasons:

1. There are better ways to help students or to persuade them to voluntarily seek aid than to use such demeaning procedures on suspected drug users. This action would increase distrust in students rather than establish rapport.
2. There is a legal question about the infringement on the rights of individuals unless the tests were voluntary and approved by parents. However, should permission be granted, there is still doubt about the appropriateness of using this procedure in schools.
3. Such procedures may not be necessary because the number of compulsive and relapse users of most drugs is not very large, except possibly in some schools. Hence the cost might be too high in terms of the results.

WHAT TO DO FOR ABUSERS

There are perhaps four situations when school personnel may need to act and, in some cases, to act quickly with regard to drug users who have been identified through any or all of the procedures previously outlined. These situations vary in their immediacy for action and are categorized as follows is descending order of importance.

1. *Emergencies and crisis intervention.* Drug use that creates a serious condition, perhaps involving life and death, depending on the drug used, is an emergency and requires crisis intervention. In an emergency situation a person may have taken an overdose of barbiturates, narcotics, or other drugs. It is a matter of life and death, and medical aid is needed quickly; the person may be unconscious. Other cases in need of prompt attention include diabetic coma, LSD bad trip, toxic psychosis or flashbacks, or student "freak-out" suicide threats. These are serious, life-threatening situations, but they may not demand as quick action as the situations previously described. All of these conditions may occur in schools but only on rare occasions.
2. *Under the influence.* When a student is under the influence of a drug it will

be obvious because he will be nauseous, drowsy, overstimulated, or otherwise unable to function. The youth may be causing a disruption in school; he may be drunk on alcohol, drowsy or sleepy on barbiturates, or very high on marijuana.

3. *Suspected of being under the influence.* Some of the signs of drug use will be evident in the student but they may not be clear. These signs may result from the use of alcohol, marijuana, stimulants, barbiturates, or other drugs.

4. *Self-identification.* When under the influence, the student may voluntarily seek help from someone in school.

All of these four situations should be included in the policies and procedures established for a given school or school district. In Chapter 11 policies and procedures will be discussed.

In addition to the aforementioned, there will be other students not under the influence who have been suspected of using drugs and who will need aid. They will not require quick action, however. Ways to help these students will be covered later in this chapter.

With regard to the procedures to follow in emergency and crisis intervention ("hurry") cases, no attempt will be made here to provide extensive details as to "what to do" but merely what are the necessary essentials. When specific, detailed information needs to be included in policy and procedure statements, school personnel should consult medical and other sources in the community.

EMERGENCIES. When a person is unconscious due to drugs or for whatever reason and has stopped breathing, this is a "hurry case" in first aid and immediate action must be taken. Such action probably must occur within 5 minutes if the person is to survive and brain damage due to the lack of oxygen is to be prevented. An emergency demands the prompt start of artificial respiration with the concurrent call for medical aid. A physician, or an ambulance for transportation to the hospital, or both may be summoned. School policies should govern the exact procedures to follow. Parents need to be notified as quickly as is feasible. Whenever possible, as a secondary action, the cause of the unconsciousness should be determined by asking people who may have witnessed the action or through tell-tale signs that may be available. This may aid the physician in treatment.

CRISIS INTERVENTION. The nature of the crisis intervention action will depend on the drug taken and the extent of the crisis. In all cases medical aid should be summoned, parents should be notified, and tell-tale evidence should be located to try to determine the drug used.

Stimulants. A speed "freak-out" is similar to a bad trip with LSD but more difficult to handle. It may be obvious by these acute signs: anxiety, paranoid feelings, rapid speech, repetitive ideation, muscle tremor, and occasional toxic hallucination. Someone should stay with the victim and help to reassure him and relieve anxieties.

Barbiturates. An overdose of barbiturates is a serious matter, especially since withdrawal without medicine is more violent and dangerous than heroin withdrawal. The drug disinhibits (like alcohol) and the release of suppressed behavior can create a serious and explosive situation. If taken in conjunction with alcohol, barbiturate overdose may be extremely serious and could lead to death due to the synergistic depressant action of the two drugs. If a large dose has been taken within 2 hours, the victim is conscious, and you are awaiting medical aid, it may be advisable to induce vomiting. Be cautious of the hazard of aspiration of vomitus material following this procedure.

Hallucinogens. Three types of situations may occur with hallucinogens: bad trips, toxic psychosis, and flashbacks. In all cases help is needed due to the anxiety reactions created.

1. *Bad trips.* Be sure to rap with the person on a bad trip and try to talk

him down. Be supportive and friendly; help the person feel warmth and acceptance. Talk about what he wants to talk about and assure him that what is happening will vanish when the drug wears off. Try to make him relax and go with the trip.

2. *Toxic psychosis.* The state of toxic psychosis produces anxiety characterized by panic, excitement, and paranoia and is due to large doses of the drug. You still must talk the person down and let him know that the experience is due to the drug and will wear off. Remain with the individual at all times.

3. *Flashbacks.* With hallucinogens it is possible to have a sudden recurrence (flashback) of a previous, probably bad, trip complete with anxiety reactions and perception distortions yet independent of any drug use. You still must talk the person down and point out that the drug has taught him to react improperly to these illusions.

UNDER THE INFLUENCE. If a student is inexplicably demonstrating abnormal behavior and is unable to function at school, yet his vital signs indicate no immediate danger, parents should be notified. The student should be removed from the classroom and placed where he can be observed by a nurse, teacher, principal, or other person while awaiting the parents' decision as to disposition. Perhaps medical consultation is advisable; it should be suggested to parents when they are contacted. The parents should come for the student; if this is not possible, the student should remain under supervision and be taken home or to a physician's office.

SUSPECTED OF BEING UNDER THE INFLUENCE. A student whose behavior indicates that he is under the influence of a drug (a little high) but still functioning within the normal school setting should be referred to the person delegated to implement school procedure in such instances. Suspension, expulsion, consultation with parents, or any other action should receive careful con-

sideration. No precipitous action should be taken (Chapter 10).

SELF-IDENTIFICATION. If a student reports his use of drugs to someone in school, and if he is under the influence, any of the procedures outlined in this section may need to become operative. If the case is one that does not involve quick action, the procedure for students under the influence would be appropriate.

FOLLOW-UP PROCEDURES

Having identified some of the drug users and abusers, including those suspected of or admitting to drug use, the school must decide what to do about helping these students. It is futile to merely locate students with problems unless something is done for them. More importantly it will be necessary to offer assistance not only to those who may seek help but to all others who are referred to school personnel for aid. The decision to provide help should be based on the school's desire to fulfill its educational obligation, that is, to provide opportunities so students can profit most from their experiences. This necessitates that pupils be at their highest levels of wellness. The use of drugs may interfere with the attainment of these states of well-being. Thus schools must be involved in the resolution of drug problems. The services rendered to help students will be referred to as follow-up procedures. They include counseling and guidance, use of community resources, and adjustment of school programs.

Counseling and guidance

The phrase "counseling and guidance" has many meanings, but it will be used here in the context of providing educational assistance mainly through a variety of informal educational procedures. Some aid may also be forthcoming from the formal educational program previously described. Counseling and guidance refer to the efforts made to provide understanding, to make interpretations about the drug problems students face, and to try to help solve these problems when desired. Counseling and guidance involve the interaction of school personnel with students and parents in a variety of settings. The purpose is to assist in formulating action plans.

PROVIDING DRUG COUNSELING

Who should and how to provide drug counseling services has not been clearly defined in schools; however, some promising efforts are offering clues. It is becoming clear that each school needs to have at least one person who is assigned this responsibility. This individual may involve others, including students, to help provide aid, but he is held accountable for the availability of such services. Ungerleider and Bowen[33] call such an individual an ombudsman, others identify him as a drug counselor, whose responsibilities might include:

1. Establishment of procedures for identification of users and abusers
2. Availability and accessibility to students for information and guidance upon request
3. Aid in the development and implementation of follow-up procedures
4. Aid in the development of policies and procedures
5. Liaison with school personnel such as teachers, nurses, psychologists, and principals
6. Management of in-service programs when necessary
7. Crisis intervention when necessary
8. Liaison with community institutions, including the police and the courts
9. Parental guidance and assistance
10. Aid in developing the drug curriculum and instructional program or as a resource when requested

The counselor may or may not be the administrator in charge of the total school drug program. This is a decision that each local school district must make. The counselor should not be confused with the drug education resource individual mentioned in Chapter 7. Although such a name is appropriate for the drug counselor, the former name identifies the person who aids teachers in the formal educational program. However, Chapter 10 provides information about administrative structure that should be considered.

The ombudsman, or counselor, should essentially possess these characteristics:

1. Be an approachable person who is able to communicate easily with students and is understanding of student problems, culture, and concerns
2. Be readily available and accessible whenever needed
3. Be willing to talk and not preach; be willing to listen and not dominate the conversation
4. Be honest and truthful in approach; one in whom students can place trust and faith
5. Not be using illegal drugs himself
6. Not be afraid to discuss drugs or anything else: sex, search for life's meaning, Vietnam war, and the draft
7. Have some preparation and ability to recognize emotional disorders, to offer guidance, and to refer students to the school nurse, psychologist, or to a community resource
8. Be knowledgeable about the drug scene, especially in the youth culture, and know how to assist those drug users and abusers who desire help
9. Can work well with school personnel and community people, including parents
10. Be interested and willing to help young people with drug problems

School districts may find it impossible to locate ombudsmen, or counselors, with these qualifications because little is being done to prepare such individuals. It will probably be necessary to select likely candidates from within the school system. These are 3 basic qualifications such individuals should possess: (1) the ability to communicate with students, (2) acceptance by students, and (3) a sincere interest in wanting to help young people. To further prepare these individuals, schools should encourage participation in a wide variety of activities, including attendance at workshops and conferences, visitations to and discussions with people working in the drug scene, meetings, and involvement with the police.

In counseling young people about drugs, Frykman[11] has identified these guidelines that may be helpful:

1. Keep all confidences a sacred trust
2. Offer help so it can be easily refused or accepted
3. Wait patiently until the person wishes to make contact and to identify with you; do not force the relationship
4. Concentrate on the articulated problem, even when you become aware of far deeper ones
5. Seek to understand the problem as he sees it, not as you see it
6. Show positive support in his struggle and interest in what he has to say
7. Try not to solve things for him; help him instead to come to some conclusion as to how to solve the problem himself
8. Gently steer the conversation toward what he is obviously leaving out; do not finish sentences for him
9. Be aware that he senses or imagines your response because of past experience with helping agents

Several additional thoughts to be considered by the counselor when dealing with students with drug problems are those expressed by Dorsey and Silverman[3]:

1. Encounters with drug users may be difficult for many reasons; the user may be confused about the need for help and be reticent to seek help
2. Students frequently engage in a reconnaissance of the counselor prior to overtly asking for help
3. Both the drug user and the counselor encounter each other with certain expectations, biases, and fears
4. The student seeking help may be uncertain about what help is
5. The student may be afraid of being "busted"
6. The student may not trust the counselor

Numerous schools are experimenting with the use of students to help with counseling in a variety of ways. Actually no easily or clearly defined methods have been established to best utilize students. There is no question that students play a role in helping their peers but how this is to occur needs clarification. Students, whether they have been addicts, or not, have been available for one-to-one relationships, in small group discussions, at drop-in centers, and on hot-lines. How successful such procedures have been has not been fully ascertained. The length of time over which such efforts have extended has not been revealed. However, students may be helpful if properly used. Schools need to accept the concept of student involvement and become innovative and creative in exploring further their usage in drug programs.

The procedure for counseling used in the Palo Alto Unified School District in California utilizes drug counselors who have been chosen by the students because they can be trusted and because students can communicate with them without fear of reprisal. Each school has a group of drug specialists among whom are teachers, administrators, psychologists, and counselors. This team has been exposed to a special inservice training program. The members are free to respond to student needs in the manner they deem appropriate and effective. They are provided with released time from teaching or other responsibilities during the day if students require help.

ILLUSTRATIONS OF TYPES AND PROCEDURES

Although the types and procedures of counseling in drug problems are still not clear, they have assumed a variety of forms and appear to be somewhat consistent in the methods used. Generally the informal educational type of program has been used. This takes place with one student or a group of students and has also involved parents. The procedures used have included any or all of the following: drop-in, rap, or informational centers (on or off school grounds) run by school personnel, students, or both; peer-group activities in which high school students visit junior high schools, or junior high schools visit fifth and sixth grades and rap with students; hot-lines on or off campus for student and parent use; school newspapers, special bulletins, and other communication procedures in schools; special notices to parents; and counseling with students or parents or both.

Various combinations of the types and procedures of counseling have been used in programs throughout the country. Programs in California, North Carolina, Ohio, New Jersey, and New York are illustrative of the efforts being made.

SAN FRANCISCO UNIFIED SCHOOL DISTRICT, CALIFORNIA. "Crash" pads have been established experimentally in four high schools where students may voluntarily go or be taken for treatment or help for the effects of drug abuse. These are rap centers where students can feel safe and talk about their drug problems with no moralizing and little judging. These centers are staffed by physicians from the community, including the public health department; nurses, psychiatric social workers and technicians, and psychologists assist at no cost to the district.

There is some discussion of using mobile vans or trailers as additional drop-in centers in each neighborhood. These would be staffed by mental health professionals working on a part-time basis at no expense to the schools with whom they will work closely.

A drug counseling workshop for students who violated narcotic laws on campus but who are not considered hard-core users or sellers was initiated. Any student who has been identified in a police report as a user and has admitted to police officials that he has used or possessed drugs on campus is required to attend. At least one parent must accompany the student to a 2-hour

meeting held one night a week for 4 weeks. The meetings are conducted by a qualified staff member or psychologist who discusses the pharmacological aspects of illegal drugs, meanings and dangers of drug use, feelings and attitudes of parent and child toward each other, and personal observations and views of guest speakers.

Selected high school students, including those with extensive drug abuse experience, visit community agencies and talk with personnel who handle young people with drug problems. These students then act as resources for their classmates and younger students in nearby high schools and upper elementary grades, serving as discussion leaders in the classroom setting.

SPARTANSBURG, NORTH CAROLINA. A storefront counseling center called STAND (Students Talk About Narcotic Drugs) has been established and is funded by contributions from local businesses. All counseling is done by junior and senior high school students. They answer telephone calls, distribute literature, provide confidential counseling, and arrange treatment for students who request it. Three doctors are on emergency call at all times.

LAKEWOOD, OHIO. A hot-line operates out of a teen-age drop-in center in the basement of the YMCA-YWCA. Some 30 to 40 young people gather nightly to talk about drug-related problems and to receive help if necessary.

WESTFIELD, NEW JERSEY. A "Speakout" program for parents and students meets weekly in small discussion groups to cover the generation gap problem, including drugs.

NASSAU COUNTY, NEW YORK. DEAN (Deputy Educators Against Narcotics) has been established by the district attorney to help teen-agers of several school districts. These young persons attend monthly meetings, usually held in the district attorney's office, and talk about the legal and medical aspects of narcotics. They also visit treatment centers. The purpose is to train these teen-agers so they may return to their schools and share this information with their peers.

MONTEREY, CALIFORNIA. A Drug Information and Youth Crisis Center has been established to inform or counsel young people and adults about drugs and related problems. The program includes education, detoxification, and rehabilitation. More specifically, the center provides the following services: (1) a 24-hour switchboard with immediate referral for medical or psychiatric assistance, (2) consultation with existing agencies, including schools, for improving drug education, (3) a library of resource materials and training aids for educators and agencies, (4) continuing institutes for the training of those involved in drug education and counseling programs for drug users and their families, and (5) rehabilitation, job placement, and follow-up contact whenever possible.

SAN DIEGO UNIFIED SCHOOL DISTRICT, CALIFORNIA. Several teachers have been selected and given in-depth preparation for drug abuse education. They are itinerant teachers, each of whom meets with a small group of eighth grade students in informal discussions for 4 days. The fifth day is spent on the individual counseling of students. These teacher specialists serve as a resource for teachers and for group presentations about drugs at grade levels 7 through 12.

CAMPBELL UNION HIGH SCHOOL DISTRICT, CALIFORNIA. Students are counseled by school personnel while in custody of juvenile authorities. Parent discussion groups and other community awareness and involvement activities are utilized.

Use of community resources

Schools will discover that after the counseling and guidance phase, some students will require the assistance of available community agencies. Pupils and parents may need help in identifying and locating local resources. Therefore the personnel assisting students and parents must know about the various private psychotherapists, private physicians, public and private

hospitals, hot lines, guidance and outpatient clinics, mental health centers, city and county agencies, religious organizations, groups such as Teen Challenge, The Family, Synanon, Damien House, and Daytop Village, and other services. Liaison and communication should be established with these agencies so that referrals and assistance with the school program become possible.

The nature and extent of community resources will depend on location. Schools centered in metropolitan areas may have more such resources than those in rural areas. In probably all cases the supply will fall short of the need. This should induce schools and school districts to take the initiative and motivate the forces in the community to provide a variety of service centers, particularly in ghetto areas. Thus the schools and the community can work together in a common cause.

If Dallas, Texas, is indicative of the limited treatment services available, it can be generalized that there is need for more throughout the nation. The Ad Hoc Committee Report on Drug Abuse[25] prepared for the Dallas Independent School District states that a wider spectrum of treatment services is needed, ranging from care for acute drug crises to a diversity of outpatient and inpatient rehabilitative agencies. The report also states that a variety of health professionals should be involved in providing this care. The school district is urged to support the development of new approaches to treating drug dependency. The claim is made that no available treatment program for any severe drug dependency consistently yields positive results. This comment was probably made before the advent of methadone, although the methadone program still needs study and is only one promising approach. However, the Ad Hoc Committee identified two urgent needs:

1. Development of outpatient, group-oriented therapy and counseling programs
2. Development of small residential cen-

ters for the intensive rehabilitation of students requiring 24-hour-a-day care

An innovative approach to community services is under way in Renton, Washington. Titled "School and Community Drug Intervention Program," it may be called a youth services program. Its emphasis is prevention and it developed out of the schools' desire to get the community to provide help in handling drug problems. Federal funding was obtained to get started. The program is multifaceted and includes the following services: residential and job placement; crisis intervention; community-recreational facilities; and social, medical, and educational aid for the school, parent, and community. It has developed a drop-in center called "Berry House" for young people. It is expected that the program will be operated by the individuals who come to the drop-in center.

Adjustment of school programs

School districts must be cognizant of the student's welfare when determining action to be taken with drug abusers and must consider the school's basic function, which is educational, in reaching any decision to suspend or expel students. Schools should try to keep students in school, perhaps through innovative approaches, or should attempt to provide educational services wherever pupils may be—in jails, juvenile halls, or other correctional institutions. Schools located in ghetto areas or in predominantly ethnic minority neighborhoods will need to give special attention to these matters.

ILLUSTRATIVE ACTIVITIES

The literature does not contain a great deal of information as to what schools are, or might be, doing with regard to adjusting their programs. However, some illustrations provided under counseling and guidance are applicable. In addition, the following are activities that give clues to what some schools are doing. These may spark local schools to create their own approaches.

CENTINELA UNION HIGH SCHOOL DISTRICT, CALIFORNIA. When students with drug problems are identified, if possible, they are allowed to remain in school but must attend a 2-week program of group counseling sessions with their parents. Whereas the program's curriculum does not focus on drugs themselves, it does, however, provide knowledge and understanding of the complexities and the multiple effects of drug misuse and abuse.

NEW YORK CITY SCHOOLS. Two programs for addicts are operative, each of which is an innovative approach to education. One deals with the addict in a special school setting; the other works with established treatment facilities.

Alpha School, a special public school, seeks to rehabilitate former addicts while they continue their high school education. It is located in a two-story former milk plant and houses 60 students, most of whom were high school drop-outs. Students spend 1 year at this school, take equivalent high school work, and receive intensive counseling before returning to their regular schools. Once back in their own schools these students are expected to help counsel their peers about drug use.

An extensive project exists whereby programs leading to a high school equivalency diploma are available within the city's narcotic treatment centers, including Daytop Village, Odyssey House, Lagos, city hospitals, and prisons. The program includes remedial reading, mathematics, counseling toward returning to school, a "college discovery" project, vocational guidance aimed at developing salable skills, and help with obtaining jobs after rehabilitation.

CORONADO SCHOOL DISTRICT, CALIFORNIA. An approach was proposed, although not implemented, that was experimental in nature and would have provided a broadened guidance program, involving school counselors, administrators, and effective volunteer teachers. It was to have been remedial and preventive in order to treat the underlying causes. The plan was to refrain from sending students identified or involved directly or indirectly with drugs into continuation schools (schools with special hours, possibly work-study programs) or to involve them with police, probation, and juvenile authorities. Instead these students would be subjected to a "contract" for 1 year, approved by parents and including the following:

1. Student and parent would agree to plan for therapy.
2. Student and parent would attend weekly encounter sessions together. The duration of attendance would depend upon student's behavior changes, evidence of parents' adaptation to an ongoing program of communication, and other factors.
3. The school counselor would be involved in individual and group counseling.
4. All agency and institutional experts would be utilized as resource people.
5. Each student was to be assigned to a specific counselor to develop individual and group therapy plans.
6. Students would return to schools in full standing upon successful completion of the plan.

• • •

Other more innovative approaches to adjustment include the Parkway School in Philadelphia, the Opportunity School in San Francisco, Project Community in Berkeley, California (Dr. William Soskin, director), and the Summerhill School in England. These schools do not focus on drug problems and drop-outs, although they are probably acquiring many drug-involved students. Rather they try to provide a meaningful, interesting, stimulating, functional type of education. The atmosphere is freer; there are no rigid dress codes and the importance of time schedules and attendance is minimized or eliminated. Teachers are not looked upon as authoritarians but as facilitators of education. Programs are tailored for individual differences and interests and often dove-tail

employment opportunities. Much use is made of the community. In a sense, these are schools without walls. Informal and open discussions on any world topics or social programs are possible. Thus the attempt is not to deal with drugs per se, but with individuals and their needs.

SUMMARY

In summary, three essential points are significant:

1. Identification of student drug misusers and abusers is not a simple procedure. Where recurrent signs and symptoms appear, pupils should be referred to physicians or clinical experts thoroughly familiar with the pharmacology of drugs for assistance.
2. Schools should provide one or more individuals who communicate easily with students and especially with drug misusers and abusers.
3. Help to students with drug problems includes knowledge of the community resources and adjustment of school programs.

References

1. Blum, R. H., et al.: Horatio Alger's children, San Francisco, 1972, Jossey-Bass, Inc., Publishers.
1a. Bowen, H., and Schroeder, W.: Drug abuse handbook, Campbell, Calif., 1970, Campbell Union High School District.
2. Cohen, A. Y.: Decisions about drugs, Paper presented in Juneau, Alaska, 1970.
3. Dorsey, D., and Silverman, M.: Counseling of students who use drugs, Calif. Sch. Health 4:15-20, 1968.
4. Drug abuse: a reference for teachers, Trenton, 1969, New Jersey State Department of Education.
5. Drug Abuse Council: Drug abuse control: administrative guidelines, Los Angeles, 1970, Los Angeles City Schools.
6. Drug abuse education, ed. 2, Washington, D. C., 1969, American Pharmaceutical Association.
7. Drug abuse: escape to nowhere, Philadelphia, 1967, American Association for Health, Physical Education, and Recreation and Smith, Kline & French Laboratories.
8. Drug crisis: schools fight back with innovative programs, Washington, D. C., 1971, National School Public Relations Association.

9. Drug education handbook, Denver, 1970, Alcoholism and Drug Dependence Division, Colorado Department of Health.

10. Drug education in Maine, Augusta, 1970, Maine State Department of Education.

11. Frykman, J. H.: A new connection: an approach to persons involved in compulsive drug use, San Francisco, 1971, Scrimshaw Press.

12. Guber, B.: Management of students suspected to be under the influence of drugs, Calif. Sch. Health 4:9-11, 1969.

13. Helm, S. T.: Predisposition to alcoholism. In Resource book for drug abuse education, Chevy Chase, Md., 1969, National Institute of Mental Health, National Clearinghouse for Mental Health Information.

14. Hubbard, H.: Drug treatment and prevention: Hope House Inc., Albany, N. Y., N.A.S.S.P. Bull. 54:95-105, 1970.

15. KQED Educational Services: Drugs the children are choosing, a supplementary manual for teachers and parents, San Francisco, 1969, (J. Fadiman, instructor).

16. Land, H. W.: How a parent can teach his child about drugs, Today's Health 49:42-45, 1971.

17. Land, H. W.: What you can do about drugs and your child, New York, 1969, Hart Publishing Co., Inc.

18. Langer, J. H.: School-law enforcement cooperation. In Guidelines for drug abuse prevention education, Washington, D. C., 1970, Bureau of Narcotics and Dangerous Drugs, U. S. Department of Justice.

19. Laufer, M. W.: Medications, learning and behavior, Phi Delta Kappan 52:169-170, 1970.

20. Leviton, D.: Crisis interventions by the health educator, Sch. Health Rev. 1:22-36, 1970.

21. Miller, C. M.: Crisis intervention and health counseling: an overview, Sch. Health Rev. 1:15-17, 1970.

22. Montgomery County Mental Health Association: A county mental health association's hotline, Sch. Health Rev. 1:27-30, 1970.

23. Moorehead, C.: Drug inspections welcomed, Times Educ. Suppl. 2900:5, 1970.

24. Pavey, S.: Crisis intervention by the counseling psychologist, Sch. Health Rev. 1:18-21, 1970.

25. Report of the Ad Hoc Committee on Drug Abuse, Dallas, 1970, Superintendent of Schools, Dallas Independent School District.

26. School board policies on drug education and drug use, Waterford, Conn., 1971, National School Boards Association.

27. Seccombe, W.: Illusionogenic crisis and effective intervention, Int. J. Addictions 8:11-14, 1971.

28. Selected drug education curricula, drugs and hazardous substances, grades K-12, San Francisco, 1969, San Francisco Unified School District.

29. Smith, D. E., and Bentel, D. J.: Drug Abuse Information Project, fourth annual report to the legislature, San Francisco, 1970, University of California San Francisco Medical Center.

30. Stamford Public Schools, Connecticut: Stamford curriculum guide for drug abuse education, Chicago, 1971, J. G. Ferguson Publishing Co.

31. A teacher resource guide for drug use and abuse, Lansing, 1970, Michigan State Department of Education.

32. Teacher's resource guide on drug abuse, Harrisburg, 1969, Division of Public Health Education, Pennsylvania Department of Health.

33. Ungerleider, J. T., and Bowen, H. L.: Drug abuse and the schools, Am. J. Psychiatry 125:105-111, 1969.

34. The voluntary health agency, Sch. Health Rev. 1:36, 1970.

35. Winston, S. L.: Drug counseling: a workshop with a purpose, Clearing House 44:227-228, 1969.

CHAPTER 9

SCHOOL ATMOSPHERE

Educational effectiveness is directly related to the atmosphere found in schools. How well students learn is not solely dependent on the imparting of factual information nor on the physical aspects of the environment, such as textbooks, resources, and buildings. Hartman[30] says learning involves the perceptions, interests, and feelings of learners. Thus any educational institution must consider the social-emotional aspects and the attitudes and interactions of students, teachers, parents, and others. The climate and the learning that takes place in schools are affected by how people feel, believe, and value as well as how people treat each other. People must be concerned with individuals and not just subject matter. School personnel should treat students with kindness and humaneness. Borton adds, "I believe that what a student learns in school, and what he eventually becomes are significantly influenced by how he feels about himself and the world outside."[2]

What is happening inside people where it is not readily apparent in tangible form but is reflected in people's attitudes may truly be identified as the school climate. School personnel must really care about students in order to provide security, happiness, independency, individuality, freedom to make decisions, interest, desire to learn, equality of opportunity, freedom from bias and prejudice, fair and just actions, and involvement. Smith and Luce[41] best describe this atmosphere in the title of their book *Love Needs Care*. They say we need to care about people to provide

love. In essence, schools must be concerned with developing the attitudes and feelings of their students. The school climate may contribute to or detract from the achievement of this goal.

The atmosphere found in schools in the United States today is best reflected in the selected statements that follow. Glines has said: "Present conventional schools are the most inhumane institutions in America. They closely rival the prisons; the only difference is that after 3:00 P.M. and on weekends we let the prisoners escape."[14]

The National School Public Relations Association reports a comment made in the *Washington Post* by Terry Beresford on the school situation: "A rigid and outdated public school system in which students are treated with distrust and often with hostility helps create for youth a climate in which escapism, rebelliousness, defiance of rules and risk-taking—all typical adolescent behavior—are given added appeal, and drug use becomes a kind of rite of initiation for passage out of childhood or out of the established order."[7] The National School Public Relations Association also claims: ". . . majority of youth are bored with their education and find schools neither meaningful nor exciting."[7] Dearden quotes this remark as having been made by a student: "Teachers seem more interested in whether we chew gum, sit in our assigned seats, or have sideburns, than they do in relating to us as human beings and students."[5]

If these comments are representative of the school atmosphere, they provide some clues to why many youth are bored with schools and with education. They provide leads to the reasons for student unrest. The lack of meaningful and challenging education as well as the overly conforming and constricting nature of many schools may be factors contributing to youth's disenchantment and encouraging them to seek escape through the use of drugs. Providing a school climate conducive to the greatest learning and helpful in reaching some of the root causes of drug misuse and abuse depends on these three factors: (1) student alienation and unrest, (2) physical and psychological needs of pupils, and (3) humaneness in the school.

STUDENT ALIENATION AND UNREST

Numerous young people have feelings of disaffection for the school, the home, and the community. Alienation with and unrest in society exists among many junior high and high school students. Although the extent of student alienation and unrest is not known today, it has occurred with sufficient frequency and intensity to warrant attention and study. It may provide clues to the drug problem.

Alienation has various meanings but herein it refers to the reaction to, and even the rejection of, the accepted values, goals, and institutions that have normally been characteristic of America as youth attempt to find self-identity. Such feelings result in disenchantment, dissatisfaction, and unhappiness with programs, teachers, parents, and social conditions, and lead to unrest and possibly rebellion among some young people.

The problems of alienation and unrest involve psychological, social, and possibly spiritual and ideological factors that affect youth. King[22] writes that Erikson says the major psychological task of the adolescent is to form a stable identity so that he can successfully pass into adulthood. The conditions for this transition to take place, for the adolescent to find this identity, can occur if (1) there exist meaningful adult roles—the greater the number found in a meaningful social context the smoother the transition is likely to be; (2) there are clearly defined transition points, or social activities, to facilitate the transition; and (3) there is stability and consensus about the value system of society—it must provide acceptable answers to the questions: Why am I here? What meaning is there to my life? How do I relate to others? Where am I going after death? Such questions have spiritual overtones and applications.

The transition of youth through adolescence is likely to be crisis oriented and to lead to upheaval and rebellion, depending on the stability of the existing social conditions. Today the social structure is undergoing a variety of changes and modifications, including shifts in political power, the explosion of knowledge, the economic structure, the family organization, the availability of increased leisure time, and the value system. In addition, there is considerable confusion and fuzziness regarding how society expects youth to behave in the adult role.

Not all students feel a sense of crisis. The majority are able to adapt to the changing conditions and to make the transition into adulthood. However, attention must be given to those who are unable to meet the situation easily, to those who encounter problems, and to those who turn to a magical solution to life's problems through the use of drugs.

The social changes taking place in this world are challenging the military complex and the war, the establishment and its bureaucracy, big business and its control over man, the dichotomy of affluence and poverty in the world, technology and its destruction of nature and man, materialism and secularism, the political system, intellectualism and the knowledge explosion, prejudice and bias, inequality, civil rights, and other values. Young people have discovered that their lives have been outlined and determined by others rather than by their own experiences, their own self-searching, and their own listening to life. They desire opportunities to experience life on their own and to be free to make decisions and changes by themselves. They do not wish to have everything programmed in a prescribed curriculum or predetermined by schools, parents, or society. They desire and need opportunities to grow up by themselves, to act responsibly, to work closely with seriously concerned adults, and to participate in other meaningful ways.

The problem of alienation has existed

for a long time among the impoverished, the minorities, and the rejected. However, the present alienation is coming from the average, affluent, and adjusted American as well as from the fortunate, talented, and privileged individual. Keniston[21] says the "new" alienation is not the bottom one third of the population concerned with poverty, exclusion, sickness, oppression, lack of choice, and lack of opportunity; it is found among those who have every possible advantage. Alienation is bound up with the technological society in which we live.

The National School Public Relations Association[7] reports that high school student unrest and protest are related to the following factors:

1. Racial issues and the black student's commitment to the renaissance of his people—demand for more black teachers, guidance counselors, and administrators; recognition of black identity, pride, and culture
2. Dress and grooming regulations—miniskirts and maxilocks
3. School smoking rules and the cafeteria
4. Censorship and regulation of school papers, the scheduling of sporting events, and social events at school
5. Lack of student voice in rule-making and in determining school policies and curriculum
6. The open versus the closed campus
7. Need for new student organizations
8. Dissatisfaction with the school program and personnel—teachers who neither like their jobs nor students; worthless counseling programs; lack of relevant curriculum; class groupings; grades; examinations; homework
9. Staff members who contribute to unrest by
   a. Tending to talk rather than listen
   b. Imposing primarily white, Anglo-Saxon value systems on students
   c. Tending to overemphasize rules, regulations, and other rigid controls
   d. Seeing pupils not as individuals but as groups
   e. Tending to "turn-off" students who display deviant behavior in terms of class performance, grooming, and dress
   f. Locking students into categories of ability or aptitude
   g. Tending to convey through a look, tone of voice, or gesture "silent contempt" for some deviant characteristic of the student

Wynne[45] claims student unrest is not only the product of war, poor teaching, racism, and poverty. He has additionally identified the following reasons:

1. Diminishing work experience—students remaining in school longer than at any period of history and hence having little contact with adults except those in the immediate family
2. Increase in suburban living, resulting in reduced contacts among intergeneration people
3. Development of shopping centers; advent of modern transportation resulting in fathers going farther away to work and children having less contact with fathers or perhaps not even knowing what father does
4. Diminishing of the extended family such as grandparents, uncles, aunts, and the like, resulting in less contact with sympathetic adults

It should be evident that the school atmosphere is not the only factor contributing to student alienation and unrest but is one of several social forces that can have a definite effect on pupil behavior. It may be one of the contributing causes to the use and misuse of drugs. The school atmosphere is directly related to effective learning. Keniston[20] states that the type of student who is prone to use drugs is the "disaffiliate," the one who rejects the prevalent American values. Kohn and Mercer[23] support this view, saying that drug use and the attitudes toward drug use may be related to a left-right, rebellious-authoritarian dimension of sociopolitical ideology. These same authorities report similar findings by Zinberg, McGlothin,

Blum, Geber, and Suchman, who indicate a greater tendency to drug use among student political activists, those opposed to restrictions on individual freedom, those exhibiting sociocultural alienation, individuals who are rebellious to authority, those opposed to parents, and individuals who reject conventional values.

Gottlieb[16] says the use of drugs is not only an attempt at personal adjustment but also a personal reaction to maladjustment. He reasons that the poor have always been discriminated against and have had difficulty in achieving economic and familial stability. Therefore delinquency and drugs are a part of life for the poor because such people are born to pessimism, futility, mistrust, negativism, and quick pleasures. Thus the young ghetto person turns to drugs to get away from unpleasant reality.

According to Keniston[21] these signs help to identify the alienated outlook of students:

1. A distrust of commitment—rejection of the American culture, rejection of group activities, realization of the futility of civic and political activities, a hesitancy to act
2. A pessimistic existential viewpoint—future looks dark and unclear, anxiety about the world, belief that meaning can only be created by the individual, finding it impossible to communicate, belief in the universe as chaotic, unstructured, and meaningless
3. Showing anger, scorn, and contempt
4. Quests for the aesthetic—desiring awareness experience, living for today, interested in self-expression, creativity, passion, emotion, and feeling, being a social outsider

PHYSICAL AND PSYCHOLOGICAL NEEDS

Physical, psychological, or emotional needs of children and youth must be considered in order to provide the most productive school atmosphere. The fulfillment of these wants helps young people develop and maintain a high level of mental health. These needs play a significant role in the preventive health program. Opportunities must be offered for the fulfillment of these needs if schools are to aid in preventing the misuse and abuse of drugs.

Physical needs include food, air, water, warmth, rest, sleep, clothing, and freedom from disease and from other health hazards. Schools may find it advisable to provide free breakfasts and lunches for needy students, to maintain a comfortable and safe environment, to establish procedures to protect, maintain, and promote the health of their students, and to prepare rest and relaxation facilities for those needing such relief. These actions are not meant to replace the functions or responsibilities of the home or the family as the primary sources of such need fulfillment, but rather to assist in a complementary capacity. When the home is unable to supply adequate food, clothing, or sleeping quarters, the school may find it necessary to help care for these student wants, especially in ghetto areas. The school acts in loco parentis and has both a legal and a moral responsibility to utilize its resources in helping to satisfy the physical needs of pupils and to assist in the improvement of learning.

More importantly perhaps, and more complex to satisfy in schools, are the psychological or emotional needs.[3] They generally include the following:

1. Affection—love
2. Security—to belong, to have roots, to have protection
3. Acceptance as an individual—free of prejudice and bias, concerned about individual differences
4. Achievement—success experiences, recognition
5. Independence—to be a creative and developing person, to be on one's own, to act under one's own guidance and and direction, to make decisions, to be self-expressive
6. Authority—guidance and direction by adults

7. Self-respect—courteous, fair, and just treatment

Failure on the part of students to adequately satisfy their physical and emotional needs may result in deviant behavior. Psychological and social maladjustments in children and youth may occur and may be manifested in behavior contrary to normal. Such social-emotional disturbances may exhibit themselves in terms of:

1. Overtimidity—withdrawing, crying easily
2. Overaggressiveness—bullying, quarreling, boisterousness
3. Excessive daydreaming—persistent inattentiveness
4. Excessive boasting or showing off
5. Poor sportsmanship
6. Undue restlessness—habit tics, stammering, nail-biting
7. Frequent accidents or near-accidents
8. Abnormal sex behavior
9. Difficulty in reading or reciting
10. Failure to advance in school at normal rate
11. Stuttering or other forms of difficulty
12. Lying, stealing, cheating
13. Resistance to authority, constant complaints of unfairness
14. Unhappiness and depression
15. Gradual deterioration and marked sudden drop in educational achievement
16. Lack of interest or motivation
17. Constantly seeking attention or popularity

Glasser[13] says identity is related to the psychological wants of individuals and is a basic human need. If a child cannot find success identity, he will follow the pathway to failure identity. Therefore the deviations previously identified may not have serious implications when they first appear, but if they persist could become significant problems. The individual will be hampered in achieving the identity necessary to attain the psychological maturity needed in adulthood.

In speaking of needs Maslow[28] places human needs in a hierarchy. At the bottom, he says, are the physiological needs (hunger, thirst). Next are the safety needs, followed by love, affection, and belonging, then personal esteem, and finally self-actualization. Self-actualization refers to becoming what one is capable of becoming. Maslow states that needs at the lower levels must be satisfied before higher needs emerge. Hence few people achieve self-actualization.

There is evidence to support relationships between the use of drugs and student maladjustments. Schools, and especially teachers, must therefore make efforts to prevent such deviant conditions from occuring by providing an environment where young people feel secure, wanted, and loved, experience success, are treated fairly and justly without bias and prejudice, are involved, and are free to express themselves openly. Teachers should observe signs and symptoms of abnormal behavior as previously described and be aware of the appropriate action to take if such signs appear. The instructional program must be motivating and meaningful, and the school must engage teachers and counselors who are interested in children and youth. This kind of a school atmosphere is necessary to provide the help needed to attain emotional maturity so that students can acquire a high level of mental health and thus be able to cope with the problems of society. Such an atmosphere will help divert young people from seeking escape through the drug scene.

CREATING HUMANENESS IN SCHOOLS

"A commitment to humanism calls for a shift in thinking from self to learner . . . to be less concerned with what we do and much more concerned with what happens in the hearts and minds of those we do things to."[30] A spiritual, ideological concept involving a moral issue and relating to learning and the learning process is emerging. It is being labeled "humanism" or "humaneness" and is an important part of the school atmosphere. Humaneness has special significance because of its relationships to preventing student maladjustments and in turn to drug misuse and abuse. Humaneness has resulted from the many rapid changes that have and are taking place in society, including technology, science, and the knowledge explosion. A series of important questions have been raised in education regarding the nature of educational goals and of the process used to achieve such goals. Junell asks, "Is rational man our first priority? Have we placed too much faith in the power of the intellect, while tragically disregarding humane values? Does public education owe its responsibility to the intellectual-academic world, or to the emotional-social one?"[19] René Dubos[24] has said that science alone cannot be trusted to determine the future of man and his civilization. Krutch[24] has remarked that science cannot make value judgements and therefore can tell us only what can be done, never what we ought to do. Foshay queries, "Is the function of the schools to make a citizen or to serve the person, to make a man?"[36] He adds that social criteria are necessary but not sufficient for humane purposes.

Humaneness or humanism has not been clearly defined in the literature and therefore has a variety of meanings. Some of the key words used to express the term include trust, self-reliance, options, human relationships, freedom, justice, equality, alternatives, values, self-reliance, friendship, and decision making. Foshay[36] has said it is to pursue humane ends in a human form. Combs[36] refers to humane people as those concerned with the feelings, beliefs, values, attitudes, and understandings of others. When humaneness is applied to learning or to education, Maslow[28] refers to it as self-actualization, achievement of those interests that are uppermost in the hierarchy of needs. He believes that we live by our personal commitments, from which the individual derives a value system that motivates his behavior. Learning therefore is related directly to the learner. What actually takes place stems from a person's own

innovations, interests, and commitments, which are internal. The emphasis on the educational process, therefore, should be to make learning become self-directed. Achievement of self-directed learning is dependent on the human atmosphere in classrooms and in the school. This atmosphere includes tolerance, friendliness, respect for the individual, freedom of choice, self-expression, decision making, and other such considerations.

The basic goal of humanism in education is to make learning so interesting that the student will say, "I want to go to school." It becomes the teacher's role to aid the student in the search, or achievement, of self-actualization. Thus the student seeks to identify himself and to become a unique entity. To achieve this, teachers must constantly help the student increase the understanding about his feelings and attitudes and aid him in the expansion of his self-awareness. It is clear that self-awareness requires help from the teacher, especially through interpersonal relationships and communications. The process of bringing about self-valuing is referred to as creating humaneness in schools.

There is no magic formula to apply in developing the concept of humaneness in schools, but perhaps the suggestions that follow will provide specific ideas that teachers, administrators, and others may find stimulating and useful:

1. Maximize individual learning through recognition of individual differences in terms of uniqueness, potential, and achievement by providing opportunities for self-direction and self-management, by allowing for independent student and individual progress, and by creating special programs and curricula—Head Start, Upward Bound, and others.

2. Encourage and increase student involvement in the educational process through their participation in curriculum development, surveys, evaluation, development of policies, and open-forum discussions, through encouraging freedom of expression and choice, and in other ways.

3. Make the curriculum, instruction, and experiences meaningful and relevant to the needs of the student and of society. Permit flexibility of subject matter, including discussion of controversial areas.

4. Prepare instructional objectives in behavioral terms that deemphasize the mere acquisition of factual information.

5. In the instructional program, efforts should be made to make success inevitable.

6. Grades and grading procedures should become noncompetitive and noncomparative in order to reduce the pressures that arise. Instead consideration should be given to nongrading techniques based on individual evaluation methods and utilizing performance criteria.

7. Permit and encourage openness in classrooms, including freedom of expression, experiences, choices, and a variety of alternative opinions or data to make student decisions possible.

8. Teachers should try to act humanly in all relationships with students. They should express the feelings and attitudes of joy, anger, laughter, and sadness that anyone would experience. Students should be accepted as they are and not as someone wishes them to be. Tolerance should be exercised in terms of dress, appearance, errors, ability, and achievement.

9. School personnel should develop trust in students as individuals. They should show interest in their pupils and should be understanding. They should treat students honestly, fairly, justly, and without bias or prejudice.

10. Encourage increased and improved communications between school personnel and students. Administrators might tour the buildings more frequently and talk with students. Teachers might have lunch with pupils on occasion.

11. Students should be listened to more frequently and more intently. When listening, school personnel should do so with interest, making no attempt at judgments or evaluations. They should listen for positive thoughts rather than disagreements and for the general ideas expressed rather than the details.

12. In junior and senior high schools flexible class scheduling should be used.

13. Disciplinary procedures should be reviewed in terms of their intent. Are they punitive or are they in the best interest of the students?

14. Teachers need to be involved to a greater extent in school affairs and should have opportunities for freedom of expression and decision making regarding curriculum, instructional practices, and other procedures.

15. The atmosphere of the school should be open for both teachers and students; freedoms should be given every consideration and the climate should be one of warmth, friendliness, and security.

Special humane consideration must be given to the poor minority and ghetto children and youth who attend schools. Washington states: "Too often deprived children encounter in the school an institution out of touch with the reality they know. All too often such factors diminish rather than enlarge the child's view of himself and his world. Children learn not what they are told but what they experience. The child who is hostile, insecure, and unsuccessful needs to know adults who are secure, successful and free of hostility."[36] She further says that the student who comes to school with the frustration and unappeased physical and emotional needs found in a life of poverty and often compounded by prejudice expects the same rejection that he has learned from society. Educators therefore must develop approaches to these compelling needs, especially for the poor minority youth.

These hypotheses for teacher-student-group relationships need consideration:

1. The student self-concept is a significant factor in his ability to learn.

2. The student must be valued as an individual.

3. Every child wants to succeed.

4. The student's belief in himself must be nurtured if he is to grow emotionally and intellectually.

5. True learning will take place only

if the student is an involved participant in the process.

6. The power structure and the learning situation must be understood and used to advantage because the child needs both the support of peers and the opportunity to differentiate himself from others.

To implement these suggestions will involve radical changes in schools today. That such changes are possible may be demonstrated in the very liberal approach to the application of the concept of humaneness found in three schools. Broad provision is made for freedom of thought and action, with the goal being that students will achieve self-actualizations toward learning. These attempts focus on the belief by certain authorities that schools need not have walls. These illustrations may be especially useful among minority youths, drop-outs, and those in deprived areas. Drug abusers could profit by experiences in these schools.

The Summerhill School in England is a small, private institution that has no requirements, rules, homework, regulation, role-taking, grades, texts, or social conventions.[9] The theory behind this approach is that a free child is a happy child and eventually becomes a responsible child. There is the feeling that true discipline comes from the self.

The Benjamin Franklin Parkway High School in Philadelphia comprises 60% black and 40% white students and also stresses much freedom and individual initiative.[17] It is a school that apparently has no schoolhouse. It says its place of learning is anywhere and everywhere. Students may be admitted with parental consent simply by showing interest. The students must meet the same requirements for graduation as in any other city school. The emphasis in the school is on making students self-reliant, self-directed, and responsible individuals who will be worthwhile members of society. The students are placed in groups of 15 with one full-time faculty member assigned to each group. The humanistic atmosphere is one of tolerance, friendliness, optional dress (no codes), with teachers and students on a first-name basis, attendance optional, people accepted as they are, no grades, no rigid requirements, no competitiveness, smoking permitted, no strict authority or discipline, and no limits on personal freedom. Students and faculty discuss together what they want to know, or learn, and teachers explain to students what they need to know. Teachers write evaluations of students' work but give no grades.

The Wilson School in Mankato, Minnesota, reaches students from ages 3 to 19 and has tried to develop a humane school.[14] It operates under these main provisions: students choose their own instructors, select their own adviser-counselors, plan their own course of study through individual conferences, have no required classes, follow an open-campus policy, may go home if nothing interesting is being offered because attendance is optional, have no established number of courses to take or required length of time to complete them, and are evaluated in terms of learning objectives through conferences with instructors and parents. The program is individually diagnosed and prescribed for each student but there are no graduation requirements. Also, students are encouraged to take as much work outside the school as possible, including trips with parents, work in local governments and in hospitals, and other experiences.

• • •

In summary, it should be evident that the school atmosphere may play a significant role in the drug misuse and abuse problems of those students prone to abuse drugs; the atmosphere is important in facilitating effective learning. To help prevent drug difficulties and to obtain the best results from the learning process, it is important that schools be cognizant of (1) the reasons for student alienation and unrest, (2) the physical and psychological needs of pupils, and (3) the significance of creating humane schools. The data reveal that there is much work ahead if schools are to develop the atmosphere necessary for student self-actualization in self-directed learning. When students in large numbers, including drop-outs and other nonachievers, begin to say, "I want to go to school," such a goal will show evidence of realization.

References

1. Alschuler, A. S.: Humanistic education, Educ. Technol. **10**:58-61, 1970.
2. Borton, T.: Reach, touch and teach: student concerns and process education, New York, 1970, McGraw-Hill Book Co., Inc.
3. Cornacchia, H. J., et al.: Health in elementary schools, ed. 3, St. Louis, 1970, The C. V. Mosby Co.
4. Dearden, M. H.: Adolescent drug abuses— a problem of interpersonal relations and school organization, J. Drug Educ. **1**:205-215, 1971.
5. Dearden, M. H., and Jekal, J. F.: A pilot program in high school drug education utilizing non-directive techniques and sensitivity training, J. Sch. Health **41**:118-124, 1971.
6. Dorr, R.: Sensitivity training, Sch. Health Rev. **1**:38-40, 1970.
7. Drug crisis: schools fight back with innovative programs, Washington, D. C., 1971, National School Public Relations Association.
8. Education USA Special Report: Individually prescribed instruction, Washington, D. C., 1968, National School Public Relations Association.
9. Emery, R. C.: Existentialism in the classroom, J. Teacher Educ. **22**:5-9, 1971.
10. Erikson, E. H.: Identity: youth and crisis, New York, 1968, W. W. Norton & Co., Inc.
11. Frankl, V. E.: Man's search for meaning, New York, 1959, Washington Square Press.
12. Gerzon, M.: The whole world is watching: a young man looks at dissent, New York, 1969, The Viking Press, Inc.
13. Glasser, W.: The effect of school failure on the life of a child. In National Association of Elementary School Principals: The elementary school: humanizing? dehumanizing?, Washington, D. C., 1971, National Education Association.
14. Glines, D. E.: Creating humane schools, Mankato, Minn., 1971, Campus Publishers.
15. Goodman, P.: High school is too much, Psychol. Today **4**:25-26, 1970.
16. Gottlieb, D.: Alienation and rebellion among the disadvantaged, Paper presented at the fourteenth Annual Conference of Mental Health Representatives of State Medical Societies, sponsored by the American Medical Association Council on Mental Health, Chicago, March 15, 1968.
17. Greenberg, J. D., and Roush, R. E.: A visit to the "school without walls," Phi Delta Kappan **51**:480-484, 1970.
18. High school student unrest, Washington, D. C., 1969, National School Public Relations Association.
19. Junell, J. S.: Is rational man our first priority? Phi Delta Kappan **52**:147-151, 1970.
20. Keniston, K.: Drug use and student values, Paper presented at the National Association of Student Personnel Administrators Drug Education Conference, Washington, D. C., November, 1966.
21. Keniston, K.: The uncommitted: alienated youth in American society, New York, 1965, Dell Publishing Co., Inc.
22. King, S. H.: Youth and society, Paper presented at the Annual Convention, National Congress of Parents and Teachers, San Diego, Calif., May 21, 1968.
23. Kohn, P. M., and Mercer, G. W.: Drug use, drug-use attitudes, and the authoritarianism-rebellion dimension, J. Health Soc. Behav. **12**:125-131, 1971.
24. Krutch, J. W.: A humanist's approach, Phi Delta Kappan **51**:376-378, 1970.
25. Lee, W. S.: Human relations training for teachers: the effectiveness of sensitivity training, Calif. J. Educ. Res. **21**:28-34, 1970.
26. Levy, N. J.: The use of drugs by teenagers for sanctuary and illusion, Paper presented at the symposium on *Our Youth: Apathy, Rebellion and Growth* at the Carnegie Endowment International Center, New York, November 12, 1966.
27. Malcolm, A.: Drug abuse and social alienation, Today's Educ. **59**:28-31, 1970.
28. Maslow, A. A.: Motivation and personality, New York, 1954, Harper & Row, Publishers.
29. Meeds, L.: Drug abuse as a reaction to the stresses of growing up, Sch. Health Rev. **1**:3-5, 1970.
30. Moustakas, C.: Personal growth: the struggle for identity and human values, Cambridge, Mass., 1969, Howard A. Doyle Publishing Co.
31. National Association of Elementary School Principals: The elementary school: humanizing? dehumanizing? Washington, D. C., 1971, National Education Association.
32. Prettyman, R. L., et al.: Drug abuse and the school scene, Sci. Teacher **35**:45-47, 1970.
33. Protest in the sixties, Ann. Am. Acad. Polit. Soc. Sci. vol. 382, March, 1969.
34. Randolph, N., and Howe, W.: Self-enhancing education: a program to motivate learners, Palo Alto, Calif., 1966, Sanford Press.
35. Roszak, T.: The making of a counter culture, Garden City, N. Y., 1969, Anchor Books.
36. Scoby, M. M., and Graham, G., editors: To nurture humaneness: commitment for the 70's,

Washington, D. C., 1970, Association for Supervision and Curriculum Development.

37. Siberman, C. E.: Crisis in the classroom: the remaking of American education, New York, 1970, Random House, Inc.

38. Simmons, J. L., and Winograd, B.: It's happening: a portrait of the youth scene today, Santa Barabara, Calif., 1966, Marc-Laird Publications.

39. Simon, S., et al.: The day the consultant looked at our grading system, Phi Delta Kappan 51:476-479, 1970.

40. Small, G. R.: Humanism in education, Clearing House 43:195-197, 1968.

41. Smith, D. E., and Luce, J.: Love needs care, Boston, 1970, Little, Brown & Co.

42. Suchman, E. A.: The hang-loose ethic and the spirit of drug use, J. Health Soc. Behav. 9:146-155, 1968.

43. Wertheimer, P. A.: School climate and student learning, Phi Delta Kappan 52:527-530, 1971.

44. Wright, T. H.: Learning to listen: a teacher's or a student's problem? Phi Delta Kappan 52:625-628, 1971.

45. Wynne, E.: Student unrest re-examined, Phi Delta Kappan 53:102-104, 1971.

46. Yablonsky, L.: The hippie trip, New York, 1969, Pegasus.

47. Yearbook 1966: learning and mental health in school, Washington, D. C., 1966, Association for Supervision and Curriculum Development.

48. Yolles, S. F.: Prevention of drug abuse. In Resource book for drug abuse education, Chevy Chase, Md., 1969, National Institute of Mental Health, National Clearinghouse for Mental Health Information.

CHAPTER 10

COORDINATION OF THE SCHOOL DRUG PROGRAM

For the school drug program to function efficiently, the segments—education, services, and atmosphere—must be coordinated. Interrelationships that exist between the segments must be clarified and an administrative organization must be established in order to mold the various aspects of the program into a smoothly functioning, effective operation that will have impact on children and youth. Thus coordination as herein described will refer to (1) resolving administrative problems, (2) establishing the administrative organizational structure, (3) developing policies and procedures, (4) financing the program, and (5) providing in-service preparation.

Although this chapter will focus primarily on matters relating to local schools and school districts, a number of problems and matters pertaining to national and state activities will also briefly be considered.

ADMINISTRATIVE PROBLEMS

At the national level three major problems need attention at present: coordination of agency efforts in resolving the drug problem, financial support to states, and the dichotomy of philosophical approach to school drug prevention programs between state and federal authorities.

1. Until the passage of the Drug Abuse Office and Treatment Act of 1972, a number of federal agencies were independently involved in drug education, treatment, rehabilitation, training, and research programs that were separately funded. The

Office of Education (OE), the National Institute of Mental Health (NIMH), the Bureau of Narcotics and Dangerous Drugs (BNDD), the Law Enforcement Assistance Administration (LEAA), among others, occasionally participated in overlapping and duplicating activities. However, Jerome H. Jaffe, M.D., was appointed by President Nixon as Special Consultant to the President for Narcotics and Dangerous Drugs* in 1971, and the Special Action Office for Drug Abuse Prevention (SAODAP) with direct communication to the President was created. The 1972 legislation gave this office the official support needed to take action. SAODAP now has authority over all federal programs or activities relating to drug abuse education, training, treatment, rehabilitation, and research, irrespective of the agencies that run them. There are 19 federal departments and agencies engaged in non-law enforcement aspects of drug abuse prevention. SAODAP's charge is to coordinate, evaluate, and help improve services. Its major task, or problem, is to mold this amorphous, diverse, and conglomerate group of independent bureaucracies into a cohesive, effective organizational structure.

2. The question of adequate and continued federal support to state educational agencies may be crucial if many of the

---

*Press release from the Office of the White House Press Secretary, June 17, 1971, regarding appointment of Dr. Jaffe as Special Consultant on Narcotics and Dangerous Drugs to the President of the United States.

drug education programs are to survive. The discontinuation of such funds will unquestionably cause numerous states to remove the administrators now employed. In addition, unless the states themselves are willing to budget funds from their own sources for these services, some programs will suffer through curtailment and others will disappear. At this writing it appears that federal funds will be available through 1972 and 1973. It also seems evident that no direct program funds to states on a per capita basis will be provided to state education departments in 1974 but these funds will be available to states for the development and evaluation of model programs on a competitive basis. It is hoped, however, that should federal monies fail to be provided beyond the identified dates, individual states will subsidize programs directly. To firmly establish school drug programs, much more time is needed beyond that included in currently funded plans.

3. The dichotomy in philosophical approach between states and the federal government regarding primary and secondary prevention emphasis is extremely important because of the confusion it causes. Although state legislatures are mandating primary prevention through education, federal agencies are prematurely generalizing that education has not been effective and plan to diminish stress on certain aspects of education, to fund programs that emphasize early recognition of drug abusers, and to focus on secondary prevention procedures. The 1973 budget apparently reflects this change through lowered financial support. Less than 3% of a total of $750 million will be provided to various educational projects emanating out of the Office of Education.

At the state level, where state department of education offices are generally responsible for school programs, funds and coordination with other state agencies are critical matters but 12 state drug education directors who attended the National Drug Education Training Center conducted at San Francisco State College in 1970 identified the following problems as the most significant in need of attention:

1. The question of state commitment to a school drug program by providing funds supplemental to those received from the federal government
2. Several state agencies participating concurrently in the development of independent drug programs, thereby creating difficulties in communication and in appeals for financial support
3. Influences of conservative-liberal and left- and right-wing groups who advocate varying approaches to program emphasis
4. Attempts by politicians to use the drug problem for political advantages and not primarily to help young people with their difficulties
5. Weak leadership by the superintendent of public instruction in refusing to consider innovative and creative approaches to the resolution of the drug problem
6. Lack of qualified leadership to conduct school drug programs together with brief, inadequate in-service preparation programs for school personnel
7. Education department difficulties in obtaining cooperation from other state agencies with regard to coordinating efforts and avoiding overlapping and duplication
8. The need for special emphasis on problems of children and youth from minority groups or ghettos
9. Recognition and clarification of the need for and the extent of the use of youth and parents, including those from the "hippie subculture," in drug programs
10. Difficulties in demonstrating accountability in schools whose evaluation procedures focus primarily on educational goals in the cognitive domain instead of in the affective and action domains; additional con-

cern in those states where financial aid is provided and expected results must be demonstrated with evidence clearly showing a reduction in drug use among students

11. Difficulties in marshaling a total community attack on the drug problem because schools are frequently omitted or schools fail to include the community

12. Methods of gaining support and involving the communication media

Although this book is not directed at solving state problems, much of the content herein is applicable and useful. It appears that funds are needed, cooperation between state agencies is necessary, the removal of politics is vital, and adequate leadership and special emphasis on ghetto problems are important in developing successful programs.

At the local level these critical administrative problems need resolution if an effective school drug program is to emerge:

1. Commitment by school districts to a drug program

2. Delegation of administrative responsibility for the program

3. Determination of school personnel responsibilities and qualifications

4. In-service training of personnel in specific terms (when, how, where, what, who, and funds available)

5. Place of drug education in the curriculum and amount of time to be permitted for it at various grade levels

6. Financial support

7. Role of the school in community action

8. Involvement of students, parents, community organizations, agencies, and other individuals, including the police

ADMINISTRATIVE ORGANIZATION

In order for the administrative problems outlined to receive consideration for resolution and if a school drug program is to have a chance of success, an organizational structure consisting of basically two essentials is necessary. These are (1) someone delegated with the responsibility to direct and conduct the drug program and (2) an advisory drug committee. Such an administrative arrangement is also necessary at federal and state levels.

At the federal level Dr. Jerome Jaffe is the director of the Special Action Office for Drug Abuse Prevention. His advisory committee, the National Advisory Council for Drug Abuse Prevention, makes recommendations to the director in regard to planning, policies, and priorities. In the fall of 1972, President Nixon appointed the 12 members to this committee; it should be noted that not one school or community educator was selected to serve. In addition, the U. S. Office of Education has a drug education branch. Dr. Helen Nowlis is the present director of this office, the functions of which include approving state project and other grants, providing leadership, aiding in program planning and evaluation, and giving technical assistance to school and community education programs. In 1972 through 1973 it established eight regional centers in the United States designed to provide training for personnel and assistance to school and community education programs. For several years a National Action Committee of 28 members, including students, educators, school administrators, psychologists, pharmacologists, community and federal agency representatives, assisted with some of these functions. The commmittee was disbanded in 1972 after the appointment of Dr. Jaffe and the reorganization of the drug education segment of the Office of Education.

At the state level practically all states have appointed a coordinator of drug programs with direct responsibility to the governor. In addition, the receipt of federal funds by state offices of public instruction and the assurance that such funds will be continued for several more years have resulted in the designation of an administrator for drug programs in every state and territory in the United States. Many of the larger states have employed several staff members. In California, drug coordinators have been designated for each county within the state. Although the functions of these leaders vary, they generally include the following:

1. Creating awareness of the problem of drug abuse among school and community personnel
2. Providing in-service training for teachers, admininstrators, counselors, and parents
3. Curriculum development or implementation or both
4. Coordination with other state agencies
5. Research and development of new techniques and evaluation
6. Providing resource information and and materials

Many states have also established advisory committees whose members include other state agencies, teachers, administrators, counselors, students, parents, and a variety of community representatives.

A number of the large school districts in this country are employing administrative personnel, identified as drug coordinators, drug education coordinators, drug program directors, and by other names, on a full-time basis with responsibility for drug programs. The frequency and extent of such action is not known. Where such specialists are found, there may also be a committee, comprising people from the school and from the community, to provide help with the program. Although no established criteria serve as guidelines in the selection of a coordinator, these personal attributes should be sought:

1. Is approachable by students
2. Is able to communicate easily with young people, teachers, and administrators
3. Has the ability to accurately articulate student concerns
4. Has interest in and empathy for children and adolescents
5. Is a good listener
6. Is able to work successfully with others, including community resource and agency personnel
7. Is familiar with the drug scene or is willing to acquire such understanding

No attempt has been made to specify the responsibilities of drug coordinators. However, sufficient information is given here for individual school districts to establish such functions locally.

In the San Francisco Unified School District, California, in addition to administrative assistance and an advisory committee, several elementary and all junior and senior high schools have drug resource teachers who (1) assist other teachers with their drug education programs and (2) help develop and maintain drug information centers in their respective schools.

In the Coronado School District, California, a specialist was employed to develop a drug abuse prevention program with a three-phased approach: (1) identification of potential high-risk takers (drug abusers), (2) a drug education program for grades K through 12, and (3) evaluation procedures.

The establishment of a school drug advisory committee is not only of value at the federal and state levels but has special significance at the local level. It is usually the motivating force behind programs and serves as the bridge between the schools and the community. The composition of this committee must be determined in each school district, but it should comprise a variety of school and community representatives, including students and parents. Responsibilities will differ, but the following are suggested functions:

1. Help develop procedures for identifying drug users and abusers.
2. Prepare procedures for referral and treatment of students using drugs.
3. Encourage the development of a comprehensive educational program.
4. Aid in efforts to coordinate the school, home, and community.
5. Aid in the development of parent education programs.

6. Support and encourage in-service programs.
7. Help prepare and determine school policies and procedures.
8. Aid in the selection of the drug coordinator.
9. Provide assistance in conducting surveys to determine the extent of the drug problem among students.
10. Assist in the selection of instructional resource materials.
11. Help design procedures for evaluating the drug program.

POLICIES AND PROCEDURES

Schools and school districts need written policies and procedures for the total drug program (education, services, atmosphere, and coordination) that (1) clearly identify the actions that school personnel may take, (2) establish the lines of authority, and (3) determine the responsibilities of all staff members. Without such statements, the boards of education, superintendents of schools, teachers, counselors, and other personnel may be unfairly obligated to handle drug problems when they are not assured of school support or are unclear about what action is to be taken. Cooperative effort on the part of both schools and law enforcement agencies in developing policies is needed if the confusion regarding the handling of students who violate the law and of other related matters is to be clarified.

In the development and implementation of administrative guidelines, school personnel should consider the student's welfare and positive therapeutic approaches to pupil's problems first rather than turn to punitive solutions. It is most important that schools make the effort to find alternatives to legal action for student drug offenders. It is felt by some that the school's authority and responsibility should be confined to student actions on school property or during regular school-sponsored activities. However, it may be necessary to extend this responsibility to relations with police, probation departments, community organizations, jails, and other agencies as long as the purpose is focused on the education of the individual.

Whenever action is to be taken regarding students, schools should consider each case on its own merit and in regard to the total behavior of the individual. In addition, procedures regarding drugs should be established whereby all avenues for correction and rehabilitation within the school setting are exhausted prior to considering suspension or expulsion. This latter action should be a "last resort," taken only when all possible efforts to help have failed.

The "hard line" approach in dealing with drug users may seriously impair the possibility of meaningful dialogue between students and school personnel regarding drugs. Such a policy undoubtedly leads to distrust, suspicion, and withdrawal by students. It ignores the argument that punishment treats the symptom and not the cause, thereby complicating the problem of rehabilitation. However, school officials agree that pressure must be brought to bear on pushers of drugs, with less severe treatment applied to those students who are only users of drugs.

In all cases involving drugs, the school principal will probably play the major role. Before making a decision, however, he should obtain as much information as possible by consulting with teachers, counselors, nurses, physicians, parents, and friends. The principal is the one who will have to interpret the policy and make adjustments in its application when necessary. This interpretation should be governed by sympathy and understanding so that any action taken will aid in the rehabilitation and continued education of students.

The policies and procedures established by school districts should cover the entire school drug program. More specifically they should include:

1. The educational phase
2. The services phase, identifying drug users and abusers and what to do for abusers in emergencies, crisis intervention situations, students under

the influence, and related conditions
3. The school atmosphere and the role of school personnel
4. Coordination of the total program with attention to law violations involving possession, sale, and other matters related to drugs whether they occur on campus or during school-related activities or off campus and not under school supervision but where schools may intervene upon request of parents, the police, or others

Material in Chapters 7 to 9 also provides information that needs to be included in the policies and procedures to be established. The following material additionally considers important student relations as well as the legal and law enforcement aspects of handling students involved in drugs.

Guidelines

These questions, many of which have been developed by the Salinas Union High School District, California, may provide assistance in determining the role of the school in handling students involved with drugs:

1. Must drug or narcotic offenses be committed while the student is under the supervision of the school for school officials to become involved?
2. What is the school's position when drug offenses are committed off campus and not under school supervision?
3. How should schools handle a student who is referred to the office by school personnel because he is under the influence or in possession of a drug or narcotic?
   a. Should the parents be notified by the school?
   b. Are there situations in which the parents may not be notified?
   c. Should juvenile authorities be notified?
   d. Should the school treat the student?
4. How should schools handle a student who voluntarily reports to the office, admits use of a drug or narcotic, and requests assistance with his problem?
   a. Should the parents be contacted if the student objects?
   b. Should juvenile authorities be notified?

5. What standards of evidence should the school use in determining whether a student has wrongfully used, sold, or been in possession of prescribed drugs or narcotics?
   a. Police record?
   b. Probation or court record?
   c. Should the school take action without due process (punitive or protective suspension)?
6. Should the school recommend professional counseling for students identified as drug users?
   a. With parental consent?
   b. Without parental consent?
   c. What agencies? Law enforcement? Probation? County medical department? Specialist employed by the school district? Others?
7. What are the legal responsibilities of the district and of school personnel?
8. How are confiscated drugs to be handled by school personnel?
9. What is to be done when outsiders are found dealing with drugs in school?
10. How can conflicts between enforcement agencies and the schools be resolved?
11. How should law enforcement personnel be handled when they come to school?
12. Should undercover policemen be used in schools to search out drug traffic?

Suggested areas to include in policies

When specific policies and procedures are being established, a school drug abuse advisory committee should be formed to assume the responsibility for developing a proposal to be placed before the school board. There are no prescriptions regarding the composition of committee membership; however, the committee should have broad representation, including students, parents, and community representatives. The committee should obtain advice from legal sources and the police in the preparation of proposals. The suggestions that follow may be used in the preparation of policies and procedures.

It should be noted that the legal concept of "in loco parentis," which has given schools parental responsibility over students, appears to be changing, is being replaced, or will be replaced by the principle of "student rights." The question of the infringement of the rights of minors is being challenged by recent court and legal actions. By way of illustration, state laws permitting students to receive venereal disease counseling and drug abuse guidance without parental approval or knowledge are indications of greater changes that may take place in the future. In addition, the questions of due process, consultation with a lawyer, avoidance of self-incrimination, identification of civil and legal rights of children, and the cross-examination of hostile witness are being considered by the courts. In an attempt toward clarity, some school districts have prepared lists of student rights. Therefore the suggestions and illustrations in this book may not be entirely applicable in some states or in the near future.

SUSPENSION AND EXPULSION. The laws of each particular state in regard to suspension and expulsion need to be given consideration. However, these thoughts should help:

1. Resort to suspension or expulsion only after careful study of all the facts and when no other approach is found to be feasible.
2. Only after due process is supported by records of testimony and not simply hearsay or supposition evidence should a student be suspended or expelled.
3. Contact parents as soon as possible to discuss appropriate action. A student showing an emotional or psychological problem should be directed to help.
4. The evidence must be definite and concrete that the student's behavior will interfere with the maintenance of discipline and the learning process of other students in the school or to the student's own physical or mental health.
5. Reputable advice from a variety of sources must indicate such action to be in the best interest of the student in terms of his intellectual and social development.
6. Advise the student as to vocational and other educational opportunities that he may be required or encouraged to pursue and that may be useful in his gaining readmission.

RIGHTS OF STUDENTS WITH REGARD TO SEARCH. Federal laws permit school authorities the "reasonable right to inspection of school property and premises" even though such areas have been set aside for the exclusive use of a particular student. Hence inspection of student lockers and their contents is permissible when the evidence supports such action. However, such search usually may not include individual belongings (pockets, purses, etc.). The right to inspect becomes a duty when parents surrender their children to the public schools (in loco parentis) and expect certain safeguards to occur. Inspections should not be undertaken without careful thought and then only for clearly compelling reasons.

In New York City these guidelines are in force:

1. School personnel may search lockers, closets, desks, and similar areas under school control "at any time."
2. A teacher seeing a student "in possession" of narcotics or a hypodermic instrument may immediately search the student or place him under a citizen's arrest for search by the police.
3. A teacher may also search any student who, in the "opinion" of the teacher, is "reasonably suspected" of possessing drugs or drug instruments. Reasonable suspicion is more than mere suspicion and should be based on "concrete personal observations," or at least on "apparently reliable" information from other students.
4. Information from student informants may be the sole basis for a search if the informant has, in the past, given information that has proved to be "consistently accurate" in two or three separate instances.
5. Indiscriminate searches are to be avoided. Although they are "not per se illegal," they offend everyone's "sensibilities" and undermine the status and credibility of school authorities.
6. All personal searches are to be made

by school personnel, with police to be called in only for protection.

In New York City the last regulation takes on added significance because of a decision by the New York State Supreme Court in the case of a teacher searching a youth suspected of possessing narcotics. The court said the teacher, acting in loco parentis, or in the place of a parent, needed only a "reasonable suspicion" to justify the search, although a policeman in the same circumstances would be bound by stricter standards of search and seizure. The case involved the arrest of a 16-year-old youth for the possession of a hypodermic needle and related equipment discovered by a teacher during a search. The court agreed, in a 2-to-1 decision, that a school official stood in the place of a parent with regard to the pupils in his care. They said the official had an obligation to protect the children from harmful and dangerous influences, which would include narcotics.

RIGHTS OF STUDENTS WITH RESPECT TO QUESTIONING. The following rights of students must be honored:

1. Notice of charges—specific charges to be made at any hearing should be given in advance to parents or to the individual defending the student.
2. Right to counsel—student may be represented by his parents or legal counsel at any hearing.
3. Right to cross-examination and confrontation—parents and others may do so.
4. Privilege against any degree of self-incrimination—parents and others should know that, according to the Fifth Amendment, students may refuse to answer questions that might incriminate themselves.
5. Right of transcript of proceedings—a copy should be available to student and parents.
6. Right of appellate review—case can be reviewed by a higher authority.

PERSONAL RECORDS. The question of whether or not to record the drug incidents of students should receive careful study. If they are to be recorded, they should be kept in a separate folder for the exclusive use of school officials in developing constructive plans for student rehabilitation. They should not be part of the student's permanent record, and access to this information should be limited to specifically designated persons.

READMISSION. Any student suspended or expelled because of drug-related problems should have the right to be readmitted. The decision should be based on a review of (1) the steps taken to seek solutions to the problems that were the basis for the suspension and (2) the medical and psychiatric records from treatment and rehabilitation agencies and other available records. School authorities should be assured that an honest attempt has been made by the student to deal with the problem while in school. It may be necessary to establish a review board.

CONFIDENTIALITY AND POLICE RELATIONS. "Most schools are uncertain about their role regarding privileged communication—whether the drug-using youngster who confides in a school representative should be reported to his parents, the police or even the school administrator."[18] The teacher, counselor, or other school official often faces the dilemma of wanting to assist students by establishing communication and trust and yet trying to resolve the question of possibly breaking the law. In order to protect himself, the individual often feels obligated to report confidential information to some authority.

It is clear that teachers, counselors, and others need to feel secure when relating to a drug-involved student and must display confidence when in this role. Policies and procedures should be clearly established so that when a student confides to a school official that he or she is using drugs, that individual is able to be honest and forthright with the student. He should try to help the student understand the full ramifications of this involvement and motivate him or her to a decision for positive action.

The law on confidentiality is vague in some states, except for such persons as doctors and lawyers. However, courts[13] in several states say that merely failing to inform public authorities about felonies that may, or may not, have been committed is not breaking the law. In Connecticut[12] the law states that any professional employee who in good faith discloses, or does not disclose, such professional communication shall be immune from any liability, civil or criminal. In Maryland[19] these legal protections are operative:

1. Whenever a student seeks help about a drug problem from a teacher, counselor, administrator, or other individual, no statement made by the student or observations of the educator are admissible in any court proceeding.
2. Educators do not have to inform parents about students seeking help about drug problems, nor must they divulge the identity of students.
3. Any young person, including those under 18 years of age, may receive treatment for a problem of drug abuse without parental consent, and the physician is not legally bound to inform the parents.

It is important to consider the role of the school as focusing on the welfare of the student. Therefore this consideration should enable confidentiality to become a tool with which the school may better fulfill its educational function. Breaking the trust of the student who reveals confidential information will shut off communication at a time when it may be vitally needed.

Counselors recognize that any information given to them during an interview usually constitutes hearsay evidence and is, therefore, not ordinarily admissible in court. However, there are exceptions to this rule and it is clear that schools must establish policies and procedures regarding this important matter or should obtain interpretations as to the legal provisions of confidentiality applicable in their individual communities.

At times schools may wish police to conduct investigations of students suspected of drug activities, or police themselves may wish to investigate. When drugs are being sold on campus, it will be necessary to take action and to work with the police to apprehend the pusher and to confiscate the drugs. In addition, police may be willing to turn over suspected drug abusers to the schools for guidance and help. Police may offer to assist with the school educational and guidance programs. They may be of help in the decision on confidentiality. In any event, schools should appoint one person to establish liaison and to coordinate actions between the police and the schools.

COUNSELING, GUIDANCE, AND REHABILITATION. The follow-up procedures schools establish to help students should include counseling, guidance, and rehabilitation (Chapter 8).

UNDERCOVER POLICEMEN ON CAMPUS. The question of using undercover policemen on campus to ferret out drug pushers is not easily resolved. Apparently parents would prefer this arrangement to having dope pushers sitting in classes with their children. However, certain students believe that police spies may produce attitudes of tension and mistrust, resulting in greater student unrest, which is not necessary in the school setting. The decision to use policemen must be weighed carefully in terms of the severity of the drug problem. Basically, an undercover operation should be the action of last resort in attempting to handle the drug situation and should only be instituted when all other means to resolve the problem have been explored and rejected.

ILLUSTRATIONS OF SCHOOL DISTRICT POLICIES AND PROCEDURES

The policies and procedures from the Newton Public Schools, Massachusetts, and the Los Angeles City Schools, California, have been selected to serve as illustrations. No attempt has been made at evaluation. These policies and procedures represent two approaches that schools and school districts may find useful.

Newton Public Schools, Massachusetts

Procedure for drug abusers

1. As soon as a student is positively identified as a drug abuser in the school, or as one who engages in drug traffic in the school, the principal will send him home after notifying the parents, inviting them in for an appointment to explain the issue (a copy of the letter should go to the superintendent). The understanding will be that the student must remain under the constant surveillance of the parents while he is at home. At this point the principal will notify the Supervisor of Attendance (using only one person as the liaison between the schools and the police should reduce the communications problem) who in turn will informally notify the police of the action taken by the principal.

2. The student will be readmitted to the school only after he has had both a physical and a psychiatric clearance. The physical evaluation can be done either by a private physician or the Newton Department of Public Health. The psychiatric evaluation can be done privately by the Newton Mental Health, Massachusetts General Hospital or some other comparable agency. If these facilities are not available, the school psychiatrists will do the evaluation. Whenever private physicians, psychiatrists, or other evaluating personnel have completed their work, they should send their reports to the Chief Psychologist of the Division of Pupil Personnel. The physical and psychiatric clearance will be an assurance that the student has enough stability to re-enter the mainstream of school activities.

3. If the student is unable to get clearance after a reasonable period of treatment, the principal shall then forward a recommendation to the School Committee that they drop the boy or girl from the school roster. The action would be a last resort, with recognition that the student's removal by no means solves his problem.

Obviously, before step one can take place the student drug abuser must be identified. To do this, each teacher will be asked to pass on any information (fact or hearsay) to the principal. Once the principal has collected enough information and proof, he may then take step one as recommended; otherwise he will continue to receive and sift the information. No one should minimize the importance of the principal's role in this very sensitive position.

The relationship between the schools and the police must be very close and continuous. Each agency has to extend itself more than they do at present. The schools must not withhold information on the grounds that the police are interested only in law enforcement. On the other hand, the police must be sensitive to the schools' interest in the student's therapy, and must not act hastily without consultation with the school authorities. The life of the boy or girl must be paramount in the minds of the members of both agencies.

The schools and the police can gain the confidence of the parents by the judicious handling of individual cases. Surely, if the parents see that both the police and the schools have compassion and concern for their children, they will respond positively toward any efforts of the public agencies. Perhaps the knowledge that public and private agencies within the community are working cooperatively on the problem will help to allay the fears of parents whose children are caught up in the use of drugs.

Los Angeles City Schools, California*

USE—Pupil suspected of being under the influence of drugs, narcotics, or other harmful substance.

I. Determination of need for medical attention
   A. Evaluate observable symptoms.
   B. Provide for examination by school nurse or physician.
   C. Interview pupil, if he is coherent, in presence of an adult witness.
      1. Question pupil regarding amount and type of narcotic consumed or substance used.
      2. Attempt to determine if pupil is in possession of drug, narcotic, or harmful substance.
      3. Confiscate all physical evidence obtained as a result of investigation.
         a. Seal evidence in an envelope bearing the name of the pupil from whom it was confiscated, the date and time it was confiscated, and the signature of the person who confiscated it.
         b. Provide law-enforcement agency with all confiscated evidence.
   D. Provide for an appropriate period of observation in a supervised, non-classroom environment.
   E. Inform parent or guardian of reasons for the investigation even if pupil is found *not* to have been involved with illegal drugs, narcotics, or other harmful substances.
   F. Refer to procedures outlined below under II if symptoms develop which indicate a need for emergency medical attention.
II. Provision for necessary emergency medical attention

---

*From Drug Abuse Council: Drug abuse control: administrative guidelines, Los Angeles, 1970, Los Angeles City Schools.

A. Provide needed attention.
1. Call ambulance, in accordance with emergency procedures listed on "Accident Instructions" card, or
2. Call law-enforcement agency, or
3. Send pupil, accompanied by a certificated employee, to authorized medical facility listed on "Accident Instructions" card, if procedure listed in 1 or 2 above is not followed.
B. Notify parent, guardian, or authorized person listed on pupil's "Emergency Information" card.
1. Call as soon as possible after emergency arrangements have been made.
2. Request that school be informed regarding pupil's progress.
C. Notify law-enforcement agency if such notification was not made when emergency arrangements were completed.
D. Conduct a thorough investigation by interviewing witnesses and/or pupil's associates and examining school records.
E. Report information, limited to obvious symptoms, to the school nurse or physician for recording on pupil's confidential "Health Record" card.
F. Suspend pupil, and schedule conference with parent and pupil after emergency medical attention has been provided and pupil has recovered from the incident.
G. Consider taking one or more of the following additional actions:
1. Provide for a rehabilitation program within the local school, including the use of one or more of the following: medical supervision, individual and/or group counseling, parent education, opportunity class, opportunity program, etc.
2. Utilize district guidance, counseling, health, and attendance services with appropriate regard for confidentiality and use of privileged information.
3. Provide information, in accordance with district policy, to parent or guardian regarding availability of public and private resource agencies for rehabilitation. . . .
4. Provide for inter-school adjustment (e.g. opportunity transfer, opportunity school).
5. Notify Los Angeles County Probation Department or California Youth Authority regarding the drug involvement of pupils whose cases are active with these agencies.
6. Refer to school physician for recommendation regarding possible need for medical exclusion.

III. Procedures when emergency medical attention is not indicated
A. Evaluate observable symptoms.
B. Provide for examination by school nurse or physician.
C. Interview pupil in presence of an adult witness.
1. Question pupil regarding amount and type of drug or narcotic consumed or of harmful substance used.
2. Attempt to determine if pupil is still in possession of drug, narcotic, or harmful substance.
3. Confiscate all physical evidence obtained as a result of investigation.
   a. Seal evidence in an envelope bearing the name of pupil from whom confiscated, the date and time it was confiscated, and the signature of the person who confiscated it.
   b. Provide law-enforcement agency with all confiscated evidence.
D. Provide for a limited period of observation in a supervised non-classroom environment.
E. Refer to procedures outlined above under item II (A through G) if symptoms indicate a need for emergency medical attention.
F. Utilize the following procedures for pupil if no further symptoms are discernible and is not involved in possession or sale:
1. Inform parent or guardian, and consult with law-enforcement agency at the time of incident. (If pupil does not have a known history of drug abuse nor significant delinquent behavior, further involvement by law-enforcement agency may not be necessary unless additional information is obtained relative to the incident and such action is in the interest of pupil and school.)
2. Schedule an early conference with parent and pupil at school.
3. Consider suspension of pupil, pending formulation of an individualized plan to aid in the solution of pupil's drug abuse problem.
4. Refer to IIG above for additional follow-up procedures, and verify pupil's participation in a rehabilitation program.
G. Determine all related aspects of incident by interviewing witnesses and/or pupil's associates and examining school records for background information.
H. Report information, limited to obvious symptoms, to the school nurse or physi-

cian for recording on pupil's confidential "Health Record" card.

POSSESSION—Pupils suspected of possessing drugs, narcotics, or other harmful substances which are illegal or have the potential for abuse

I. Determination of pupil involvement
   A. Interview pupil in presence of an adult witness.
   B. Request pupil's cooperation in conducting a search of his person and possessions.
      1. Search may include pupil's lockers and other locations at school where it is suspected that illegal drugs, narcotics, or other harmful substances may be hidden.
         a. The search should be made by a school administrator or his delegated certificated representative in the presence of an adult witness.
         b. The search should not be conducted by a security agent unless the pupil has been placed under arrest.
         c. Security agents should not be present when searches are conducted by other school personnel.
      2. Law-enforcement agency should be notified if the pupil continues to be uncooperative after a reasonable effort has been made to gain his cooperation. (A reasonable effort may include requesting parental assistance in gaining pupil's cooperation.)
   C. Determine all related aspects of incident by interviewing witnesses and/or pupil's associates and examining school records for background information.
   D. Confiscate all physical evidence obtained as a result of investigation.
      1. Seal evidence in an envelope bearing the name of the pupil from whom it was confiscated, the date and time it was confiscated, and the signature of the person who confiscated it.
      2. Provide law-enforcement agency with all confiscated evidence.
   E. Inform parent or guardian of reasons for the investigation even if pupil is found *not* to have been in possession at school of illegal drugs, narcotics, or other harmful substances.

II. Procedures when possession is established
   A. Notify law-enforcement agency.
   B. Notify parent or guardian.
      1. If an arrest is made and the pupil is removed from school, a representative of the law-enforcement agency should notify the parent or guardian prior to

the time that the pupil would normally return home from school.
      2. A member of the school staff also may notify the parent or guardian if a pupil is in the custody of a law-enforcement agency.
   C. Suspend pupil, and schedule an early conference with parent and pupil.
   D. Examine pupil's records to aid in determining an appropriate course of action, which may include one or more of the following:
      1. Provide for a rehabilitation program within the local school, such as medical supervision, individual and/or group counseling, parent education, opportunity class, opportunity program, etc.
      2. Utilize district guidance, counseling, health, and attendance services with appropriate regard for confidentiality and use of privileged information.
      3. Provide information to parent or guardian in accordance with district policy regarding the availability of public and private resource agencies for rehabilitation. . . .
      4. Provide for inter-school adjustment (e.g., opportunity transfer, opportunity school).
      5. Notify Los Angeles County Probation Department or California Youth Authority regarding the drug involvement of pupils whose cases are active with these agencies.
      6. Request [Area] Superintendent to initiate expulsion proceedings [when facts warrant such actions].
   E. Follow procedures referred to in "Sale" section (item II) if it is established that the pupil sold or furnished a dangerous drug, narcotic, or other harmful substance to another person, or persons.

SALE—Pupils suspected of selling or furnishing a dangerous drug, narcotic, or other harmful substance to another person, or persons.

I. Determination of pupil involvement
   A. Interview pupil in presence of an adult witness.
   B. Request pupil's cooperation in conducting a search of his person and possessions.
      1. Search may include pupil's lockers and other locations on campus where it is suspected that illegal drugs, narcotics, or other harmful substances may be hidden.
         a. Search should be made by a school administrator or his delegated cer-

tificated representative in the presence of an adult witness.

b. Search should not be conducted by a security agent unless the pupil has been placed under arrest.

c. Security agents should not be present when searches are conducted by other school personnel.

2. Law-enforcement agency should be notified if the pupil continues to be uncooperative after a reasonable effort has been made to gain his cooperation. (A reasonable effort may include requesting parental assistance in gaining pupil's cooperation.)

C. Determine all related aspects of incident by interviewing witnesses and/or pupil's associates and examining school records for background information.

D. Confiscate all physical evidence obtained as a result of investigation.

1. Seal evidence in an envelope bearing the name of the pupil from whom it was confiscated, the date and time it was confiscated, and the signature of the person who confiscated it.

2. Provide law-enforcement agency with all confiscated evidence.

E. Inform parent or guardian of reasons for the investigation even if pupil is found *not* to have been selling or furnishing a dangerous drug, narcotic, or other harmful substance to another person, or persons.

F. Follow procedures referred to in the sections on "Use" and/or "Possession" if it is determined that pupil was involved in use and/or possession.

II. Procedures when sale is verified

A. Notify law-enforcement agency.

B. Notify parent or guardian.

1. If an arrest is made and the pupil is removed from school, a representative of the law-enforcement agency should notify the parent or guardian prior to the time that the pupil would normally return home from school.

2. A member of the school staff also may notify the parent or guardian if a pupil is in the custody of a law-enforcement agency.

C. Suspend pupil, and schedule an early conference with parent and pupil.

1. Provide information, in accordance with district policy, to parent or guardian, regarding the availability of public and private resource agencies for rehabilitation. . . .

2. Inform parent or guardian that pupil will continue to be suspended pending

further investigation and final disposition of the case.

D. Request [Area] Superintendent to initiate expulsion proceedings when facts warrant such action.

ROLE OF SCHOOL PERSONNEL

The entire school staff has responsibility for the drug program. Counselors' functions have been covered in Chapter 9. The duties of psychologists, social workers, and other personnel will need identification. We will now provide what is essentially to be expected of the primary personnel.

1. Superintendent and school board
   a. Provide commitment to a school drug program.
   b. Approve policies and procedures.
   c. Provide funds for a drug coordinator and for conducting the drug program.
   d. Delegate appropriate authority for the development and implementation of the program.

2. Principal
   a. Manage the overall drug program.
   b. Assist in motivation, implementation, and evaluation.
   c. Aid in home and community communication.
   d. Assure compliance with state laws in school policies and procedures.
   e. Help in the selection of qualified teachers.
   f. Encourage and support in-service programs.
   g. Make concerted efforts to improve the school atmosphere.
   h. Give primary consideration to student welfare before taking disciplinary action in drug cases.

3. School physician (where available)
   a. Aid in identifying drug users and abusers.
   b. Serve as liaison with home and community resources.
   c. Assist particularly in the development and implementation of the drug services program.
   d. Serve as a resource person in planning and developing the drug education curriculum and instructional program.

4. School nurse
   a. Be primarily responsible in the drug services program.
   b. Advise both students and teachers regarding drug problems and program.
   c. Respond to emergency situations in schools.
   d. Act as liaison between physicians, school, home, and community resources.
   e. Serve as a resource person in curriculum development and in the instructional program.

5. Teacher
   a. Help identify drug users and abusers through observations of symptomatic behavior.
   b. Be familiar with procedures for handling students with drug problems
   c. Provide school atmosphere conducive to learning.
   d. Conduct drug instructional program.

FINANCING

Perhaps the most crucial aspect of any drug program is the availability of funds for development and implementation. Without financial aid for schools, especially in this tight money period, no program can be planned or made operative. Without federal funds it is questionable whether the wide variety of school programs now under way would ever have been started or could be maintained. It is estimated that it will take at least 3 to 5 years for drug programs to become operational and firmly established. Therefore, unless federal monies are continued and possibly expanded for some years hence, many such programs will suffer or disappear despite excellent funding provided by numerous state governments and local school districts. Such state and local aid, unfortunately, has not been universal nor broad enough to maintain or initiate large numbers of programs to date.

The availability of funds in itself does not assure quality programs. The achievement of quality necessitates the commitment of school boards to drug programs, qualified personnel to conduct these programs, and other factors described in this text. Our major concern, therefore, is to motivate school districts to give high priority to conducting programs that are effective in the lives of children and youth. This book is a result of our concern.

Financial support for drug programs, primarily educational, has come from three governmental levels—federal, state, and local school districts.

At the federal level the primary source of school financial aid has been the Office of Education. Between 1968 and 1970, President Nixon released $3.5 million under the Education Professions Development Act. Each state department of education and territory in the United States was awarded between $40,000 and $210,000, depending on population, to develop educational programs primarily for training teachers. Approximately $500,000 was used to establish the four National Training Centers in Drug Education in the United States previously referred to (we directed one in San Francisco) and to establish the National Action Committee (an advisory group to the Office of Education). Before such funds were available, a number of projects in schools and school districts had been financed under the Bureau of Higher Education Act, Title I, and the Elementary and Secondary School Education Act, Titles III and V.

In 1970 the United States Congress passed the Drug Abuse Education Act of 1970 (Mondale-Meeds Bill), which provided $29 million to be authorized for drug education and prevention over a 3-year period as follows: 1970, $5 million; 1971, $10 million; and 1972, $14 million. Due to the late passage of this legislation, these funds were rescheduled for distribution from 1971 to 1974. This money was designated for institutions of higher education, state and local educational agencies, community programs, and research. At the state education level, support was provided for drug coordinators and for the training of school personnel. About $2.5 million per year has been available to state departments of education, but few or no funds pass to school districts directly. In 1972 through 1973 a large portion of the total budgeted funds was utilized for a variety of community education projects. It is estimated that less than 1% of the entire 1973 to 1974 budget for combating the drug problem in the United States will be allocated to state departments of education.

The Drug Abuse Office and Treatment Act of 1972 established a Special Action Office for Drug Abuse Prevention within the office of the President. The bill provided the needed coordination of all federal agencies involved in drug programs and gave the Special Action Office direct responsibility for all major federal drug abuse prevention, education, treatment, rehabilitation, training, and research programs. Of the $155 million designated over a 3-year period, $100 million was set aside for the treatment and rehabilitation of addicts and $10 million for education. The 1973 budget shows these funds to be greatly increased in the following manner: $244 million for law enforcement; $313 million for treatment and rehabilitation; $105 million for research, evaluation, and coordination; and $66 million for education and training.

Table 10-1 provides information regarding the federal funds provided for drug

Table 10-1. Federal funds for drug abuse programs by category and agency*†

CATEGORY AND AGENCY	MILLIONS OF DOLLARS		
	1969 Estimate	1970 Estimate	1971 Estimate
Law enforcement			
Department of Justice:			
Bureau of Narcotics and Dangerous Drugs (BNDD)	14.8	21.9	27.7
Other	2.4	2.3	3.2
Treasury Department	3.1	12.1	15.7
Subtotal	20.3	36.3	46.6
Treatment and rehabilitation			
Department of Health, Education and Welfare:			
National Institute of Mental Health (NIMH)	21.9	24.7	29.6
Social and Rehabilitation Service	0.6	0.9	1.0
Department of Justice:			
Bureau of Prisons	1.0	1.8	3.1
Law Enforcement Assistance Administration (LEAA)	0.4	6.8	11.2
Office of Economic Opportunity	2.2	4.0	4.0
Subtotal	26.1	38.2	48.9
Education and training			
Department of Health, Education and Welfare:			
Office of Education	0.2	3.7	3.7
NIMH	1.2	3.5	4.3
Department of Justice:			
BNDD	0.4	1.5	1.8
LEAA	0.2	1.2	2.6
Subtotal	2.0	9.9	12.4
Research and other support			
Department of Health, Education and Welfare:			
NIMH	14.1	16.3	18.3
Department of Justice:			
BNDD	3.0	4.0	4.9
Subtotal	17.1	20.3	23.2
Total	65.5	104.7	131.1

*From a Special Report by Bureau of the Budget for the White House, dated February 12, 1970, and updated July 9, 1970.
†1973 estimate (millions of dollars): law enforcement, 244.2; treatment and rehabilitation, 313.0; education and training, 66.4; and research and other support, 105.8.

abuse programs from 1969 to 1971. From $131.1 million in 1971, the estimated total is expected to be increased to almost $750 million in 1973. Of the $66 million scheduled for education and training, approximately $12 million will go to the U. S. Office of Education.

The following are some current sources of federal funds for drug abuse education programs[5]:

Office of Education
Bureau of Educational Personnel Development
Division of Program Resources
Drug Education Branch
400 Maryland Avenue, S.W.
Washington, D. C. 20202

Authority: Drug Abuse Education Act of 1970 (P.L. 91-527)
Purpose: School and community education
Who is eligible: Institutions of higher learning, state and local educational agencies, other public and private education and research agencies, institutions, organizations, and community education projects

Office of Education
400 Maryland Avenue, S.W.
Washington, D. C. 20202

Authority: Elementary and Secondary Education Act, Title III
Purpose: Demonstration projects in drug education
Who is eligible: Only local education agencies

Law Enforcement Assistance Administration
633 Indiana Avenue, N.W.
Washington, D. C. 20530

Authority: Omnibus Crime Control and Safe Streets Act of 1968 (P.L. 90-351)
Purpose: Reduce crime in United States by permitting criminal justice agencies to initiate or participate in drug abuse prevention and education
Who is eligible: Grants only to states and local units of governments and combinations of local units

It is advisable to contact state drug coordinators or administrators in departments of education for further information and assistance regarding these federal sources of funding.

Numerous state governments have provided funds supplementary to the federal support for drug education programs. Arizona, California, Colorado, Oregon, and Washington are illustrative of the states who have made provisions. Colorado's State Department of Education was awarded $153,000 in 1970; its State Department of Health received $100,000 for use in dealing with alcoholism and drug abuse. These funds were in addition to the $40,000 received from the Office of Education. Colorado's departments of education and health worked cooperatively on their educational programs. Many states have continued to provide supportive funds for school training programs in recent years.

The extent of funds provided by local school districts to support drug education programs is not known but many districts have provided moneys. The San Francisco Unified School District, California, made $92,000 available for each of the years 1969, 1970, and 1971 to develop programs for 90,000 students in 137 schools. These funds were used to pay the prorated values and overhead costs of the central office staff, services for former drug users, clerical help, secondary school resource teachers, 15 in-service training courses, and fees for instructional aids and supplies. Many additional professional services and some funds were provided by community agencies and organizations.

Financial support for drug programs in local school districts should be sought through the federal, state, and local sources identified. For federal and state funds it may be advisable to contact the state drug coordinator or director.

IN-SERVICE PREPARATION

Despite the numerous in-service programs for school personnel that have been conducted in the last few years, there is still a great need for continuance and expansion in this area. Many individuals have not been reached to date and a great deal of new research on drugs and new approaches to treatment and rehabilitation are appearing in the literature, making it necessary to keep individuals up to date with current information through periodic refresher meetings or in other appropriate ways. Therefore the material presented in this section is designed to supply ideas for the content and presentation of a variety of orientation programs for those individuals needing an introduction to the drug scene and of updating and growth programs for those in need of such assistance.

Despite the in-service programs that have been conducted, great confusion and lack of understanding still exists regarding the nature of the school drug program. The conceptual model developed herein is unique in its organization for schools. Implementation by a variety of school people is needed if effective programs are to result from this model. Many school programs are greatly fragmented and have developed in piecemeal fashion without identifying any overall purpose. This program, based on clearly identified concepts and purposes, is known to few individuals.

The information that follows should provide suggestions and ideas for those with responsibility for conducting in-service programs for school personnel.

PARTICIPANTS

Programs may be prepared for a variety of school and community people. The schools may desire to include such school personnel as board members, superintendents, assistant superintendents, principals, teachers, counselors, and school nurses; students; and community individuals, including parents, policemen, lawyers, physicians, psychiatrists, and health department staff members. It may be advisable to have small meetings just for counselors, school nurses, or teachers, depending on the problem facing the school. If the gathering is a first in-service meeting for sensitization purposes, it may be advisable for a variety of school personnel, students, and community representatives to participate. The goals to be achieved should determine which groups will participate.

OBJECTIVES

The goals for in-service programs should not only be cognitive in emphasis but also affective and action oriented if at all possible. Thus concern should be given to the attitudes and practices of those in attendance as well as the knowledges and understandings that they should acquire. In addition, emphasis should be given to the spectrum of health, including physiological, pharmacological, social, psychological, and spiritual aspects. These objectives should be adapted according to the nature of the audience, the length of the meeting, and other factors. By way of illustration, a session for school board members and superintendents might try to arouse their interest in and make them feel the need for a drug program that deals humanely with drug users and abusers. A program for teachers may stress cognitive, affective, and action aspects but may also be concerned with the improvement of communication skills in the classroom.

To be specific, an all-inclusive coverage of the drug field is provided in the following overall purposes, from which the appropriate goals may be selected for any given program. These purposes are stated in behavioral terms and are categorized so as to be of practical help in establishing objectives for in-service programs.

1. Cognitive domain
   a. Explain the nature, extent, and significance of the drug problem in society, especially relative to children and youth in the ghetto areas.
   b. Identify the national, state, and local drug laws.
   c. Identify the pharmacological, psychological, sociological, and possibly spiritual effects of drugs on man and society.
   d. Recall the nature of the community organization for effective drug abuse programs.
   e. List the community resources available to help drug abusers.
   f. Explain a variety of significant school drug education programs.
   g. Describe a variety of ways to effectively communicate with children, youth, and the community in order to effect behavioral and attitudinal changes.
   h. Identify a variety of approaches used and community resources available for rehabilitation and treatment of drug users and abusers.
   i. Identify symptomatic behavior of students

who may be misusing and abusing drugs.

j. Recall the school district's policies and procedures for handling drug abusers.

k. Identify the physical and psychological needs of children and youth and understand the relationship of these needs to drug misuse and abuse.

2. Affective domain

a. Appreciate the reasons why youths misuse and abuse drugs.

b. Be interested in developing ways to make the community more aware of the need for drug education programs in schools.

c. Feel more sympathetic toward young people and the stresses and problems facing them in society.

d. Feel more sympathetic toward young misusers and abusers of drugs.

e. Believe that a school drug program is necessary.

f. Feel the need for greater student involvement in school drug programs.

g. Value the need for a school atmosphere conducive to learning.

h. Believe that the stress on students to develop values is necessary in the educational program.

3. Action domain

a. Assess and help others to analyze the drug culture in schools and in society.

b. Organize the community resources to support, assist with, and improve school drug education programs.

c. Help pupils identify alternatives to drug use.

d. Develop a humane classroom atmosphere in school.

e. Plan and develop a curriculum in drug education for grades K through 12.

f. Involve students to a greater degree in school drug programs.

g. Participate in the development of drug education curricula using the concept approach.

h. Demonstrate a variety of techniques for evaluating the school drug program.

i. Evaluate and select drug instructional materials.

j. Provide competent guidance assistance for student drug users and abusers.

k. Provide leadership in the development of policies and procedures for the school drug program.

l. Demonstrate improved skills in the counseling and guidance of drug users and abusers.

m. Develop and improve school drug programs.

n. Prepare others to develop, promote, and improve school drug programs.

o. Help students in their search for identity and for self-actualization in learning.

p. Demonstrate a variety of effective drug education teaching techniques.

ESSENTIAL PROGRAM COMPONENTS

The following brief outline provides in capsule form those essential components, the content, to be included in a total school drug program. In-service programs can utilize whatever portions of the following that they deem appropriate:

1. Physiological or pharmacological aspects—drug classification, definitions, types, methods of administration, form available, effects on body, and medical use

2. Psychological aspects—why drugs used and abused, alternatives to drug use, personalities predisposed to use of drugs, physical and psychological needs of children and youth, and characteristics of abusers and potential misusers

3. Sociological aspects—extent of drug problem (including ghetto areas), youth drug culture, youth alienation and unrest, factors affecting drug use, rehabilitation and treatment, the courts and the law, controls and prevention, history of drugs, and religion and drugs

4. Spiritual aspects—value systems, moral implications, and humanism

5. The school drug program

a. Education—curriculum development, problems, techniques of teaching, resources, youth involvement, and parent education

b. Services—identification of abusers, counseling and guidance, community resources, and adjustment of programs

c. Atmosphere—mental health needs, student unrest, and creating a humane atmosphere

d. Coordination—problems, administrative organization and advisory committee, drug coordinator, and policies and procedures

e. Evaluation

6. Communication procedures—group processes, youth involvement, peer values and pressures, community awareness, and use of multimedia approach.

7. Community resources

ACTIVITIES AND EXPERIENCES

It is recommended that a variety of activities and experiences be provided, with opportunities for selection by participants if individual needs are to be satisfied. This may not be possible where training sessions are of 1 and 2 days' duration, where sufficient staff help is not available, and where community and other resources are limited. Nevertheless the concept of using different approaches is important in planning for in-service programs. These suggestions are not meant to be exhaustive

in nature but rather illustrative of ideas
that have been workable:

1. Large group sessions—speakers, panels, and
   debates
2. Small group sessions to:
   a. Discuss speaker presentations
   b. Exchange ideas
   c. Air biases, prejudices, and views regard-
      ing the drug scene, drug users, youth un-
      rest, and other issues
   d. Meet, communicate with, and even chal-
      lenge youthful drug abusers in or out of
      the drug scene
   e. Learn techniques of improving communi-
      cation
   f. Be exposed to a variety of communica-
      tion exercises and games
   g. Participate in a variety of formal and in-
      formal discussions
   h. Be involved in problem solving centered
      on those problems introduced by partici-
      pants, using such techniques as role play
      and psychodrama
3. Field trips—halfway houses, juvenile deten-
   tion centers, community clinics, youth "drop-
   in" centers, mental hospitals, drug treatment
   units, courtrooms covering drug cases, the
   drug street scene, rock music houses, and
   other community resources concerned with
   drug rehabilitation and treatment
4. Discussions with youths, drug users and
   abusers, and ex-addicts
5. Utilization of community resource speakers—
   police, lawyers, judges, physicians, pharmacologists, psychiatrists, sociologists, and psychologists or, where speakers are not available,
   videotapes or audiotapes (Check with local
   medical centers and other community resources for materials.)
6. Film series, "The Social Seminar," developed
   by the National Institute of Mental Health
   (Address: Box 2305, Rockville, Maryland
   20852.)
7. Time for individuals and groups to view films,
   evaluate resource materials, or read independently whenever possible
8. Workshop periods for curriculum development,
   program planning for teachers, development
   of evaluative instruments, development of
   policies and procedures for school districts,
   and other activities
9. Pretests and posttests of participants' knowledge and attitudes (Suggestions and ideas
   may be found in Chapter 11.)
10. Group process activities[9] to improve com-
    munication and awareness skills
    a. Experimental
       (1) Communication exercises—a person
           speaks precisely to an audience and
           the speech is taped and played back
           to check points covered
       (2) Simulated experiences of acceptance
           and rejection[9]
       (3) Exercises to increase skill in observa-
           tion
       (4) Exercises using group resources
    b. Group processes
       (1) Sensory stimulation—exploring and
           discovering the refreshing and relax-
           ing appeal of the multimedia process,
           including hi-fi records, tapes, TV, films,
           and psychedelic lights
       (2) Peer-group pressure—participants sit
           in a circle and leader asks for a volun-
           teer to walk inside circle. As person
           walks, leader asks if someone wishes
           to join him. Stroller is encouraged
           to describe feelings of being alone
           inside circle. Leader continues to ask
           if anyone will join stroller, to help
           him out. As participants in inner circle
           are added, they are asked to describe
           their feelings and opinions about them-
           selves and the group. Exercise con-
           tinues until leader stops to review
           and analyze the participants' remarks
           (discourse tends to correspond closely
           to discourse of drug users [inner
           group] and nonusers [outer group]).
       (3) Breaking down formalized structures—
           provide different seating arrangements
           and organization of conference each
           day; rearrange chairs; sometimes have
           speaker address from lectern or sitting
           on floor for meetings; occasionally
           move into the community, etc.
       (4) Illustrations of frustrations

ORGANIZATIONAL ARRANGEMENT

When possible, and provided the in-
service session is to continue for 2 to 3
days or more, it is advisable to provide
a "live-in" experience. This is an arrangement where all participants are involved
in close proximity for a specific period of
time at a pleasant location that is removed
from the general work routine. A place
should be selected that is relaxing and
comfortable, and where participants can
communicate during the major part of the
day. The live-in experience offers an excellent opportunity to be informal, to dress
optionally, to get to know participants better, including the students attending, and to
discuss many topics that may not be presented in the planned sessions. Opportunities for social and recreational activities
should be provided. The live-in experience

is a functional, unusual, and effective way to bring about human relationships. It is a continuous training session during which a great deal of work can be accomplished. If a live-in is not possible, sites for in-service training should be selected that will permit informality, comfort, and limited sociability.

There is no single best length of time for a training session. How long it lasts should be determined on the basis of the goals to be achieved and a variety of other logistical factors. It may meet for 1 to 3 hours once a week for 2 or more weeks, 4 to 6 hours for 1 day, 8 to 16 hours over 2 or 3 days (weekend), 1 week, 2 weeks, or longer. To take advantage of the many activities previously identified and to feel somewhat knowledgeable about the drug scene, perhaps a 2-week live-in session, or a comparable series of experiences, is the minimum training to be received. This is especially true if the trainees are to assume leadership roles in schools. Shorter periods might be workable but the attitudinal effect of the drug scene and the possibility of field trips become difficult to realize in short, periodic meetings.

When possible and desirable, the session might be offered through a local college or university so that credit toward a degree or in lieu of class hours could be obtained.

TRAINEE TASKS

When in-service training workshops are conducted with 50 to 100 or more participants and a variety of activities are taking place concurrently, it will be necessary to establish a working arrangement for the participants that will assure total involvement and will also meet the needs of each individual and each group in attendance. This can be accomplished by establishing a series of trainee tasks from which each person chooses those he wishes to complete. These tasks should be a series of feasible performance goals established by the participant with the consent of the workshop director. They should include flexible deadlines for completion. The pro-

cedure used at the National Training Center in Drug Education for State Leaders held at San Francisco State College during the summer of 1970 illustrates this concept. Note that teams of state leaders were in attendance; hence both individual and group tasks have been presented in the excerpt that follows.

TRAINEE TASKS FOR NATIONAL TRAINING CENTER

The purpose of these tasks is to help participants to direct their efforts and energies during this four week period so that they will be as productive as possible. They are designed to assist you in your leadership training.

The elective activities are not meant to be prescriptive, nor to be all-inclusive. They are suggestions that can be modified and changed in any way to fit the needs of those in attendance.

Each person will be expected *to prepare in writing*, on the forms distributed . . . a brief plan of action in terms of tasks to be accomplished during the next four weeks. Please prepare copies and turn in before you leave the building on Monday, July 20th.

Prepare your tasks in terms of:
1. Identification of the individual and team tasks in which you are to be involved weekly.
2. The accomplishments to be achieved at the end of each week.

At the end of each week you should review your plans . . . in accordance with possible modified goals.

It is recommended that you carefully review the program given you and the trainee tasks that are listed below. It is further suggested that as teams you confer together regarding State and territorial needs and decide on accomplishments to be achieved at the Training Center.

Individual tasks

Required:
   1. A written report on tasks to do.

Elective:
   1. Review and evaluate films.
   2. Review and evaluate materials distributed.
   3. Participate in a variety of field trips.
   4. Improve communication skills.
   5. Develop skills in curriculum development.
   6. Attend a variety of program presentations.
   7. Read a variety of books, pamphlets and other materials.
   8. Participate as a team member in planning for the implementation of the State proposal and other activities.
   9. Participate in the presentation of:

a. a discussion on drugs to ghetto youths (to be videotaped)
b. a parent-pupil discussion on drugs (to be videotaped)

Team tasks

Required:

1. Develop clear, concise and detailed procedures for implementation of the State proposal. Leave a copy of this plan with the Director before you leave the Training Center on August 14th.

Elective:

1. Develop a survey form for determining the nature of community drug resources.
2. Prepare a survey form for assessing the extent of the student drug problem in school, school district, or a community.
3. Prepare suggestions of suitable teaching methods for drug education by grade levels that will improve communications.
4. Develop, or start to develop, a curriculum guide in drug education for grades K-8, 8-12, K-12.
5. Prepare a program for community action in drug education for parents, the general public, and others, using a variety of communication media.
6. Plan an in-service training program for teachers, counselors, and others.
7. Prepare a resource manual containing guidelines for teachers and/or administrators on drug education.
8. Plan a program to improve communications between the school and the community.
9. Develop plans and procedures for evaluation of the drug education program in your school, school district, or community.

EVALUATION

Periodic assessment of the training session, or the in-service program, should take place. Suggestions and illustrations of procedures that might be usable are given in Chapter 11.

References

1. Colorado Interdepartmental Committee on Alcohol and Drug Abuse: Progress report to Colorado General Assembly, Denver, 1971, Colorado Drug Education Program, State Department of Health, Education, Institutions and Social Services.
2. Colorado State Department of Education, Colorado drug abuse education program: an interdepartmental project—training workshop, Colorado, December 6-11, 1970.
3. Drug abuse: a reference for teachers, rev., Trenton, N. J., 1968, Division of Curriculum and Instruction, New Jersey State Department of Education.
4. Drug Abuse Council: Drug abuse control: administrative guidelines, Los Angeles, 1970, Los Angeles City Schools.
5. Drug abuse programs: a guide to federal support, report series no. 7, Washington, D. C., 1971, National Institute of Mental Health, National Clearinghouse for Drug Abuse Information.
6. Drug crisis: schools fight back with innovative programs, Washington, D. C., 1971, National School Public Relations Association.
7. Finlater, J.: The drug scene: the scope of the problem faced by the schools. In Teaching about drugs: a curriculum guide, K-12, Kent, Ohio, 1970, American School Health Association.
8. Hamilton, L. D.: Drugs: what can the schools do about the problem? Educ. Canada 10: 30-36, 1970.
9. How to plan a drug education workshop for teachers, Washington, D. C., 1969, National Institute of Mental Health, National Clearinghouse for Mental Health Information.
10. Langer, J. H.: School-law enforcement cooperation. In Guidelines for drug abuse prevention education, Washington, D. C., 1970, Bureau of Narcotics and Dangerous Drugs, U. S. Department of Justice.
11. Report of the Ad Hoc Committee on Drug Abuse, Dallas, 1970, Superintendent of Schools, Dallas Independent School District.
12. School board policies on drug education and drug use, Washington, D. C., 1971, National School Boards Association.
13. School drug policies: a guide for administrators, Boston, 1969, Division of Curriculum and Instruction, Massachusetts Department of Education.
14. Stamford Public Schools, Connecticut: Curriculum guide for drug abuse education, Chicago, 1971, J. G. Ferguson Publishing Co.
15. A statewide plan for drug abuse prevention education in Arizona, Phoenix, 1971, Arizona State Department of Education.
16. Tate, C. P.: In-service education for teachers, Sci. Teacher 37:49-50, 1970.
17. Teacher's resource guide in drug abuse, Harrisburg, 1969, Division of Public Health Education, Pennsylvania Department of Health.
18. Ungerleider, J. T., and Bowen, H. L.: Drug abuse and the schools, Am. J. Psychiatry 125:1691-1697, 1969.
19. Wiggins, X.: Public schools and drug education: report of a conference, Atlanta, 1972, The Southern Regional Education Board.

PART IV · CONCLUSION

CHAPTER 11

EVALUATION

The school drug program and its component parts as described in this book need to be evaluated just as any other facet of the school program must be assessed. The information about the drug program should clearly outline the nature and extent of evaluation necessary and offer helpful suggestions to schools and school districts. It is the purpose of this chapter to offer assistance and to identify the specific details of evaluation.

The complexity of the drug program, the newness of its emergence, the lack of available devices, and the limited attention paid to the development of instruments will make it impossible to provide a comprehensive program of evaluation. However, an attempt will be made to define the scope of what is to be assessed, to state some guiding principles of operation, to introduce a variety of illustrative devices, and to provide some sources for other instruments.

SCOPE

The nature of the drug evaluation program should include the total program as well as the segments of drug education, drug services, the school atmosphere, and coordination. The following outline illustrates the matters to be focused upon in evaluating these phases.

I. The total school drug program
II. The educational program
  A. Effects on students
    1. Objectives
    2. Content
    3. Methods or pupil learning activities
    4. Resource materials
    5. Course, unit, or informal program
    6. Teacher, counselor, or administrator

  B. Effects on parents
III. The services program
  A. Appropriateness of drug user identification procedures
  B. Adequacy of procedures for handling drug users and abusers
  C. Effect of guidance and counseling on the rehabilitation of students
  D. Adequacy of community resources to aid students
  E. Effect of school program adjustments on students in terms of learning and drug abuse problems
IV. The school atmosphere
  A. Effect on student alienation and unrest
  B. Extent of success in satisfying physical and emotional needs
  C. Impact of humane school atmosphere on learning and on the control and prevention of student misuse and abuse of drugs
V. Coordination of the program
  A. Effectiveness of the drug coordinator
  B. Value of school drug advisory committee
  C. Adequacy of financial aid
  D. Effectiveness of organizational structure
  E. Usefulness of established policies and procedures
  F. In-service program values

PRINCIPLES OF EVALUATION

The general guiding principles that will be helpful in evaluating the school drug program will be identified within these headings: (1) how to evaluate, (2) who evaluates, (3) when to evaluate, and (4) problems in attempting to conduct an evaluation program.

How to evaluate

Schools should utilize a variety of procedures to determine present status, for baseline purposes, and to discover the progress made toward the achievement of desired goals. Such procedures may include observations by teachers, students, counselors, and others; checklists; questionnaires; self-tests; pretests and posttests; opinionnaires; practice inventories; and analysis of records. The evidence obtained can be of a subjective nature when it is collected in empirical form, or it can be of an objective nature, so that it may be statistically analyzed through the use of mechanical devices or by other quantitative means. Whenever possible, objective evidence should be acquired but subjective data may be the only kind obtainable because appropriate instruments are not available or due to other inhibiting factors.

A broad spectrum of assessment methods to gather both quantitative and qualitative data should be used. Educational evaluation processes all too frequently merely attempt to discover how many of something exists or to answer the following questions: Do we have a program? Are there qualified teachers? Are there adequate resource supplies? It is imperative that evidence be obtained to determine the effectiveness of the drug program. Evaluation should attempt to determine what impact the program has had on students. This is more difficult to achieve and may be an impossible process at times, especially if behavioral objectives in the educational program have been established. Nevertheless, such data are necessary to best demonstrate accountability. What a program does to students is more relevant than determining how much of something a school may possess.

A number of illustrative evaluation instruments have been prepared by a variety of individuals, many of whom have limited experience in the evaluative process, although expert help has been used in some instances. Certain relevant weaknesses may be evidenced including the reference of the instruments to local situations. There are few, if any, standardized instruments available at this writing and there are no known devices to assess the individual drug program components categorized as services, atmosphere, and coordination. (See "Criteria for Evaluating the School Drug Program," p. 266.) Perhaps the dearth of published instruments is due to the emphasis on the development and implementation of the programs that are now taking place in schools rather than the evaluation process. Schools, school districts, and school personnel therefore will have to utilize or adapt those instruments found in this chapter in addition to devising methods to meet their own local needs.

Who evaluates

Students, school personnel, including teachers, counselors, administrators, and nurses, and the community, especially parents, should be involved in assessing the school drug program. The individuals who should participate will be selected depending on the goal or goals to be achieved.

It should be stressed that students may provide such useful services to teachers or administrators as (1) responding to questionnaires to determine the effect of classroom educational experiences; (2) helping to assess the value of films and pamphlet materials to be used, or purchased, for the drug educational program; (3) conducting surveys of student drug misuse and abuse; (4) aiding in determining the meaningfulness of the content of the drug education program; and (5) aiding in determining whether teachers and counselors have the ability to communicate with students effectively. Students should be included in the evaluative process.

One of the functions of the school drug advisory committee may be involvement in evaluation. This committee may participate in the development of procedures, support the need for assessment, or decide to delegate this responsibility.

When to evaluate

Frequently it has been said that evaluation is a continuing process; there is a beginning, but no end. Such a statement applies to the school drug program.

More realistically, no evaluation program of great intensity and length can continue over an indeterminate period of time. However, teachers, administrators, and others should at least minimally participate in the periodic assessment of their activities. The nature and degree of intensity together with the frequency of what takes place will differ depending on the time available, the people involved, the nature of the program, and numerous other variables. In the classroom the teacher might well consider pretesting and posttesting behaviors during a course or unit related to drugs, or merely use personal observations to find results. In the school or school district, short- and long-range goals should be established to assess the various segments of the total drug program.

In any event consideration must be given to the establishment of a time period over which the entire program will be measured. The specific procedures, timing, personnel involved, and other matters should be determined at the local level to meet local needs. It is suggested that drug programs now under consideration, or in the process of being established, include provision for the evaluation process.

Problems in evaluation

One significant problem in drug education programs is the community expectation in some areas that a dramatic reduction in the numbers of students using, misusing, or abusing drugs should take place after relatively brief instructional programs. Knowledge of the difficulties in the process of behavioral change indicates that the achievement of such a goal is impossible. In addition, the strength of the social forces and factors outside the school—television and other mass media, peer influence, adult use of drugs—makes it clear that schools by themselves cannot solve this widespread drug problem. In fact schools may not be able to have much effect at all. They may be able to aid in the limited reduction of some drug use, but support and cooperative assistance from the total community are needed for even partial success.

The question may be raised as to whether young people are to be turned off of all drugs, including aspirin, alcohol, and tobacco. Therefore it is important that the goals established in school drug programs be reasonable in their potential for achievement and within the limitations of the funds, facilities, resources, teacher competencies, and learning atmosphere available. Emphasis in the drug program may start with cognitive aspects and then increasingly focus on the affective and action domain achievements. Guidance in terms of educa-

tional goals to be reached may be obtained by referring to Chapter 8.

A second problem in evaluation is the assessment of action domain goals when much of the student behavior involving drug use and misuse occurs outside the school setting. Such actions are unobservable and difficult, if at all possible, to assess. Therefore expecting schools to turn pupils off drugs in any dramatic fashion after only 1 or 2 years of conducting drug programs is unreasonable. Schools will find it difficult to know what they have achieved in this regard. This is not to imply that such an outcome should not be included in the program. Some of the suggestions given here will be helpful in both short- and long-range plans.

It may take 3 to 5 years just to establish a drug program that begins to demonstrate consistent degrees of effectiveness in terms of knowledge and attitude purposes. If such a program is ongoing for a number of additional years, if it is a total program as described in this book, if it utilizes personnel who are able to communicate effectively with students, and if sufficient funds and competent teachers are available, perhaps more effective results in the reduction of certain drug use can be achieved despite the difficulties of assessing behavioral changes.

A third problem in evaluation concerns the use of performance objectives that are primarily cognitively oriented. This emphasis is brought on by the need for schools to demonstrate educational accountability. The approach has dangers when applied to the drug problem because schools may again place themselves in the trap of trying to treat the symptom, and of imparting solely subject matter rather than being concerned with students, their feelings, and their attitudes. Although there is no quarrel with the performance objectives concept, the program should not be solely oriented toward knowledge and understanding. The need for an approach emphasizing attitudes and practices will present a challenge to teachers and schools. They will need to establish reasonable, achievable objectives in these categories as defined in Chapter 8 as well as devices to assess these goals. School personnel will therefore need to carefully review the attitudinal and practice inventories presented here and adapt, devise, or create others so these inventories are functional. Thus schools will be better able to provide data that will enable them to demonstrate accountability in the affective and action domains as well as in the cognitive domain.

There is no easy solution to the matter of evaluation in the school drug program. It is expected that the material and inventories in this chapter will not only provide assistance but will also motivate school personnel to develop improved assessment procedures.

ILLUSTRATIVE EVALUATION INSTRUMENTS
Total program evaluation instrument

"Criteria for Evaluating the School Drug Program" is a useful instrument that will help in the gross assessment of the total school drug program both from a quantitative and a qualitative standpoint. It seeks primarily subjective evidence but the data could be collected objectively if a sufficient number of individuals take part. This involvement would remove the possibility of bias that may develop from the use of a small number of observers. If the advisory drug committee wishes to authorize this device to be self-administered by a representative committee from each school in the district, the compiled information would provide greater objectivity in the data collected. (See p. 266.)

Education program evaluation instruments

A variety of devices usable in the instructional program are presented in this section. These instruments are listed according to the following categories and subcategories:

1. Objectives
   a. Knowledge instruments
   b. Attitude instruments
      (1) Related to drugs
      (2) Related to youth alienation, unrest, problems, social and psychological needs, and interests
   c. Practices survey forms
   d. Knowledge-attitude instrument
2. In-service
   a. Knowledge instrument
   b. Attitude instruments
3. Resource materials
   a. Films and filmstrips
   b. Materials

OBJECTIVES

The instruments to measure objectives will include those to assess knowledge (cognitive domain), attitudes (affective domain), and practices (action domain). They are designed to be used in a variety of ways: (1) to pretest students and utilize the data to determine needs, interests, and problems for curriculum development and course content; (2) to posttest students following instruction to determine behavioral changes; and (3) to serve as self-tests to help initiate discussion. These devices may need modification and adaptation to local situations and communities.

KNOWLEDGE INSTRUMENTS. Four knowledge devices will be given:

1. The "High School Drug Knowledge Questionnaire" contains 46 multiple-choice questions prepared by the Colorado State Department of Education for high school students. (See p. 270.)
2. The "High School Drug Knowledge Test" includes 91 true-false and multiple-choice questions prepared by the Great Falls Public Schools, Montana, for ninth graders. (See p. 276.)
3. The "Simplified Drug Fact Sheet" consists of 23 questions organized and adapted from an examination prepared by the Baltimore County Board of Education, Maryland, for sixth graders. (See p. 280.)
4. The "Revision of the University of Illinois Smoking Knowledge Test" is a set of 44 questions prepared for use in the University of Illinois smoking project for grades 7 to 12. (See p. 281.)

ATTITUDE INSTRUMENTS. There are two groups of attitude instruments. One group contains five techniques related to attitudes about drugs. The second group includes four instruments related to the alienation, unrest, problems, needs, and interests of students.

Drug attitudes

1. The "Alcohol and Alcoholism—Attitudinal Measure" presents a series of statements relating to the use of alcohol, teaching about alcohol, the drinking problem in school, and the person with a drinking problem. Weir used this device in a study of high school students in Canada. (See p. 286.)
2. The "Attitude Toward Smoking Marijuana" instrument may be helpful to measure attitudes toward smoking marijuana ranging from favorable to unfavorable. This scale may be used to determine the feelings toward marijuana of one individual or of a group. (See p. 287.)
3. The "Drug Attitude Survey" is a useful self-test to start a classroom discussion. (See p. 288.)
4. The "Drug Abuse Attitudes and Opinions Pre-Test and Post-Test" contains 30 questions prepared for high school students by the Utah State Board of Education. (See p. 289.)
5. "Opinions on the Use and Control of Beverage Alcohol" consists of 33 questions prepared by the Great Falls Public Schools, Great Falls, Montana, for seventh grade students. (See p. 292.)

Alienation, unrest, problems, interests, and needs of students

1. The "Youth Alienation Survey" will help to determine the concerns young people have with individuals and society. It may help to get at the root causes of youth unrest and the drug problem. (See p. 295.)
2. The "Youth Attitude Questionnaire" will aid youth in finding out about their feelings toward life and society. (See p. 297.)
3. The "Pupil Problems, Interests, and Needs" instrument was prepared by the Dallas Independent School District, Texas, to help young people gain insight into what is troubling them. (See p. 298.)
4. "My Checklist" was prepared by the Oregon State Board of Education to help discover some of the psychological difficulties young children may be experiencing. (See p. 299.)

PRACTICE SURVEY FORMS. The three techniques identified as practice survey forms may be useful in surveying students at the junior and senior high school levels to determine the extent of their use and misuse of drugs. These devices also have utility as pre- and posttests to determine behavioral changes.

1. The "Student Drug Use Survey Form" covers many of the major drugs of abuse by young people. It is simple in design and easy to complete so that information may be gathered and tabulated quickly. (See p. 300.)
2. The "Survey Form Used in 1970" in San Mateo, California, where such surveys have been conducted for the past 4 years on thousands of junior and senior high school students. (See p. 301.)
3. The "Confidential Questionnaire" is used by the schools in Lovell, Wyoming, and is simple in design. It provides attitudinal information that may be useful for discussion or curriculum purposes. (See p. 302.)

KNOWLEDGE-ATTITUDE INSTRUMENT. The "Alcohol Education Pretest" was prepared by the Michigan Department of Education. It may be useful in gathering information and determining high school students' feelings about alcohol in order to ascertain the nature of the content to be covered. Parts I and II may serve for pretest and posttest purposes. (See p. 303.)

IN-SERVICE

The instruments provided in this section are illustrative of some of the devices usable in determining the effectiveness of in-service programs. These techniques permit assessment of information and attitudes that may be adapted to pre- and posttesting in order to determine behavioral changes. Two very helpful procedures are included. One is a device to measure opinions about the program at weekly intervals, and the second is a procedure to be used as a culminating, or final, program evaluation instrument.

Knowledge instrument
1. The "Drug Information Test" was prepared for use in the California drug education training program, 1970-1971. (See p. 306.)

Attitudes instruments
1. The "Drug Attitude Survey" was also prepared for use in the California drug education training program. (See p. 310.)
2. The "Weekly Program Opinions" were used each week during the 4-week session of the National Training Center in Drug Education held at San Francisco State College in 1970. (See p. 313.)
3. The "Final Program Evaluation" was the culminating evaluation measurement used at the National Training Center in Drug Education held at San Francisco State College in 1970. (See p. 314.)

RESOURCE MATERIALS

The volume of films, filmstrips, records, books, pamphlets, cassettes, and other resource materials that is being produced demands ways of determining the best ones for the educational program. Evaluation procedures must be available to determine the quality of these items. The following three devices will be helpful with the assessment task.
1. The "Film Rating Scale" is a simple device that can help to quickly arrive at a conclusion regarding a film. It may also be used for filmstrips by omitting inappropriate criteria. (See p. 315.)
2. "Evaluation of Materials" is an instrument to evaluate a variety of printed publications using a few essential criteria. (See p. 316.)
3. "Material Evaluation" was prepared by the Mental Health Planning Committee of Milwaukee County, Wisconsin. It is a multi-itemed evaluation procedure that is more complex than the others previously introduced. It may be better suited to the needs of some schools and school districts than the "Evaluation of Materials." (See p. 317.)

Text continued on p. 318.

CRITERIA FOR EVALUATING THE SCHOOL DRUG PROGRAM

Instructions:
1. Place a check ($\checkmark$) in the appropriate box under "Provision" for each criterion.
2. Place a number in the appropriate box under "Effectiveness" that best illustrates the effectiveness of the criterion. Scale: POOR 0 1 2 3 4 5 GOOD
3. Add appropriate comments under "Needed changes."

CRITERIA	PROVISION			EFFECTIVENESS	NEEDED CHANGES
	yes	no	partly		
BASIC OBJECTIVES					
1. Familiarity with nature and extent of drug problem among students					
2. Operation of a school drug program					
3. Drug program includes more than education					
4. Goals are behaviorally centered					
5. Treatment of students based on causal relationships rather than symptomatic behavior					
6. Focus on improvement of interpersonal relations and helping students find identity					
7. Students actively participate in a variety of ways					
8. Community involved in the program					
9. Related to and coordinated with community efforts					
FORMAL EDUCATION					
1. Organization of program					
a. Part of health education					
b. Correlated with other subjects					
2. Curriculum					
a. Graded program K through 12					
b. Curriculum guide available					
(1) Concept approach used					
(2) Behavioral objectives provided					
(3) Content includes					
(a) Pharmacological aspects					
(b) Psychological aspects					
(c) Sociological aspects					
(d) Spiritual aspects					

    (4) Variety of stimulating and interesting
        methods of teaching
    (5) Realistic assessment procedures estab-
        lished
  3. Teachers
    a. Communicate well with students
    b. Qualified to teach about drugs
  4. Resources
    a. Variety of materials available
    b. Resource teacher in each school
    c. Use of community
  5. Instructional program for parents

INFORMAL EDUCATION
  1. Opportunities through
    a. Rap sessions—one-to-one or small groups
    b. Drop-in centers
    c. Hot-lines
    d. Others
  2. Individuals available for "rapping"
    a. Teachers
    b. Counselors
    c. Nurse
    d. Students
    e. Ex-addicts
    f. Physicians
    g. Others
  3. Parents
    a. Personnel available and procedures estab-
        lished to help with
        (1) Information
        (2) Guidance and assistance
  4. Use of community resources

SERVICES
  1. Identification of drug abusers and users
    a. Procedures established
    b. Personal familiarity with procedures

Continued.

CRITERIA FOR EVALUATING THE SCHOOL DRUG PROGRAM—cont'd

CRITERIA	PROVISION			EFFECTIVENESS	NEEDED CHANGES
	yes	no	partly		
2. Handling of drug users and abusers					
a. Procedures established					
b. Personnel roles identified					
c. Availability of teachers, counselors, nurses, or others for help when needed or requested					
d. Rehabilitation and treatment help for students					
3. Personnel familiar with community resources available to help students					
4. Coordination with community resources					
5. Adjustments of school program for drug abusers to help with rehabilitation					
SCHOOL ATMOSPHERE					
1. Personnel awareness of student alienation and unrest					
2. Action to reduce student alienation and unrest					
3. Action to satisfy students' physical and psychological needs					
4. Action to satisfy students' psychological and social needs					
5. Action toward more humaneness in school with attention to					
a. Individualized instruction					
b. Student involvement					
c. Meaningful learning					
d. Success opportunities					
e. Performance objectives criteria					
f. Freedom of student expression					
g. Improved human relationships					
h. Listening to students					
i. Flexible scheduling of classes					

i. Greater teacher involvement in school affairs and decisions
k. Provision for warm, friendly, secure atmosphere

COORDINATION
1. Availability of drug coordinator for school system
2. Drug advisory committee
3. Written policies and procedures that include:
   a. Educational program
   b. Services program
   c. Identification of roles of personnel and students
   d. Handling students using, suspected of using, or under the influence of drugs
   e. Handling law violations and other conditions, including:
      (1) Suspension and expulsion
      (2) Student search rights
      (3) Student questioning rights
      (4) Personnel records
      (5) Readmission
   f. Confidentiality and police relations
   g. Counseling, guidance, and rehabilitation
   h. Possession or sale of drugs
   i. Undercover police on campus
4. Financial support
5. In-service programs for school personnel

HIGH SCHOOL DRUG KNOWLEDGE QUESTIONNAIRE*

1. Drugs that are more likely than others to cause dream images are
   a. stimulants.
   b. depressants.
   c. hallucinogens.
   d. opiates.
   e. none of the above.

2. Physical dependence on drugs is a condition in which
   a. the body needs the drug.
   b. larger doses are required.
   c. a strong desire for the drug has developed.
   d. the body always suffers pain.
   e. none of the above.

3. Tolerance has developed when
   a. the body rejects the drug.
   b. the drug makes the user sick.
   c. the body gets used to the drug.
   d. the drug must be injected into the blood.
   e. withdrawal symptoms set in.

4. Drugs that stimulate the central nervous system and give a feeling of being pepped up are
   a. barbiturates.
   b. amphetamines.
   c. hallucinogens.
   d. opium products.
   e. THC derivatives.

5. A condition that may be caused by misuse of amphetamines is
   a. withdrawal illness.
   b. a depressed feeling.
   c. the need for larger doses.
   d. sleepiness.
   e. all of the above.

6. Amphetamines are used medically for the relief of
   a. drowsiness and mild depression.
   b. fear and excitement.
   c. feelings of restlessness.
   d. nervousness.
   e. none of the above.

7. A person who has taken an amphetamine is likely to be
   a. calm, quiet, and inactive.
   b. unsteady.
   c. talkative and restless.
   d. unable to stay awake.
   e. losing sense of time and space.

8. The most common medical use of barbiturates is
   a. to produce sleep.
   b. to relieve pain.
   c. for weight control.
   d. for research studies.
   e. to combat depression.

9. Misuse of barbiturates is likely to cause
   a. broken speech.
   b. slowness of thought.
   c. poor balance.

*From Measures used in the drug evaluation, Appendix A, unpublished data, Colorado Department of Education.

HIGH SCHOOL DRUG KNOWLEDGE QUESTIONNAIRE—cont'd

      d. drowsiness.
      e. all of the above.
10. Continued use of barbiturates over a period of time can cause
      a. tolerance.
      b. physical dependence.
      c. emotional dependence.
      d. none of these.
      e. all of the above.
11. Barbiturate users are likely to
      a. stay awake for long periods.
      b. fall asleep easily.
      c. feel restless and excited.
      d. experience loss of appetite.
      e. none of the above.
12. The effects of marijuana on the body are closely related to those caused by
      a. stimulant drugs.
      b. depressant drugs.
      c. hallucinogenic drugs.
      d. opiate derivatives.
      e. none of the above.
13. The long history and widespread use of marijuana have
      a. established evidence that the drug is harmless.
      b. shown that the drug causes recklessness.
      c. created confusion about the effects of the drug.
      d. shown that it leads to heroin use.
      e. none of the above.
14. Marijuana does not cause
      a. an effect on the central nervous system.
      b. emotional dependence.
      c. physical dependence.
      d. an effect on the sense of time.
      e. occasional fear and anxiety.
15. A dose of cocaine would most likely cause the body to become
      a. depressed.
      b. stimulated.
      c. sleepy.
      d. nauseated.
      e. none of the above.
16. The strongest of the following opium drugs is
      a. morphine.
      b. heroin.
      c. codeine.
      d. cocaine.
      e. all are the same strength.
17. The effects of heroin will most likely cause
      a. a dulling of senses of fear, tension, and anxiety.
      b. excitement and increased energy.
      c. restlessness and oxygen in the blood.
      d. inability to sleep or relax.
      e. mild hallucinations.
18. Some cough medicines can cause drug dependence if misused because they contain
      a. meperidine.
      b. Benzedrine.
      c. codeine.

Continued.

HIGH SCHOOL DRUG KNOWLEDGE QUESTIONNAIRE—cont'd

    d. morphine.

    e. Methedrine.

19. Hallucinogens are sought because they
    a. relax tension, induce elation.
    b. increase alertness, reduce sleepiness.
    c. produce a sense of calm, well-being.
    d. cause exciting visions and increased intelligence.
    e. cause varying illusions and escape from reality.

20. Abuse of airplane glue, gasoline, and other solvents causes
    a. excitement, weightlessness.
    b. depression, laziness, relaxation.
    c. intoxication, confusion, tissue damage, and comas.
    d. hallucination, depression.
    e. feelings of temporary restored alertness and energy.

21. Which of the following drugs causes psychological dependence but not physical dependence?
    a. Seconal
    b. Benzedrine
    c. Morphine
    d. Heroin
    e. Dilaudid

22. There is scientific evidence to indicate that physical dependence can be established with use of marijuana.
    a. Definitely false
    b. Probably false
    c. I do not know
    d. Probably true
    e. Definitely true

23. Most people who use marijuana will also try heroin.
    a. Definitely false
    b. Probably false
    c. I do not know
    d. Probably true
    e. Definitely true

24. Alcoholism is our primary national addiction problem.
    a. Definitely false
    b. Probably false
    c. I do not know
    d. Probably true
    e. Definitely true

25. LSD is addicting in the sense of producing physical dependence.
    a. Definitely false
    b. Probably false
    c. I do not know
    d. Probably true
    e. Definitely true

26. Of the people you know personally, who do you feel is best informed about drugs?
    a. My teachers or counselors
    b. A friend or group of friends
    c. My parents
    d. My doctor
    e. Other _____

27. If you were having trouble handling drugs (a bad trip, etc.), where would you go for help?
    a. To my parents

HIGH SCHOOL DRUG KNOWLEDGE QUESTIONNAIRE—cont'd

    b. To a close friend
    c. To a teacher
    d. To my doctor
    e. To a drug center (assuming one were available)
28. Why do you feel parents and students have trouble communicating about drugs?
    a. Parents are not willing to listen.
    b. Students are not willing to listen.
    c. Parents do not know enough about drugs and drug-related problems.
    d. Parents and students do not have enough common activities.
    e. The value systems of parents are too different from the value systems of students.
29. How comfortable do you feel talking to your parents about drugs?
    a. Extremely uncomfortable
    b. Fairly uncomfortable
    c. Fairly comfortable
    d. Extremely comfortable
30. Who do you talk with most about drugs?
    a. My parents
    b. A certain friend
    c. A group of my friends
    d. My teachers
    e. No one
31. Why do people your age use drugs?
    a. They enjoy drugs.
    b. Drugs help them communicate with people.
    c. Their friends use them.
    d. They help them understand themselves.
    e. They are curious about the effects.
32. Why do people your age not use drugs?
    a. They are afraid of the possible harmful physical consequences (addiction, deformed children, etc.).
    b. They are afraid of the possible harmful psychological consequences (nervous breakdown, hysteria, etc.).
    c. Their parents are against drugs.
    d. Their friends advised against using drugs.
    e. They are afraid of getting arrested and having a legal record.
33. Families who have good channels of communication between parents and children are less likely to have drug abuse problems.
    a. I strongly disagree
    b. I disagree but with reservations.
    c. I have no feelings about this issue.
    d. I agree but with reservations.
    e. I strongly agree.
34. It is possible to identify drug users by their physical appearance.
    a. I strongly disagree.
    b. I disagree but with reservations.
    c. I have no feelings about this issue.
    d. I agree but with reservations.
    e. I strongly agree.
35. The mass media have made the use of illegal drugs appear attractive to youth.
    a. I strongly disagree.
    b. I disagree but with reservations.
    c. I have no feelings about this issue.
    d. I agree but with reservations.
    e. I strongly agree.
36. There can be no single successful method of prevention or treatment of drug abuse for all individuals.
    a. I strongly disagree.

Continued.

HIGH SCHOOL DRUG KNOWLEDGE QUESTIONNAIRE—cont'd

    b. I disagree but with reservations.
    c. I have no feelings about this issue.
    d. I agree but with reservations.
    e. I strongly agree.

37. Drug abuse by an individual is merely a symptom of a deeper underlying personal problem.
    a. I strongly disagree.
    b. I disagree but with reservations.
    c. I have no feelings about this issue.
    d. I agree but with reservations.
    e. I strongly agree.

38. Adults must modify their use of drugs such as tobacco and alcohol before they can expect youth to modify their use of drugs such as marijuana and LSD.
    a. I strongly disagree.
    b. I disagree but with reservations.
    c. I have no feelings about this issue.
    d. I agree but with reservations.
    e. I strongly agree.

39. The great majority of drug abusers are youth under age 21.
    a. I strongly disagree.
    b. I disagree but with reservations.
    c. I have no feelings about this issue.
    d. I agree but with reservations.
    e. I strongly agree.

40. The elimination of dangerous drugs from society would only bring about the abuse of other dangerous substances.
    a. I strongly disagree.
    b. I disagree but with reservations.
    c. I have no feelings about this issue.
    d. I agree but with reservations.
    e. I strongly agree.

41. One of the best solutions to the drug abuse problem is to crack down on the users by enforcing stiff penalities.
    a. I strongly disagree.
    b. I disagree but with reservations.
    c. I have no feelings about this issue.
    d. I agree but with reservations.
    e. I strongly agree.

42. Every community has a potential drug abuse problem.
    a. I strongly disagree.
    b. I disagree but with reservations.
    c. I have no feelings about this issue.
    d. I agree but with reservations.
    e. I strongly agree.

43. There are as many causes for drug abuse as there are drug abusers.
    a. I strongly disagree.
    b. I disagree but with reservations.
    c. I have no feelings about this issue.
    d. I agree but with reservations.
    e. I strongly agree.

To what extent do you feel each of the following drugs should be legalized?

44. Narcotics
    a. Totally prohibited
    b. Available only by prescription or for research.

HIGH SCHOOL DRUG KNOWLEDGE QUESTIONNAIRE—cont'd

      c. As available as liquor
      d. As available as tobacco
      e. No restrictions

45. Marijuana
      a. Totally prohibited
      b. Available only by prescription or for research.
      c. As available as liquor
      d. As available as tobacco
      e. No restrictions

46. Psychedelics
      a. Totally prohibited
      b. Available only by prescription or for research.
      c. As available as liquor
      d. As available as tobacco
      e. No restrictions

HIGH SCHOOL DRUG KNOWLEDGE TEST*

TRUE-FALSE QUESTIONS

T   F   1. The term "drug" applies only to substances that are used as medicines.

T   F   2. The medical meaning of the term "narcotic" differs from the legal meaning of the term.

T   F   3. Drug dependence is said to exist only when a person is physically and psychologically dependent on a drug.

T   F   4. Psychological dependence on a drug is easier to overcome than physical dependence.

T   F   5. When a person has developed tolerance to a drug, he needs increasing amounts of that drug in order to react satisfactorily to its presence.

T   F   6. Amphetamine, when self-administered to prevent sleepiness while driving, may cause intoxication which affects the driver's ability to handle his car safely.

T   F   7. Barbiturates, taken in excessive amounts, cause a severe depression of the central nervous system, which may result in unconsciousness or death.

T   F   8. When alcohol and barbiturates are taken together, the drugs tend to neutralize each other, causing a relatively mild reaction.

T   F   9. Barbiturates, if taken repeatedly, may cause total drug dependence comparable in severity to heroin dependence.

T   F   10. Amphetamine may be self-administered with relative safety because it does not lead to drug dependence.

T   F   11. The dangerous drugs differ from the narcotics in that their excessive use leads only to psychological dependence, whereas narcotic abuse leads to both psychological and physical dependence.

T   F   12. The young person who abuses dangerous drugs is likely already to have a history of delinquent behavior.

T   F   13. It has been shown through experimentation that the use of amphetamines can substantially improve athletic performance.

T   F   14. The organic solvents present in glues and plastic cements are capable of damaging the brain, affecting liver and kidney functions, and interfering with the blood-forming function of the bone marrow.

T   F   15. There is no evidence that glue sniffing leads to the development of dependence.

T   F   16. It is believed that the abuse of volatile chemicals will soon be solved through the development of nonintoxicating solvents to replace those now present in glues and plastic cements.

T   F   17. Marijuana is an important medicinal drug because of its effectiveness as a pain-killer.

T   F   18. Marijuana is a contraband drug, and whoever produces or distributes it is guilty of a crime punishable as a felony.

T   F   19. Most marijuana entering the United States today comes by way of Mexico.

T   F   20. The plant Cannabis sativa, from which marijuana is derived, grows only in warm, humid climates.

T   F   21. The plant from which marijuana is derived has been known and used as a drug for several thousand years.

T   F   22. A person who feels he must take marijuana (or any other drug) in order to enjoy life or to belong in a group has failed to make a normal, wholesome adjustment to life and has not learned to function as an independent, responsible member of society.

T   F   23. If other people are using marijuana (or some other drug), it is best for you to use it too, so as not to appear different.

T   F   24. If you can not find success or enjoyment in life, it is wise to try to forget your sense of failure by drinking alcohol or taking drugs.

*Adapted from Tabacco, drug, alcohol unit, ninth grade, Great Falls, Mont., 1971, Great Falls Public Schools.

HIGH SCHOOL DRUG KNOWLEDGE TEST—cont'd

T   F   25. Since most marijuana users today do not progress to heroin, there is little reason not to use marijuana.

T   F   26. Marijuana contains a powerful chemical that appears to incite its users to commit acts of violence.

T   F   27. There is now believed to be little or no relation between the use of marijuana and the commission of acts of violence.

T   F   28. A person who forms a **habit** of marijuana use may find it exceedingly difficult to break that habit.

T   F   29. The use of marijuana opens the way for many persons to the use of other drugs.

T   F   30. When a drug is said to be "nonaddicting" it means that a person using the drug can stop any time he wants to.

T   F   31. A person should make decisions in terms of his own standards and convictions rather than in terms of the pressures and practices of other people.

T   F   32. Marijuana, while apparently acting as a stimulant, dulls the higher control centers of the brain so that one's conduct may become socially unacceptable, for one's normal inhibitions no longer prevail.

T   F   33. A person under the influence of marijuana is able to think more clearly and act more efficiently than he would under normal conditions.

T   F   34. When a person has taken marijuana, he is likely to experience a period of stimulation followed by a period of depression.

T   F   35. LSD may be used only for purposes approved by the Federal Food and Drug Administration.

T   F   36. Any licensed physician can obtain LSD from the Food and Drug Administration for the purpose of conducting scientific investigations.

T   F   37. People with stable personalities seldom experience adverse effects after taking LSD.

T   F   38. Since the early 1940s, scientists have known that LSD causes hallucinations.

T   F   39. LSD is one of the most potent drugs known to man.

T   F   40. LSD has an accepted place in medical practice.

T   F   41. After a user takes LSD, his mind "expands" and he becomes more aware of his surroundings.

T   F   42. Psychological dependence may result from the use of LSD.

T   F   43. A user taking the same amount of LSD in the same surroundings a second time will have an experience similiar to the one he had the first time.

T   F   44. Hallucinations experienced after a person has taken LSD can recur several months later, even though he has not taken any more of the drug.

T   F   45. An individual's value system often changes after he has taken LSD.

T   F   46. After taking LSD, the user becomes more social; that is, he relates more closely to those around him.

T   F   47. A number of persons have committed suicide after taking LSD.

T   F   48. Some people use LSD in order to withdraw from reality.

T   F   49. A person who has used LSD several times can predict the kind of side effects, if any, that a new user might expect.

T   F   50. Persons who use LSD seldom use any other drugs.

T   F   51. In Montana it is illegal to have LSD in one's possession.

T   F   52. LSD is derived from the sacred mushroom, which has long been used by the Indians in Mexico.

T   F   53. LSD is a relatively mild drug that can be used safely in large amounts.

T   F   54. Once it is brought under medical control, LSD promises to be a "miracle drug" in that it helps people to solve their problems and adjust better to life.

T   F   55. LSD and other hallucinogens are now subject to the same federal controls as the dangerous drugs.

T   F   56. The use of LSD is frequently accompanied by severe and dangerous side effects.

Continued.

HIGH SCHOOL DRUG KNOWLEDGE TEST—cont'd

T F 57. Physicians prescribe LSD for persons who have symptoms of anxiety and depression.

T F 58. LSD has a special attraction for adolescents who are searching for identity.

T F 59. LSD can help adolescents resolve the conflicts of "growing up."

T F 60. Involvement in narcotic use, if it occurs, is likely to take place only after prior experience with other drugs.

T F 61. Heroin is legally used in the United States today as a medicinal drug.

T F 62. The process of injecting heroin (or any other foreign substance) directly into the veins carries serious danger of infection.

T F 63. Since heroin appears not to damage body tissue, its use is not serious from the standpoint of health.

T F 64. The use of heroin leads rapidly and almost inevitably to total drug dependence.

T F 65. The recent increase in sex crimes throughout the United States is attributable, in part, to the increase in narcotic use.

T F 66. Narcotic dependence may be said to be cured when a person has been relieved of the physical aspects of dependence.

T F 67. The narcotic addict in Great Britain, once he has registered with designated authorities, is entitled automatically to receive a supply of drugs to maintain his desired level of dependence.

T F 68. The "clinic plan" of administering sustaining doses of narcotics to addicts was tried in the United States in the 1920s and deemed a success at the time.

T F 69. The American Medical Association has come out in favor of the adoption of the British method of narcotics control in the United States.

T F 70. The United States has made significant progress in international narcotic control.

T F 71. In the United States the dispensing of drugs by a physician to an addict for the gratification of his desire or need for drugs is now considered by the courts to fall within the province of legitimate medical practice.

T F 72. Whereas control of drug abuse in the United States rests largely in the hands of law enforcement personnel, control in Great Britain is vested in the medical profession.

T F 73. Since the drug abuse pattern in the United States differs drastically from that in Great Britain, it is doubtful that this country will ever move toward wholesale adoption of the British method of narcotic control.

T F 74. Under Montana law the mere possession of marijuana or of a narcotic (other than one prescribed by a physician) is illegal.

MULTIPLE-CHOICE QUESTIONS

_____ 1. "A substance that produces sleep, lethargy, and relief of pain" is the definition of (a) a drug; (b) a sedative; (c) a narcotic; (d) an opiate; or (e) an analgesic.

_____ 2. A substance, other than food, that affects body structure and functions is called (a) a depressant; (b) a narcotic; (c) an analgesic; (d) a drug; or (e) an intoxicant.

_____ 3. The term "narcotic" is used medically in reference to (a) marijuana; (b) the barbiturates; (c) the opiates; (d) the hallucinogens; or (e) the hypnotics.

_____ 4. "A state arising from repeated administration of a drug on a periodic or continuous basis" is the definition of (a) drug abuse; (b) depression; (c) drug dependence; (d) analgesia; or (e) euphoria.

_____ 5. Substances that depress body functions are (a) the barbiturates and amphetamines; (b) barbiturates and opiates; (c) amphetamines and opiates; (d) cocaine and marijuana; or (e) amphetamines and cocaine.

_____ 6. Substances that stimulate body functions are (a) barbiturates and amphetamines; (b) barbiturates and opiates; (c) amphetamines and opiates; (d) cocaine and marijuana; or (e) amphetamines and cocaine.

HIGH SCHOOL DRUG KNOWLEDGE TEST—cont'd

_____ 7. "A generalized feeling of well-being in the absence of any objective justification for such feeling" is the definition of (a) euphoria; (b) tolerance; (c) analgesia; (d) dependence; or (e) hallucination.

_____ 8. One of the following statements about the dangerous drugs is correct: (a) they are outlawed both legally and medically; (b) they may be used legally without a doctor's prescription; (c) they may be used legally only with a doctor's prescription; (d) they fall under different regulations depending on the drug involved; or (e) they are mild drugs comparable to alcohol in their effects.

_____ 9. The most hopeful approach to the solution of the glue-sniffing problem at present appears to lie in (a) more stringent laws; (b) more stringent enforcement of existing laws; (c) voluntary control by distributors of glues and plastic cements; (d) replacement of volatile chemicals by nonintoxicating solvents; or (e) education of children concerning the hazards of introducing foreign substances into the body.

_____10. In the United States marijuana is most frequently taken into the body by (a) chewing; (b) sniffing; (c) eating; (d) drinking; or (e) smoking.

_____11. The odor associated with the use of marijuana is most like (a) dried alfalfa or hay; (b) alcohol; (c) garlic; (d) decaying fruit; or (e) burning wood.

_____12. The body system most affected by the use of marijuana is (a) the nervous; (b) the circulatory; (c) the digestive; (d) the respiratory; or (e) the muscular.

_____13. In laboratory research, LSD has proved to be (a) safe and effective for the treatment of epilepsy; (b) safe but not effective for the treatment of alcoholism; (c) neither safe nor effective for the treatment of any disease; or (d) safe but not effective for the treatment of psychosis.

_____14. From among the following side effects, the one which has not resulted from the use of LSD is (a) distortion of perception; (b) withdrawal illness; (c) delusions; or (d) severe depression.

_____15. A person who takes LSD often continues to take it because (a) it improves his ability to concentrate; (b) it causes sexual stimulation; (c) it creates a sensation which he likes; or (d) it brings on a physical craving.

_____16. The part of the opium poppy from which raw opium is derived is (a) dried flowers, (b) dried leaves; (c) unripe seed pods; (d) ripe seeds; or (e) unripe seeds.

_____17. The federal law that forms the basis of our government's control over narcotics by requiring registration and payment of an occupational tax by those who deal in narcotics is (a) the Boggs Act; (b) The Narcotic Control Act; (c) The Harrison Narcotic Act; (d) The Opium Poppy Control Act; or (e) The Narcotic Drugs Import and Export Act.

SIMPLIFIED DRUG FACT SHEET—GRADE 6*

T   F   1. A great deal of confusion exists regarding the facts of drug use and drug abuse.

T   F   2. All the drugs commonly abused are "narcotics."

_____ 3. Barbiturates are safe to take (a) whenever one wants to; (b) when a friend offers some; (c) if they are in a family medicine chest; (d) only when prescribed by doctors.

_____ 4. There is a growing trend to abuse (a) barbiturates; (b) amphetamines; (c) both of these drugs.

T   F   5. Any experimental drug may be dangerous.

_____ 6. Experimental means that experts (a) know all the good effects; (b) know all the bad effects; (c) both of the above; (d) do not know all the good or bad effects.

_____ 7. The effects of marijuana are (a) consistent—always pleasant; (b) variable—sometimes pleasant.

T   F   8. The abuse of alcohol is a serious problem.

_____ 9. The major effects of all the drugs are (a) on the mind; (b) on the body; (c) on both the mind and the body.

_____ 10. Kinds of changes or "alterations" these drugs can produce in the mind include (a) changes in moods (anxiousness, happiness, and sadness); (b) changes in consciousness (awareness of things); (c) feelings; (d) all of these things.

_____ 11. A particular drug, given in the same amount or dosage, will affect (a) all people the same way; (b) different people in different ways.

_____ 12. A specific drug taken by the same person at different times may produce (a) somewhat different results each time; (b) the same result always.

_____ 13. These other factors that will modify (change) the basic action of a drug are (a) a person's physical condition; (b) his personality and mood; (c) both his physical condition and his personality and mood.

T   F   14. Can a person's expectations (what he wants to happen) influence how the drug will affect him?

_____ 15. When taking a drug, a person will react according to (a) his expectations of the drug (what he wants it to do); (b) the social setting where it is given; (c) both.

_____ 16. A habit means a person (a) really needs the drug; (b) feels that he needs the drug; (c) does not need the drug at all.

_____ 17. What does "tolerance" mean? Does it mean that the original drug effects continue to be produced by (a) the same amount of the drug; (b) only smaller amounts of the drug; (c) only larger amounts of the drug?

T   F   18. All drugs can become habit forming.

_____ 19. Physical dependence, that is, physical addiction, can develop with (a) all drugs; (b) some drugs; (c) no drugs.

_____ 20. If a person addicted to a drug, physically dependent on it, can not get his drug (a) he gets better; (b) he gets sick; (c) nothing happens.

T   F   21. All drugs can be dangerous.

_____ 22. The success of a law or regulation depends on (a) the number of law enforcement persons; (b) the harshness of the regulation; (c) the power of the medical profession; (d) the willingness of people to obey the law.

_____ 23. A person's decisions about drugs should be based on (a) what his teachers want him to do; (b) what his friends want him to do; (c) what he knows about drugs and what he wants to do.

*Adapted from Drug abuse education, grades 6, 9, 12, Towson, Md., 1969, Baltimore County Board of Education.

REVISION OF THE UNIVERSITY OF ILLINOIS SMOKING KNOWLEDGE TEST*

1. A study of the smoking habits of American teen-agers reveals that
   a. more teen-agers than adults smoke cigarettes.
   b. more junior high students smoke than high school students.
   c. approximately 30% of all teen-agers smoke cigarettes.
   d. more teen-age girls than teen-age boys smoke cigarettes.
2. Cigarette commercials no longer show professional athletes smoking. Which of the following is **not** true of cigarette advertisements?
   a. Cigarette advertisers sponsor athletic contests on TV.
   b. Some athletes give testimonials against smoking for poster displays.
   c. Cigarette commercials include the health effects of smoking.
   d. Cigarette smoking is associated with participation in recreational activities.
3. The work load of the heart of a cigarette smoker is increased due to
   a. carbon monoxide reducing the oxygen-carrying capacity of the blood.
   b. the acceleration of the clotting time of blood.
   c. increased thickening of the walls of the arterioles and small arteries.
   d. all of the above.
4. Surveys indicate that most teen-agers smoke because they
   a. like the taste of tobacco.
   b. are rebelling against authority.
   c. want to belong to the group.
   d. say it calms them down.
5. Nicotine, an ingredient in cigarette smoke, is
   a. stimulating to the nervous system.
   b. depressing to the nervous system.
   c. both stimulating and depressing.
   d. neither stimulating nor depressing.
6. The reason most adult smokers would advise teen-agers not to start smoking is that
   a. doctors are against smoking.
   b. it is unlawful for teen-agers to smoke.
   c. cigarette ads do not give the whole truth.
   d. it is easier not to start than to give up smoking.
7. One reason scientists think cigarette smoking is a cause of lung cancer is due to the
   a. increased activity of the cilia of smokers.
   b. thickening of respiratory membranes of smokers.
   c. higher incidence of lung cancer among cigarette smokers.
   d. all of the above.
8. Which of the following is **not** true of coronary heart disease?
   a. Coronary heart disease is the leading cause of death.
   b. It kills 2½ times more smokers than lung cancer each year.
   c. It claims a majority of its victims in the 20 to 30 age group.
   d. It is a greater health hazard for smokers rather than nonsmokers.

Please study the following table concerning the rate of smoking by sex and education. Use this information for answering question 9.

number of years of education	MALES (100%)			FEMALES (100%)		
	never smoked regularly	former smokers	present smokers	never smoked regularly	former smokers	present smokers
5 to 8	24.3	20.1	55.5	64.8	4.8	30.0
9 to 12	30.1	17.6	52.2	55.9	8.4	35.5
13 and over	36.3	22.6	41.1	53.7	12.0	34.1

*Adapted from Creswell, W. H., Jr., et al.: Youth smoking behavior characteristics and their educational implications, Washington, D. C., 1970, U. S. Public Health Service.

Continued.

REVISION OF THE UNIVERSITY OF ILLINOIS SMOKING KNOWLEDGE TEST—cont'd

9. The table given on p. 281 does **not** indicate that
   a. the percentage of female smokers generally increases with an increase in education.
   b. a higher percentage of males than females smoke.
   c. the more highly educated females quit smoking more often than do the highly educated males.
   d. the percentage of male smokers generally decreases with an increase in education.
10. Emphysema in recent years has
    a. increased slightly for both men and women.
    b. increased moderately for men; remained unchanged for women.
    c. increased considerably for men and is increasing for women.
    d. remained the same for both men and women.
11. Metastasis relates to the
    a. thickening of the walls of the arteries.
    b. spreading of cancer cells to other parts of the body.
    c. destruction of the tiny air sacs of the lungs.
    d. result of poor circulation in the body extremities.
12. The percentage of high school girls who now smoke is
    a. shown to be gradually decreasing.
    b. progressively approaching that of high school boys.
    c. greater than that of high school boys.
    d. greater than that of adult women.
13. A disease characterized by a progressive reduction of blood flow to the extremities has long been recognized as due primarily to the use of tobacco. This disease is called
    a. Buerger's disease.
    b. bronchitis.
    c. coronary heart disease.
    d. emphysema.
14. Most people continue to smoke because of
    a. psychological factors.
    b. addiction to nicotine.
    c. physiological effects.
    d. aesthetic reasons.
15. Cigarette smokers tire easily because
    a. the lungs decrease in size.
    b. dirt and dust cannot be filtered.
    c. of inefficient gas exchange in the lungs.
    d. the membranes lose their elasticity.
16. Which of the following best describes the effect of nicotine?
    a. It dilates the blood vessels.
    b. It constricts the blood vessels.
    c. It has no effect on the blood.
    d. Little is known on the subject.
17. The person **most** likely to get lung cancer is the
    a. pipe smoker.
    b. cigar smoker.
    c. cigarette smoker.
    d. ex-smoker.
18. Which of the following acts directly as a cleaning and filtering system for the lungs?
    a. Bronchi
    b. Cilia
    c. Trachea
    d. Alveoli

REVISION OF THE UNIVERSITY OF ILLINOIS SMOKING KNOWLEDGE TEST—cont'd

19. Approximately how many cigarettes does it take to affect the pulse rate?
    a. One
    b. Five
    c. Ten
    d. Twenty
20. The "smoker's cough," a type of chronic bronchitis, is
    a. the result of constriction of nasal passages of the smoker.
    b. caused by irritation of mucous membranes of the respiratory tract.
    c. due to the chemicals in the cigarette paper.
    d. not really related to smoking.
21. The purpose of studying about smoking is to
    a. create an awareness of health hazards.
    b. present both sides of the issues.
    c. help with individual decision making.
    d. accomplish all of the above.
22. The pattern of cigarette smoking among women reveals that
    a. more women than men smoke.
    b. the number of women smokers has decreased.
    c. approximately 30% of the women smoke.
    d. women start smoking earlier than men.
23. The ingredient in cigarette smoke that is believed to be the cause of lung cancer is
    a. nicotine.
    b. carbon monoxide.
    c. tobacco tars.
    d. charcoal.
24. An immediate effect of cigarette smoking is the
    a. dilation of the pupils.
    b. increase in body temperature.
    c. increase in blood pressure.
    d. slowing down of pulse rate.
25. Smoking affects the diet by
    a. leading to an increase in the appetite.
    b. increasing the sensitivity of the taste buds.
    c. decreasing the flow of gastric juices.
    d. increasing the level ot blood sugar.
26. Cancer is generally described as a (an)
    a. inflammation of the membranes in the throat.
    b. irritation of cells in the bronchi.
    c. uncontrollable growth of abnormal cells.
    d. break up of cells within the lungs.

Read the information concerning the following four teen-agers and then answer questions 27 and 28.

    Margaret—majority of her close friends smoke; boyfriend smokes
    Joyce—a few of her friends smoke; boyfriend smokes
    Bill—neither father nor mother smokes; friends mainly nonsmokers
    Donald—both father and mother smoke; friends mainly smokers

27. The two teen-agers **most** likely to become smokers are
    a. Joyce and Margaret.
    b. Donald and Margaret.
    c. Bill and Joyce.
    d. Donald and Joyce.
28. The two teen-agers **least** likely to become smokers are
    a. Bill and Donald.
    b. Margaret and Donald.
    c. Donald and Joyce.
    d. Joyce and Bill.

Continued.

REVISION OF THE UNIVERSITY OF ILLINOIS SMOKING KNOWLEDGE TEST—cont'd

29. A loss of elasticity of the tiny air sacs in the lungs is most characteristic of
    a. Buerger's disease.
    b. cancer.
    c. bronchitis.
    d. emphysema.

30. Cigarette commercials do **not** include appeals to one's
    a. emotional feelings.
    b. smoking pleasures.
    c. rational thought.
    d. sexual awareness.

31. When compared to nonsmokers, cigarette smokers tend to have
    a. a greater life expectancy.
    b. a shorter length of life.
    c. the same mortality rate.
    d. the same morbidity rate.

32. The walls of the blood vessels of cigarette smokers are apt to be
    a. thinner than nonsmokers.
    b. thicker than nonsmokers.
    c. more brittle than nonsmokers.
    d. more elastic than nonsmokers.

33. Unlike the tars in cigarettes, nicotine has the greatest effect on
    a. respiration.
    b. circulation.
    c. digestion.
    d. excretion.

34. In patients with emphysema
    a. there is a paralysis of the alveoli.
    b. cancerous growths appear in the lungs.
    c. there is a decreased blood flow to the extremities.
    d. air cannot flow freely out of the lungs.

35. Through advertising, people are persuaded to buy certain brands of cigarettes because they
    a. are under the subtle influence of suggestion.
    b. identify cigarette smoking with social pleasures.
    c. associate smoking with beautiful, sophisticated people.
    d. are influenced by all of the above.

36. The reason most people fear lung cancer is because it is
    a. the leading cause of death.
    b. a permanent handicap.
    c. nearly always fatal.
    d. difficult to diagnose.

The following boys are on the high school track team:
    Rob—distance runner
    Bill—discus thrower
    Bob—sprinter
    Paul—pole vaulter

37. Of the above athletes, the one whose performance will probably be **least** affected by smoking is
    a. Rob.
    b. Bill.
    c. Bob.
    d. Paul.

REVISION OF THE UNIVERSITY OF ILLINOIS SMOKING KNOWLEDGE TEST—cont'd

38. Of the above four trackmen, the one whose performance will probably be **most** affected by smoking is
    a. Rob.
    b. Bill.
    c. Bob.
    d. Paul.
39. One of the first serious effects of smoking is the
    a. paralysis of the cilia.
    b. lowering of the blood pressure.
    c. tar that accumulates on the lips.
    d. heat of the smoke in the lungs.
40. Studies have shown that many high school boys do not smoke because of their
    a. awareness of the health hazards.
    b. inability to afford the expense.
    c. participation in athletics.
    d. aesthetic considerations.
41. Cigarette smoking produces all of the following **except** a (an)
    a. decrease in temperature in the extremities.
    b. reduction of the oxygen in the blood.
    c. rise in the blood sugar level.
    d. increase in body weight.
42. The body part most affected by pipe smoking is the
    a. lungs.
    b. trachea.
    c. lips.
    d. bronchial tubes.
43. As a result of regular cigarette smoking there is
    a. an overall decrease in reaction time.
    b. a slowing of the blood flow through the capillaries.
    c. an increase in the total vital capacity of the lungs.
    d. an overall increase in the body's temperature.
44. The health hazards of cigarette smoking increase with
    a. the number of cigarettes smoked.
    b. the number of years a person smokes.
    c. the amount of smoke inhaled.
    d. all of the above.

ALCOHOL AND ALCOHOLISM—ATTITUDINAL MEASURE*

Instructions: Read the following group of seven statements and mark a 1 in front of the statement you **like** the most. Then mark a T in front of any other statements you agree with. Next mark a 2 in front of the statement you **dislike** the most. Then mark an F in front of any other statements you do not agree with. You need not mark all the statements if you do not want to. Read all seven statements before you mark any of them. There are three groups to be done this way.

1. As far as the use of alcohol is concerned:
_____ There should be no restrictions as to when and who can use alcohol.
_____ The present laws should not be as strict as they are toward the use of alcohol.
_____ People should be able to ignore some of the laws about the use of alcohol at times.
_____ People should be able to make a free choice as to how they want to use alcohol as long as they don't interfere with the choice of others.
_____ People who develop a problem because of alcohol should not be allowed to use it.
_____ Strict laws should be enforced as to when and who can use alcohol.
_____ No one should be allowed to use alcohol in any form.

2. In teaching about alcohol and problem drinking the school should present:
_____ Any true or false facts that will keep people from drinking.
_____ Any true facts that will keep people from drinking.
_____ The true facts but should lean toward convincing people not to drink.
_____ The true facts so a person can make a choice based on hearing both sides of the story.
_____ Only facts that the students and parents want to hear.
_____ Only the bare minimum facts required by state law.
_____ Absolutely nothing, since this area is not the school's concern.

3. A person who has a drinking problem:
_____ Is completely incompetent and should be put in an institution for his own good.
_____ Is such a weakling that he should be forced to accept treatment.
_____ Is dealing with his own personal problem and society should not interfere.
_____ Is physically, mentally, socially, and/or spiritually ill and should be treated as any other ill person.
_____ Should be given a chance to make restitution with the law and to promise that he won't drink anymore.
_____ Should be held responsible for his actions against the law when drinking, the same as when he is not drinking.
_____ Is a threat to society and should be treated as any other criminal.

*From Weir, W. R.: J. Alcohol Educ. **15**:1-8, 1969.

ATTITUDE TOWARD SMOKING MARIJUANA*

Recently increasing publicity has been given to smoking marijuana. The following scale is meant to explore some of your **feelings** toward smoking marijuana. It is **not** meant to test what you know about marijuana. Read each item carefully and **circle** the number opposite each statement with which you **agree**. Make **no marks** opposite the statement with which you **disagree**.

(S)

4.9	149.	Smoking marijuana is a requirement for successful living.
4.7	147.	Smoking marijuana is necessary if one is to achieve his potential.
4.5	145.	Smoking marijuana is an excellent way to increase one's understanding of the world about him.
4.3	143.	Smoking marijuana is too good a thing to be given up.
4.1	141.	Smoking marijuana can be a helpful way of adjusting to the world around us.
3.9	139.	A person should be allowed to smoke marijuana if he wants to.
3.7	137.	Smoking marijuana can be justified.
3.5	135.	Smoking marijuana is all right in some cases.
3.3	133.	The benefits of smoking marijuana depend entirely upon the individual.
3.1	131.	Smoking marijuana is not necessarily wrong.
2.9	129.	Smoking marijuana is one way of trying to be different.
2.7	127.	Smoking marijuana is not absolutely bad but it is not good either.
2.5	125.	I question whether or not it is morally right to smoke marijuana.
2.3	123.	Smoking marijuana is not a necessary part of life.
2.1	121.	Smoking marijuana is an emotional "crutch."
1.9	119.	Smoking marijuana is a foolish thing to do.
1.7	117.	Smoking marijuana is wrong.
1.5	115.	Smoking marijuana is bad.
1.3	113.	Smoking marijuana is a foolish way to try and escape reality.
1.1	111.	Smoking marijuana shows an utter lack of self-respect.

SCORING THE SCALE

Each statement has a scale value. These scale values are indicated in column (S). This column is not to be included in the scale given to the student and is shown here only to simplify the explanation of scoring. The scale encompasses statements that reflect a point of view that can be rated on a five-point continuum: 5 = very favorable; 4 = favorable; 3 = neither favorable nor unfavorable; 2 = unfavorable; and 1 = very unfavorable.

The individual "score" or measure of attitude is the scale value of the middle or median value of those statements to which the student responds. For example, if a student agrees with and responds to statements 137, 131, 129, and 117, his median score is 2.9. According to the scoring system, 2.9 indicates that this student's attitude toward smoking marijuana is neither favorable nor unfavorable. Let us further assume that a student agrees with and responds to statements 121, 119, 117, and 115. Here his median or middle "score" would be 1.8, which indicates an unfavorable attitude toward smoking marijuana. Individual "scores" from a class may be averaged to obtain a class mean score toward smoking marijuana. The numerical value of this mean score indicates the class attitude toward smoking marijuana. For example, the scores of 35 students in a classroom average a mean score of 2.23. From our scoring values we may ascertain that the attitude of this class toward smoking marijuana is unfavorable since 2.0 indicates an unfavorable expression of attitude.

*From Vincent, R. J.: J. Sch. Health **40**:454-456, 1970.

DRUG ATTITUDE SURVEY

Directions: Give your feeling about each of the items below by marking in the column to the right the number, 1 to 5, which most accurately expresses your opinion at this time.

1. Strongly agree
2. Agree
3. Neither
4. Disagree
5. Strongly disagree

NUMBERS

1. When in a group, go along with the group view because it is usually right. _____

2. Parents should let kids experiment with drugs if they want to. _____

3. If your friends use marijuana, you should too so that you are not different. _____

4. If you can not succeed in or enjoy life, you have a good reason to want to forget it all by drinking or taking drugs. _____

5. Since marijuana use today does not lead to heroin use, there is little reason against using marijuana. _____

6. The laws against marijuana should be made more lenient. _____

7. There is little or no harm in using marijuana so long as a person does not indulge too frequently. _____

8. A user of LSD experiences mind expansion and greater awareness of his surroundings. _____

9. Taking LSD makes you become more sociable and more closely related to those around you. _____

10. Some people withdraw from reality through the use of drugs. _____

11. The side effects, if any, that a new user might expect can be predicted by a person who has used LSD several times. _____

12. LSD promises to be a "miracle drug," once it is brought under medical control, because it helps people solve problems and adjust to life. _____

13. Adolescents trying to resolve the conflicts of growing up can be helped by LSD. _____

14. People who use drugs are stupid. _____

15. People who use drugs are just trying to find out what it is like. _____

16. The laws about drugs should be more strict and enforced more. _____

17. The laws about drugs should be made more lenient for the first offense. _____

18. The laws about drugs should be eliminated. _____

19. Anybody who gives or sells drugs to kids should not be punished any more than someone who takes it. _____

20. Anybody who furnishes kids with drugs should be severely punished. _____

DRUG ABUSE ATTITUDES AND OPINIONS PRE-TEST AND POST-TEST*

Directions: Indicate by placing a check (✓) in the appropriate column to the right your feelings and opinions to the statements listed.

	AGREE	DISAGREE	CANNOT DECIDE

1. The decision to use or not to use any drug is a personal decision which each individual must make for himself.
2. Every time a person takes a drug as an attempt to help in solving his problems, he loses an opportunity to develop his own resources for solving the problems.
3. If you don't use drugs it is risky to associate with those who do because they might influence you to begin.
4. The decision to use drugs affects only the person who chooses to use them.
5. People who are curious about drugs should satisfy their curiosity by trying them.
6. Driving an automobile after smoking marijuana is safer than driving after drinking alcoholic beverages.
7. Students who use drugs tend to lose interest in school, to get lower grades, to subsequently drop out of school.
8. If a person has will power, he can take almost any drug and be able to stop when he wants.
9. Drugs are good for some people because they help them escape from their problems.
10. Marijuana use frequently leads to, or is associated with, the use of other drugs.
11. The use of heroin leads a person quickly toward total drug dependence from which it is very difficult and often impossible to recover.
12. Marijuana is a harmless drug that does not cause physical or mental damage.
13. Drug users are likely to be persons who never learn to solve problems or to adjust to life.
14. Adults who use and often abuse alcohol are unfit to advise young people about the use of marijuana.
15. State and federal laws restricting the use of drugs constitute violations of the individual's constitutional rights.
16. The amphetamines are mild and fairly harmless drugs with which students can safely experiment.

*From Senior high school health guide, unit IV, drug abuse and health, Salt Lake City, 1971, Utah State Board of Education.
Continued.

DRUG ABUSE ATTITUDES AND OPINIONS PRE-TEST AND POST-TEST—cont'd

	AGREE	DISAGREE	CANNOT DECIDE

17. Some users of LSD experience mental disturbances which endanger their mental health.
18. Suppose you discover that a classmate is abusing drugs. What should be done?
    a. It is his own business—nothing should be done.
    b. Offer your help.
    c. Talk to trusted adults about him.
    d. Inform his parents.
    e. Inform the police about him.
19. Giving students information about drugs will
    a. have no effect on their decision to use or not to use drugs.
    b. make students curious who never thought about using drugs before.
    c. encourage drug abuse.
    d. help stop drug abuse.
    e. encourage experimentation to merely find out what it's all about.
20. Lack of parental discipline is a **major** cause of drug use and abuse.
21. Too strict parental discipline is a **major** cause of drug use and abuse.
22. Permissiveness in homes and in society is a **major** cause of drug use and abuse.
23. Most drug users have valid and workable plans for improving America, its schools, its government, its policies.
24. The nature and extent of drug abuse among students (high school, junior high, and elementary) has been exaggerated.
25. One of the primary mistakes of teachers who are trying to conduct drug education programs is that they make no distinction between various patterns of drug use—experimental, occasional, regular, compulsive.
26. Drug use among students is largely due to Communists and their plans to overthrow the U. S. government.
27. School programs that continue to be planned for the college-bound, the socially motivated, and the athletically gifted, contribute to the drug use and abuse problem.
28. Students often use drugs as a means of attacking their parents.

DRUG ABUSE ATTITUDES AND OPINIONS PRE-TEST AND POST-TEST—cont'd

	AGREE	DISAGREE	CANNOT DECIDE

29. What has been your experience with people?
   a. There is a lot of good in all people.
   b. There is some good in most people.
   c. People are about as good as they have to be.
   d. A surprising number of people are mean and dishonest.
   e. Most people are just no good.

30. Which of the following best describes your feelings toward most people?
   a. I have very few close friends. Generally I do not meet and make friends easily.
   b. I have a few close friends. Generally I meet people and make friends fairly easily although probably not as easily as most people do.
   c. I have probably a little less than the average number of close friends since I generally do not have the time or the interest to spend with them.
   d. I have about the average number of close friends, and I meet people and make friends about as well as most people do.
   e. I have many close friends and I try to take an interest in most of them. I meet people and make friends easier than most people do.

OPINIONS ON THE USE AND CONTROL OF BEVERAGE ALCOHOL*

Directions: The following statements are concerned with the use and effects of alcohol as a beverage. Some of the statements deal with facts and some reflect opinions. You are asked to consider each of the statements and indicate your choice in the proper column. If you are in agreement with what the statement says, place an "X" opposite the statement in the column headed "agree." If you disagree with the statement, place an "X" in the column headed "disagree." If you do not know whether you agree or disagree with the statement, or if you are doubtful, place an "X" in the column marked "uncertain."

	AGREE	DISAGREE	UNCERTAIN
1. Even among the experts, very little is known of the effects of alcohol upon the human body.			
2. Frequent drunkenness and alcoholism means the same thing.			
3. Drinking alcoholic beverages, though begun in moderation, will lead eventually to alcoholism.			
4. The present trend in the consumption of alcoholic beverages in the United States indicates a decrease in per capita consumption.			
5. The increase in alcohol is the fundamental cause of most alcoholism.			
6. Most people who drink alcoholic beverages do so moderately.			
7. Alcohol is directly responsible for a large proportion of the crimes committed.			
8. Alcoholic beverages are a form of poison.			
9. Alcohol, in the form of a beverage, is a good stimulant and, therefore, effective in the treatment of snakebite, shock, or a common cold.			
10. There are several kinds of alcohol, but ethyl alcohol is the one contained in alcoholic beverages.			
11. The alcohol content of alcoholic beverages produced by fermentation is greater than that of beverages produced by distillation.			
12. The chemical effect of alcohol on the body is similar to that of ether and acts as an anaesthetic or depressant on the nervous system.			
13. Alcohol beverages are a form of food.			
14. The same amount of alcohol taken in the form of whiskey is more "potent" than that taken in the form of wine.			
15. Alcohol may, when taken in small amounts, serve a beneficial purpose in bringing about relaxation, lessening body tension, and acting as a "social lubricant."			
16. People who drink alcoholic beverages do not make good parents.			

*From Tobacco, drug, alcohol unit, seventh grade, Great Falls, Mont., 1971, Great Falls Public Schools.

OPINIONS ON THE USE AND CONTROL OF BEVERAGE ALCOHOL—cont'd

	AGREE	DISAGREE	UNCERTAIN

17. Excessive drinking produces serious physical and mental diseases.

18. Alcohol in high concentration is known to be irritating to body tissues; therefore, when whiskey, containing 50% alcohol by volume, is taken into the body, it irritates and causes inflammation of the organs of the body, especially the brain.

19. Alcohol taken into the body in beverage form is absorbed from the stomach and taken directly into the bloodstream without change.

20. Most people can drink alcoholic beverages without injury to their health.

21. The habit of excessive drinking puts a great strain upon the heart and is thus responsible for much heart disease.

22. Prohibition of the manufacture, sale, and use of alcoholic beverages prevents people from drinking and thereby solves the problems of excessive drinking and alcoholism.

23. The best known method for measuring the amount of alcohol in the brain is to measure the concentration of alcohol in the blood.

24. Magazines and newspapers containing liquor advertisements should not be patronized.

25. Scenes which show persons drinking alcoholic beverages, with or without ill effects, should not be permitted in the movies.

26. The use of alcoholic beverages has existed for thousands of years in all countries despite all legal and social attempts to prohibit it.

27. Many persons can increase their skill in operating an automobile after taking a little alcohol.

28. Chronic alcoholics are more susceptible to respiratory diseases, especially pneumonia, and are less able to survive them than nonalcoholics.

29. Any use of alcoholic beverages by the state encourages drinking by giving it official approval.

30. The use of alcoholic beverages in the home is not necessarily harmful to good family life.

31. Various attitudes toward serving and drinking alcoholic beverages are found among different groups in our society.

Continued.

OPINIONS ON THE USE AND CONTROL OF BEVERAGE ALCOHOL—cont'd

	AGREE	DISAGREE	UNCERTAIN
32. Judgment, vision, and reaction time in individual performance are frequently impaired by even small amounts of alcohol.			
33. The money obtained from taxes on alcoholic beverages should not be used for the support of schools or for the aged.			

YOUTH ALIENATION SURVEY

This is a survey to determine your opinions on a few general issues. Since opinions are of a personal nature, there are no right or wrong answers. Please try to answer as honestly as possible. All responses will be kept in the strictest of confidence.

Directions: Indicate in the column on the right the number that best represents your opinion.

1. Disagree strongly
2. Disagree
3. Neutral
4. Agree
5. Agree strongly

NUMBERS

1. Nowadays a person has to live pretty much for today and let tomorrow take care of itself. _____

2. Religion is playing an important role in solving today's problems. _____

3. None of the political candidates running for election ever represents my view. _____

4. I usually have the courage of my convictions. _____

5. Deep down I know I am not the person I would like to be. _____

6. With the advance of science, the world is daily becoming a better place to live. _____

7. The best way to get things done is to operate within the channels of the existing political system. _____

8. If people are allowed to do whatever they want, they are likely to cause trouble. _____

9. The stuff they teach in schools just does not seem useful in the real world. _____

10. Having pull is more important than ability in getting a good job. _____

11. Parents today are not strict enough with their children. _____

12. More and more I feel helpless in the face of what is happening in the world today. _____

13. I used to think my prospects for success were pretty good, but now I am beginning to wonder. _____

14. Most of the decisions made by the courts are unfair. _____

15. Our society may not be ideal, but things are not as bad as most people claim. _____

16. You can always find friends if you try. _____

17. Most people would not work if they did not have to eat. _____

18. Ask not what your country can do for you; ask instead what you can do for your country. _____

19. No one has the right to tell me how to run my life. _____

20. Despite what others may say, I know I am on the right track in life. _____

21. Nobody really cares about anybody's problems but his own. _____

22. A factory worker can lead just as full a life as anyone else. _____

23. It is important to teach young people strict obedience to their parents. _____

24. The future is so unpredictable that there is not much point in making long-range plans. _____

25. Active discussion of politics can eventually lead to a better world. _____

26. Family responsibilities come first, even at great personal cost. _____

27. Other people seem to find it easier to decide what is right than I do. _____

28. Everyone is always trying to tell me what to do.

29. Most people in public office are genuinely interested in the problems of the average person. _____

30. I would take a boring job if I thought the chances for promotion were good. _____

31. We are just so many cogs in the machinery of the system. _____

32. Young people must be made to realize that there is a lot they can learn from their elders. _____

Continued.

YOUTH ALIENATION SURVEY—cont'd

NUMBERS

33. This world is run by only a few people in power. _____

34. It is worthwhile to have friends, no matter how much trouble they may seem to be. _____

35. Most religious leaders are really out of touch with what is happening today. _____

36. You can't fight city hall. _____

37. As long as no one is hurt, the police ought to mind their own business. _____

38. One thing I know I can always fall back on is my religion. _____

39. Marriage is out of date. _____

40. Any job can be interesting if you work hard at it. _____

41. If I had my life to live over, I would probably do the same things. _____

42. Even if the odds seem against you, it is possible to come out on top by persisting. _____

43. When I am really honest with myself I realize that I just do not have what it takes. _____

44. My friends would not let me down if I really needed them. _____

45. It takes a few nonconformists to show the rest of the world how to shape up. _____

46. I think I could make a go of almost anything if I really put my mind to it. _____

YOUTH ATTITUDE QUESTIONNAIRE

This questionnaire is designed to find out what different young people think about the world and their part in it. It asks questions about you and your attitudes. Please answer the questions frankly and seriously. Your names are not requested.

Indicate in the blank space the number (1 to 5) that best represents your feelings:

1. Good
2. Somewhat good
3. Don't care
4. Somewhat bad
5. Bad

Here are some things that people feel differently about. Illustrate your feelings about each by placing to the right the number that best represents that feeling, using the rating scale above.

Your school	_____	The churches	_____
Your city	_____	Business and industry	_____
The armed forces	_____	Your parents	_____
School teachers	_____	Boy Scouts	_____
U. S. government	_____	Girl Scouts	_____
The police	_____	YMCA-YWCA	_____
Hippies	_____	City officials	_____

Here are some statements representing common attitudes. Place the number that best represents your feeling to the right of the statement, using the rating scale below:

1. Completely agree
2. Mostly agree
3. Mostly disagree
4. Completely disagree

1. I am the master of my fate.   _____
2. Sometimes I cannot understand why I do the things I do.   _____
3. What a person makes of his life depends on him.   _____
4. Getting what you want is mostly a matter of getting the breaks.   _____
5. There are days when nothing seems to matter.   _____
6. I am sure of my feelings about things that affect my life.   _____
7. In life, some people are intended to be happy, others are not.   _____
8. Most of life is pretty boring.   _____
9. When things go bad, I try harder.   _____
10. Most of my experiences are interesting ones.   _____
11. Most people will not really do anything to make this a better world.   _____
12. Parents want for their child only that which is for the child's own good.   _____
13. With the present situation, most people would be better off if they were never born.   _____
14. Nobody really cares about anyone else.   _____
15. Parents are always looking for things to nag their children about.   _____
16. Marijuana should be legalized.   _____
17. Smoking or possession of marijuana should be considered misdemeanors rather than felonies.   _____

If you had a personal problem, which of the following people would you be most likely to talk it over with? Parents, friend of own age and sex, friend of own age of opposite sex, adult outside the family, would not talk it over with anyone.   _____

PUPIL PROBLEMS, INTERESTS, AND NEEDS*

Your teacher is interested in finding better ways to help you identify your problems, interests, and needs. You can help by answering the following questions. Please feel free to write what you think. This information will be kept in confidence and will help us to more effectively plan for your future. No names are requested on this paper.

1. What is now giving you the greatest satisfaction?

2. What do you like most about your school?

3. What do you like least about your school?

4. What is your greatest problem at the present time?

5. What are you most afraid of?

6. What do you like to do in your spare time? What is your strongest interest?

7. What kind of work would you most like to do when you finish school?

8. What kind of work will you probably have to do when you finish school?

9. What was your greatest problem when you first came to this school?

10. What will probably be your greatest problem when you leave this school?

11. What person do you usually go to for help with your problems?

12. What is the one most important thing the school should do for you?

*From Drug abuse education curriculum guide and resource materials for grades K-12, Dallas, 1970, Superintendent of Schools, Dallas Independent School District.

MY CHECKLIST*

Name_____Grade_____Age_____Date_____

	MAKES ME HAPPY	MAKES ME UPSET OR ANGRY	DON'T CARE
Accidentally breaking something			
Sleeping late in the morning			
Being scolded, even though I didn't mean to cause trouble			
A quiet, orderly house			
Being called to get up			
Being told I did wrong			
Having to say ''sorry,'' even though I should			
Having to eat what I don't like			
Winning a game			
Being teased or called names			
Going places I want to go			
Being shoved around			
Being told how nice I am			
Having someone take my things without asking			
Doing my lessons well			
Not being allowed to do what I want to do			
Being told that I have done a good job			
Knowing I have made a mistake			
Being told to go to bed			
Being kind to someone			
Being told to ''hurry up'' when I am already hurrying			
Losing a game			
Brothers and sisters being mean			
Being able to tell my troubles to someone I like			
Someone else being teased or bothered			
Feeling guilty about something			
Other			

This is what I wish:

*Adapted from Toward responsible drug education, grades K-4, Salem, 1970, Oregon State Board of Education.

STUDENT DRUG USE SURVEY FORM

Instructions: Place an "X" in the appropriate column for each drug used.

DRUGS	TIMES EVER USED					
	0	1 to 2	3 to 6	6 to 9	10 to 49	50+
Alcohol						
Barbiturates						
Cocaine						
Cough syrup						
Hallucinogens						
Heroin						
Marijuana						
Solvents						
Stimulants						
Tobacco						
Tranquilizers						

DRUGS	TIMES USED IN THE LAST 6 MONTHS					
	0	1 to 2	3 to 6	6 to 9	10 to 49	50+
Alcohol						
Barbiturates						
Cocaine						
Cough syrup						
Hallucinogens						
Heroin						
Marijuana						
Solvents						
Stimulants						
Tobacco						
Tranquilizers						

SURVEY FORM USED IN 1970*

Instructions: This survey is being made in county schools to get some facts. NO ONE IN YOUR SCHOOL WILL SEE THIS REPORT AFTER YOU FILL IT OUT. YOU CANNOT BE IDENTIFIED. Please do not report any drug used because a doctor or dentist prescribed it for you, or gave it to you. We appreciate your help. The only way we can get a fair picture is to come directly to the persons who know.

THIS REPORT WAS MADE BY:

☐ MALE   ☐ FRESHMAN   ☐ SOPHOMORE   ☐ GRADE 7
☐ FEMALE   ☐ JUNIOR   ☐ SENIOR   ☐ GRADE 8

I have used (during the past 12 months)	0	1 to 2	3 to 9	10 to 49	50+
Tobacco					
LSD					
Marijuana					
Alcoholic beverages					
Amphetamines (meth, speed, bennies, pep pills)					
Barbituates (downers, reds, yellow jackets, blues)					
Anything else you would like to name or say?					

*Adapted from Five mind-altering drugs (plus one), San Mateo, Calif., 1970, Department of Public Health and Welfare.

CONFIDENTIAL QUESTIONNAIRE*

> **Directions:** Place a check mark after any statements that apply. Do not sign your name. YOU ARE PROMISED THAT YOU WILL NOT BE IDENTIFIED FROM THIS QUESTIONNAIRE. School District No. 3 is asking for your cooperation in answering the following questions.

1. Are drugs used by students in your school?　　　　　　　　YES_____　NO_____
2. If yes, please check the ones you know about.
   a. Marijuana　　　　　　　　　　　　　　_____
   b. Hallucinogens (LSD, acid, cubes, big D, DMT) _____
   c. Amphetamines (speed, pep pills, dexies, bennies, footballs)　　　　　_____
   d. Deliriants (airplane glue, freon)　　　　_____
   e. Barbiturates (goofballs, red birds, yellow-jackets, blue heavens)　　　_____
   f. Heroin (hard stuff, junk)　　　　　_____
   g. Other　　　　　　　　　　_____
3. Have you ever used any of these drugs?　　　　　　　　YES_____　NO_____
4. If yes, which drugs and to what extent (how many times) have you used them?
   a. Marijuana　_____　Times: a. _____
   b. Hallucinogens　_____　b. _____
   c. Amphetamines　_____　c. _____
   d. Deliriants　_____　d. _____
   e. Barbiturates　_____　e. _____
   f. Heroin　_____　f. _____
   g. Other　_____　g. _____
5. How do you feel about the use of drugs?
   a. Would like to try using drugs.　　YES___　NO___　MAYBE___
   b. Think it's OK for others to use.　　YES___　NO___　MAYBE___
   c. Think it's OK for me.　　YES___　NO___　MAYBE___
   d. Would like more information on drugs and their use.　YES___　NO___　MAYBE___
   e. Would never try using drugs.　　YES___　NO___　MAYBE___
   f. Feel it's wrong for others to use drugs.　YES___　NO___　MAYBE___
6. Any comments you care to make would be appreciated:

*Adapted from Curriculum guide for drug education, grades K-12, Lovell, Wyo., 1970, Superintendent of Schools.

ALCOHOL EDUCATION PRETEST*

General instructions: This booklet contains a collection of statements concerning alcohol and its use. We are going to study this topic, and to insure that our sessions are of maximum value to all members of the class, we must know as much as possible about the needs of our class for knowledge about alcohol. Please answer all questions as frankly and completely as you can. It will not be necessary to sign your name or otherwise identify yourself personally, since it is group rather than individual results we want to consider. Nonetheless, each of your responses will be important in determining what we stress in this series, so please read each item carefully before answering.

Part I.   How much do you know about alcohol?

Below are some statements concerning alcohol and its use. If you think that the statement is **True,** encircle the letter **"T"** before the statement. If you think that the statement is **False,** encircle the letter **"F"** before the statement. Be sure to answer every question. If you don't know the answer make a guess.

T   F   1. Alcohol, the chemical found in all alcoholic beverages, is a stimulant.

T   F   2. Drinking alcohol will warm you up by increasing body temperature.

T   F   3. Alcohol in small amounts can increase athletic skill.

T   F   4. Two or three drinks can reduce your ability to operate a machine.

T   F   5. It's a sign of manliness to be able to drink a lot.

T   F   6. Some people are better drivers after a couple of drinks because they purposely drive more carefully.

T   F   7. Alcoholic drinks are necessary at a party if people really want to have a good time.

T   F   8. Alcohol is good for colds.

T   F   9. Excessive drinking of alcohol may injure body organs by "pickling" them.

T   F   10. Drunkenness of a person clearly shows he is addicted to alcohol.

T   F   11. There are fewer alcoholics among those who stick to beer and wine than among those who drink hard liquor.

T   F   12. The earlier the alcoholic patient looks for help, the better are his chances of recovery.

Part II.   How do you feel about alcohol?

A number of statements concerning alcohol and its use are listed below. Please indicate your agreement or disagreement with each statement by checking the column to the right of each statement which comes nearer to describing your feeling. There are no right or wrong answers. Your first reaction to the statement is what we are interested in. Make a choice for every statement. Check only one column for each statement.

                                                        AGREE   DISAGREE
1. The general public is already sufficiently informed about the facts of alcoholism.

2. If an alcoholic wanted to be cured, he could accomplish the matter himself.

3. The alcoholic suffers from a severe illness and needs treatment to a much greater degree than the usual medical complaints.

4. Drinking on some social occasions should be done if it helps the individual to fit in with others.

5. Only people like physicians, social workers, and the like should receive information concerning alcoholism.

6. Alcoholism is the direct result of a sick society.

7. No one should criticize the alcoholic without knowing why he drinks.

*Adapted from A curriculum guide for alcohol education for teachers, bulletin no. 371, Lansing, 1970, Michigan Department of Education.

Continued.

ALCOHOL EDUCATION PRETEST—cont'd

AGREE   DISAGREE

8. General hospitals should not accept alcoholics for treatment.
9. More research programs are needed about alcoholism.
10. Drinking alcoholic beverages should be classed with the illegal use of dope.
11. The alcoholic has no one to blame for his troubles but himself.
12. The facts about alcohol should be taught in every high school in America.
13. The families of alcoholics should encourage them to seek expert treatment for their condition.
14. Alcoholism begins as the sin of drinking and ends as a sinful habit.
15. Information on alcoholism should be available to any citizen who has the interest to write for it.
16. Doctors who spend their time treating alcoholics are wasting their time.
17. Public education concerning alcohol is a waste of time and money.
18. Alcoholic beverages are harmless when used in small amounts.

Part III.   What would you like to know about alcohol?

Rate the following topics according to their importance to you. Put the number ''1'' on the blank line in front of the topic you most want to learn about, the number ''8'' in front of the topic which interests you least and assign numbers ''2'' to ''7'' to the balance of the items in order of their importance to you. If two topics are equally important to you, rate them with the same number and omit the next number.

_____ The effects of alcohol on emotions, mental processes, and body organs (including hereditary effects).

_____ The physiological effects of alcohol with emphasis on its effect on behavior.

_____ Knowledge about the symptoms, causes, treatment, and hope for recovery in alcoholism.

_____ Knowledge of drinking customs with emphasis on why people drink, why young people shouldn't drink, and the variations in current drinking patterns and practice.

_____ Legal regulations about alcoholic beverages, and enforcement of these regulations, including justification for sale of such beverages in our society.

_____ The relationship of alcohol use to such areas as driving and social interaction, including its effect on sexual promiscuity.

_____ What is being done and what can be done to help solve school-related alcohol problems.

_____ What is alcohol and what are the differences between alcoholic beverages.

Feel free to comment below about this questionnaire, alcohol education, alcoholism, or anything related to alcohol use. Use the back of this page if you need more space.

SCORING AND INTERPRETING THE PRETEST

Part I.   Correct answers are: F,F,F,T,F,T,F,T,F,F,F,F,T.

Score one point for each correct answer. Sum all items for total score. Sum overall total scores and divide by the number of students for the group score. The higher the score, the better informed is the group.

Average score	Interpretation
11-12	Well-informed group
8-10	Somewhat better than chance
5-7	Chance performance. No knowledge
0-4	Misinformed

ALCOHOL EDUCATION PRETEST—cont'd

Part II.	Item	Favorable	Weight	Item	Favorable	Weight
	1.	Disagree	3.0	10.	Disagree	3.7
	2.	Disagree	2.9	11.	Disagree	2.2
	3.	Agree	1.7	12.	Agree	3.1
	4.	Agree	1.4	13.	Agree	3.7
	5.	Disagree	2.6	14.	Disagree	2.8
	6.	Disagree	2.7	15.	Agree	2.7
	7.	Agree	2.1	16.	Disagree	3.7
	8.	Disagree	2.4	17.	Disagree	3.7
	9.	Agree	2.4	18.	Agree	2.1

Score each item answered as above with the weight for that item. Sum all weights for total score. Sum overall total scores and divide by the number of students for the group score. The higher the score, the more favorable the group attitude toward education about alcohol use and treatment of alcoholism as an illness.

Average score	Interpretation
33.8 to 48.6	Highly favorable attitudes
22.2 to 33.7	Moderately favorable attitude
11.8 to 22.1	Neutral attitudes
5.2 to 11.7	Moderately unfavorable attitudes
0.0 to 5.1	Highly unfavorable attitudes

Part III. Sum across students for a total score on each topic. Divide the total score for each topic by the number of students rating that topic. Rank order the topics with the lowest score first. The lower the score, the higher the group interest in that topic.

Any remarks made in response to the invitation to "Feel free to comment" in Part III may be interpreted as evidence of strong concern on the part of the respondent about the topic mentioned. Particularly in topic areas suggested spontaneously by two or more students, some opportunity to clarify or discuss these topics should be provided in subsequent class sessions.

DRUG INFORMATION TEST

MULTIPLE CHOICE QUESTIONS

Directions: Place the correct letter in the space provided on the left that represents the best answer.

_____ 1. The greatest societal problem in the United States today is abuse of
  a. cocaine.
  b. heroin.
  c. alcohol.
  d. marijuana.
  e. LSD.

_____ 2. The active ingredients in marijuana have been extracted and synthesized. They are known collectively as
  a. psilocybin.
  b. DMT.
  c. lysergic acid diethylamide.
  d. THC (tetrahydrocannabinol).
  e. STP.

_____ 3. Which of the following is **not** a psychedelic drug?
  a. THC
  b. LSD
  c. STP
  d. IRT
  e. DMT

_____ 4. After repeated use the marijuana smoker
  a. develops a marked tolerance.
  b. develops little or no tolerance.
  c. develops an aversion to marijuana.
  d. usually goes to heroin.

_____ 5. The effects of cocaine are those of a
  a. stimulant.
  b. depressant.
  c. narcotic.

_____ 6. Studies of the effects of marijuana indicate tentatively that
  a. heart rate and respiratory rate go down.
  b. pupil size does not change.
  c. automobile driving performance is severely impaired.
  d. heart rate increases and blood sugar level drops markedly.

_____ 7. Which of the following is **not** a psychopharmacological agent?
  a. Narcotics
  b. Tranquilizers
  c. Antidepressants
  d. Psychotomimetics
  e. Antibodies

_____ 8. Tolerance to drugs refers to the fact that
  a. decreasing amounts of the drug are necessary to get the same effect.
  b. increasing amounts of the drug are necessary to get the same effect.
  c. no matter how large a dose one cannot obtain the original effect.
  d. none of the above.

_____ 9. Which of the following is **not** usually a morphine withdrawal symptom?
  a. Death
  b. Nausea, chills, prostration
  c. Cramps
  d. Anxiety
  e. Vomiting and weight loss

_____10. If an individual told you he had in his medicine cabinet secobarbital (Seconal), chlordiazepoxide (Librium), and meprobamate (Equanil), one could say that he had a fair amount of
  a. psychostimulants.

DRUG INFORMATION TEST—cont'd

      b. psychotomimetics.

      c. minor tranquilizers.

      d. antidepressants.

_____ 11. The effects of chlorpromazine (Thorazine) include

      a. inhibition of the effects of barbiturates.

      b. blocking of LSD psychosis.

      c. high abuse potential.

_____ 12. Which of the following is true of alcohol and barbiturates?

      a. Both are general stimulants.

      b. Barbiturates inhibit the effects of alcohol.

      c. Alcohol potentiates the effects of barbiturates.

      d. Their effects are completely different.

      e. Both drugs may be used in treating LSD psychosis.

_____ 13. Chronic use of "speed" can lead to

      a. cardiovascular involvement.

      b. malnutrition.

      c. paranoid psychosis.

      d. all of the above.

      e. only a and b of the above.

_____ 14. The drug which, according to its users, allows one to "experience death" is

      a. marijuana.

      b. heroin.

      c. "smack."

      d. LSD.

      e. alcohol.

_____ 15. Which of the following drugs is generally **not** hallucinogenic?

      a. LSD

      b. DMT

      c. Psilocybin

      d. Phenobarbital

      e. Mescaline

_____ 16. The effects of marijuana include

      a. sedation and relief of anxiety.

      b. disinhibition or excitement.

      c. perceptual changes.

      d. all of the above.

      e. only b and c of the above.

_____ 17. The known chromosomal effects of LSD include

      a. chromosome breaks in germ cells of mice.

      b. chromosome breaks in human white blood cells.

      c. abortion in baboons.

      d. all of the above.

      e. only a and c of the above.

_____ 18. LSD has been considered for therapy in which of the following ways?

      a. Reactivate repressed memories

      b. Allow psychiatrists to experience psychosis

      c. Provide therapeutic aid for terminal cancer patients

      d. All of the above

      e. Only b and c of the above

_____ 19. Which drug does **not** have the same effects as the others?

      a. Hash

      b. Crystals

      c. Speed

      d. Meth

      e. Bennies

Continued.

DRUG INFORMATION TEST—cont'd

_____ 20. The "rushes" refers to
    a. New York subway system.
    b. a bad trip on LSD.
    c. the first few seconds following an I.V. dose of speed.
    d. convulsions due to an overdose of barbiturates.
    e. a series of LSD flashbacks.

_____ 21. Which of the following is considered to be relatively safe to inhale or sniff?
    a. Toluene
    b. Propane
    c. Butanol
    d. Freon
    e. None of the above

_____ 22. The action of glue on the CNS is similar to that of
    a. major tranquilizers.
    b. Librium.
    c. Methedrine.
    d. alcohol.
    e. LSD.

_____ 23. Dependence on alcohol includes
    a. psychological dependence.
    b. physical dependence.
    c. tolerance.
    d. withdrawal produces physical symptoms.
    e. all of the above.
    f. only a and c of the above.

_____ 24. Dependence on hallucinogens like LSD includes
    a. psychological dependence.
    b. physical dependence.
    c. tolerance.
    d. withdrawal produces physical symptoms.
    e. all of the above.
    f. only a and c of the above.

_____ 25. Dependence on amphetamines includes
    a. psychological dependence.
    b. withdrawal produces physical symptoms (as in heroin withdrawal).
    c. tolerance.
    d. all of the above.
    e. only a and c of the above.

_____ 26. Dependence on barbiturates includes
    a. psychological dependence.
    b. physical dependence.
    c. withdrawal can produce convulsions and death.
    d. all of the above.
    e. only a and b of the above.

_____ 27. Dependence on marijuana includes
    a. psychological dependence.
    b. physical dependence.
    c. tolerance.
    d. withdrawal produces physical symptoms (as in narcotic withdrawal).
    e. all of the above.
    f. only b and d of the above.

_____ 28. Dependence on heroin includes
    a. physical dependence.
    b. psychological dependence.
    c. withdrawal produces an adverse physical reaction.

DRUG INFORMATION TEST—cont'd

d. tolerance.

e. all of the above.

f. only a and c of the above.

Directions: Please circle the correct answer to the left.

T   F   29. Death in human beings using LSD usually has been the result of suicide or accident.

T   F   30. All things can be poisonous; the variety of toxicity is in the dose and the individual's sensitivity.

T   F   31. We are exposed to many chemicals whose toxicity is in general unknown.

T   F   32. The initial discovery and testing of drugs are based on the assumption that experimental animals will react to the chemical being tested in the same way as the human being.

T   F   33. The drug aspirin is the chemical most frequently implicated in childhood poisoning.

T   F   34. As a result of the use of insecticides such as DDT, probably every living animal in the world now contains some insecticide.

T   F   35. LSD produces dilation of pupils.

T   F   36. The mechanism of action of virtually all drugs is unknown.

T   F   37. Physical dependence is an adaptive state that manifests itself by intense physical disturbances when the administration of the drug is suspended.

T   F   38. Drug dependence of the morphine type may be created within the dosage range generally used for therapeutic purposes.

T   F   39. Morphine-dependent individuals become tolerant to many of the effects of morphine but still retain the characteristic pinpoint pupils.

T   F   40. Death from morphine overdosage is usually due to respiratory depression.

T   F   41. The leaves of the female marijuana plant are considerably more potent than those of the male plant.

DRUG ATTITUDE SURVEY

Directions: Give your opinion about each of the items below by placing the number in the space on the right which most accurately expresses your opinion.

1. This is a completely accurate statement.
2. I strongly agree with this statement.
3. I tend to agree with this statement but with reservations.
4. I really could not say.
5. I tend to disagree with this statement but with reservations.
6. I strongly disagree with this statement.
7. This statement is patently untrue.

NUMBERS

1. Young people who abuse drugs are inadequate or immature individuals who need a crutch to cope with reality. _____
2. The only successful education and prevention programs are those which involve ex-addicts or ex-users. _____
3. Virtually every category of substance that has some effect on mood, feeling, or perception is being misused at this time. _____
4. It has been shown that LSD stimulates or enhances creativity. _____
5. The nature and extent of drug abuse among high school and elementary school children has been exaggerated. _____
6. Marijuana leads to sexual orgies. _____
7. No drug prevention program in school or community will be successful unless young people are involved at every state of planning and execution. _____
8. Like the heroin addict, the "speed freak" will do anything to obtain his supplies. _____
9. There is total agreement among competent scientists and physicians that marijuana is not a narcotic drug either pharmacologically or medically. _____
10. A drug is any substance that affects the structure and function of the living organism and all drugs act according to the same basic principles. _____
11. An important motive for drug use is a need to belong to a clique which happens to be engaged in drug use. _____
12. For total amount of damage done to our society, alcohol is more dangerous than any other drug. _____
13. Children should not be continually exposed to the idea that the stresses of daily life require chemical relief. _____
14. Marijuana leads to violent crimes. _____
15. Small groups honestly and freely discussing problems of adolescents would do more toward solving the drug problem in schools than reaching every young person with the most comprehensive and honest information about the potential dangers of nonmedical drug use. _____
16. Each use of a drug involves a decision that the good which will come about through its use will overbalance the detrimental effects that may occur. _____
17. Today drug abuse is a problem of equal magnitude in upper, middle, and lower socioeconomic class children. _____
18. People who abuse drugs are trying to cope with overwhelming stress in their environment. _____
19. Society should judge adults who misuse liquor or drugs by the same standards that it judges young people. _____
20. Marijuana is harmless. _____
21. The principal reason for the ineffectiveness of most drug education efforts is that they make no distinctions among various patterns of use—experimental, occasional, regular, compulsive. _____
22. An important motive for drug use is the obvious approval of drug use by legitimate adult sources. _____

DRUG ATTITUDE SURVEY—cont'd

NUMBERS

23. Every pharmacologically active drug is dangerous at some dose in some individuals under some circumstances. _____

24. Marijuana use, although spreading throughout the country, is still primarily seen in Mexican-American communities. _____

25. Society's attitude to the use of a specific drug is the most important factor in determining the nature of abuse of that drug. _____

26. An important motive for drug use is a desire to experience God. _____

27. Education about drugs is meaningless unless society evolves strategies to deal with the physical, psychological, and social conditions that predispose to drug dependence. _____

28. Excessive drug use in a mother will affect any children she bears while on drugs.

29. Drug abuse in young people is largely the fault of Communist elements. _____

30. It is now known that drug users have lower than average IQs. _____

31. The number of people in the United States of all ages who have tried marijuana is 20 million or more. _____

32. An important reason for drug use is easy access to drugs. _____

33. Public health experience shows that no social disease of man has ever been managed by attacking the disease directly. Massive frontal attacks on drug abuse will only intensify the problem. _____

34. Marijuana should be legalized. _____

35. In the final analysis, one must use drugs in order to really know their effects. _____

36. Investigations into chromosomal changes, birth defects, and brain cell alterations following LSD use are not conclusive. _____

37. An important motive for drug use is dissatisfaction or disillusionment with the prevailing social system. _____

38. The estimates of extent of heroin use throughout the general population are based entirely on speculation. _____

39. One of the main factors contributing to the drug problem has been its political exploitation. _____

40. Heroin addiction should be considered a disease rather than a crime. _____

41. Young people can be effectively involved in persuading other young people not to use drugs, but only if they have been carefully selected and trained in the dangers of drug abuse. _____

42. When your child is found to be using drugs, an excellent source of help is your clergyman. _____

43. Drug abuse among young people is largely the fault of criminals who make a profit from them. _____

44. One important motive for drug use is the tendency of persons with psychological problems to seek easy solutions with chemicals. _____

45. School programs in the area of drug education cannot be successful without continuous community involvement. _____

46. In some countries, narcotic addicts can and do lead relatively normal lives. _____

47. It is almost always possible to obtain medical help on drug abuse without incurring legal penalties. _____

48. Within the past few years narcotic addiction has spread from the ghetto to the middle class youth. _____

49. Children often abuse drugs as a means of attacking their parents. _____

50. Since feeling and subjective experience are influenced by and enhanced by drugs, we must attack the problem through emotional means if we are serious about drugs and youth. _____

Continued.

DRUG ATTITUDE SURVEY—cont'd

NUMBERS

51. The increasing degree of alienation is a basic cause of drug abuse. _____

52. There is no generation gap in the abuse of stimulants and sedatives. _____

53. Even with extensive use, marijuana users develop little or no tolerance. _____

54. The single, most important factor in drug use by young people is permissiveness of parents and teachers. _____

55. When your child is found to be using drugs, an excellent source of help is the police. _____

56. Very few chronic users of marijuana go on to heroin use. _____

57. Drugs that are nonaddicting are harmless because a person can stop at any time he wants to. _____

58. An important reason for drug use is the development of an affluent society that can afford drugs. _____

59. Most true drug abusers are multiple drug users. _____

60. The greatest danger of marijuana use is arrest for a felony. _____

61. Almost all heroin addicts have a basic character defect which leads to addiction. _____

62. The use and abuse of drugs is a private matter. _____

63. People who work for socially beneficial goals seldom use drugs. _____

64. There can be no single successful method of prevention or treatment of drug abuse for all individuals. _____

65. In moderate amounts the effects of any drug are determined more by presonal and social factors than by the drug itself. _____

66. It will soon be possible to use an assessment of personality traits to predict which kind of drug an individual will abuse. _____

67. Even though marijuana is illegal, it is better to smoke pot than it is to drink liquor because of the bodily harm that can result from the use of alcohol. _____

WEEKLY PROGRAM OPINIONS

Directions: Please rate the program presentations to the extent they helped achieve the goals of the Training Center by recording the appropriate number in the boxes provided using the following scale:

NOT EFFECTIVE   1   2   3   4   5   6   7   HIGHLY EFFECTIVE

Week no. **TRAINING CENTER GOALS**	PROGRAM												
	Allure of drugs	Turn on without drugs	Discussion group	Social psychology	Discussion group	Over-the-counter drugs	Predrug users	Discussion group	Field trip	Drug scene 1970	Amphetamines	Marijuana	Youth and the community
Pharmacological effects													
Psychological effects													
Sociological effects													
Community action— resources													
Leadership training													
Laws, police, courts													
Medical, rehabilitation and treatment													
Communication procedures													
Curriculum development													
Teaching strategies													
Resource materials													
Counseling and guidance													
Illustrative school program													
Administrative problems													

FINAL PROGRAM EVALUATION

I. What is your overall rating of the Training Center Program? (check one item)

_____ Excellent

_____ Very good

_____ Good

_____ Fair

_____ Poor

II. Content and activities of Training Center

Please indicate the degree to which you believe each of the following helped prepare you for participation in a drug education program. Circle the appropriate number from "1" (poor) to "5" (excellent) for each of the six areas. Also, please make any comments or suggestions in the space provided for each area.

	POOR				EXCELLENT
1. Lectures by staff Comments:	1	2	3	4	5
2. Lectures by visiting consultants Comments:	1	2	3	4	5
3. Field trips Comments:	1	2	3	4	5
4. Group discussions Comments:	1	2	3	4	5
5. Films Comments:	1	2	3	4	5
6. Resource/reading material Comments:	1	2	3	4	5

7. If you were planning a training center such as this
    a. what aspects would you retain?
    b. what aspects would you eliminate?
    c. what aspects would you modify, and in what ways?

III. Structure of Training Center

Please judge each of the following and make any comments you feel appropriate.

	POOR				EXCELLENT
1. Living arrangements Comments:	1	2	3	4	5
2. Organization of Training Center Comments:	1	2	3	4	5
3. Tempo or pace of activities Comments:	1	2	3	4	5
4. Physical setting of lectures/meetings Comments:	1	2	3	4	5
5. Psychological climate Comments:	1	2	3	4	5

Additional comments:

FILM RATING SCALE

Scale: 1 = POOR; 2 = FAIR; 3 = AVERAGE; 4 = GOOD; 5 = EXCELLENT

QUALITIES TO BE RATED	FILM TITLES								
	1.	2.	3.	4.	5.	6.	7.	8.	9.
Is the content accurate?									
Is the film up to date?									
Is the film well organized?									
Are the objectives clear?									
Is the film a good source of information?									
Rate the following technical qualities:									
Photography									
Sound									
Music									
Voice									
For what grade level is the film suited? (Is this a teacher reference?)									
What overall rating would you give the film?									

EVALUATION OF MATERIALS

Scale: 1 = POOR; 2 = FAIR; 3 = GOOD; 4 = VERY GOOD; 5 = EXCELLENT

NAME OF PAMPHLET	information scientifically accurate	minimal or no advertising	organization and appropriateness of illustrations	up to date	stimulates interest	grade level suitability*	your overall rating
1.							
2.							
3.							
4.							
5.							
6.							
7.							
8.							
9.							
10.							
11.							
12.							
13.							
14.							
15.							
16.							
17.							
18.							
19.							
20.							

*Grade levels use these symbols: P = Primary grades; I = Intermediate grades; J = Junior high schools; S = Senior high schools.

MATERIALS EVALUATION*

I. Title _____

II. Subject emphasis _____

III. Understanding—education level:

K-3 _____ 4-6 _____ 7-9 _____ 10-12 _____

IV. Commercial references made—frequency

High _____ Medium _____ Low _____

V. In accordance with the above determinations, rate the material's presentation attributes.

	EXTENT			QUALITY		
	high	medium	low	superior	good	poor
1. Subject coverage						
a. Scientific facts						
b. Objective approach						
c. Judgments made based on scientific validity						
d. Moralizing on the subject						
e. Currency of facts						
f. Stimulation of thought and discussion						
g. Continuity						
h. Relevance to intended audience						
2. Overall subject coverage rating						
3. Multiethnic considerations						
4. Readability (when applicable)						
5. Audio-understandability (when applicable)						
6. Currency of visual appeal						
7. Relevance of visual appeal to intended audience						
8. General value in relation to cost						
9. General value in relation to length						

VI. General recommendations and level of use

Schools only _____ Adults only _____ Schools and adults _____

Reference _____ No possible use _____

VII. Additions or comments on any of the above information _____
_____
_____

VIII. Evaluation summary

_____ Book

_____ Pamphlet

_____ Film

_____ Slides or transparencies

_____ Film strip

_____ Poster

_____ Casette or audiotape

_____ Record

Evaluator _____

Place of employment _____

Position _____

Evaluation date _____

Overall quality of material

Superior _____ Good _____

Poor _____ Inadequate _____

*Adapted from Guidelines for the prevention of drug abuse problems through education, interim report, Milwaukee, 1971, Mental Health Planning Committee of Milwaukee County, Wisconsin.

SOURCES OF INSTRUMENTS

It has previously been stated that there are not many sources from which to obtain drug evaluation instruments. Most of those available are unpublished. The sources listed below will provide additional assistance for schools and school districts in search of evaluation instruments.

1. Arizona State Department of Education
   Drug Abuse Education Consultant
   State Capitol Building
   Room 165
   Phoenix, Ariz. 85007

   "Values Inventory of Behavioral Responses," devised by Nancy D. Seiders and Edward N. Sanford, Jr., Grades 4 to 6, 1970.

   Using the Lasswell Framework of Values, attempts to register children's value choices.

2. Family Life Publications, Inc.
   Box 427
   Saluda, N. C. 28773

   "A Drug Knowledge Inventory," by Gelolo McHugh and J. C. Williams, 1969, is available.

3. Maribeth L. Murphy, Ph.D.
   5283 Countryside Drive
   San Diego, Calif. 92115

   "The Murphy Inventory of Values," Grades K-8 primarily, 1969.

   This is a projective instrument for assessing self-image to facilitate teaching and counseling toward developing responsibility. It is designed for teachers, counselors, and school psychologists. It is based on Lasswell's Framework of Values.

4. Major Associates
   P. O. Box 8063
   Roseville, Minn. 55113

   "Mood Altering Substances: A Criteria Referenced Inventory," by Marion B. Pollack, 1971.

5. Professor Richard E. Carney
   Department of Psychology
   U. S. International University
   3902 Lomaland Drive
   San Diego, Calif. 92107

   "What Do You Think: Risk-Taking Attitudes," Grades 4, 5, 1969.

   An inventory to assess what young people think and how they feel about some of the risks people take.

6. Psychiatry Service
   Boston City Hospital
   249 River Street
   Mattapan, Mass. 02126

   This office has prepared a "Drug-Abuse Research Instrument Inventory" that lists a variety of instruments, some of which are usable in schools and communities. Most of the devices are unpublished and for a nominal charge duplicated copies are available on request.

References

1. Conceptual guidelines for school health programs in Pennsylvania, Harrisburg, 1970, Division of Health, Physical and Conservation Education, Pennsylvania Department of Education.
2. Cornacchia, H. J., et al.: Health in elementary schools, ed. 3, St. Louis, 1970, The C. V. Mosby Co.
3. Creswell, W. H., Jr., et al.: Youth smoking behavior characteristics and their educational implications, Washington, D. C., 1970, U. S. Public Health Service.
4. A curriculum guide for alcohol education for teachers, bulletin no. 371, Lansing, 1970, Michigan Department of Education.
5. Curriculum guide for drug education, grades K-12, Lovell, Wyoming, 1970, Superintendent of Schools.
6. Drug abuse education curriculum guide and resource materials for grades K-12, Dallas, 1970, Superintendent of Schools, Dallas Independent School District.
7. Drug abuse education, grades 6, 9, 12, Towson, Md., 1969, Baltimore County Board of Education.
8. Five mind-altering drugs (plus one), San Mateo, Calif., 1970, Department of Public Health and Welfare.
9. Guidelines for the prevention of drug abuse problems through education, interim report, Milwaukee, 1971, Mental Health Planning Committee of Milwaukee County, Wisconsin.
10. Measures used in the drug evaluation, appendix A, Colorado Department of Education.
11. Pargman, D.: Teacher evaluation of the school drug education program, Sch. Health Rev. 1:14, 1970.
12. Pollock, M. B.: Mood-altering substances: a behavior inventory, J. Educ. Measurement 7: 211-212, 1970.
13. Richards, L. G.: Evaluation in drug education, Sch. Health Rev. 2:22-27, 1971.
14. Senior high school health guide, Unit IV, Drug abuse and health, Salt Lake City, 1971, Utah State Board of Education.
15. Survey of drug use among junior and senior high school students in the state of Idaho, Boise, 1970, Idaho State Department of Public Instruction.
16. Tobacco, drug, alcohol unit, seventh grade, Great Falls, Mont., 1971, Great Falls Public Schools.

17. Tobacco, drug, alcohol unit, ninth grade, Great Falls, Mont., 1971, Great Falls Public Schools.

18. Toward responsible drug education, grades K-4, Salem, 1970, Oregon State Board of Education.

19. Vincent, R. J.: A scale to measure attitude toward smoking marijuana, J. Sch. Health **40**: 454-456, 1970.

20. Weir, W. R.: Alcohol and alcoholism education: attitude development and change, J. Alcohol Educ. **15**:1-8, 1969.

APPENDIX

DRUG ABUSE IN SPORTS

Enough has been written about the unwarranted use of drugs by athletes to consider this an important part of the school drug abuse problem. Yet the actual extent of such drug use by high school players is difficult, if not impossible, to accurately determine. One reason for this is that competition, secrecy, and ethical considerations prevent coaches, players, or team doctors from talking much about such use even when it is discovered. In fact there is an official attitude of negativism against all forms of drug misuse, and also, typically, total denial that drugs are a problem on the playing field.

Perhaps more important than the actual extent of such drug use is a careful definition of just what is meant by "drugging" or "doping," terms that are confusing and frequently misused. In widely varying circumstances the simplistic term "doping" will be used in conjunction with any situation involving drugs and athletes. Doping is typically defined as "the use of *any* chemical substances not normally present in the body, and not essential to a healthy person competing in athletics." Both medical and athletic organizations concerned with regulating competitive sports have officially condemned doping of athletes.

When the issue of such use or abuse is to be considered, several confusing aspects must be separately examined. Are we talking about use by an athlete of a specific drug taken just prior to a game to improve his short-term athletic performance, to relieve pain, or to build up body tissue? Or

are we talking about legitimate pharmaceuticals administered to an athlete by a physician to counteract injury or to treat disease? Or perhaps is the real issue illegal drug use or abuse as part of an athlete's personal life-style or of his peer-group associations having no direct relevance to his athletics?

Athletes, just like other students, smoke marijuana, get drunk, smoke cigarettes against the coach's orders, and sometimes even take dangerous drugs like LSD, amphetamines, or heroin. Such drug abuse may be part of a compulsive pattern or merely part of a life-style not at all related to athletics, although it may cause a problem on the playing field. In fact such misuse is typically reflected only in impaired athletic performance and generally deteriorated health.

An athlete may self-medicate with legitimate preparations to deal with real or imagined problems with no intention of directly affecting his performance. For example, he may "snitch" some Darvon Compound from the family medicine cabinet to stop an aching knee, or he may dose himself with vitamin pills.

Yet in another completely different circumstance, the athlete may be examined, diagnosed by a team physician, and legitimately prescribed medicine to combat illness or pain. This is precisely where the most ambivalent "gray area" of medicine and ethics begins. The team physician may also assist the players in coping with pain or injury in a situation where the player should, for his best health interests, not be allowed to continue to participate. Even the coach may provide, or allow to be provided, drugs or substances ill-advised for sports play. Where should these fine distinctions be drawn? For example, exactly how badly should a player be injured before he should stop playing? To what extent should drugs be administered to an injured player so he can continue to play? No one knows exactly, of course, except probably the team physician. Every physician will exercise a slightly differing human judgment but, perhaps at the same time, be subtly influenced by the acute demand that the players be allowed to play and that the team win!

The most dramatic and the most publicized circumstances occur when the players take, with the coach's and team physician's approval, pep pills and other improper substances merely to improve performance. This is usually what is meant by the expression "doping." It would be safe to say that the use of amphetamines, or pep pills, is generally more of a problem on college teams and in professional athletics where the stakes are high and the winning edge narrow. Nevertheless the school must be aware that high school and junior high school students do take stimulants not condoned, and generally unknown, by either the coach or the team physician.

It has been reported, however, that the practice of doping flourishes at all levels of organized sports despite official disapproval. The problem of utilization of drugs to increase an athlete's performance is acknowledged in professional athletics and, to a much lesser degree, among high school and college athletes. The high school athlete is not yet owned by the institution but the motivation for optimal performance is perhaps just as strong as at the college or "pro" level. Coaches will obviously go to great lengths to gain a competitive edge. In fact some feel that just to keep up with the competition, the athlete *must* use amphetamines for that extra drive, anabolic steroids for body building, or pain medication to mask the symptoms of a disabling injury. This reputedly happens in high schools and colleges and in international competition, not just in professional sports. The fact that these are potentially dangerous drugs, totally unsuitable for sports, is well known, at least to the medical profession. Yet it has been suggested that some team physicians are a party to this underground practice; they cannot approve drug use, but by turning their backs on it they are tacitly condoning it.

Baugh[1] has stated that there is a general belief that by taking "dope" athletes improve their playing performance. The accusation has been made, sometimes irresponsibly, that team doctors dope injured players with pain killers to keep them in the game, or at least that these physicians are openly permissive about the use of stimulants—"speedies" or "greenies"—by players who want some quick pep.

One of the largest drug abuse problems among young athletes is not associated with nonprescription drugs, but with the socially acceptable drugs alcohol and tobacco, use of which represents a violation of good training practices.

Dr. Robert K. Kerlan,[6] an orthopedic surgeon, team physician for the Los Angeles Lakers and the Los Angeles Kings, and consulting physician for the California Angels and the San Diego Padres, has organized all athlete's medications into three classes. Group one, the harmless and useless group, includes vitamins, dextrose (sugar), or those agents that will not harm unless taken to excess. Excessive use of vitamin B_{12}, for example, should be discouraged unless a rare case of pernicious anemia exists. Group two includes drugs with definite value in the treatment or sequelae of specific injury, such as the anti-inflammatory and pain-killing agents. Phenylbutazone is used principally for relief of muscular and skeletal problems such as arthritis and gout, indomethacin is an anti-inflammatory agent, hydrocortisone is an anti-inflammatory steroid, and trypsin is an enzyme used to dissolve blood clots. These agents must be administered under the constant supervision of a physician. With phenylbutazone, for example, regular blood checks must be made, and with indomethacin the gastrointestinal tract must be observed. Group three is made up of all the useless and potentially dangerous agents—the stimulants, or pep pills, the depressants, or downers, and the various hormones, including the anabolic steroids. Anabolic- or metabolic-increasing steroids are male sex hormones that can powerfully affect the physical growth and sexual maturity of the young athlete. Artificial introduction and use of such hormones in excess of normal body production may create abnormal increases in height and body weight with disturbances in the masculinity of the male. Artificial use of such hormones may profoundly disturb the individual's normal growth processes; thus these are considered by most physicians to be totally unsuitable for general use.

Dr. Kerlan believes that drugs in groups one and two may occasionally be necessary adjuncts to treating athletes. However, those drugs in group three are for diseases rarely encountered among healthy male athletes. Their use must be substantially restricted; they have no place in sports.

Unfortunately athletes of any age or level tend to be fetishists, somewhat superstitious, and remarkably given to embracing ritual or any drug or food substance that has the reputation of making athletes excel. For example, the world's best fed athletes consume millions of unnecessary vitamin capsules and tablets each year. Athletes participating in individual sports seem to be more prone to drug fads than team sports members, and so may have to be particularly cautioned concerning the dangers involved. Weight lifters and field event athletes seem especially susceptible in their quest to gain greater body weight and size, which they equate with increased strength. The use of these anabolic steroids is to be particularly condemned because of virilization, liver involvement, and possibly increased incidence of carcinoma of the prostate. Athletes should be made aware of the potential dangers involved in the use of steroids as well as of the doubtful advantages.

Consumption of honey, sugar preparations, and glucose just prior to game time is also typical even on the high school playing field. Use of sugar is perhaps more logical than any other nutritional aid, since there is an increased utilization of carbohydrates during strenuous activity. However, there is *no* evidence that sugar as a pre-event supplement increases athletic performance. Nevertheless there is much honey-water sipping, or chocolate-bar eating by athletes during or preceding competition. Such practices, often encouraged by coaches, add credibility to the concept that ergogenic (energy-producing food substances) aids really work. Coaches should encourage athletes to rely only on healthful living and the physiological outcomes of activity for performance rather than on "gimmicks," "fads," or superstition.

References

1. Baugh, R. J.: The use and misuse of drugs among high school athletes, Paper presented at the American School Health Association, Chicago, Oct., 1971.
2. Clarke, K. S.: Drugs, sports and doping, J. Maine Med. Assoc. 61:55-58, 1970.
3. Food facts and fallacies, tips on athletic training VII, Chicago, 1965, American Medical Association.
4. Fowler, W. W.: The facts about ergogenic aids and sports performance, J. Health, Phys. Educ. Recreation 40:37-42, 1969.
5. Fulton, G. B.: Personal communication, April 28, 1971.
6. Kerlan, R. K.: Personal communication, Jan. 8, 1973.
7. Murphy, R. J.: The use and abuse of drugs in athletics, Paper presented at the American Medical Association Convention, Chicago, June, 1970.

INDEX

Laws—cont'd
  Narcotic Control Act, 115
  Narcotic Drugs Import and Export Act, 113
  Narcotics Manufacturing Act, 115
  Opium Poppy Control Act, 114
  Uniform Act, 118
Learning principles, 166
Le Dain Commission Interim Report, 135
Lennard, H. L., 8
Lewin, L., 69
Lewis, D. C., 135
Lindesmith, A. R., 27
Lipscomb, W. R., 8
Louria, D., 8
LSD, 36, 86
Luce, J., 228

M

Magazines and journals, 195
Magazines and newspaper articles, as teaching
    technique, 174
Mandell, A. J., 97
Map, as teaching technique, 174
Marijuana; *see* Drug(s), depressants; Drug(s),
    marijuana
Martin, P., 12
Maslow, A. A., 231, 233
Maslow, A. H., 143
Mellinger, G. D., 40
Mercer, G. W., 230
Mescaline, 36
Messer, M., 46
Methadone, 102
Methods of teaching; *see* Curriculum, teaching
    techniques
Meyers, F., 82
Mikeal, R. L., 135
Millman, R. B., 16
Morphine, 65, 88
Mural, as teaching technique, 174
Music, as teaching technique, 174

N

Narcotic antagonist, 101
Narcotics; *see* Drug(s), commonly abused;
    Drug(s), narcotics
National Action Committee, 240
National Advisory Council for Drug Abuse Pre-
    vention, 240
National Association of State Drug Abuse Program
    Coordinators, 10
National Clearinghouse for Drug Abuse Informa-
    tion, 108-109, 187, 189, 205
National Coordinating Council on Drug Abuse
    Education, 189, 205
National Institute of Mental Health, 43, 82, 103,
    109, 110, 121, 122, 189, 238
National School Public Relations Association, 230
National Training Centers, 5
Needs and interests, student, 147-150
Nervous system, 60
New York State Narcotic Addiction Commission, 9
Newsletters, 194-195
Nicotine; *see* Drug(s), stimulants, tobacco
Niederhoffer, A., 45
Nixon, R. M., 5, 17, 19, 25, 89, 238, 240, 251

Notebook, as teaching technique, 182
Nowlis, H., 26, 38, 131, 240
Nurses, 206, 250-251, 261
Nyswander, M. E., 16, 69, 90, 102

O

Objectives, drug education, 146-147, 152-157
Odyssey House, 225
Office of Economic Opportunity, 5
Office of Education, 5, 110, 122, 238, 240, 251,
    253
Opiates; *see* Drug(s), narcotics
Opinionnaires, as teaching techniques, 168, 174
Over-the-counter drugs; *see* Drug(s), commonly
    abused; Drug(s), over-the-counter

P

Palo Alto Unified School District, California, 222
Panel discussion, as teaching technique, 174, 256
Parent educational programs, 207-208
  formal, 207-208
  informal, 208
Parent involvement, 175, 182
Parkway School, Philadelphia, 226
Parodies, as teaching technique, 182
Parsons, T., 45
Patterns of drug abuse, 43-44
Patterns of instruction, health education, 136-140
  correlated, 137-139
    advantages, 138
    problems, 139
  direct, 136
    advantages, 139-140
    problems, 140
Peer groups, as teaching technique, 175
Penalties for illegal sale and possession, California,
    119
Percodan; *see* Drug(s), narcotics
Personnel, school; *see* School personnel, role of
Phoenix House, 101, 102
Physicians, 206, 250
Police, 245-246
Policies and procedures for school; *see* School co-
    ordination
Posters, as teaching technique, 175, 182, 184
Pretests, as teaching technique, 168, 175, 182
Prevention, 132
  educational approaches, 10
  school-community coordination, 12
Problem solving, as teaching technique, 168, 175,
    182, 185
Problems, 131, 139-140, 238-240, 262-263
  drug, 25-26
  school, 6-7
Program(s), 3
  community, 11; *see also* specific programs
  coordination, 238-258
  governmental
    federal, 108-111
    local, 112
    state, 111-112
  school drug, 3, 133-134
    adjustment for abusers, 225-226
    principles, 212-226
Projects, as teaching technique, 175
Psychedelics; *see* Drug(s)